Contemporary Foundations for Teaching English as an Additional Language

This engaging volume on English as an Additional Language (EAL), argues persuasively for the importance of critical participatory pedagogies that embrace multilingualism and multimodality in the field of TESOL. It highlights the role of the TESOL profession in teaching for social justice and advocacy and explores how critical participatory pedagogies translate into English language teaching and teacher education around the world.

Bringing together diverse scholars in the field and practicing English language teachers, editors Polina Vinogradova and Joan Kang Shin present 10 thematically organized units that demonstrate that language teaching pedagogy must be embedded in the larger sociocultural contexts of teaching and learning to be successful. Each unit covers one pedagogical approach and includes three case studies to illustrate how English language teachers across the world implement these approaches in their classrooms. The chapters are supplemented by discussion questions and a range of practical sources for further exploration. Addressing established and emerging areas of TESOL, topics covered include:

- Critical and postmethod pedagogies

- Translingualism

- Digital literacy and multiliteracies

- Culturally responsive pedagogy

- Advocacy

Featuring educators implementing innovative approaches in primary, secondary, and tertiary contexts across borders, *Contemporary Foundations for Teaching English as an Additional Language* is an ideal text for methods and foundational courses in TESOL and will appeal to in-service and preservice English language teachers as well as students and teacher educators in TESOL and applied linguistics.

Polina Vinogradova is Director of the TESOL Program at American University, USA.

Joan Kang Shin is Associate Professor of Education at George Mason University, USA.

D1597349

Contemporary Foundations for Teaching English as an Additional Language

Pedagogical Approaches and Classroom Applications

Edited by Polina Vinogradova
and Joan Kang Shin

Routledge
Taylor & Francis Group

NEW YORK AND LONDON

First published 2021
by Routledge
52 Vanderbilt Avenue, New York, NY 10017

and by Routledge
2 Park Square, Milton Park, Abingdon, Oxon, OX14 4RN

Routledge is an imprint of the Taylor & Francis Group, an informa business

Library of Congress Cataloging-in-Publication Data
Names: Vinogradova, Polina, editor. | Shin, Joan Kang, editor.
Title: Contemporary foundations for teaching English as an additional
    language : pedagogical approaches and classroom applications / edited by
    Polina Vinogradova, Joan Kang Shin.
Description: First edition. | New York : Routledge, 2021. | Includes
    bibliographical references and index.
Identifiers: LCCN 2020022126 | ISBN 9780367026325 (hardback) |
    ISBN 9780367026356 (paperback) | ISBN 9780429398612 (ebook)
Subjects: LCSH: English language—Study and teaching—Foreign speakers. |
    English language—Study and teaching—Foreign countries. | English
    language—Study and teaching—Foreign countries—Case studies.
Classification: LCC PE1128.A2 C687 2021 | DDC 428.0071—dc23
LC record available at https://lccn.loc.gov/2020022126

ISBN: 978-0-367-02632-5 (hbk)
ISBN: 978-0-367-02635-6 (pbk)
ISBN: 978-0-429-39861-2 (ebk)

Typeset in Joanna MT & Frutiger
by Apex CoVantage, LLC

Contents

List of Figures ix
List of Tables xi
Foreword xii
JoAnn (Jodi) Crandall
Preface xv
Acknowledgments xvii

UNIT 1
Introduction   1

1   **Introduction: Teaching English as an Additional Language in the 21st Century**   3
    Joan Kang Shin

UNIT 2
Critical Pedagogies and TESOL   13

2   **Disrupting Method: Critical Pedagogies and TESOL**   15
    Benjamin "Benji" Chang and Spencer Salas

2.1   **Awakening Critical Consciousness in Japanese University EFL Students Through Student Journalism**   23
    David Leslie

2.2   **Implementing Critical Pedagogy in a Standards-Driven Context in Turkey: Making Room for Teacher and Student Voices**   28
    Hale Hatice Kizilcik

2.3   **Critical Pedagogy in a Postgraduate TESOL Professional Development Course in México: Using the NACTIC Model**   38
    Leticia Araceli Salas Serrano, Rebeca Elena Tapia Carlín, and Celso Pérez Carranza

UNIT 3
Postmethod Pedagogy in ELT   45

3   **Postmethod Pedagogy and Its Role in Contemporary English Language Teaching**   47
    Doaa Rashed

3.1 Course Planning in the Postmethod Era: Ideas From a Practicum Experience in Thailand   56
Lucas Edmond

3.2 Enacting Postmethod Pedagogies in IELTE Programs in Argentina: Do as I Say, or as I Do?   66
María Alejandra Soto

3.3 Towards a Context-Sensitive Theory of Practice in Primary English Language Teaching Through Theme-Based Instruction in Serbia   77
Vera Savić

UNIT 4
Culturally Responsive Pedagogy in ELT   89

4 Culturally Responsive Pedagogy in TESOL   91
M'Balia Thomas and Marta Carvajal-Regidor

4.1 Why Are There So Many Immigrants Here?: Problem-Posing With Middle Schoolers in Hawai'i   100
Gordon Blaine West

4.2 Teaching ESL Through Social Justice Themes in China: Developing a Critical Consciousness   107
Hetal Patel

4.3 Applying Culturally Responsive Pedagogy to Engage With Cultural Differences in an ESL Composition Course in the U.S.   113
Zhenjie Weng, Mark McGuire, and Tamara Mae Roose

UNIT 5
Translingualism in TESOL   119

5 Translingualism in the Teaching of English: Theoretical Considerations and Pedagogical Implications   121
Eunjeong Lee

5.1 Leveraging Translanguaging in Role-Plays in a U.S. University   131
Katja Davidoff and Zhongfeng Tian

5.2 Translingual Practices in an Adult ESL Literacy Class in the U.S.   135
Sarah Young Knowles

5.3 Koryoin (고려인/КОРЁ CAPAM) Children's Translingual Practices for Learning English: A Case Study of Russian-Korean Children in South Korea   139
Youngjoo Yi and Jinsil Jang

UNIT 6
Multiliteracies in TESOL   **149**

6   **A Pedagogy of Multiliteracies and Its Role in English Language Education**   151
Shakina Rajendram

6.1   **Using Art to Spark Conversation With Recently Arrived Immigrant English Language Learners in the U.S.**   160
Brian Tauzel

6.2   **Exploring Places and Spaces of Migration and Immigration Using Google Earth: A Multiliteracies Approach for English Learners in the U.S.**   175
Natalia A. Ward and Amber N. Warren

6.3   **Rappin' on Campus: Multiliteracies in Action in Japan**   181
David Dalsky and Jueyun Su

UNIT 7
Collaborative Technologies and TESOL   **189**

7   **Teaching With Collaborative Technologies Across Borders**   191
Ilka Kostka

7.1   **Developing Skills for Independent L2 Writers in Hawai'i: Democratic Participation in Classroom Assessment**   200
Mitsuko Suzuki

7.2   **Borderless Learning Using Online Writing and Videoconferencing: A Case of Agriculture Students in Indonesia**   204
Mushoffan Prasetianto

7.3   **Implementing Flipped Classrooms in Uzbek and Karakalpak EFL Teacher Education**   209
Gena Bennett, Aybolgan Borasheva, and Dilnoza Ruzmatova

UNIT 8
Digital Literacy and TESOL   **215**

8   **English Language Education and Digital Literacy in the 21st Century**   217
Richmond Dzekoe

8.1   **Affordances of Mobile Devices in Teaching English as a Foreign Language in Brazilian Public Schools**   227
Cristiane R. Vicentini, Inês Cortes da Silva, and Luciana C. de Oliveira

8.2   **A Lesson in Hedging With Online Corpus Data in an Academic Research and Writing Course in the U.S.**   235
Erik Voss

8.3 The Effect of Mobile Learning on Learner Autonomy in the United Arab Emirates   240
Hussam Alzieni

UNIT 9
Advocacy and TESOL   247

9   **Advocacy for Student and Teacher Empowerment**   249
Heather A. Linville

9.1 **Educators Influencing Policy: The Language Opportunity Coalition
and the Seal of Biliteracy in the U.S.**   257
Rachel Thorson Hernández and Nicholas Close Subtirelu

9.2 **Caring as a Form of Advocacy for Literacy-Emergent Newcomers With
Special Education Needs: The Community-Building Pedagogical
Approach in the U.S.**   265
Luis Javier Pentón Herrera

9.3 **Building Communities of Practice: Advocacy for English Teachers in Rwanda**   270
Richard Niyibigira and Jean Claude Kwitonda

UNIT 10
TESOL Teacher Education   275

10   **Preparing English Language Teachers for Participatory Teaching**   277
Polina Vinogradova

10.1 **Reflective Teaching and Critical Language Pedagogy in a Thai EFL Context**   288
María Díez-Ortega and Hayley Cannizzo

10.2 **From Teachers to Young Learners: Integrating Personal Development
Instruction into Foreign Language Teaching in Serbia**   294
Danijela Prošić-Santovac

10.3 **Preparing Teachers to Create LGBTQ+ Inclusive Classrooms in the U.S.**   298
Joshua M. Paiz

Index   306

Figures

1.1   P21 framework for 21st-century learning   4

1.2   United Nations Sustainable Development Goals   5

2.1.1   Student articles published to the Life in Kochi website https://lifeinkochi.net   26

2.2.1   Padlet brainstorming session   31

2.3.1   Screenshot of a digital autobiography   41

2.3.2   The Prompt for the Final Project   42

3.1.1   A model for a postmethod approach to design   59

3.1.2   Project parts 1 and 5   64

3.1.3   Interview write-up by a student   65

3.2.1   A sample learner reflection for the task above   75

3.3.1   Illustrations for *The Ant and the Grasshopper*   84

3.3.2   Sample worksheet for *The Ant and the Grasshopper*   88

4.1.1   Restored and replica buildings, including houses built by various ethnic groups that lived and worked on the plantations   102

5.3.1   Koryoin children utilize three languages and non-linguistic resources   141

5.3.2   Stepan's drawing of a comic strip after reading multiple versions of texts   141

5.3.3   The school vocabulary chart in English, Korean, and Russian displayed in the classroom   142

5.3.4   Artur's reading workbook written in English and Korean   143

5.3.5   Image from the search for words 'Roman public bathrooms'   144

5.3.6   Signpost explaining recycling in six languages   145

5.3.7   Bus map written in multiple languages   146

6.1.1   Winslow Homer, *Dressing for the Carnival*, 1877, Metropolitan Museum of Art   162

6.1.2   Ralph Earl, *Elijah Boardman*, 1789, Metropolitan Museum of Art   163

6.1.3   Edward Hopper, *Tables for Ladies*, 1930, Metropolitan Museum of Art   164

6.1.4   Diego Rodríguez de Silva y Velázquez, *Juan de Pareja*, 1650, Metropolitan Museum of Art   166

6.1.5   *Tughra (Insignia) of Sultan Süleiman the Magnificent*, 1555–1560, Metropolitan Museum of Art   168

6.2.1   Google Earth tour created by a student   178

6.2.2   Student journal entry uploaded to Google Earth tour   178

7.2.1 Examples of student's topic discussions on the OCEP platform 206

7.2.2 A videoconference in progress 208

7.3.1 Google Classroom setting 211

7.3.2 A glance at Google Classroom process 211

7.3.3 Telegram interface 212

8.1.1 Screenshot from Portuguese Dictionary app. 229

8.1.2 Using the mobile app for vocabulary and pronunciation development 230

8.1.3 PDF handout 231

8.1.4 Creating a digital poster 232

8.2.1 Screenshot of Michigan Corpus of Upper-Level Student Papers (MICUSP) Simple showing results for the word "might" in student research papers in Linguistics 237

8.2.2 Screenshot of Michigan Corpus of Upper-Level Student Papers (MICUSP) Simple showing results for the word "might" in student research papers in Economics 238

8.3.1 The rubric for the Managing Expenses WebQuest 243

8.3.2 An Emotional Intelligence Task 244

9.1.1 LOC blog post on testifying on behalf of the LOOK Act 260

9.1.2 LOC's guidelines for testifying before the Joint Committee 261

9.1.3 Blogpost announcement of a LOC webinar 262

10.1.1 Scaffolded worksheet for classroom rules negotiation 290

10.1.2 Examples of students' final Critical Poster Project 292

10.1.3 Scaffolded brainstorming worksheet for final poster project 293

10.2.1 An example of a thematic unit web created by the teachers 296

10.3.1 Recreations of participant drawings from narrative illustration activity 301

Tables

1.1	Traditional vs. contemporary approaches to teaching	8
2.2.1	The draft rating scale	34
2.3.1	Organization of the course: three modules	40
3.1.1	Final course and project schedule	63
3.3.1	Sample materials and activities developed by the participants	79
4.2.1	Presentation task grading rubric	112
5.2.1	Contrasting a "traditional" approach to ESL literacy instruction with a translanguaging approach	137
6.2.1	Books and websites to use with students	180
7.1	Overview of selected tools to support collaborative English language learning	193
8.2.1	Example phrases that include "might" from Linguistics and Economics texts	239
10.2.1	Stories used in the activity	297

Foreword

JoAnn (Jodi) Crandall

....

As this volume makes clear, much has changed in the field of TESOL, especially in how we conceptualize both teaching and learning. Those of us who have been in the field for some time will remember one of our first courses that was known briefly as a "Methods" course, where we learned about Grammar-Translation, Direct, and Audiolingual Methods and Communicative Language Teaching, along with a number of other methods or approaches in what Rashed refers to as a "constant search for the best method" (p. 47). Each new method gave rise to new techniques, textbooks, and language policies, without consideration of the local contexts of teachers or learners, leaving teachers to try to adhere to the required method and materials, while still trying to meet the individual needs of their learners by integrating activities from a number of methods in their teaching.

It's not surprising, then, that many TESOL teacher education programs changed the name of that central course from "Methods" to "Methodology," in recognition that few teachers were actually teaching according to a particular method, except perhaps when attempting to teach using the highly structured methods of Silent Way, Community Language Learning, or Suggestopedia, but often with limited success.

But TESOL has now moved from a focus on "methodology" to a postmethod period, challenging the view that there can be one approach, method, or set of activities for all learners. Language learning, especially English language learning, has become much more complex when viewed from the multiple sociocultural and sociolinguistic contexts of its use by diverse individuals. Differences in class, race, ethnicity, gender, sexual orientation, migration, and other ways in which learners are marginalized has led to a more critical stance, questioning traditional views of language, literacy, culture, or learning (Chang & Salas, Ch. 2 of this volume). As many of the chapters underscore, language teaching pedagogy must be embedded in the larger sociocultural contexts of teaching and learning, with teachers empowered to help learners sustain or revitalize their linguistic and cultural identities while also providing relevant English instruction (Thomas & Carvajal-Regidor, Ch. 4 of this volume).

The field of TESOL recognized this sociocultural shift in multiple special issues of *TESOL Quarterly*, from 1997 to 2004, focusing on "language and identity, critical approaches to TESOL, gender and language education, language and race, and critical pedagogy" (Rashed, Ch. 3 of this volume, p. 47). Increasingly, as well, teaching English became viewed as a "political act" (Chang & Salas Ch. 2 of this volume, p. 15), which has also led to an increased focus on the importance of advocacy to address inequities and injustices (Linville, Ch. 9 of this volume). So instead of expecting learners to mimic "native speakers" (a contested term, for who are those speakers?), there is greater recognition that there are multiple Englishes and English speakers within countries and around the globe, multiple multilingual speakers who use their repertoire of languages when speaking with others who share those languages in translingual conversations (Lee, Ch. 5 of this volume), and multiple users of English as a lingua franca among speakers who do not share a common language, for whom English is not a "foreign" language but rather an "additional" language (Shin, Ch. 1 of this volume).

While there are numerous postmethod pedagogies discussed in this volume, such as critical (Chang & Salas, Ch. 2 of this volume), culturally responsive (Thomas & Carvajal-Regidor, Ch. 4 of this volume), and participatory (Vinogradova, Ch. 10) pedagogy, translingualism (Lee, Ch. 5 of this volume), multiliteracies (Rajendram, Ch. 6), and multimodal pedagogy (Kostka, Ch. 7 and Dzekoe, Ch. 8 of this volume), they share a number of common features. Among these is a recognition that teaching in an ELT classroom must begin by learning about students and their linguistic and cultural experiences, what Luis Moll and his colleagues have referred to as "funds of knowledge" (Moll, Amanti, Neff, & Gonzalez, 1992). While we as ESL/EFL/EAL teachers may have been trained to draw upon students' background knowledge, today that has a much deeper and richer meaning of including learners' linguistic and cultural experiences, their homes and communities, and their ways of communicating (including through digital and multimodal means) in our instruction. These pedagogies take a critical stance in recognizing that English language instruction does not and should not exist in isolation. For example, culturally responsive pedagogy "sustains and revitalizes the cultural products, practices, and ways of knowing of students' home and communities" (Thomas & Carvajal-Regidor, Ch. 4 of this volume, p. 99) while also helping them develop linguistic and cultural skills needed for academic or professional success. These pedagogies view learners from an "asset" perspective rather than a deficit one, or as Linville points out (Ch. 9 of this volume), as emergent bilinguals rather than English learners with deficiencies to correct.

These pedagogies also recognize the personal and global value of multilingualism, given the many ways in which people communicate across linguistic, cultural, and other boundaries, especially through digital technology, and the importance of bringing this translanguaging or translingualism into the language classroom (Lee, Ch. 5 of this volume). They require us to view language learning from a dynamic, multilinguistic perspective, with language constantly evolving as learners use their linguistic resources, rather than from a monolinguistic perspective (with what Lee, Ch. 5 of this volume refers to as "parallel monolingualism").

These pedagogies also recognize the role of multiliteracies and multimodal communication, occasioned especially through the use of digital technology, reflecting the ways in which today's students communicate (see Rajendram, Ch. 6; Kostka, Ch. 7; and Dzekoe, Ch. 8 of this volume). Digital technology has changed (and greatly augmented) the ways in which learners communicate, beyond the printed text and the traditional language skills of listening, speaking, reading, and writing (which are still important) to a multimodal approach, using "text, images, video, sound to express their ideas, consume information, and create new content" through social media, podcasts, blogs, webinars, and so on (Rajendram, p. 153). As Kostka (Ch. 7 of this volume) notes, many of today's students are digital natives who "have become accustomed to how easy it is to communicate and collaborate across the globe," making it "difficult to imagine second language (L2) learning without it" (p. 193). And as Dzekoe (Ch. 8 of this volume) reminds us, we need to think in terms of digital literacies – not only in terms of basic language skills but also in terms of a broader "discourse competence" or "sociocultural literacy" (p. 222) and the 21st century skills discussed by Shin (Ch.1 of this volume).

A related theme that emerges in these chapters is the importance of creating contexts in which learners can collaborate with each other and the teacher or take charge of their own learning, whether through participatory (Chang & Salas, Ch. 2, and Vinogradova, Ch. 10 of this volume) or culturally responsive pedagogy (Thomas & Carvajal-Regidor, Ch. 4 of this volume), or the use of collaborative digital technologies and computer-mediated support, enabling learners to work alone or with others both inside and outside of class, locally and globally (Kostka, Ch. 7 of this volume). Technology allows learners to explore and share language and literacy from personal or community perspectives, for example, through videoconferencing, digital stories, photo essays, and collaborative writings.

Although these pedagogies provide exciting and enriching ways of bringing learners' (multi)linguistic, multimodal, and cultural experiences and communities into the classroom, several chapters note the challenges of integrating them into traditional curricula with high-stakes standardized assessments. In addition, they note that most English language teachers have limited preparation in critical, culturally responsive, translingual, digital, multiliteracies, or multimodal pedagogy, either in their preservice TESOL education or in-service professional development.

This collection can help provide some of that much-needed professional development. The chapters and the three case studies that follow each chapter provide concrete examples of how various pedagogical approaches can be or have been implemented in classrooms or programs from a range of educational levels (primary and secondary, but especially postsecondary levels of adult, university, or TESOL professional programs) and from a range of linguistic and cultural contexts.

These include examples from ESL contexts such as engaging newly arrived immigrant middle school students in researching their new home in Hawai'i; using art in a multiliteracies approach for 12th grade high school students in New York City; translanguaging in an intensive course at a Boston university; and advocating for recognizing the bilingualism of English language learners with the Seal of Biliteracy in the United States.

Examples from EAL contexts include a journalism project to develop critical consciousness for Japanese university students; student and teacher collaboration in implementing critical pedagogy in Turkey; using smartphones for collaboration both online and offline with a 9th grade class in Brazil and mobile technologies with technology college students in the United Arab Emirates; and implementing a flipped classroom in Uzbekistan.

In addition to these examples, the chapters in this collection provide a number of suggestions on how English language teachers can develop needed training. These include engaging in action research and participatory action research (Chang & Salas, Ch. 2; Rashed, Ch. 3; and Vinogradova, Ch. 10 of this volume), examining multilingual students' daily language practice through interviews and literacy products (Lee, Ch. 5 of this volume), implementing critical pedagogy as the foundation for a TESOL professional course (Serrano, Carlin, & Carranza, Case Study 2.3 of this volume), designing a project-based summer course based on students' interests and expectations as a practicum experience in Thailand (Edmond, Case Study 3.1 of this volume), and engaging TESOL candidates in activities such as teaching and learning autobiographies, interviews of experienced language educators, and development of teaching philosophies, with teachers modeling participatory teaching and critical reflective practice (Vinogradova, Ch. 10 of this volume). As Vinogradova notes (p. 284), "In order to empower EL learners and create educational spaces that embrace critical participatory pedagogy, implement CRT, create translingual space, and foster development of digital literacies, TESOL candidates need to experience this type of learning themselves."

This collection provides both novice and experienced teachers and teacher educators around the globe with much of the current thinking about English language teaching and learning. The chapters discussing the background, theoretical concepts, implications for English language education, future directions – along with discussion questions and case studies – are certain to give rise to rich discussions and promising directions for English language teaching and learning.

REFERENCE

Moll, L. C., Amanti, C., Neff, D., & Gonzalez, N. (1992). Funds of knowledge for teaching: Using a qualitative approach to connect homes and classrooms. *Theory Into Practice*, 31(1), 132–141.

Preface

In the past decade, scholars and language educators have been extensively discussing and developing methodological approaches in second language education that build on critical pedagogy, emphasize language teacher and language learner empowerment, demonstrate the need for multiliteracies development in addition to functional and academic literacies, argue the value of multilingualism, and incorporate the use of various technologies that facilitate collaborative language learning (see Canagarajah, 2013; Kessler, 2018; Kumaravadivelu, 2003; Ortega, 2013, 2017; Shin, 2016; Vinogradova, 2017). These issues and methodological approaches have been discussed in various TESOL academic publications, including TESOL methods textbooks, scholarly articles, and classroom case studies. Considering the urgency and importance of these themes for 21st century learning, we wanted to create one space – one book – that will highlight and give an overview of contemporary methodological approaches to English language teaching. Within this space, we wanted to accomplish several things. First, we saw the need to provide a platform for educators who themselves represent diverse multilingual voices in TESOL—that is, for educators in whom current English language learners can see themselves and recognize what is possible for them. Second, we wanted to invite TESOL-ers who could showcase important and innovative work they do in various parts of the world, thus shifting from the Anglo-centric focus to the perspective of World Englishes and multilingualism. Third, we wanted to include teacher voices that are often left unheard in scholarly and academic publications in the English-speaking world. And finally, we wanted to offer innovative examples of how English language educators around the world interpret, implement, and appropriate complex themes and concepts of critical participatory pedagogy and challenge monolingual, hegemonic, and heteronormative discourses.

Three years after initially brainstorming and conceptualizing this volume, we are thrilled to see it being published. As we originally envisioned, the goal of this volume is to represent contemporary pedagogical approaches to teaching and learning English as an additional language informed by critical participatory pedagogy. This volume unpacks such methodological approaches as postmethod, a pedagogy of multiliteracies, and culturally responsive pedagogy; demonstrates how these pedagogical approaches can be incorporated in English language teaching using collaborative technologies; explores the role of translingual practices and advocacy; and connects theoretical considerations and scholarship with actual teaching practices. Although the book seemed to develop according to plan, we could not have predicted how beautifully the themes would cut across chapters as well as how well the case studies would illustrate the conceptual chapters.

Through this labor-intensive but invigorating process we have been privileged to work with thoughtful, caring, and outstanding English language educators who care deeply about students, colleagues, and the TESOL profession. We were amazed to see the level of innovation and creativity that is happening in English language classrooms in Argentina, Brazil, China, Indonesia, Japan, Mexico, Rwanda, Serbia, South Korea, Thailand, Turkey, the United Arab Emirates, the United States, and Uzbekistan. And within each of these countries and classrooms, the English language learners, their teachers, as well as the authors, represent great linguistic, cultural, and ethnic diversity. We believe that the end result of this endeavor will prove to be a worthwhile read for both budding and seasoned English teaching professionals who are passionate about contributing to the global TESOL community.

References

Canagarajah, S. (2013). *Translingual practice: Global Englishes and cosmopolitan relations*. New York, NY: Routledge.

Kessler, G. (2018). Technology and the future of language teaching. *Foreign Language Annals*, 51(1), 205–218. https://doi.org/10.1111/flan.12318

Kumaravadivelu, B. (2003). *Beyond methods: Macrostrategies for language teaching*. New Haven, CT: Yale University Press.

Ortega, L. (2013). SLA for the 21st century: Disciplinary progress, transdisciplinary relevance, and the bi/multilingual turn. *Language Learning*, 26(1), 1–24. https://doi.org/10.1111/j.1467-9922.2012.00735.x

Ortega, L. (2017). New CALL-SLA research interfaces for the 21st century: Towards equitable multilingualism. *CALICO Journal*, 34(3), 285–316. https://doi.org/10.1558/cj.33855

Shin, J. K. (2016). Building a sustainable community of inquiry through online TESOL professional development. In J. A. Crandall & M. A. Christison (Eds.), *Global research on teacher education and professional development in TESOL* (pp. 143–160). New York, NY: Routledge.

Vinogradova, P. (2017). Teaching with digital stories for student empowerment and engagement. In M. Carrier, R. M. Damerow, & K. M. Bailey (Eds.), *Digital language learning and teaching: Research, theory, and practice* (pp. 127–139). New York, NY: Routledge & TIRF.

Acknowledgments

We are grateful to the authors in this volume for their hard work, thoughtfulness, and enthusiasm. We have learned so much from the amazing work that you all do! We are also grateful for your care and support of your students.

We also want to extend words of gratitude to the Language, Literacy, and Culture PhD Program and give a shout out to our professors and classmates at the University of Maryland, Baltimore County (UMBC). That is where we met and where our friendship and academic collaboration started more than a decade ago. And a special thank you goes to our professor and mentor, Dr. JoAnn (Jodi) Crandall, who has been supporting and inspiring us for years and who kindly agreed to write the Foreword for this volume.

Polina Vinogradova would like to thank her husband, Ayhan Kose, for patiently listening to book ideas and regular progress updates, for offering feedback, and for always being cheerful, enthusiastic, supportive, and encouraging. She would also like to thank Heather Linville for reading and commenting on the drafts of Chapter 10. And thank you to AU TESOL students and colleagues who are the constant source of my learning and inspiration.

Joan Kang Shin would like to thank her husband, Jeremy Hurley, for his love, understanding, and never-ending support every day of our life together, especially on Fridays (aka writing days). She would also like to thank her parents, who taught her about commitment and perseverance, which are two necessary ingredients for completing a book. Huge thanks go to my colleagues at George Mason University, who have inspired me to strive for excellence in scholarship while keeping the heart of a teacher and the spirit of a learner.

We both thank Woomee Kim and Dildora Khakimova for their help in preparing and formatting the figures and tables for this volume.

UNIT 1
Introduction

CHAPTER I

Introduction

Teaching English as an Additional Language in the 21st Century

Joan Kang Shin

FRAMING THE ISSUE

Here is what we know about communication in the 21st century. We live in a multilingual world. We live in a multimodal world. In this multilingual and multimodal landscape, English has emerged as the world's lingua franca. English is a global language. It is linked closely to areas such as diplomacy, business, air traffic control, and tourism. The use of English in diverse contexts requires the ability to communicate and collaborate across borders. It is the language of science and technology, and it is the most widely used language on the World Wide Web. Using English requires the ability to interpret information critically from multimodal sources as well as produce and distribute messages utilizing an array of media and genres. With so much information and media being consumed and produced globally through English, the world's lingua franca of the 21st century is inextricably tied to digital, information, and new media literacies.

Considering this global and multimodal use of English, we have had to change our mindset from the 20th-century representation of so-called "native speakers" of English coming from Kachru's (1992) "inner circle" countries, like the US, UK, Australia, Canada, and New Zealand. This 20th-century construct may have been a necessary developmental turn. It helped many English language educators understand that English was being learned and used by millions of people around the world and why. Kachru constructed the "outer circle" with countries like India, Kenya, and Singapore, where English is an official second language, as well as the "expanding circle" with countries like Brazil, China, Russia, and Saudi Arabia, where English is not commonly spoken but is being learned as a foreign language (Kachru, 1992). In this century, we can see how these distinctions of circles of English speakers are becoming less defined and perhaps less important for educators. The British Council (2013) predicted that there would be over 2 billion people using or learning English in classrooms around the world by 2020, and Crystal (2019) has estimated that the total number of English speakers in the world is just over 2.3 billion. With Crystal's (2019) estimation of approximately 388 million native speakers of English—that is, from Kachru's inner circle countries—it is widely accepted that there are many more learners and speakers of English as a second, third, or as we want to emphasize in this volume, an *additional* language. Therefore, to learn or use English does not necessarily require conforming to cultural or even linguistic norms of the inner circle countries, which have historically been presented through English language teaching materials as US or British. In the 21st century, speakers of English are not from a particular country or culture; instead, speakers of English represent many countries and cultures.

Understanding this new world of global English speakers is the first step toward a multilayered understanding of how challenging it is to be an English language teacher in the 21st century. First, if most speakers of English are learning it as an additional language, we must recognize that English learners are bi/multilingual and bring to the classroom diverse linguistic and cultural identities and varying perspectives on education and ways of knowing. Additionally, the contexts mentioned here, such as diplomacy, business, tourism, science, and technology, typically use English as the international language among people with diverse ways of communication. Now factor in our new ways of 21st-century multimodal communication that integrate digital, social, and collaborative technologies. Here is where we should consider more broadly how the field of education as a whole is trying to keep up with and meet the challenges of our complex world in the 21st century.

CONCEPTS AND THEORETICAL CONSIDERATIONS

In the broader field of education, there has been a focus on building so-called 21st century skills since the turn of the century. Although these skills were not necessarily discovered in the 21st century or new to the field of education, the world in this century demands the mastery of these skills more urgently. According to Richard Riley, former U.S. Secretary of Education, "We are currently preparing students for jobs that don't yet exist . . . using technologies that haven't yet been invented . . . in order to solve problems we don't even know are problems yet." (Trilling & Fadel, 2009, p. 3). Because of our rapidly changing world and the uncertainty of our future, we know that beyond learning new technological skills our next generation needs skills such as critical thinking, problem solving, and creativity to meet the demands of our ever-changing world.

Frameworks for 21st-Century Skills

One of the most widely recognized and used frameworks for understanding 21st-century skills comes from the Partnership for 21st-Century Learning (P21), which was previously referred to as Partnership for 21st-Century Skills. P21 has developed a "Framework for 21st-Century Learning," described as "[a] unified vision for learning to ensure student success in a world where change is constant and learning never stops" (Battelle for Kids, 2019, p. 1). It recognizes that "all learners need educational experiences in school and beyond, from cradle to career, to build knowledge and skills for success in a globally and digitally interconnected world" (p. 2). Currently P21 is considered part of Battelle for Kids (www.battelleforkids.org), which is a national not-for-profit organization that creates networks of all schools systems and communities focused on bringing 21st-century learning to all students. Figure 1.1 shows P21's framework for 21st-century learning.

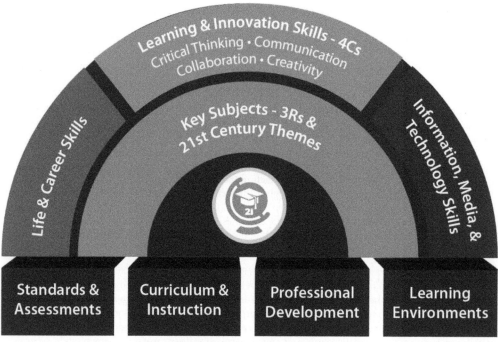

Figure 1.1 P21 framework for 21st-century learning

Source: © Battelle for Kids. All Rights Reserved. www.battelleforkids.org

This framework shows the combination of knowledge and skills that educators should integrate into curriculum and instruction as well as standards and assessments. It includes mastery of key subjects, such as language arts, world languages, arts, mathematics, economics, science, geography, history, government, and civics, which are typical in K-12 curricula worldwide. Additionally, the P21 framework supports integration of interdisciplinary 21st-century themes that cut across all subject areas, such as global awareness; financial, economic, business, and entrepreneurial literacy; civic literacy; health literacy; and environmental literacy (Battelle for Kids, 2019).

These interdisciplinary 21st-century themes intersect with the United Nations Sustainable Development Goals or SDGs (www.un.org/sustainabledevelopment). These are 17 goals to transform our world. As educators, the SDGs are a useful framework for integrating the cross-cutting 21st-century themes. As the UN website states: "The Sustainable Development Goals are a call for action by all countries . . . to promote prosperity while protecting the planet. They recognize that ending poverty must go hand-in-hand with strategies that build economic growth and address a range of social needs including education, health, social protection, and job opportunities, while tackling climate change and environmental protection." Figure 1.2 shows the UN's SDGs.

The United Nations also established a holistic and transformational educational approach called Education for Sustainable Development (ESD). This approach integrates the SDGs into the curriculum while promoting "an action-oriented, transformative pedagogy, which supports self-directed learning, participation and collaboration, problem-orientation, inter- and transdisciplinarity and the linking of formal and informal learning" (UNESCO, 2017, p. 7). The intended goal for ESD is empowering learners to "take informed decisions and responsible actions for environmental integrity, economic viability and a just society for present and future generations" (p. 7).

Similarly, Trilling and Fadel (2009) emphasize that

> [e]ducation's big goal, preparing students to contribute to the world of work and civic life, has become one of our century's biggest challenges. In fact, all the other great problems of our times—solving global warming, curing diseases, ending poverty, and the rest—don't stand a chance without education preparing each citizen to play a part in helping to solve our collective problems.
>
> (p. 40)

Figure 1.2 United Nations Sustainable Development Goals

Source: United Nations

Students today need to be prepared for life and work in our dynamic, multimodal world that is rapidly changing and ever more complex day by day. According to the P21 framework, we should develop the following types of skills to meet the challenges of our complex 21st-century world:

Learning and Innovation Skills

- Creativity and Innovation
- Critical Thinking and Problem Solving
- Communication
- Collaboration

Information, Media, and Technology Skills

- Information Literacy
- Media Literacy
- ICT (Information, Communications, and Technology) Literacy

Life and Career Skills

- Flexibility and Adaptability
- Initiative and Self-Direction
- Social and Cross-Cultural Skills
- Productivity and Accountability
- Leadership and Responsibility

(Battelle for Kids, 2019, p. 2)

For some educators, technology is at the forefront of their goals for preparing students for their future. Therefore, many educators use another framework for 21stcentury skills focused on technology which comes from the International Society for Technology in Education (ISTE). As ISTE (2020) describes: "Today's students must be prepared to thrive in a constantly evolving technological landscape. The ISTE Standards for Students are designed to empower student voice and ensure that learning is a student-driven process." The focus is on transformative learning with technology, and the standards are presented from the student perspective. Next are the components of the framework for the ISTE standards developed in 2016:

Empowered Learner: Students leverage technology to take an active role in choosing, achieving and demonstrating competency in their learning goals, informed by the learning sciences.

Digital Citizen: Students recognize the rights, responsibilities and opportunities of living, learning and working in an interconnected digital world, and they act and model in ways that are safe, legal and ethical.

Knowledge Constructor: Students critically curate a variety of resources using digital tools to construct knowledge, produce creative artifacts and make meaningful learning experiences for themselves and others.

Innovative Designer: Students use a variety of technologies within a design process to identify and solve problems by creating new, useful or imaginative solutions.

Computational Thinker: Students develop and employ strategies for understanding and solving problems in ways that leverage the power of technological methods to develop and test solutions.

Creative Communicator: Students communicate clearly and express themselves creatively for a variety of purposes using the platforms, tools, styles, formats and digital media appropriate to their goals.

Global Collaborator: Students use digital tools to broaden their perspectives and enrich their learning by collaborating with others and working effectively in teams locally and globally.

(ISTE, 2020)

21st-Century Skills vs. Digital Skills

P21 and ISTE provide two of the most widely known and used frameworks for understanding 21st-century skills as well as technology and digital skills. These clearly overlap. Based on a systematic review of the literature, van Laar, van Deursen, van Dijk, and de Haan (2017) examined the relationship between 21st-century skills and digital skills. They concluded that 21st-century skills are broader than digital skills and are not grounded in ICT. van Laar et al. (2017) developed a framework of seven core skills that are considered "fundamental for performing tasks that are necessary in a broad range of occupations," and five contextual skills, which are skills "required to take advantage of the core skills" (p. 582). These skills outlined here will look familiar because they are well-aligned with P21 and ISTE.

Core Skills

- Technical: The skills to use (mobile) devices and applications to accomplish practical tasks and recognize specific online environments to navigate and maintain orientation.

- Information management: The skills to use ICT to efficiently search, select, organize information to make informed decisions about the most suitable sources of information for a given task.

- Communication: The skills to use ICT to transmit information to others, ensuring that the meaning is expressed effectively.

- Collaboration: The skills to use ICT to develop a social network and work in a team to exchange information, negotiate agreements, and make decisions with mutual respect for each other toward achieving a common goal.

- Creativity: The skills to use ICT to generate new or previously unknown ideas, or treat familiar ideas in a new way and transform such ideas into a product, service or process that is recognized as novel within a particular domain.

- Critical thinking: The skills to use ICT to make informed judgements and choices about obtained information and communication using reflective reasoning and sufficient evidence to support the claims.

- Problem solving: The skills to use ICT to cognitively process and understand a problem situation in combination with the active use of knowledge to find a solution to a problem.

Contextual Skills

- Ethical awareness: The skills to behave in a socially responsible way, demonstrating awareness and knowledge of legal and ethical aspects when using ICT.

- Cultural awareness: The skills to show cultural understanding and respect other cultures when using ICT.

- Flexibility: The skills to adapt one's thinking, attitude or behavior to changing ICT environments.

- Self-direction: The skills to set goals for yourself and manage progression toward reaching those goals in order to assess your own progress when using ICT.

- Lifelong learning: The skills to constantly explore new opportunities when using ICT that can be integrated into an environment to continually improve one's capabilities.

(van Laar et al., 2017, p. 583)

Traditional vs. Contemporary Approaches to Teaching

In order to develop these skills and prepare our students to succeed in our world, we must find new ways to teach. Trilling and Fadel (2009) suggested that we have a balance between the traditional teaching and

Table 1.1 Traditional vs. contemporary approaches to teaching

Traditional approaches	Contemporary approaches
Teacher-directed	Learner-centered
Knowledge	Skills
Content	Process
Basic skills	Applied skills
Facts and principles	Questions and problems
Theory	Practice
Curriculum	Projects
Time-slotted	On-demand
One-size-fits-all	Personalized
Competitive	Collaborative
Classroom	Global community
Text-based	Web-based
Summative tests	Formative evaluations
Learning for school	Learning for life

Source: Adapted from Trilling and Fadel (2009, p. 38)

learning approaches and the newer approaches based on the demands of the 21st century. Table 1.1 represents two ends of a continuum between more traditional versus more contemporary approaches.

As Trilling and Fadel (2009) note, "Clearly it will take the best from the entire range of learning practices represented to successfully prepare our students for their future, with the approaches on the right side of the chart becoming more and more important as we move through our century" (p. 40). Although approaches to teaching and learning are not binary categorizations, we can see the shift from the one-size-fits-all, knowledge-based approaches that are the hallmark of traditional approaches to a more contemporary approach that puts learners and the skills they need to succeed in our ever-changing world at the center of our educational goals. These approaches are representative of education from a broad perspective and align with what we consider 21st-century, contemporary approaches to teaching English as an additional language.

IMPLICATIONS FOR ENGLISH LANGUAGE EDUCATION

It is important to remember that the status of English as the world's lingua franca makes it a key subject in the P21 framework, as it has become an important language for global communication and collaboration. As the British Council (2013) describes it:

> English is the dominant international language of the 21st century. It is spoken at a useful level by some 1.75 billion people – a quarter of the world's population. As the language of communications, science, information technology, business, entertainment and diplomacy, it has increasingly become the operating system for the global conversation.

(p. 5)

David Graddol (2006) describes this shift in English becoming a global language:

> The next stage of global development will be as dramatic as that of the industrial revolution and the rise of nation states. We are rapidly shifting to a completely new social, economic and political order and with it a new world order in languages. English is proving to be a key part of this process. On the one hand, the availability of English as a global language is accelerating globalisation. On the other, the globalisation is accelerating the use of English.

(Graddol, 2006, p. 22)

In response to this evolving status of English around the world, TESOL International Association (2008) published a Position Statement on English as a Global Language. In this position statement, TESOL emphasizes the importance of English worldwide and suggests its conceptualization as an "additional" language rather than a "foreign" one.

> Given the broad geographic spread of English, and the variety of world Englishes being spoken globally, English is seen less and less as a "foreign" language, and more as an additional language. In other words, learning English is no longer viewed as something optional, but essential. English has become the most widely taught language in the world, and numerous countries have instituted English as a required subject for all students, often starting at very young ages. With English being taught globally for very diverse purposes, a singular or monolithic approach to the modeling of English is no longer tenable. . . . TESOL urges English language teachers to make informed decisions at local, regional, and/or national levels, taking into account the purposes and contexts of use that are most relevant to their learners.
>
> (TESOL, 2008, p. 1)

As English language educators, we have many considerations when developing appropriate pedagogies for such an important and impactful global language. Can we promote global communication and collaboration to prepare our students for 21st-century problem solving? Can we position English as an additional language as an important tool for the 21st century? Can our English teaching pedagogies also reflect UNESCO's (2017) Education for Sustainable Development that is learner-centered, action-oriented, transformative, participatory, collaborative, problem-posing, inter- and transdisciplinary, and real-world oriented? Can we ensure that English language teachers make informed decisions that take into account local, regional, national, and international considerations that affect their learners?

As mentioned in the Introduction, there are some important characteristics of English being used as a global language in this century as well as English being learned as an additional language that should lead the discussion of contemporary approaches to teaching it. These are the following:

- English is a global language spoken by a quarter of the world's population.
- Speakers of English as a second or foreign language far outnumber people who speak it as a first language.
- English does not belong to any one country or culture.
- English speakers come from diverse backgrounds both culturally and linguistically.
- English is the world's lingua franca and used as a common language in these fields: science, information technology, business, entertainment, diplomacy, air traffic control, and tourism.
- English is the most widely used language on the World Wide Web (w3techs.com).
- Use of English is multimodal and requires new and diverse literacies, or *multiliteracies*, for communication.

If 21st-century English learners are bi/multilingual with diverse backgrounds and varied purposes for using the language to communicate across borders and cultures, we have to change our understanding of what it means to be teachers of this global language. Certainly the one-size-fits-all approach is no longer relevant in this postmethod era. English language teachers must be sensitive to the needs of their learners and their local teaching contexts in order to create their own English teaching pedagogies and classroom procedures (Rashed, Ch. 3 of this volume). Furthermore, recognizing English learners' diverse cultural and linguistic backgrounds, teachers must enact culturally responsive and culturally sustaining pedagogies (Thomas & Carvajal-Regidor, Ch. 4 of this volume) while steering away from English-only, monolingual perspectives in language learning, teaching, and practice in an effort to emphasize translingualism in ELT (Lee, Ch. 5 of this volume).

If 21st-century communication is inextricably linked to skills like collaboration, creativity, critical thinking, problem solving, and digital literacies, then we must incorporate these skills into how we teach English as a global language. No longer is learning a language limited to text-based communication. Therefore, English teachers should integrate a multiliteracies approach that includes both comprehension and production in English that integrate linguistic, visual, audio, gestural, tactile, and digital modalities (Rajendram, Ch. 6 of this volume). In order to communicate globally across borders, English learners should have authentic experiences using collaborative technology in the classroom (Kostka, Ch. 7 of this volume) and build their critical thinking, collaboration, creativity, and problem-solving skills in constructing and decoding digital messages (Dzekoe, Ch. 8 of this volume). Using more contemporary approaches, like projects and problem posing that encourage students to apply 21st-century skills and practice real communication will help prepare them to use English outside of the classroom, which is the goal.

In its report *The English Effect*, the British Council (2013) provides evidence that English drives growth and international development. "For developing and emerging economies, there is enormous demand and need for English in public education systems to boost stability, employability and prosperity" (p. 3). The report also shows how English has become "the language of opportunity and a vital means of improving an individual's prospects for well-paid employment" (British Council, 2013, p. 3). Considering English's gatekeeping status internationally, it is important for teachers to be aware of the importance of English for opportunity for students as individuals as well as a country's economic growth. In countries where English is commonly spoken, English learners face the gatekeeping status differently and often have an immediate need to learn English to both survive and thrive. Given the potentially high stakes for learners of English in many contexts, teachers must take an advocacy stance in order to ensure inclusivity and equitable teaching practices (Linville, Ch. 9 of this volume). English teachers need to commit to critical participatory (Freirian) pedagogies, which are humanizing pedagogies for the English language classroom that will encourage both English teachers and students to be critically conscious of the role English plays both globally and locally in their lives (Chang & Salas, Ch. 2 of this volume).

These implications of 21st-century knowledge and skills in ELT are explored in great detail through both theoretical chapters and practical case studies following this Introduction. These chapters and case studies will illustrate contemporary pedagogical approaches to teaching and learning English as an additional language. Furthermore, a thorough discussion about how these contemporary approaches to teaching English impact TESOL teacher education and how to prepare teachers to be transformative intellectuals who are able to enact critical, participatory, and culturally responsive pedagogies in this postmethod era (Vinogradova, Cha. 10). These contemporary approaches to ELT and TESOL teacher education are interconnected and informed by the needs of our world in this century, the role of English for global communication, and the cultural and linguistic diversity of our 21st-century English learners.

FUTURE DIRECTIONS

Based on the parameters set by our world in the 21st century, English language educators must respond with approaches that are grounded in postmethod, translingual, multimodal, and critical pedagogies. Creating educational spaces that are equitable and participatory requires cultural responsiveness and advocacy on multiple levels. English language educators must represent more than just linguistic value in the classroom. They have a responsibility to bring the world to the classroom, but to also allow each student to bring their world to the classroom. Whatever worlds enter each classroom and however they may interact and perhaps even collide, English language teachers should find ways to equip their learners with the skills needed to use English effectively as the world now seems to demand it.

The following conceptual chapters in this volume delve deeply into the contemporary foundations for teaching English as an additional language. Each proposes future directions that when combined work together toward creating more empowered and innovative 21st-century learners who can use English to communicate and collaborate effectively in our multimodal, multilingual world.

Discussion Questions

1. What 21st-century framework presented in this chapter seems the most relevant to your own educational experiences and/or your current classroom context? What aspects of this 21st-century framework have not been addressed in your own educational experiences or in your current classroom context?
2. Reflect on your educational experiences in the past and present (including your own classroom if you are currently teaching). Now take a look at Table 1.1 that shows traditional versus contemporary approaches to teaching and discuss whether or not your experiences have been more traditional or contemporary.
3. Think about the use of English in your country or context. Next, reflect on the ways English is taught and learned in your context. Is English a gatekeeper for opportunity? Discuss what kinds of opportunities might depend on one's ability to use English for communication. How might this affect your approach to teaching English?
4. Find an English language textbook that is used in your country or context. What countries or cultures are represented in the content and images? How is your country or culture represented in this textbook? Does this textbook show that English does not belong to any one culture? Why or why not?
5. Describe how 21st-century skills frameworks align with contemporary approaches to teaching English as an additional language.

Resources for Further Exploration

1. Battelle for Kids. (n.d.). *Partnership for 21st Century Learning (P21)*. https://battelleforkids.org/networks/p21
   The Partnership for 21st Century Learning (P21) is the most well known and widely used framework for understanding 21st-century skills. It is now a part of Battelle for Kids, which is a national not-for-profit organization that collaborates with school systems and communities to bring 21st-century learning to every student. This website provides many resources as well as networks that educators and school systems can join.
2. Graddol, D. (2006). *English next: Why global English may mean the end of 'English as a Foreign Language'*. British Council.
   This book explores recent trends in the use of English worldwide and its changing relationships with other languages. It is a helpful resource for English language educators who seek to better understand the role of English as a global language and how it is used and positioned around the world.
3. ISTE. (n.d.). *International Society for Technology in Education*. www.iste.org/
   The International Society for Technology in Education (ISTE) is a community of global educators who focus on how to use educational technology to transform teaching and learning. This website provides information about ISTE Standards, educational resources, and professional development opportunities, including information about membership in the community.
4. TESOL (n.d.). TESOL International Association. www.tesol.org
   This website for the TESOL International Association provides many resources for learning about English language teaching, which include publications, conferences, and a variety of

professional development opportunities. This is an association representing Teachers of English to Speakers of Other Languages. It publishes standards for teaching English and position statements to improve public policy and understanding of English language teaching.
5. UNESCO. (n.d.). *17 Goals to Transform Our World*. www.un.org/sustainabledevelopment/ The United Nations has developed 17 Sustainable Development Goals (SDGs) that work toward a better and more sustainable future for all. The SDGs address global challenges, such as poverty, inequality, climate change, environmental degradation, peace, and justice. This website not only explains the SGDs but also provides resources for educators to integrate them into teaching and learning, with information about how to promote UNESCO's Education for Sustainable Development.

REFERENCES

Battelle for Kids. (2019). *Partnership for 21st century learning: Framework for 21st century learning*. Retrieved from http://static.battelleforkids.org/documents/p21/P21_Framework_Brief.pdf

British Council. (2013). *The English effect: The impact of English, what it's worth to the UK and why it matters to the world*. British Council.

Crystal, D. (2019). *The Cambridge encyclopedia of the English language* (3rd ed.). Cambridge: Cambridge University Press.

Graddol, D. (2006). *English next: Why global English may mean the end of "English as a Foreign Language"*. British Council.

ISTE. (2020). *ISTE standards for students*. International Society for Technology in Education. Retrieved from www.iste.org/standards/for-students

Kachru, B. B. (1992). *The other tongue: English across cultures* (2nd ed.). University of Illinois Press.

TESOL. (2008). *Position statement on English as a global language*. TESOL International Association. Retrieved from www.tesol.org/docs/pdf/10884.pdf?sfvrsn=2&sfvrsn=2

Trilling, B., & Fadel, C. (2009). *21st century skills: Learning for life in our times*. Jossey-Bass.

UNESCO. (2017). *Education for sustainable development goals: Learning objectives*. United Nations Educational Scientific and Cultural Organization.

van Laar, E., van Deursen, A. J. A. M., Van Dijk, J. A. G. M., & de Haan, J. (2017). The relation between 21st-century skills and digital skills: A systematic literature review. *Computers in Human Behavior, 72*, 577–588.

Unit 2
Critical Pedagogies and TESOL

CHAPTER 2

Disrupting Method
Critical Pedagogies and TESOL

Benjamin "Benji" Chang and Spencer Salas

FRAMING THE ISSUE

In 2016, TESOL International celebrated its 50th anniversary as a flagship professional organization for English language teaching and learning. Across those years, a number of changes have taken place in and around the discipline. These changes included how we conceptualize language, culture, and literacies, and how those conceptualizations intersect with the work we do and the meanings we make of it. We have witnessed these changes in our own teaching lives. For example, in 1994 during a semester-long English as a Second Language teaching practicum in a large urban U.S. high school, Salas worked under the tutorship of a mentor trained in "Suggestopedia" by the same Bulgarian psychotherapist, Georgi Lozanov, who had developed it (see Larsen-Freeman, 2011). The mentor fervently believed that the Bulgarian Baroque music he played during the somewhat hypnotic sessions of watching a subtitled version of Robin Williams's "Mrs. Doubtfire" film was exactly what his and, perhaps, all English Learners needed. Granted, by 1994, methodological allegiance to Suggestopedia was an anomaly. Yet the mentor's commitment to a method was mirrored across the discipline even as TESOL entered a new millennium and a "postmethod" condition (Kumaravadivelu, 1994). The long-standing disciplinary argument went that teaching language effectively required understanding how languages were learned. With that knowledge in hand, the discipline might then develop a subsequent method for accelerating language learning with derivative teacher training teaching products for large-scale replication.

Shortly after a series of policy reforms that began in the late 1990s, market-oriented paradigms of school achievement quickly entered the larger project of U.S. K-12 public education with policy makers embracing notions of accountability, performance, value, and big data. U.S.-based TESOL largely followed that lead – and is still in search of a method-like package in forms such as a Sheltered Instruction Observation Protocol (SIOP), WIDA K-12 Can Do Descriptors, and an arcade of evidence-based teaching products for a large-scale market. Here the argument shifted somewhat. A traditional focus on language learning gave way to the development of academic literacy/literacies whereby K-12 learners especially might gain access to academic content, and, as a consequence, academic achievement was often measured through large-scale standardized assessments and with a reward/punishment system for schools that met or failed to meet annual yearly progress goals.

By the late 1990s, from within and outside the profession, activist scholarship consistently challenged the limitations of method and of market to forward the notion of teaching and learning as a political act of reading the word and the world. More than language learning or academic literacies development, TESOL was also a potential space for teachers and learners to interrogate, disrupt, and reimagine themselves, each other, and their communities through liberatory and humanizing critical pedagogies. Here, critical pedagogies go beyond the depoliticized versions of "critical thinking" which are often associated with Bloom's Taxonomy charts found in many classrooms and generic conceptualizations of "21st century skills" or "higher-order thinking." In their broad ensemble, critical pedagogies in TESOL have focused on challenging deficit representations of language learners and related subtractive paradigms of language, literacy, and culture with keen attention to a nexus of sociocultural factors such as majority-minority relations, social class difference, linguicism, patriarchy, language attitudes and prestige, and others.

In this chapter, we outline shared concepts of critical pedagogies in TESOL, their theoretical origins, and elaborations of participatory social justice approaches. We provide examples of the intersections of critical pedagogies with English language teaching – organizing them into pedagogical processes of recognition, collaboration, and solidarity. We conclude with a discussion of future directions for the field with potential resources for further exploration.

CONCEPTS AND THEORETICAL CONSIDERATIONS

As we have noted, contemporary scholarship and praxis in TESOL has elevated social justice as a disciplinary characteristic. Social justice related work has included discussions surrounding issues of class, gender, sexual orientation, race, ethnicity, privilege, colonization, imperialism, migration, and other sites of marginalization and inequity. To address these issues, some of the literature within TESOL has drawn inspiration and influence from various movements led by and/or for women, indigenous peoples, Lesbian Gay Bisexual Transgender Queer Intersex (LGBTQI) communities, working-class families, immigrants, people of color, and other minoritized populations. These movements have urged the TESOL field to be more diverse, inclusive, and transformative in its conceptualization of English and Englishes, and teaching with those who do not speak English as their first or primary language. As English has continued to be one of the major languages of power and imperialism for over 300 years, critical voices within TESOL have been understandably concerned with inequities related to the teaching of English for some time (Benesch, 1993). Globalization and the explosion of the internet and digital technologies have enabled unprecedented access to people, places, and data that facilitate new methods and analyses with TESOL (Norton & Toohey, 2011). Yet these developments have also further enabled calls for large-scale standardization and commodification of knowledge, education, and TESOL that are highly inequitable to minoritized populations (Ramanathan & Pennycook, 2008). These calls and their subsequent policies have been labeled as a 'flattening of the world' where the standards, evaluations, rankings of language and culture (i.e., standard English), knowledge and research (i.e., "scientific empirical study"), and achievement (i.e., PISA scores), are determined and brokered by an ever-shrinking few (Darling-Hammond, 2007). Such reductions and consolidations can lead to inequitable power distributions and social injustices (Luke, 2008).

From the 1970s onward, critical pedagogy has become one of the most significant areas of scholarship to address issues of power and social injustice in education. Critical pedagogy's origins have been commonly associated with the work of Brazilian educator Paulo Freire, with roots in critical theory (e.g., Marx and Engels, the Frankfurt School, Gramsci), decolonizing traditions (e.g., Fanon, Memmi), and liberation theology (Freire, 1985). Early iterations of critical pedagogy often applied Freire's notions of education toward developing one's critical consciousness and agency (conscientization), the centering of the experiences and concerns of the oppressed, and the dialogical relationships between colonizer and colonized. In addition, this literature also applied sociological, philosophical, and psychological lenses to education, tackling forms of social reproduction, resistance, and agency within schooling structures and institutions. As Freire's work became more widely translated and known in English, enthusiasm and critique of critical pedagogy in TESOL also grew.

Some of critical pedagogy's most prominent critiques came from feminist and poststructural scholarship interrogating how patriarchy, the "straight" male body, and Eurocentrism could be found in critical pedagogy literature across fields, and that these could perpetuate certain forms of oppression, even with the best of intentions. At this locus, poststructural and feminist scholarship pushed critical pedagogy to reexamine its assumptions and standpoints (Davis & Skilton-Sylvester, 2004). In doing so, one result was that much of the critical pedagogy field reconsidered its emphases and metanarratives (which often leaned toward issues of class), and looked at more diverse forms of oppression and agency such as those faced by women and LGBTQI communities. "Critical pedagogies" became a more widely used term, often to signify the range of approaches to social justice education and TESOL, beyond solely Marxian and Freirean traditions. In addition, over the last 15-plus years, there has been a strong emergence of critical pedagogies scholarship, often by scholar-practitioners of color, that utilizes poststructural and feminist lenses but also re-centers issues of race, ethnicity, imperialism, and white supremacy through fields like postcolonial theory, critical race theory, and whiteness studies (Kubota & Lin, 2006).

Another significant body of literature within TESOL, which is often associated with critical pedagogies work in Anglophone nations such as the Americas, the UK, and Australia, is action research (Esposito & Evans-Winters, 2007). While its applications have spread among educational research around the world, action research can be historically tied to critical theories and pedagogies. These ties are perhaps most evident in the ways that action research can challenge positivist and Eurocentric notions of detached researcher objectivity and the over-privileging of large quantitative data research through its qualitative explorations of local communities and their knowledge, practices, and reflexivity toward improving educational spaces. Action research has most often been deployed in school sites to improve teaching and outcomes, typically with teachers, students, and administrators examining their own practices: this is often categorized as participatory action research (PAR). Whether it is teachers observing and analyzing their own pedagogy and those of their grade-level peers, or students going out into their neighborhoods to record and analyze data on their communities' socioeconomic conditions, PAR and other forms of action research have continued to emerge in traditional academic and social justice spaces, given their track record of being able to develop "21st-century academic skills" as well as forms of agency (e.g., social, civic, political) for participants (Lau, 2013; Morrell, 2006).

Similar to action research, sociocultural learning approaches have also developed separately and concurrently with critical pedagogies and other social justice-oriented frameworks, with significant influence in TESOL over recent decades. Broadly speaking, sociocultural frameworks emphasize the idea that human development involves a process whereby "higher functions originate as actual relations between human individuals" (Vygotsky, 1978, p. 57). From a sociocultural perspective, activities such as teaching English to speakers of other languages are situated and distributed in human interactions. Likewise, such activities are generated and sustained in dominant social practices, language, and ideological discourses. Consequently, sociocultural research in TESOL closely examines the ESL/EFL classroom as an ensemble of cultural historical artifacts – or what in Vygotskian parlance might be understood as a means for enabling or, in some cases, disabling institutional and individual identities (see Portes & Salas, 2011). In U.S. K-12 contexts, sociocultural theory has been leveraged to challenge gross and often deficit generalizations about English learners by deconstructing the implicit and explicit cultural practices and assumptions surrounding schools, schooling, and the discipline of TESOL in and of itself.

As sociocultural frameworks generally see learning as a locally contextualized, constructed, and ever-changing process, they can be strongly connected to scholarship that is concerned with meaning-making such as critical literacy and New Literacy Studies (NLS). When NLS was first developed in the 1990s, the term "New" was used to highlight rapidly changing forms of communication and texts, especially those tied to the digital and internet age and shifting forms of capitalism. These changes were seen as paradigm shifts in how students and teachers were reading, writing, listening, speaking, and making meaning in their everyday lives, which in turn had a huge impact on their teaching and learning in schools. Since that time period, critical literacy and NLS have pushed TESOL to look at much of what happens in learning, teaching, and their outcomes as literacies and literacy practices. At this juncture, we can revisit the significant emphasis of critical pedagogies on critical consciousness and agency, both of which can be challenging notions to operationalize and study. Critical literacy and NLS have developed methodologies around practices and meaning making that can support critical teachers and action researchers in their efforts to promote practices of critical consciousness and agency in their TESOL pedagogies (Lau, 2013). The research method of most dominance within these frameworks of TESOL has been critical discourse analysis (CDA), given its wide applicability in studying text and talk as social and linguistic practices that constitute and reify one other, especially within the context of power relations (Rogers et al., 2016).

IMPLICATIONS FOR ENGLISH LANGUAGE EDUCATION

In engaging with poststructural, feminist, sociocultural, and New Literacy frameworks, among others, TESOL as a field has been engaged with critical pedagogies and social justice efforts to resolve issues of marginalization and inequities within English Language Education. As English persists as the most hegemonic language of power around a very diverse and interconnected globe, it is not unexpected that critical pedagogies' work reminds us that there is not just one approach that all practitioners should employ with their students toward developing greater equity and empowerment. However, three general pedagogical themes that have demonstrated some significant implications for promoting social justice in TESOL are the processes of recognition, collaboration, and solidarity.

Recognition

Critical pedagogies within and outside of TESOL can be broadly conceptualized along themes of recognition, collaboration, and solidarity with diverse communities and peoples (Chang, 2015). For one, this can mean recognizing and understanding the different forms of cultural practices, histories, and ways of knowing that students and teachers may come from. As opposed to simply evaluating students according to predetermined standards of ability and achievement (which often correspond to legacies of British and/or U.S. English hegemony and white supremacy), teachers, students, and other stakeholders can assume a more active role in critically recognizing each other's identities, what they bring to classrooms or other educational spaces, and how they might contribute to and improve those spaces. These recognitions may take place in the contexts of educational settings which continue to devalue World Englishes, especially those of the Global South and people of color. Another context where such recognitions may occur is the tracking of pupils with a perceived lack of English skills into courses and programs that are not intended for futures in higher education. Rising above superficial legacies of multiculturalism, it is here that critical, poststructural, feminist, and New Literacy approaches are particularly useful, as they help challenge the false binary of "non-native" and "native" English speakers, and encourage all to interrogate their worldviews and recognize practices, experience, and knowledge beyond what is defined by the status quo (Norton & Toohey, 2011). As it can clearly challenge the official curriculum, this recognition process may initially take more time to plan and implement. However, the long-term sustainable benefits of this process are transformative as the active recognition and understanding of participants facilitates more humanizing interactions and relationships in TESOL.

The inclusive process of recognition, and its subsequent outcomes, can help concretize the process of collaboration among participants in educational spaces, including parents, administrators, and other stakeholders. Sociocultural learning frameworks are instructive here in helping us see that learning often occurs most effectively within collaborative and experiential environments where participants in an educational space, with their range of skills and experiences, can help one other to develop more holistic understandings of linguistic and literacy practices and push themselves beyond what they could do alone (Garcia & Sylvan, 2011). Here, action research methodologies pair well with sociocultural approaches to illustrate how TESOL educators might teach critical inquiry to students as well as be reflexive about refining their own pedagogy.

Collaboration

More specific examples of collaboration within critical pedagogies include PAR and youth PAR (YPAR) projects, where in-service TESOL teachers and their students might do ethnographies of their schools, or elementary students might take their learning home and critically inquire about the World Englishes of their family members or their classmates (Irizarry & Antrop-González, 2013; Lau, 2013; Morrell, 2006). Such action research endeavors afford interdisciplinary opportunities for new or revised collaboration with family members, school staff, university researchers, and others as participants not only develop academic English skills within the official curriculum (e.g., digital literacy skills, qualitative research skills) but also raise critical consciousness through applying critical methods of inquiry (i.e., critical discourse analysis or CDA). A popular criticism of doing such collaboration is that such teaching methods are time-consuming and require an extra amount of physical resources (Chang, 2017). However, it has been demonstrated that the types of collaboration discussed here can raise the capacity of all participants as they engage more students over longer periods of time, connect teachers to the much-needed support of other invested stakeholders, and reduce teacher burnout.

Solidarity

When engaging the processes of recognition and collaboration, critical pedagogies in TESOL can also lead to solidarity, or a sense of purpose and community, among an educational space's stakeholders and participants. At the root of many critical pedagogies in TESOL is helping participants to become in solidarity with one other toward collective goals beyond individualized access to official indicators of achievement like high standardized test scores, college admissions, and various forms of privilege that can sometimes be accumulated through elite forms of schooling and achievement. Shared experiences of empathy, support, and belonging are brought out when developing this process of solidarity, which can help endure and overcome the often dehumanizing effects of imperialism, neoliberalism, and heteronormative patriarchy. This approach to building solidarity is informed by different social movements that have emphasized "bottom-up" or grassroots strategies of bringing people together toward equity and justice (Tarlau, 2015). Examples of such solidarity in TESOL can take the shape of students working with their teacher to establish a more inclusive curriculum for minoritized students in the class, or holding administration accountable for making the best use of limited campus resources. Solidarity may also materialize when disparate stakeholders of an educational space set aside their differences, recognize their respective needs, and support one another in efforts to change the policies or cultural practices of their respective institutions. These are just a few examples of efforts to build unity and power which appear to be more and more necessary as schooling structures and institutions have adopted neoliberal forms of management that increasingly conflate people with quantitative data, flatten diversity in teaching and learning, and undermine the rights of workers and students to organize themselves and represent their concerns (Morgan & Ramanathan, 2005).

There are many pathways to promoting social justice in TESOL through critical pedagogies. This section has highlighted just a few of them through organizing the many paths along the themes of recognition, collaboration, and solidarity in order to provide a generative starting point to engage with the growing bodies of work within TESOL. As new dilemmas of access and technology quickly emerge along perennial issues like homophobia and ableism, it should be clear that there is an important body of critical pedagogies work that engages theory, practice, and change in TESOL.

FUTURE DIRECTIONS

In this chapter, we have broadly outlined the potential of TESOL as a generative space for teachers and learners to interrogate, disrupt, and reimagine themselves, each other, and their communities through liberatory and humanizing critical pedagogies. We have highlighted the intersections of critical pedagogies with poststructural, feminist, sociocultural, and New Literacy frameworks to underscore the participatory social justice pedagogical processes of recognition, collaboration, and solidarity. Thinking about future directions for the field, we begin by noting a series of unresolved tensions surrounding critical pedagogies as they relate to English language teaching and learning.

First, the nomenclature and by consequence undergirding identity of TESOL (Teaching English to Speakers of Other Languages) is in and of itself problematic in an increasingly globalized world where the binary between native and non-native speaker of English has become increasingly contested as a postcolonial artifact (Lin & Luke, 2006). Questions include What counts as English? Who counts as a native speaker? Who gets to decide? In U.S. K-12 contexts, for example, the lion's share of "English Language Learners" in public school classrooms are actually U.S. born and U.S. educated, English-dominant, second-generation Latinx children and adolescents (see Salas & Portes, 2017).

Second, and related to our previous point, enactments of critical pedagogies are potentially context-specific. For example, discussions of critical pedagogies in U.S. K-12 ESL education are often located in highly racially segregated urban school districts where the terms "English Learner" and "Latinx" are used interchangeably. However, the category of English Learner might have a very different distinction in another social-geographic context such as mainland China or Romania. To that end, we emphasize the need for critical pedagogies to recognize and embrace the specificity of the communities in which such pedagogies are enacted. We suggest that such enactments be preceded, accompanied, and followed by individual reflection and participatory dialogue within and between schools and their communities – and that such discussions inform TESOL globally.

Third, critical pedagogies are by their nature meant to disrupt and interrogate. However, such disruption can also take on visceral forms that potentially place individual teachers, students, and larger communities at risk in ways that are difficult sometimes to foresee. For these reasons, such pedagogies are more sustainable when they are generated from communal dialogue and collective action committed to not just whistleblowing but to tangible change.

Despite these and other tensions within critical pedagogies, what we do recognize in the face of populist, xenophobic, and racialized nationalistic discourse is that TESOL can no longer be content with method, postmethod, or market as its disciplinary guideposts. The historic disciplinary fixation on method was a naïve underestimation of the political nature of teaching and learning. Teaching is a political act; and, English language education is more than growing academic literacies. Rather, the spaces we create in our classrooms, curricula, and institutions are ones wherein we might glimpse the possibility of a world where individuals are valued and honored for who we are and who we are still in the process of becoming.

Discussion Questions

1. In TESOL, analytic thinking and critical thinking are sometimes used interchangeably. In the context of critical pedagogies for English language education, how are these ways of thinking similar? How are they different?
2. Critical pedagogies often focus on the dynamics of power. What is a power-differential in your classroom or community? How is it constructed? How might it be deconstructed?
3. What is an issue that you and your students are collectively concerned about? How might you bring it into your English language curriculum as a theme to explore along with the development of communicative proficiency?
4. Amid the rhetoric of "fake news," how might critical pedagogies within TESOL help support learners in your educational context to develop their own thoughtful and well-informed views, whether concerning themselves or the broader, interconnected world around them?
5. What sort of resistance might teachers employing critical pedagogies potentially face in their classrooms and school communities? How might teachers wanting to take up critical pedagogies start to build a network of support within and across communities?

Resources for Further Exploration

1. Gallo, S. (2017). *Mi padre: Mexican immigrant fathers and their children's education*. New York: Teachers College Press, Columbia University.
   In this recent book-length qualitative study, Gallo leverages critical theory to examine gendered constructions of immigrant fathers' commitment to their young children's education.
2. Paris, D. (2011). *Language across difference: Ethnicity, communication, and youth identities in changing urban schools*. Cambridge, UK: Cambridge University Press.
   Humanizing frameworks for teacher education/teacher leadership have focused on the asymmetry between institutionally valued communication patterns and local linguistic codes and cultural styles of thinking and doing. In this ethnography of an urban school, Paris seeks to problematize readers' subjectivities in regard to the academic potential of urban youth with a focus on linguistic multivocality and the cognitive fluidity it represents.
3. Cervantes-Soon, C. (2017). *Juárez girls rising: transformative education in times of dystopia*. Minneapolis, MN: University of Minnesota Press.
   In her participatory ethnography of high school girls in Ciudad Juárez, Cervantes-Soon theorizes the young women's understandings of how education can promote self-empowerment and resistance against injustice and violence.

4. www.gse.upenn.edu/cue/forum/video_library
The Ethnography in Education Research Forum at the University of Pennsylvania Graduate School of Education has a video collection of its annual conference keynote presentations from 2010 to 2016 – many of which leverage critical pedagogies.
5. www.tolerance.org
A project of the Southern Poverty Law Center, Teaching Tolerance was founded in 1991 to provide social justice teaching resources to teachers free of charge.

REFERENCES

Benesch, S. (1993). Critical thinking: A learning process for democracy. TESOL Quarterly, 27(3), 545–548. doi:10.2307/3587485

Chang, B. (2015). In the service of self-determination: Teacher education, service-learning, and community reorganizing. Theory Into Practice, 54(1), 29–38. doi:10.1080/00405841.2015.977659

Chang, B. (2017). Building a higher education pipeline: Sociocultural and critical approaches to "internationalisation" in teaching and research. The Hong Kong Teachers' Centre Journal, 16(1), 1–25.

Darling-Hammond, L. (2007). Third annual Brown lecture in education research: The flat Earth and education: How America's commitment to equity will determine our future. Educational Researcher, 36(6), 318–334. doi:10.3102/0013189x07308253

Davis, K. A., & Skilton-Sylvester, E. (2004). Looking back, taking stock, moving forward: Investigating gender in TESOL. TESOL Quarterly, 38(3), 381–404. doi:10.2307/3588346

Esposito, J., & Evans-Winters, V. (2007). Contextualizing critical action research: Lessons from urban educators. Educational Action Research, 15(2), 221–237.

Freire, P. (1985). The politics of education: Culture, power and liberation. London, UK: Bergin & Garvey.

Garcia, O., & Sylvan, C. E. (2011). Pedagogies and practices in multilingual classrooms: Singularities in pluralities. The Modern Language Journal, 95(3), 385–400. doi:10.1111/j.1540-4781.2011.01208.x

Irizarry, J. G., & Antrop-González, R. (2013). RicanStruction sites: Race, space, and place in the education of DiaspoRican youth. Taboo: The Journal of Culture and Education, 13(1), 7. doi:10.31390/taboo.13.1.07

Kubota, R., & Lin, A. (2006). Race and TESOL: Introduction to concepts and theories. TESOL Quarterly, 40(3), 471–493. doi:10.2307/40264540

Kumaravadivelu, B. (1994). The postmethod condition: (E)merging strategies for second/foreign language teaching. TESOL Quarterly, 28(1), 27–48. doi:10.2307/3587197

Larsen-Freeman, D. (2011). Techniques and principles in language teaching (3rd ed.). New York, NY: Oxford University Press.

Lau, S. M.-C. (2013). A study of critical literacy work with beginning English language learners: An integrated approach. Critical Inquiry in Language Studies, 10(1), 1–30. doi:10.1080/15427587.2013.753841

Lin, A., & Luke, A. (2006). Coloniality, postcoloniality, and TESOL . . . can a spider weave its way out of the web that it is being woven into just as it weaves? Critical Inquiry in Language Studies, 3(2–3), 65–73. doi:10.1080/15427587.2006.9650840

Luke, A. (2008). TESOL in the corporate university. TESOL Quarterly, 42(2), 305–313. doi:10.1002/j.1545-7249.2008.tb00125.x

Morgan, B. D., & Ramanathan, V. (2005). Critical literacies and language education: Global and local perspectives. Annual Review of Applied Linguistics, 25, 151–169. doi:10.1017/S0267190505000085

Morrell, E. (2006). Critical participatory action research and the literacy achievement of ethnic minority groups. National Reading Conference Yearbook, 55, 1–18.

Norton, B., & Toohey, K. (2011). Identity, language learning, and social change. Language Teaching, 44(4), 412–446. doi:10.1017/S0261444811000309

Portes, P. R., & Salas, S. (Eds.). (2011). Vygotsky in 21st century society: Advances in cultural historical theory and praxis with non-dominant communities. New York, NY: Peter Lang.

Ramanathan, V., & Pennycook, A. (2008). Articulating identities: Communities, histories, migrations. TESOL in Context, 18(2), 22–41.

Rogers, R., Schaenen, I., Schott, C., O'Brien, K., Trigos-Carrillo, L., Starkey, K., & Chasteen, C. C. (2016). Critical discourse analysis in education. *Review of Educational Research*, 86(4), 1192–1226. doi:10.3102/0034654316628993

Salas, S., & Portes, P. R. (Eds.). (2017). *US latinization: Education and the New Latino South*. Albany: State University of New York Press.

Tarlau, R. (2015). How do new critical pedagogies develop? Public education, social change, and landless workers in Brazil. *Teachers College Record*, 117(11), 1–36.

Vygotsky, L. S. (1978). *Mind in society: The development of higher psychological processes* (M. Cole, V. John-Steiner, S. Scribner, & E. Souberman, Trans.). Cambridge, MA: Harvard University Press.

Awakening Critical Consciousness in Japanese University EFL Students Through Student Journalism

David Leslie

Perhaps Paolo Freire's most important insight is that schools often inculcate a certain intellectual passivity in students that serves to preserve unjust social structures by rendering them invisible. A significant challenge for teachers is to find a way to wake students from this passive acceptance of *things as they are* and encourage them to imagine how *they might be instead*. A particularly useful approach is through student-written journalism. This case study looks at an attempt to awaken critical consciousness through the act of student journalism.

A key feature of critical pedagogy is that it rejects the traditional "banking" method of teaching wherein the teacher "deposits" knowledge into the passive and presumably hitherto empty student mind. Instead, it recognizes that students have much to teach if only given a chance. In the "Life in Kochi Project," ESL student journalists are empowered to be the primary generators of knowledge. They are tasked with using their interests and personal contacts to explore and report on the local community. They identify what they deem to be interesting stories and then serve as "bridge-bloggers" by bringing their insights and observations about the life and culture around them to the broader English-speaking world. The students are indeed writing as part of a class, but the fact that their articles reach an audience beyond the classroom means that this is not "practice" journalism; it is alternative journalism. At its best, however, it is also more than that. Citizenship is a legal status, whereas *active citizenship* describes a behavior – acting like a citizen by participating in the broadly political aspects of community life. As Harcup (2011) pointed out, journalism is not just for citizenship; it is citizenship in action. Dewey (2008) argued that what happens in the classroom should, in some way, generate a broader social good. This project attempts to do just that.

THE SETTING

This case study examines the "Life in Kochi Project," an EFL composition course taught within the intensive, semester-long English Program for International Communication (EPIC) of the Faculty of Humanities and Social Science at Kochi National University in Kochi, Japan. The EPIC program began in 2004 and was designed to meet the needs of intermediate to upper-intermediate EFL students. It aimed to prepare students with the foundational skills (e.g., small-group discussion, academic writing) required for more specialized English studies and study abroad. The program consists of six English-medium classes per week taught by three different teachers. While individual courses operate independently, the three teachers work closely to coordinate the curriculum so that students get a wide variety of language skill instruction and classroom experiences.

The focus unit of this case study, the "Life in Kochi Project," began in 2010 to give EPIC students experience in EFL composition for an audience beyond the classroom. As of this writing, more than 100 articles have been published on the Life In Kochi (*https://lifeinkochi.net/*) website, and over the last three years the site has attracted more than 30,000 unique visitors from more than 150 different countries.

DESCRIPTION OF ENGLISH LANGUAGE LEARNERS

For most of its history, EPIC has mainly attracted upper-intermediate, second-year university students majoring in English or International Communication. A typical year, however, also finds students from other faculties as well as the occasional international students here to study Japanese. While there have been a few students at the C1 Level of the Common European Framework of Reference for Languages (CEFR), most students are at the B1 or B2 CEFR Levels. Entrance to the EPIC program is restricted to students who are at the B1 Level or higher as determined by a written sample and an oral interview conducted by the three EPIC teachers. Lingley (2005) points out that students seeking to enter the program typically have complex motivations. The workload tends to be more substantial than a typical Kochi university class, but EPIC has a word-of-mouth reputation for offering a unique experience and tends to attract students who are seeking something different and more meaningful than a typical English class. Many students have been abroad and are eager to maintain their oral communication skills. All are looking to study English through the medium of English itself, which is still uncommon in Japan. Additionally, since the class meets for six periods a week, students often form deep personal connections with each other, and it is not uncommon for them to socialize outside of class.

PEDAGOGICAL APPLICATION AND INNOVATION

It may be strange to think of Japanese university students as suffering under a "pedagogy of the oppressed." Unquestionably, they come from a background significantly more privileged than Freire's Brazilian sugarcane workers. Yet it remains true that the "banking method" of language learning dominates Japan's high-stakes, test-driven secondary education. While this may produce students who score well on such tests, a blowback effect of this can be to create what Smith (1983) identified as the "mental stultification" that occurs when students are dependent on authority to do their thinking for them (p. 1). In general, Japanese university students, while good at taking notes when directed to, rarely ask questions and seldom challenge any idea presented in class. Though it can indeed be argued that silence in the face of authority has roots in the unique context of Japanese history and culture, this conspicuous lack of student agency creates a barrier for students to progress much beyond an intermediate level of communicative competence in English. Especially when it comes to writing, students often struggle to express unique points of view. Awakening what Freire (1970) described as critical consciousness, then, is key to both the development of higher levels of English proficiency and the general promotion of active citizenship among Japanese university students.

The "Life in Kochi Project" seeks to accomplish these two goals in several ways. One is the writing task itself. Students produce extended "feature" articles (as opposed to just-the-facts "hard news" stories) in English. Kochi Prefecture is a poor, rural community for which there is little information in English. This creates an opportunity for students to write for a real audience. In small-group discussions, students are invited to consider the significance of local journalism and the broader role of a free press in a democracy. The project has been running since 2010, and recent students have the benefit of reading and reflecting upon articles written by earlier students. Initially, they are often surprised at the sophistication of previous articles and intimidated by what is expected of them. By the end of the semester, however, students report that they feel proud of accomplishing what at first seemed beyond their abilities.

The search for relevant and manageable local stories also nudges students toward active citizenship. They must turn their critical attention beyond the university and toward the wider local community. While some of the best stories have come from personal connections to people or organizations doing newsworthy things, it is often the case that students whose hometowns are in other prefectures end up exploring this wider local community for the first time.

In their search for stories, students are not always sure what constitutes "local news." For this project, local news must meet two criteria. The first is that it must be something that *has* happened recently, *is* happening now, or *will* happen soon. Next, it must be significant to the wider community, not just to the writer. At times, students are attracted to a topic for reasons they do not fully understand and cannot explain. This lack of clarity is where individual editorial conferencing begins, as they may need assistance in finding a manageable story within that topic. This conferencing takes place one-on-one in the classroom, with the teacher asking questions to draw out the student's intentions and to clarify the focus of the article.

The feature article the students write follows a structure that is itself an exercise in critical consciousness. All articles follow the four-box feature article structure described by McGill (2007) where the four boxes are (1) The Anecdotal Lead, (2) The Nut, (3) The Messy Middle, and (4) The Kicker. This easily teachable structure helps students think critically about their stories.

To clarify the mechanics of this structure, a recent student article, "Where Local People Save Children's Smiles," is examined next. (See *https://lifeinkochi.net/2018/08/04/where-local-people-save-childrens-smiles/* for the full article.)

The four-box article opens with the *Anecdotal Lead*. Often written in the present progressive, it is taken from direct writer observation and serves to pull readers into the story while grounding the news in a human context:

> Because it is raining outside, an elementary school-age girl is playing house, while half-a-dozen noisy boys play tag in the playroom. From the kitchen comes the smell of spicy curry that Dai-chan (Mr. Manabe, manager of Kodomo Shokudo) is preparing with the help of university student volunteers.
>
> "What's for dinner?" one of the boys asks as he smells something delicious.
>
> "Curry and rice," Dai-chan answers while giving a sweet smile.

The second box, the *Nut*, clarifies the news value and makes explicit why and to whom this story is important:

> The 22 children, from the ages of four to eleven, gathered Wednesday afternoon at the *Kodomo Shokudo*, literally "children's cafeteria," in Koda City, Kochi. The Kodomo Shokudo aims to be a place where anyone can get together and have dinner for free. The concept of the Kodomo Shokudo is to be a safe place for the children to learn to be independent as well as for them to play with their friends and to eat dinner together.

This is by far the hardest segment for students to write, not because of the content they need to produce in English, but because of the critical analysis they need to offer. In this critical analysis, the students need to answer the question, "What is this story really about?" This requires students to engage critical consciousness by reflecting on the deeper significance of the scene they have described in the anecdotal lead.

While it is often true that writing is a way of discovering meaning as one writes, this is not the case for the Nut of the feature articles. Here, students often require conferencing for real story growth to happen. As Lingley and Isemonger (2018) note, these individual conferences are time-consuming yet critical for successful EFL writers. Making clear what is "at stake" in the article requires patient and persistent dialogue between the teacher and a student journalist.

Students are expected to deliver several drafts of their stories, and individual one-on-one conferencing happens continually as stories develop. The first written draft is a Lead and Nut only draft, as these two boxes define what the story will be about. Once this perspective is developed in the writer's mind, the rest of the article can then be written relatively easily.

The third box, the *Messy Middle*, consists of statistics, translated direct quotes and paraphrases that explain the who, what, when, where, and why of the Nut. This section requires writers to synthesize information from various sources and demonstrates the CEFR B2.1 level of written ability sought in the EPIC program. Here is an example of the *Messy Middle* box of the same story, "Where Local People Save Children's Smiles":

> In the world, lots of people think that Japan is rich enough to buy food. However, one in six people in Japan are faced with poverty. . . . In Japan, poverty does not mean only about money, it is also about mental issues.

"Some children eat dinner alone at night because of their parent are working. Therefore, the Kodomo Shokudo would be a place for these children to gather," Dai-chan explains. "Conversation at the dinner table is crucial for kids to describe their feeling."

The final box, the *Kicker*, provides an emotionally satisfying conclusion to the story. Typically, this is the most memorable quote of the piece. The Kicker can also involve picking up the action where the lead ended or the aspirations of the story's main character:

Even though there is about 50 Kodomo Shokudo in Kochi prefecture, they are only open once a month. According to Mr. Manabe, he feels that this is not enough as it made the Kodomo Shokudo to be like an event. He wishes that the Kodomo Shokudo that he manages could be a model for the other Kodomo Shokudo.

"If I can, I would want to open the Kodomo Shokudo every day, not once a week so that the children could eat dinner and have a place where they can be themselves every day."

At school, there are a lot of mental problems that made the children do not want to go to a school such as bullying and unreasonable punishment from the teachers.

"So Kodomo Shokudo is not only a place where the children could eat a meal, but also a safe place for everyone to gather."

The last day of class becomes the last stage in the development of critical consciousness. On this day, the articles are published to the Life in Kochi website (see Figure 2.1.1). Students use that final class period to read and comment on each other's articles. It is a joyful moment. Publication of their articles is an affirmation that their voices count; it is evidence that they are generators of knowledge. From the first class, students know that when finished, their articles will be published and read by a genuine audience beyond the classroom. This awareness raises the stakes for the writers as it requires the topics to be interesting and the writing to be clear. In the end, however, the best articles are written not necessarily by the students with the highest English language proficiency but rather the ones who can most carefully and critically reflect on the world around them and then write about it compellingly.

Life in Kochi

A student-written journal about Kochi Prefecture, Japan   Feature Articles   The Writers   Contact

Field Guide ⌄   About this Journal

Evers Link: Co-existence for Humans and Other Animals

Yosakoi Immigration: The solution to Kochi's Aging Society?

By Rena Nagayama, Rina Yamao, Rika Yamao Beautiful mountains and

One-Day Restaurant Challenge

By Yui Tateishi About a dozen people

Figure 2.1.1 Student articles published to the Life in Kochi website https://lifeinkochi.net

Source: David Leslie

CONCLUSION

Many students report that the writing they do in the Life in Kochi project is the most challenging they have ever done, in English and in Japanese. Through topic exploration, research, and most importantly, substantive revisions of the content of their articles, students are challenged to look carefully and critically at the society around them. The hope is that students come away from this experience not only with personal satisfaction at having accomplished a daunting task in English but also with a deeper appreciation of, and more active membership in, their communities.

REFERENCES

Dewey, J. (2008). *The school and society.* New York, NY: Cosimo Classics.

Freire, P. (1970). *Pedagogy of the oppressed* (M. B. Ramos, Trans.). New York, NY: Continuum, 2007.

Freire, P. (1973). *Education for critical consciousness* (Vol. 1). Chicago, IL: Bloomsbury Publishing.

Harcup, T. (2011). Alternative journalism as active citizenship. *Journalism, 12*(1), 15–31.

Lingley, D. (2005). Sustaining motivation through course design. *JACET Chugoku-Shikoku Research Bulletin (JACET-CSCRB),* 2, 55–72.

Lingley, D., & Isemonger, I. (2018). Producing an L2 campus newspaper: Pedagogic support for authentic writing, active learning and task-based interaction. *Research Reports of the International Studies Course, Faculty of Humanities and Social Sciences, Kochi University, 19,* 57–70.

McGill, D. (2007). The largemouth journalism manual. *The McGill Report: Media for Global Citizens.* Retrieved from www. mcgillreport.org/largemouth.htm

Smith, F. (1983). *Essays into literacy.* Portsmouth, NH: Heinemann.

CASE STUDY 2.2

Implementing Critical Pedagogy in a Standards-Driven Context in Turkey

Making Room for Teacher and Student Voices

Hale Hatice Kizilcik

This case study explores how Freirean critical pedagogies can be implemented in settings where the standardized syllabus leaves little space for taking initiative for teachers. In such contexts, teachers have to navigate and bridge the differences between the institutional goals and standards, their own teaching philosophy and background, and students' beliefs, attitudes, knowledge and needs. Here, the case study shows how teachers and students can collaborate and shape certain aspects of the course through "critical and liberating dialogue" (Freire, 1970, p. 65). The aim is to empower the teachers and students by involving them in the decision-making process while moving them from being merely consumers of knowledge in the banking model of education toward becoming problem-posers and problem-solvers (Freire, 1970).

THE SETTING

This case study took place at a large international state university in Turkey. The medium of instruction of this university is English; therefore, the university requires the students to take an institutional English proficiency exam (EPE) that assesses listening, reading, and writing skills as well as vocabulary. At present, due to the large number of students taking the exam, speaking is not tested. Students who are admitted to the university take EPE in September before the beginning of the first semester. The passing score for the test is a composite score of 60 out of 100, and the students who do not reach this minimum score are enrolled in a year-long pre-sessional English intensive program (Prep). Only after successfully completing the Prep, are they qualified to start their coursework in their majors. In the undergraduate programs regardless of their majors, they take further compulsory and elective English courses offered by the Department of Modern Languages (DML).

ENG 311: Advanced Communication Skills

ENG 311: Advanced Communication Skills is offered to the third- and fourth-year students with the overall aim of developing communication skills relevant to work-related contexts. It is a required course for some departments and an elective for others. The major tasks are divided broadly into two categories: job-seeking skills (e.g., writing CVs and cover letters, filling in application forms, and interviewing) and on-the-job skills (e.g., socializing, telephoning, giving presentations, and holding meetings).

The syllabus is designed by the curriculum committee, consisting of experienced lecturers at DML, and the instructors are expected to closely follow it. The assessment is standardized to a great extent, with exams prepared and rated by faculty other than the class instructor, and the final exam and interview count for 40% of the final grade (20% each). Other assessment tasks are designed and implemented by the class instructor aligned with the parameters set by the committee. In this case study, I zoom in on three assessed tasks: (1) making presentations, (2) leading meetings, and (3) composing and responding to emails. These tasks were revised implementing the principles of critical pedagogy. As Freire (1970) indicates action should be preceded by "serious reflection" (p. 65), and in this case study, combining two key terms in critical pedagogy, reflection and dialogue, the term reflective dialogue is used to refer to written or oral communication between the participants that requires deep and systematic thinking and evaluation. Identified tasks were adapted to encourage the students and the teacher to reflect while engaging in a dialogic interaction through speaking and writing. These reflections assisted the teacher and students in posing and solving problems in order to make the tasks more relevant and meaningful. As the case study demonstrates, praxis was achieved; that is, reflection led to action that brought about the desired changes.

DESCRIPTION OF ENGLISH LANGUAGE LEARNERS

This case study focuses on the two sections of the ENG 311 course, where 48 third- and fourth-year students were enrolled. The course was compulsory for all of them. In the first section, there were 13 female and 11 male students, and in the other, there were 14 female and 10 male students. There were international students in both sections, representing Pakistan, Syria, Taiwan, and the United States. With the exception of the international students, the students' native tongue was Turkish. The U.S. student was bilingual in Turkish and English, and the other international students spoke their native tongues (Arabic, Urdu, and Taiwanese Mandarin) and varied in their Turkish language proficiency, at a minimum meeting the general Common European Framework of Reference (CEFR) A2.

The students' English language proficiency, especially their speaking skills, varied significantly. A few students were at C1 and C2 levels, whereas some others' speaking abilities were barely B1. They were from six different disciplines – Chemistry, Education, Engineering, History, Physics, and Statistics.

As young adults approaching graduation, the students had long been in the educational system. They had views about effective and unproductive educational practices, and these reflections could be utilized to improve the instructional design. In addition, a considerable number of students already had some job experience, and thus accumulated rich and diverse knowledge and experience in the major tasks addressed in ENG 311, such as interviews and presentations. For example, some students had given presentations in professional settings. There were students who had already participated in job and graduate school interviews and who had worked part-time jobs. Therefore, they possessed tacit knowledge; that is, implicit knowledge obtained unconsciously through experience. Tacit knowledge or "know-how" may be difficult to verbally communicate and explain to others, and one of the aims of this course was to empower students by encouraging them to explore their tacit knowledge through reflective dialogue.

PEDAGOGICAL APPLICATION AND INNOVATION

Students are invaluable and often underestimated resources in the classroom. Following a prescriptive syllabus constrains both the teacher and students and may leave little room for incorporating what students bring into the class. In Frerian terms, a prescriptive syllabus oppresses the teachers and students by dictating the instructional practices and ignoring students' specific needs and potentials. This approach sees students as empty vessels and attempts to fill them with the knowledge dictated by those in power, the oppressors. Critical pedagogy aims to overhaul this banking model of education. This case study demonstrates the role of reflective dialogue in liberating the students and teacher by allowing them to share their views and experiences to shape their future experiences. Reflective dialogue is characterized by its quality to encourage deep thinking that evaluates issues at hand from various angles. This dialogue is not adversarial in nature and presumes power symmetry among the participants. It entails attentive listening, open-mindedness, argumentation skills, and commitment to positive change. Reflective dialogue can be practiced using both oral and written communication channels.

Reflective dialogue was initiated by adapting the tasks in the required syllabus so as to maintain open communication channels about the tasks and the course in general. Students and the teacher posed problems and worked on generating solutions. Without omitting any course outcomes, the tasks (e.g., presentation, meeting, and email writing) were modified to incorporate student voices. Above all, praxis was achieved by putting the results of these reflections into action by sharing them with the curriculum committee and initiating changes in the course syllabus.

The Presentation Task

In the English for Academic Purposes (EAP) courses offered at the department, the students are introduced to how to prepare and deliver effective presentations. These presentations vary in topic and length, and are graded using the rating scale developed by the curriculum committee. In ENG 311, the students are expected to deliver a presentation related to the main themes in the syllabus (e.g., ethics in the workplace), and this presentation constitutes 10% of the students' overall grade.

With the presentation task, the focus was on revising the assessment criteria which the students had long been criticizing. As documented in the program evaluation report, the students thought that in the DML courses, the presentations were unreasonably demanding because they were rigidly structured and required students to follow a template. It was also indicated that grading was unfair since there was undue emphasis on minor problems (DML, 2014). However, there was not sufficient information regarding what was actually perceived as rigid and unfair nor specific feedback on what would be a better way to assess the presentations. In this case, reflective dialogue was used to elicit the students' views on effective presentations and to design a new student-generated rating scale.

To develop this new rating scale, the teacher investigated the students' perceptions regarding the distinguishing features of effective presentations. Here, a rating scale is defined as "a set of generic descriptions of student performance which can be used to assign scores to an individual student's performance in a systematic fashion" (Carr, 2015, p. 125). Intuitive scale development methods require "principled interpretation of experience" to develop the scale (Council of Europe, 2001, p. 208). Although teachers are sometimes involved in the scale development, students are hardly ever viewed as a resource in such undertakings. As Akbari (2008) states, teachers and students "are either left out of any serious treatment of the profession or represented superficially detached from their real-life experiences" (p. 27). Critical pedagogy aims to include them in shaping the instructional practices.

When devising the presentation rating scale, the students and teacher engaged in reflective dialogue and drew on their experience. The teacher and students followed the procedure described here when developing the assessment scale.

- The teacher explained to the students the rationale behind revising the rating scale referring to earlier criticisms from fellow students.

- The teacher told the students that they all had notions of successful and unsuccessful presentations based on their experience as presenters and members of the audience.

- In groups of two, the students reflected on the presentations they had given and attended and brainstormed the qualities of effective and ineffective presentations.

- After the brainstorming session, the students used their mobile phones to post their opinions on Padlet (See Figure 2.2.1), a free online application allowing users to instantly share information. All posts were projected on the board.

- As a class, the students discussed the opinions posted.

- After class, the instructor combined the data collected from both sections and analyzed them following a basic coding and quantifying methodology. The umbrella categories were delivery (n= 42), content (n=14), language (n=15), organization (n=13), visuals (n=5), and time management (n=6). When the weights for the categories were determined, the number of descriptors under each category and their frequency were considered.

- The teacher used material and ideas generated by the students and combined it into an oral presentation scale for the class. She brought a draft of this scale for another round of student revisions.

- The class reviewed the scale and worked to specify some vague expressions such as "the content is appropriate," "proper language," and "clear language." At this stage, a descriptor related to the range and accuracy of the structures and vocabulary was introduced by the teacher.

- The revised version of the oral presentation assessment scale was piloted in class through peer assessment. The students were satisfied with the new scale and did not suggest further modifications.

At the end-of-course meeting, the teacher shared the final version of the scale with the curriculum committee to be considered as an alternative to the existing scale in the following semester. The committee found the scale appropriate and with minor modifications, they replaced the old scale with the student-generated scale (see Table 2.2.1 in Appendix A for the draft rating scale).

The Meeting Task

The second revised component of ENG 311 was the meeting task that created opportunities for the students to explore and practice the conventions of academic and business meetings. To assess this task, the curriculum committee suggested various meeting options that evaluated the students' ability to effectively

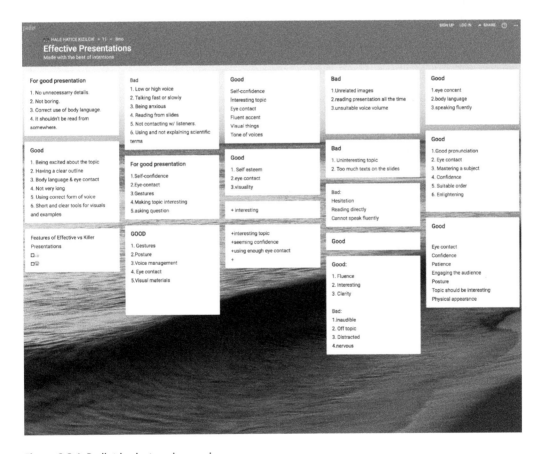

Figure 2.2.1 Padlet brainstorming session

Source: Hale Kizilcik

participate in a meeting. As an innovation, the teacher organized a course appraisal meeting which asked the students to discuss the strengths and weaknesses of the course. At the core of the course was reflective dialogue among the students. They were informed that for the meeting to be considered effective, they needed to go beyond problem posing and focus on generating solutions that could be put into action.

The teacher prepared and emailed the meeting agenda to the students a week before the meeting (See Appendix B). Four separate meetings were held with groups of 12 students, and one student chaired each group meeting. These students were chosen by the teacher based on their performance throughout the semester. They had good command of English and had actively participated in class discussions. The teacher took the minutes and participated in the meeting from time to time. However, her participation was kept to a minimum to reduce teacher power and pressure and to allow students to lead and actively engage in the meetings. The minutes were typed by the teacher and emailed to the students for any corrections and additions. The final version of the minutes was sent to the students, the curriculum committee, and department administration. The feedback in the minutes was utilized both by the teacher and the curriculum committee and resulted in course revisions. For example, the students wanted to practice video-interviews done via Skype, FaceTime, or another videoconferencing application, which have become widespread in business circles. As a result, the teacher agreed to include video-interviews in the following semester. Furthermore, the interview questions and procedure were revised by the committee based on the feedback provided by the students.

The Email Writing Task

Once again, the students were expected to engage in critical reflection on their experience with the email writing task leading to praxis. The curriculum committee did not provide specifications for the email task other than that it should focus on writing formal emails using appropriate register and style. The teacher designed email tasks to incite students to reflect on different aspects of the course and suggest action. For example, in one of the emails, the students were encouraged to review the emailed minutes and reply to the teacher about its accuracy and scope. See Appendix C for the email writing task.

In addition, at the end of the first week, which amounts to nine lessons in a summer school term, the teacher asked the students to send an email giving feedback on how the lessons were executed (see Appendix D for a sample student response). In their emails, the students asked the instructor to speak slowly and give more time to complete in-class tasks, which were justifiable concerns. On the other hand, some of the feedback was considered unreasonable from the teacher's perspective. For instance, some students criticized the teacher's strict policy against using mobile phones for personal use during the lessons and requested more tolerance. Other students were unhappy with the teacher's insistence on students using only English in class. The teacher shared all the relevant feedback in a lesson, and through reflective dialogue the class developed a course of action, which did not include changing the rules for mobile phone and language use in the classroom. This resulted from a discussion about what would be sound practice and what might be in conflict with the long-term benefit of the whole group.

CONCLUSION

The key Frerian concepts at the heart of this case study are reflection, dialogue, problem-posing, problem-solving, action, and praxis. As Freire emphasizes, in-depth reflection is essential before taking action. Here, dialogue is considered as a reflective tool that allows the participants to share their accumulated knowledge, experience, beliefs, and attitudes with others. Through dialogue, reflection becomes deeper, and reflective dialogue emerges as a means to identify problems, seek solutions to the problems, plan action, and bring about change. The present case study exemplified how critical pedagogy can be applied even in contexts where a standard syllabus prescribes the content and assessment. It demonstrated how reflective dialogue yielded to praxis and initiated change.

The students and the teacher were continuously engaged in reflective dialogue as students developed the new rating scale for the presentations, discussed both course content and instructional practices with their classmates in the course appraisal meeting, and shared their feedback by email. They not only practiced the target skills in the required course syllabus, but also shaped these components by taking a critical stance. As a practitioner of critical pedagogy, the teacher was a part of the dialogue and helped orchestrate changes by communicating with both students and the curriculum committee.

REFERENCES

Akbari, R. (2008). Transforming lives: Introducing critical pedagogy into ELT classrooms. ELT Journal, 62(3), 276–283.

Carr, N. T. (2015). Designing and analyzing language tests. Oxford, UK: Oxford University Press.

Council of Europe. (2001). Common European framework of reference for languages: Learning, teaching, assessment. Cambridge, UK: Cambridge University Press.

Department of Modern Languages (DML). (2014). Program evaluation report. Middle East Technical University, Ankara, Turkey.

Freire, P. (1970). Pedagogy of the oppressed (M. B. Macedo, Trans.). New York, NY: Continuum.

APPENDIX A
The Draft Rating Scale

The italics mark suggestions by the teacher, numbers in parenthesis are frequencies of the codes, and the question marks indicate vague points to be clarified before the scale is finalized.

Table 2.2.1 The draft rating scale

Content (n=15) 4 3 2 1 0	A topic that would appeal to the interest and level of general/educated audience is identified (8). The presentation is informative (the presenter is knowledgeable about the topic) (3) & *addresses all parts of the research topic* The ideas are supported with well-integrated concrete arguments or examples (2). References are cited (1). The content is made clear to the audience (1).
Organization (n=13) 3 2 1 0	The presentation has a clear beginning and conclusion, and the parts are balanced in terms of length. The presentation is well organized by logically ordering the ideas and using transitions and signposts. The presentation is focused on the topic.
Delivery (n=42) 4 3 2 1 0	The presenter looks confident (neither too relaxed nor too tense) (10). Effective eye-contact with the audience is maintained throughout the presentation (12). Body language including gestures and facial expression is used effectively (13). Movements are purposeful (3). The speech is audible (1). Intonation is used effectively (8); Voice quality (?). The presentation is delivered at an appropriate speed – not too fast or slow (4).
Language (n=15) 4 3 2 1 0	The speech is fluent with little or no hesitation (8). Clear language, Clarity, appropriate language (7) (?). *A range of structures and vocabulary is used accurately.* *Words are correctly pronounced (with some possible slips in unfamiliar vocabulary).* *The language has the features of formal spoken English.*
Ground rules	
Time management (n=6)	*The presentation is completed at the designated time.
Visuals (n=5)	The visuals are relevant, and well-prepared (?). The note cards look professional. Note cards are used effectively.

* + 1 min: deduct one over 10 points/1:30 min: stop the presentation (?).

Band Score Interpretation

3–4 – Meets/exceeds all/almost all of the criteria in the band.

2 – Meets some of the criteria in the band.

1 – Meets few of the criteria in the band.

0 – Provides little or no evidence to make judgements.

Appendix B
The Meeting Agenda

ENG 311 Course Evaluation Meeting, [name of the university]

Objective: To discuss the effectiveness of ENG 311 to provide feedback for curriculum designers.

Date: May 15, 2018

Time: 10:40

Location: MM 316

Agenda

1. Brainstorm the benefits of the course for [name of the university] students.

2. Brainstorm the aspects of the course that are in need of improvement and that decrease its appeal for [name of the university] students.

3. Prioritize the most important handicaps of the course and brainstorm solutions.

4. Organize the presentation for the curriculum team.

5. Closing

Appendix C
ENG 311 Email Assignment

You've received an email from the DML representative at the meeting asking you to review and confirm the minutes.

Review the minutes and write a reply doing one or two of the following:

- Point out a piece of missing information that was discussed at the meeting but is not included in the minutes.
- State a mistake/information that may lead to misunderstanding.
- Make a point that you forgot to bring out or failed to explain at the meeting.

Follow the conventions of a formal email. In your email:

- Greet the person.
- Thank the person for sending the minutes.
- State the purpose of your email.
- Deliver your message.
- Closing.

Assessment Criteria

An effective email has the following features:

- Effectively fulfills its communicative aim
- Is written at the right level of formality
- Is concise
- Follows the format associated with the genre (subject, salutation, closing, etc.)
- Is written using correct language (spelling, punctuation, capitalization included)

APPENDIX D
An Example of an Email From a Student

(Spelling and grammar are original)

Dear Hale Hocam, [an expression accepted as formal in the context]

Thank you for sharing the minutes of the meeting. I am writing this email to explain a comment I made about the interview questions. First, I want to thank to the interviewers for creating a successful role-play environment. I'd like to comment on the questions that you asked. The questions were about discovering positive sides in me but there were no questions that tried to find out negative sides of me. Example questions that might be asked to me were "why you failed two years in the university" or "why is your CGPA low?" I hope this feedback helps you while creating the interview questions.

Sincerely,
[Name Surname]

CASE STUDY 2.3

Critical Pedagogy in a Postgraduate TESOL Professional Development Course in México
Using the NACTIC Model

Leticia Araceli Salas Serrano, Rebeca Elena Tapia Carlín, and Celso Pérez Carranza

This case study focuses on the experiences of one cohort of English teachers in an MA program in ELT in Puebla, Mexico, and how they explored their teaching of both vulnerable groups and students with special needs in their English classroom. Critical pedagogy was used as the foundation to design the course "Professional Development Portfolio" and to establish the exploration of the participants' language teaching practices as its general purpose in order to transform their teaching by acknowledging who the students are and what their individual needs are in opposition to general and not personalized instruction. Following Norton and Toohey (2011), who regarded language as the "practice that constructs the way learners understand themselves, their social surroundings, their histories and their possibilities for the future" (p. 1), the Professional Development Portfolio course aimed to take the MA candidates on a journey along their teaching development and practice. According to Ares (2006), learning must occur from the critical examination of social order that leads to action for social justice as the purpose of education, including the area of ELT through the use of technology as a tool for innovation and reflection. Therefore, an MA course in TESOL with an approach on critical pedagogy might allow MA candidates to professionally develop as English teachers who, besides the linguistic instruction, are also aware of students' needs in their surrounding contexts.

THE SETTING

In Mexico, proficiency in English is seen as a way to get a better job or a scholarship, and this is the main reason why the number of English learners has increased during the past few decades. This has resulted in the creation of ELT BA and MA programs all over the country to keep up with the growing demand for qualified English teachers. Similar to the challenges facing Mexico's education system as a whole, English language education in Mexico also faces the challenge of unequal access to high-quality instruction at the different levels of the educational system in the country. In an attempt to meet the need of English teachers, the School of Languages at *Benemérita Universidad Autónoma de Puebla*, (BUAP) in Mexico has offered a BA program in ELT since 1984. Then, in 2005, an MA in ELT was created in order to give graduates of the BA program and other teachers a space for professionalization and continuous professional development (CPD). The setting of this implementation was the MA program which receives a new cohort every two years.

DESCRIPTION OF ENGLISH LANGUAGE LEARNERS

The candidates for the MA in ELT program must possess a B2 level in English proficiency based on the Common European Framework of Reference for Languages (CEFR) as well as basic digital skills. The aspiring candidates for the MA program must also have at least three years of English teaching experience as an entry requirement. An additional requirement is to submit a description of the research project they will carry out during their studies that will result in a thesis project at the end of the Master's program.

This case study focuses on the cohort of the MA in ELT students from 2017 to 2019. This cohort consisted of 16 candidates, all of them Mexican, between the ages of 28 and 55. Their native language was Spanish, and their academic background was in most cases a BA in ELT. These students earned a place in the MA program after a rigorous process of selection. Approximately 70 candidates submitted research project proposals and went through interviews and meetings with the program's Academic Committee. At the end of the process, these 16 teachers were accepted to become part of the new cohort.

PEDAGOGICAL APPLICATION AND INNOVATION

Since its establishment as a profession, the field of TESOL has made an impact on English learners' lives, either by providing them with a different perspective of the world or by giving them English language and communication tools to improve their careers or skills (Burns & Richards, 2009). Pennycook (1999) recognized the importance of incorporating critical issues, such as research and self-reflection, when teaching English in order to meet inequalities and needs in each classroom. By the same token, Gee (1994) has also acknowledged that "English teachers stand at the very heart of the most crucial educational, cultural, and political issues of our time" (p. 190).

Awareness of local and specific student needs has taken greater relevance in the context of learner-centered instruction in language teaching (Brown, 2008). Such instruction acknowledges learning differences in students and finds it important to identify social, economic, and health situations that might make English learning difficult.

Professional Development Portfolio Course

The facilitators of the Professional Development Course had the initiative to raise awareness in the MA candidates about some of the challenges that might be occurring in their teaching contexts and the urgency to address them instead of ignoring them. This way, the NACTIC model was developed. NACTIC stands for *Necesidades de alumnos en su Contexto por medio de TIC* (Students' needs in their Context through ICT). The NACTIC model was created to make MA candidates aware of current social, economic, and health issues taking place in their surroundings and the identification of learners' needs, especially in contexts where students from vulnerable groups or with special needs attend school. The model was based on the work of Kirkwood and Kirkwood (2011), who stated that "people can explore their reality and awareness so that their knowledge is deeper and start practicing what they learn" (p. 172). Critical pedagogy provided the foundation for teachers to examine their practices and look for social change through an exploration of theory and praxis (Freire, 1985). Using critical pedagogy, teachers and learners engaged in dialogue in order to acknowledge their reality. Accordingly, the steps to implement the NACTIC model were established as:

- Identifying students' needs in the MA teaching contexts, including learners from vulnerable groups and learners with special needs.

- Developing awareness and reflecting on students' needs based on the MA candidates' teaching experiences throughout their praxis.

- Taking action by designing instruction to meet the students' needs.

New courses are always opportunities to start new experiences. Therefore, we, as a research group, wanted to make the new MA in ELT cohort aware that by teaching English, teachers can make a difference not only in educational but also in social and affective situations. The course *Professional Development Portfolio* was chosen to implement the NACTIC model developed by the facilitators of the course so that MA candidates had the opportunity to reflect on their past, present, and future teaching practice. MA candidates were expected to engage with the objectives of the course:

- Develop awareness of how to work with English language learners with special needs and/or from vulnerable groups.

- Reflect on their past teaching experiences when they had students with special needs and from vulnerable groups in their classes.

- Create or adapt appropriate materials that would meet the needs of English language learners with special needs.

- Create an English teaching intervention project appropriate for English language learners of vulnerable groups.

The course was organized in three modules following the principles of the NACTIC model. Three generative themes were identified and established in order to enhance reflection as well as lead the making of the tasks of the course (see Table 2.3.1):

Table 2.3.1 Organization of the course: three modules

	Theme	Assignment
Module 1	Awareness and identification of individual teaching needs	The first e-narrative was assigned and the participants were asked to develop a collage and a digital narrative to summarize their autobiography.
		Task: An autobiography: to identify and establish the teacher as a source for needs awareness through a reflection process, writing about his/her own life and experiences.
Module 2	Raising awareness at the local context	An e-narrative about their past, present, and future experiences was assigned as the second task. The participants had to create a time line of key moments in their career and relate them to their professional development.
		Task: Time line of teaching experiences: to reflect on previous or present challenges faced in their English classrooms.
Module 3	Taking action	For the final project, participants were asked to develop an intervention research project based on 1) their previous professional experiences; 2) the knowledge acquired by exploring the needs of students in the local contexts; and 3) what they thought they could do to start changing their teaching contexts regarding social justice to improve ELT.
		Task: Preparation for future teaching: to plan an English teaching intervention that meets identified needs of English learners in the MA candidates' teaching contexts.

The course was considered an example of blended learning, as ten face-to-face, four-hour weekly sessions were scheduled and as a complement to the course, a class on the *Edmodo* platform (www.edmodo.com) was created as the common space to share materials and collect students' work.

During the first session of the course, the topics of special needs and inclusive education were introduced. This was the innovation for this course. The MA candidates became aware of the foundation of inclusive pedagogy and their students' education needs. They also explored the challenges they might encounter in their classrooms at the time of the course and in their future teaching. Then, the MA candidates shared their own experiences and listened to the experiences that their peers had had. In sessions two to nine, the content of the course stayed the same and was taught similarly to previous years. The topics included sessions on classroom management, teaching strategies and techniques, and syllabus design among others.

In the final session, the facilitator and the MA candidates discussed and reflected on the diversity of students in the different English classrooms where they had taught, but also on the vulnerable and special needs groups and how the specific needs of the students might ideally create meaning for social justice (Freire, 1970) and change. The facilitator and the MA candidates also expressed how the identification of needs led them to take action in their language classrooms.

Samples of Student Work

The students in the *Professional Development Portfolio* course had to create final teaching portfolios. To create their portfolio, the MA candidates were encouraged to use digital resources to develop their tasks, and all tasks were submitted through the Edmodo platform. Here are some examples of the work the students created.

TASK ONE – AN AUTOBIOGRAPHY

As previously mentioned, the first task for students was to create their autobiography, emphasizing their academic development, the problems or challenges they faced, and how they overcame those challenges. This exploration had the objective to make students aware of their own life and context (see Figure 2.3.1).

Figure 2.3.1 Screenshot of a digital autobiography

TASK TWO – TIMELINE OF TEACHING EXPERIENCES

For this task, the MA candidates had to reflect on five milestones or significant moments that had been critical in their development as teachers. This exploration allowed them to have insights on their teaching practices so that they could transform their teaching in a more meaningful way for them and their students. In the following example, the MA candidate realized that he likes to talk to young people and inspire them with his own experience.

> One of my most important achievements and special days was when I was asked by a friend specifically the director of the high school: David Alfaro Siqueiros to invite me to the s 3rd. Forum, entitled perseverance and growth mentality, to be held on December 9, 2016, at the Pedro Infante Auditorium in the city of San Martin Texmelucan. I was in front of 150 students telling them my story where I came from what I have been to, my dreams and passion, the opportunities that we have to change our lives. And have people coming up to me for a motivational to tell young people that you can be whatever you want to be. Neil Anderson mentions that "There is a treasure chest of heavenly direction awaiting your discovery among messages of general conference".

Each student had their own perspectives on looking at their professional development and what they needed to do to meet local social needs.

TASK THREE – THE FINAL PROJECT

The final project was to design an intervention plan in order to meet the needs that each MA candidate identified for their teaching contexts (see Figure 2.3.2).

Final project
Submit 12/12 11:45PM

Instructions

In this assignment, you will be asked to develop an intervention research project based on your previouse professional experience following these guidelines: Title, a descriptive short title of no more than 12 words. 1.- Introduction. A description of the content of the research and the need to do this project, a description of the problem and your personal motivation to conduct this research. 2. Literature Review. A report of of the works that have been done regarding the problem at an international, Latin American, national and local level. 3. A description of the target population, the treatment using technological and non-technnological tools/materials/ resources, research methodology and instruments that you will use to conduct the research. 4. A description of the expected results and limitations of the study. 5. Some conclusions or final thoughts on your study. 6 References, at least 10. 7. Appendixes (e.g. sample material, instruments). The paper must be written in a word text in Arial 12 double spaced. Between 2000 and 2500 words

Figure 2.3.2 The Prompt for the Final Project

Some of the projects that resulted from the course were:

- Teaching English to children with ADHD in elementary school
- What's for breakfast? Nutrition in the English classroom
- Girls' leadership through English learning
- Vision impairment in the English classroom
- Music for vulnerable students in the English classroom
- Inclusive education for kids with behavior problems in the EFL classroom
- Peer-tutoring for students in the English classroom

At least three of the final projects developed in the *Professional Development Portfolio* course are thesis projects.

The implementation of the NACTIC model in the *Professional Development Portfolio* class in an MA in ELT program in Puebla, Mexico, raised awareness of the necessity to explore the language learning and teaching setting in order to transform the teaching practices that might lead to social change by following the principles of critical pedagogy. In many classes, the number of students or the urgency to cover the language program do not always allow teachers to get a deeper insight of the individual or special needs their learners might have. By giving the MA candidates a framework to explore their own perspectives and teaching settings, the course increased the possibility of making changes in the near future.

CONCLUSION

In the lookout for social justice and equity in education, English teaching can make valuable contributions by incorporating some of the issues that concern the communities in which ELT instruction takes place around the world. This case study has presented the development and implementation of the NACTIC model, which allowed MA ELT candidates in Puebla, Mexico, to explore their own teaching practices and to develop strategies for supporting and meeting the needs of vulnerable groups of students and students with special needs. This exploration was informed by critical pedagogy and provided enriching and reflective experiences in MA candidates' development as ELT professionals.

This approach raised the candidates' awareness of social issues that they might not have considered as part of their teaching contexts before. By exploring and analyzing their teaching settings and social issues their students might be facing, they realized the need for transforming their teaching practice for social change. This course was developed in hopes that these empowered MA ELT candidates will take future initiatives to create classrooms where equal opportunities for learning English could lead to contexts where social justice and social change become a reality.

REFERENCES

Ares, N. (2006). Political aims and classroom dynamics: Generative processes in classroom communities. *Radical Pedagogy*, 8(2), 12–20.

Brown, J. K. (2008). Student-centered instruction: Involving students in their own education. *Music Educators Journal*, 94(5), 30–35.

Burns, A., & Richards, J. C. (2009). *The Cambridge guide to second language teacher education*. Cambridge, UK: Cambridge University Press.

Freire. P. (1970). *Pedagogy of the oppressed*. New York, NY: Continuum Publishing.

Freire, P. (1985). *The politics of education: Culture, power and liberation*. London, UK: Bergin & Garvey.

Gee, J. P. (1994). Orality and literacy: From the savage mind to ways with words. In J. Ê Maybin (Ed.), *Language and literacy in social practice* (pp. 168–192). Clevedon, UK: Multilingual Matters.

Kirkwood, G., & Kirkwood, C. (2011). *Living adult education: Freire in Scotland*. Rotterdam, Netherlands: Sense Publishers.

Norton, B., & Toohey, K. (2011). Identity, language learning, and social change. *Language Teaching*, 44(4), 412–446. https://doi.org/10.1017/S0261444811000309

Pennycook, A. (1999). Introduction: Critical approaches to TESOL. *TESOL Quarterly*, 33(3), 329–348. https://doi.org/10.2307/3587668

Unit 3
Postmethod Pedagogy in ELT

Postmethod Pedagogy and Its Role in Contemporary English Language Teaching

Doaa Rashed

FRAMING THE ISSUE

Teachers and learners stand at the heart of the language teaching and learning profession. Together they shape, construct, and evaluate its practices, consequently defining its successes. Attempts to develop language teaching and learning methods without input from both teachers and learners are, and have proven to be, unsuccessful efforts. Those efforts have been aimed at searching for the best applicable method across various contexts. The main driving assumption of each method was that its teaching practices were more effective and had stronger theoretical foundations than the one before. This constant search for the best method resulted in a succession of methods, each bringing different teaching practices to the field based on new beliefs about the purpose and nature of language and language learning. From the Grammar Translation Method to Communicative Language Teaching (CLT) and Task-Based Language Teaching (TBLT), professionals and theorists continued their search for the best method for all ELT contexts. Every time a new method gained popularity among professionals and practitioners, new textbooks were developed and language policies changed to reflect the adoption of that method in the field. Methods are organized sequentially with assigned roles for both teachers and learners without consideration of the local environments where they were adopted. Teachers who conformed to the principles of each new method were left with very little practical application to meet their students' needs and address contextual teaching and learning challenges. They were struggling to provide an engaging comprehensive learning experience to their students while at the same time following one specific teaching method assigned by their administration.

This widespread dissatisfaction with methods led teachers to adopt an eclectic approach to language teaching, which allowed them to implement parts of different methods according to the specific factors of their teaching settings. In other words, teachers were already taking charge of their classroom teaching practices, choosing from a plethora of teaching strategies and adopting new ones that met their learners' needs. This eclectic approach to language teaching reflected not only teachers' dissatisfaction with the ineffectiveness of methods but also confidence in their ability to address the realities and challenges of their different contexts outside of the constraining principles of any single teaching method.

In the 1990s, the TESOL field took a critical turn in examining and understanding the profession and recognizing how language teaching shapes the knowledge and life experiences of language teachers and learners. In fact, *TESOL Quarterly* – one of the field's leading professional refereed research journals – provided multiple opportunities for professionals to discuss emerging topics, such as language and identity, critical approaches to TESOL, gender and language education, language and race, and critical pedagogy (for more details on the critical approach in language education, see *TESOL Quarterly* Special Issues 1997; 1999; 2002; 2004). The critical approach toward language education inspired practitioners to question the nature and scope of methods and contributed to the development of postmethod pedagogy. Postmethod pedagogy, first put forward by Kumaravadivelu in 1994, is closely related to the principles of critical pedagogy as well as its emphasis on social justice and social transformation through education. A critical practice of language teaching goes beyond teaching the phonology, morphology, and syntax of the language and views language as an ideology that is influenced by political and cultural contexts. Such critical practice, then, extends "the educational space to the social, cultural, and political dynamics of language use" (Kumaravadivelu, 2006a, p. 70). In its conceptual framework for language teaching, postmethod pedagogy aims to empower teachers to construct and implement their own teaching practices and examine their effectiveness with the goal of developing their own language teaching and learning theories. In other words, teachers are encouraged not only to be independent practitioners of their own teaching methods but also critical thinkers who can theorize their practice. However, such a conceptual framework has yet to deliver tools to help teachers achieve those goals and address the challenges in their local teaching contexts that may hinder their success.

In this chapter, I briefly trace the history of methods in the ELT field, and the shift from methods to postmethod, highlighting the conditions that led the ELT field to embrace such a shift. I also summarize the parameters and guiding principles of the postmethod pedagogy as introduced by Kumaravadivelu (1994, 2003, 2006a, 2006b) and share research findings on the application of those parameters and strategies, including the extent to which they were effective. I then conclude with a discussion of future directions for the ELT field.

Concepts and Theoretical Considerations

An Overview of Methods

The concept of method refers to "a systematic set of teaching practices based on a particular theory of language and language learning" (Richards & Rodgers, 2014, p. 3). Methodology, on the other hand, refers to "what teachers do in their classes" (Akbari, 2008, p. 650). In other words, the term method refers to prescribed classroom procedures based on a predetermined theory while methodology describes the reality of language teaching in diverse classrooms and how teachers construct their teaching practices. Richards and Rodgers (2014) analyzed over sixteen ELT methods and approaches that rose and declined, starting with the study of Latin in the 16th century with the purpose of translating and decoding other languages into Latin. This approach to learning foreign languages became the standard approach until the 19th century when an increased interest in learning languages other than Latin led to the emergence of the Grammar-Translation Method, with its emphasis on reading and writing, and lack of interest in developing learners' oral proficiency. This lack of interest in developing communication skills in the foreign language changed in the mid-19th century when, influenced by children's first language acquisition, François Gouin (1831–1896) defined the concept of language learning as a way of thinking and expressing real life, and proposed his Series method. Gouin's method led to the rise of the Direct Method, which described foreign language learning in the same way a first language is learned, with a great amount of oral input and minimum to no grammar instruction. Half a century later, it was clear that the Direct Method was time-consuming, which made it less popular in public school settings, resulting in the continuous use of different modifications of the Grammar-Translation Method and its reliance on reading and writing. In the 1940s and 1950s, the fields of linguistics and behavioral psychology contributed to the development of the Audiolingual Method. Linguistics introduced the descriptive analysis of languages, emphasizing the importance of practicing patterns of language through drills and repetition. Behavioral psychologists introduced conditioning and habit-formation models of learning. The Audiolingual Method gained popularity because of its emphasis on oral proficiency, but it did not provide instruction for long-term sustainability of learning. However, the influence of the Audiolingual Method can still be seen in teachers' use of drills in modeling and practicing some language patterns. Frustrated by the meaningless language learning experiences in these methods, practitioners sought guidance from research on second language teaching and learning which contributed to the development of new language teaching methods such as Community Language Learning, Suggestopedia, the Silent Way, Total Physical Response (TPR), and the Natural Approach. Each of these methods had its merits in classroom practices, but none addressed all learners and teachers' needs in different teaching contexts. For instance, TPR, which is based on asking learners to listen and respond physically to commands, continues to be widely used in teaching English to young and adult learners with low literacy skills. TPR activities demand very little, if any, linguistic production, which reduces learner stress. Nevertheless, James Asher, who developed TPR, has emphasized that TPR is compatible with other techniques and should be used in association with other methods.

New developments in teaching English known as the Notional-Functional Syllabuses (NFS) focused on developing curriculum that incorporates functions of using English, such as identifying, analyzing, reporting, requesting, and denying. NFS led to the rise of Communicative Language Teaching (CLT) with its four components: grammatical, discourse, sociolinguistic, and strategic, which is grounded in Canale and Swain's (1980) theoretical framework of communicative competence. Canale and Swain first proposed three main competencies or fields of knowledge and skills: grammatical, sociolinguistic, and strategic. Later, Canale (1984) proposed a fourth competence: discourse. According to Canale and Swain, grammatical competence refers to mastery of the linguistic code of the language. Sociolinguistic competence describes knowledge of rules and conventions that guide the appropriate comprehension and use of the language in different settings. Discourse competence refers to mastery of rules that determine how forms and meanings are combined meaningfully in spoken or written language. Finally, strategic competence includes knowledge of verbal and non-verbal strategies that compensate for interruptions in communication resulting from lack of competence in the other competencies.

CLT continues to influence the ELT field today with many methods developed based on its principles, such as Task-Based Language Teaching, Content-Based Language Teaching, Theme-Based Instruction, and Text-Based Language Teaching to name a few. Each of these methods focused on specific language features (e.g., functional items), and proposed a set of language teaching strategies that focus on such features (e.g., tasks). In their attempt to develop the ultimate method in teaching all learners in all contexts, these methods, with their narrow views of language teaching and learning, failed to address all learners' needs or to present language teaching in meaningful comprehensible teaching strategies.

Transitioning to an Eclectic Approach

The continuing emergence of new methods reflected a change in professionals' beliefs about learning and teaching foreign languages and engaged the ELT field in a reflective and evaluative debate. This highlighted the ineffectiveness of each method, resulting in a shift in the nature and scope of the concept of method itself. Scholars (e.g., Allwright, 1991; Pennycook, 1989; Prabhu, 1990; Stern, 1992) cautioned that these methods were not based on actual classroom practices and noted that classroom-based research showed that teachers were not following a specific method with all its guiding principles. Instead, they were adapting principles suitable for their teaching contexts. In other words, the reality in the language classroom (i.e., methodology) was far from the expectations put forward by the principles of the guiding theories (i.e., methods). This disconnect between theory and practice led teachers to adopt an eclectic approach to language teaching where teachers choose and implement different teaching practices adopted from different methods as long as they meet their students' needs and the demands of their teaching contexts.

Moving from a method-driven to an eclectic approach left teachers confused, unguided, and unsupported in their search for language teaching pedagogies. Despite its free approach to teaching, eclecticism offered "no criteria according to which we can determine which is the best theory, nor [did] it provide any principles by which to include or exclude features which form part of existing theories or practices" (Stern, 1992, p. 11). It did not provide any specific framework for teachers to "develop the knowledge, skill, attitude, and autonomy necessary to devise for themselves a systematic, coherent, and relevant personal theory of practice" (Kumaravadivelu, 2003, p. 40). These evaluative debates on the ineffectiveness of methods and the eclectic approach to ELT led to what Kumaravadivelu called the "postmethod condition."

Postmethod Pedagogy

The postmethod condition called for a search for an alternative to method where teachers have complete autonomy to choose and develop teaching strategies suitable for their classrooms with the guidance of principled pragmatism (Kumaravadivelu, 2003). This means teachers develop and implement teaching strategies suitable for their students' needs within their local settings without the constraints of following a specific method or methods. At the same time, and unlike the eclectic approach, teachers will be guided with principled pragmatism, where the relationship between theory and practice, ideas and their actualization and utilization, can only be realized through teaching. Teachers should make the crucial decisions about teaching and learning and decide what works or does not work in their classrooms based on actual classroom practices.

Therefore, postmethod pedagogy encourages teachers to practice what Prabhu (1990) called a "sense of plausibility" (p. 172) in determining the effectiveness of their teaching strategies and classroom practices based on local contextual factors. This sense of plausibility frees teachers from the routines and constraints of their teaching, and allows them to develop their own theory of practice. In that sense, the postmethod condition is a practice-driven phenomenon that encourages teachers to theorize language teaching and learning based on their practice within their teaching and learning contexts and use their findings to guide their future practice. This led to the emergence of postmethod pedagogy that enabled second language (L2) teachers to be sensitive to their teaching localities as they create their own teaching practices and classroom procedures.

It is important to note here that postmethod pedagogy is not a method; it is instead an alternative to method that empowers teachers to utilize a bottom-up approach to ELT as they reflect on and examine their teaching practices and generate their own theories of teaching. Many scholars introduced frameworks for postmethod pedagogy that include guiding principles for teachers to use in developing and implementing their own teaching theories. Most notable of these frameworks are Stern's (1992) Three-Dimensional framework, Allwright's (1991) Exploratory Practice framework, and Kumaravadivelu's (1994) Ten Macrostrategies framework. Stern's Three-Dimensional framework advocates for a curricular agenda that transcends the concept of methods. Allwright's Exploratory Practice emphasizes teachers' understanding of the quality of classroom life through classroom-based research. Kumaravadivelu's framework is the one that gained popularity and has been widely researched in the ELT field thus far. It proposes ten macrostrategies as "guiding principles derived from historical, theoretical, empirical, and experiential insights related to L2 learning and teaching" (Kumaravadivelu, 2003, p. 38).

The ten macrostrategies are:

1. Maximizing learning opportunities

2. Minimizing perceptual mismatches

3. Facilitating negotiated interaction

4. Promoting learner autonomy

5. Fostering language awareness

6. Activating intuitive heuristics

7. Contextualizing linguistic input

8. Integrating language skills

9. Ensuring social relevance

10. Raising cultural consciousness

Postmethod teachers and learners are expected to take on an active, engaged, and mindful role inside and outside the language classroom and to go beyond the constraints of their local environments as they construct context-specific language teaching and learning experiences.

Supported by ten macrostrategies, postmethod pedagogy centers around three parameters: particularity, practicality, and possibility, which have the potential to help teachers develop and maintain a context-sensitive language pedagogic framework. Particularity stresses the importance that language pedagogy be sensitive to a particular group of teachers and a particular group of learners and their learning needs in a particular local situation. Practicality aims for teachers to construct their own context-sensitive theory of practice and to utilize language teaching pedagogy that is meaningful and feasible in their local settings. In a postmethod pedagogy framework, a theory of practice results from "pedagogical thoughtfulness" (Van Manen, 1991) and reflective thinking (Freeman, 1998) – "a state of being engaged in what is going on in the classroom that drives one to better understand what is happening – and can happen – there" (p. 14). This constant reflection helps teachers develop their own concept of their teaching practices that lead to desired learning outcomes. It is, then, the teachers who adopt a "sense of plausibility" (Prabhu, 1990,

p. 172) or "ethic of practicality" (Hargreaves, 1994, p. 12) that guides the theorizing of their teaching. The third parameter, possibility, pertains to the relationship between pedagogy, power, and dominance that create and sustain social inequalities. Language teaching settings are influenced not only by the teachers' and the learners' experiences but also by the social, political, and economic localities. Therefore, the parameter of possibility is concerned with language learners' identities in the classroom and the need to empower language learners to construct their sense of who they are. Although separate in their focus, the parameters of particularity, practicality, and possibility emphasize applying a critical stance in the L2 classroom, highlight the values of critical practice and community development, and utilize classroom input and interaction as effective instruments of transformation.

Postmethod Views of Language Teachers and Learners

Postmethod pedagogy views language teachers and learners as autonomous contributors to the construction and implementation of language teaching. Autonomous learners utilize metacognitive, cognitive, social, and affective strategies to determine their learning goals, choose content, monitor their progress, and assess learning outcomes. They are independent learners who can set their own learning goals and create learning experiences that help them achieve those goals. Therefore, autonomous learners aim not only to learn but also to develop agency and take action. According to Kumaravadivelu (2006b), "If *academic autonomy* enables students to be effective learners, *liberatory autonomy* empowers them to be critical thinkers" (p. 177). Liberatory autonomy helps learners recognize and seek to change the sociopolitical barriers in their contexts. To achieve liberatory autonomy, Kumaravadivelu suggests that a postmethod pedagogy encourages learners to (1) critically investigate language as an ideology, (2) reflect on their identities through diaries and journal entries, (3) form socially cohesive, mutually supportive groups of learning communities that seek self-awareness and self-improvement, and (4) explore diverse topics of interest and share their perspectives on them in class.

Much like postmethod learners, postmethod autonomous teachers are reflective, analytical about their teaching, willing to take the initiative, and effective evaluators of such initiatives. Autonomous teachers can use their prior knowledge, skills, and experiences in teaching to develop their own theories of practice and then test and evaluate those theories. According to Kumaravadivelu (2006b), postmethod teachers "can become autonomous only to the extent they are willing and able to embark on a continual process of self-development" (p. 179).

In summary, postmethod pedagogy puts the teacher and learner in the heart of the ELT field and emphasizes their significant roles in ensuring its success in not only teaching English but also in transforming the lives of learners, teachers, and those who live in the local community. However, postmethod pedagogy does not explain how teachers could help their learners achieve those goals or how they could be agents in such a transformative approach to teaching.

IMPLICATIONS FOR ENGLISH LANGUAGE EDUCATION

Understanding Teacher Localities

A quick review of the literature on postmethod pedagogical implementation in ELT reveals concerns related to teachers' lack of understanding of its main concepts, not having the tools to implement its macrostrategies, and not having the ability to address specific challenges pertaining to teachers' local teaching settings. These concerns led to what can be seen in the literature as a conflicted attitude toward postmethod pedagogy. Postmethod teachers and learners struggle to address all the demanding responsibilities of postmethod pedagogy and to overcome local challenges. One of those challenges is using the appropriate teaching materials and textbooks. In many EFL contexts, textbooks are chosen and assigned by the ministries of education in their countries and are usually developed based on a prescribed language teaching and learning method. These textbooks come with specific learning objectives, classroom activities, and accompanying quizzes and tests. They are also, for the most part, aligned with the standardized tests adopted by the countries where the books are used. This structured and connected system can pose a challenge in the postmethod classroom. For example, Khany and Darabi (2014) observed 21 Iranian high school teachers to determine if they were implementing the macrostrategies of postmethod pedagogy in their teaching. The teachers noted that the textbooks they were using were very structured, unchallenging to the learners, and relied heavily on the presentation of grammar and sentence structure as opposed to a more communicative and interactive approach to language learning, which negatively influenced their freedom to adopt new classroom practices. It is worth noting that two of the macrostrategies – minimizing perceptual mismatches and ensuring social relevance – were not included in the study. Similarly, Mardani and Moradian (2016) noted that the textbooks used by 30 Iranian teachers in private language schools were more suitable for an eclectic approach than a postmethod approach. The teachers explained that the textbooks constrained their autonomous role in choosing topics relevant to their students and that they could not deviate from the prescribed curriculum. Learner freedom to suggest lessons and topics was not possible, as the teachers had to cover the content in the textbooks. However, the teachers had autonomy in developing their lesson plans and adopting different teaching strategies. It seems from these examples that teachers are expecting to have textbooks that would guide them in implementing a postmethod approach to teaching. This can mean that some teachers still view postmethod as an alternative method to replace the previous ones. None of these studies actually examined teachers' understanding of the concepts and the parameters and macrostrategies of postmethod pedagogy, and teachers did not report real classroom practices or their effectiveness in language teaching and learning.

Along with assigned textbooks, postmethod teachers have to address the challenge of language policy and resistance from learners, parents, and administrators at their schools. This particular challenge can cause teachers to lose their jobs if their practices do not conform with school policy. Postmethod pedagogy does not provide guidance for teachers to navigate those difficult situations or protect themselves from any financial or professional consequences. In a study that examined 30 Iranian public school teachers' perception of the parameters of particularity, practicality, and possibility, Mardani and Moradian (2016) reported that teachers were concerned that following these parameters could be unwelcomed by parents, learners, and policy makers. The teachers preferred to follow an eclectic approach to teaching that gave them flexibility to adjust instruction based on learners' needs and their own teaching styles, without having to deal with any social or political issues in their local communities.

Supporting In-Service Postmethod Teachers

In its attempt to empower teachers to construct their own practice and to engage their learners in the teaching and learning process, postmethod pedagogy put great responsibilities on both teachers and learners. Missing from the postmethod pedagogy is the means to achieve its ultimate goal – empowering teachers and learners to create a teaching and learning experience that is specific to their localities and that transforms their lives. Although postmethod pedagogy gives teachers the freedom to make classroom instructional decisions, it does not take into account the social and professional constraints English professionals face in different teaching contexts (Akbari, 2008; Huda, 2013). For example, the concept of learner autonomy may not be familiar in some cultural and educational profiles where learners are expected to be passive recipients of the content and teachers are the main source of knowledge. Likewise, teacher autonomy may pose a challenge for teachers in local settings where curriculum is strict and modifications of content and teaching procedures are not allowed. In other words, neither teachers nor learners have much freedom in their choices and decision making in the classroom.

Postmethod can be empowering yet somewhat problematic in its assumption that the teachers "will eventually construct their own theory of practice" (Kumaravadivelu, 2006b, p. 180). Such an assumption aims to encourage teachers to critically examine their teaching and learning localities, determine their teaching goals and develop their own instructional practices, and then reflect on their teaching and develop their own teaching theory. However, the expectation that teachers can theorize from their practice could be overwhelming to teachers, especially when they are not equipped with the knowledge and skills they need. Teachers are not necessarily prepared to be researchers or to generate and test theories from their practice. For example, in Bangladesh, teachers reported that despite being useful and applicable, some aspects of the postmethod pedagogy are not practical because it expects them to theorize from their practice and practice what they theorize (Huda, 2013). According to Huda, teachers are not all prepared or trained to "understand and identify problems, analyze and assess information, consider and evaluate alternatives, and then choose the best available alternative that is then subjected to further critical evaluation" (Kumaravadivelu, 2006b,

p. 173) because of the many contextual, academic, and personal limitations in their contexts. In another ELT setting, Iranian language teachers raised similar concerns about lack of knowledge and skills needed to theorize from their practice, as well as not being familiar with the concept of learner autonomy or of how to increase learners' political and social awareness (Mardani & Moradian, 2016). Similarly, Hazratzad and Gheitanchian (2009) noted that teachers do not receive adequate training on current teaching approaches that helps them navigate between theory and practice. They also do not see a necessity to adopt a communicative approach to teaching because the focus of instruction is to prepare learners to pass the tests. Given such concerns from the field, there is a need to prepare in-service and preservice teachers for the demanding role of researcher. One approach to achieve this is through participatory action research where ELT researchers and teachers engage in classroom research experiences that connect theory and practice by seeking input from the teachers as well as the learners about their language teaching and learning practices. Such experiences will expose teachers to the skills they need to be effective researchers, such as being able to reflect on their teaching, draw commonalities, find and implement solutions, collect and analyze data, and examine results. Those skills could ultimately help teachers develop into reflective practitioners who can theorize from their own teaching.

Recognizing Teachers' Readiness for a Change

Despite its lack of practical guidance on implementation, postmethod pedagogy seems to be well perceived by language teachers in different language contexts. In Saudi Arabia, teachers agreed that postmethod pedagogy would compensate for the limitations in different methods and allow teachers the flexibility to consider the sociopolitical situation where they teach (Soomro & Almalki, 2017). In South Africa, teachers felt a sense of ownership of their teaching practice as they extended their research skills, reflected on the teaching process, and adopted a critical approach toward their profession (Motlhaka, 2015). Similarly, in Thailand, (Saengboon, 2013), university language teachers viewed the parameters of postmethod pedagogy to align with and go beyond Communicative Language Teaching. They considered it a break away from the traditional methods and an empowering pedagogy that went beyond linguistic input, incorporated a humanistic stance toward English teaching, and integrated form, function, and meaning. It is clear that these teachers valued postmethod pedagogy because the principles helped them realize the limitations of method-based pedagogies. They also felt empowered by those principles to develop context-sensitive strategies in their classrooms. Empowered teachers can utilize their potential to produce knowledge, incorporate learners' needs, develop classroom activities suitable for different learning styles, and engage learners in meaningful classroom interactions.

FUTURE DIRECTIONS

The field of TESOL is experiencing an era of awareness, inclusion, and global perspectives that results from the growing influence of critical pedagogy of the linguistic and cultural hegemony of English language teaching. In this new era, postmethod teachers "ensure that their practice results in social transformation and the improvement of society by taking into account the life histories of their students" (Akbari, 2008, p. 642). What is missing from the discussion is language teachers and learners' perspectives on how postmethod pedagogy improves their different teaching and learning contexts and consequently the quality of their lives. Studies that looked at the effectiveness of implementing a postmethod pedagogy did not examine the transformation of teachers and learners' localities and their contributions to such transformations, which are key to understanding postmethod notions of particularity and possibility. There is a need to conduct research where both teachers and learners are participants in the analysis of their local contexts and can connect their teaching and learning settings with the communities where they live. It is important to understand how teachers connect their teaching practices to both local and global communities and how this connectivity influences learner involvement in the learning experience.

Discourse on postmethod pedagogy should transition from ideological and conceptual frameworks to pedagogical and practical applications. More specifically, practitioners should focus on real implementations of the postmethod parameters of practicality, particularity, and possibility and investigate how they manifest in different contexts. How do teachers and learners construct learning experiences that align with these parameters? We need to understand the contextual challenges teachers face, such as assigned textbooks, standardized tests, and the financial constraints. These limitations and constraints force teachers to comply with the local rules in order to keep their jobs and protect their careers from the consequences of challenging the status quo. There is a need to transform the local contexts where teachers and learners can engage in and implement a postmethod pedagogy. What do we know about the local societal, political, economic, cultural, and educational realities in these contexts? What is their current, and consequently future, impact on language teaching and learning? How do teachers and learners construct and implement their own teaching methods? What challenges do they face both inside and outside the classroom? What local, national, and international resources do they utilize to navigate and overcome those challenges?

Postmethod pedagogy recognizes the prevailing socioeconomic, cultural, and ideological forces in language teaching and learning in local contexts. Its three parameters of particularity, practicality, and possibility provide English language teachers and learners a new and dynamic perspective on classroom practices. Teaching practices are no longer determined by a single factor, nor are they derived from a prescribed method. Instead, they are fluid in their applicability and usefulness for different learners and teachers in different teaching contexts. The ten macrostrategies expect teachers and learners to be co-constructors of the learning experiences available inside and outside the classroom. To prepare teachers for such roles, those macrostrategies should expand to include specific strategies for teachers to adapt in new and different teaching situations. They should also include evaluative techniques so that teachers can reflect on their pedagogical decisions. Postmethod teachers need the knowledge, skills, and experiences necessary to develop and evaluate their own personal teaching theory informed by their own practices.

Discussion Questions

1. How have perceptions of the concept of method changed over the last two decades? How have these changes influenced classroom practices in teaching and learning English as an additional language? Share examples from your experience as a learner and as a teacher, and describe the types of classroom interactions that took place.
2. Diamond (1993) called for *transformative* teacher education programs where teachers construct, through personal pedagogical exploration, their own personal meaning of teaching. Share what you consider a transformative experience in your development as a teacher. What knowledge and skills were gained through this experience? How do the knowledge and skills gained relate to your local teaching contexts and your language learners?
3. Discuss how a postmethod pedagogy to language teaching and learning is different from a teaching method you are familiar with. How do these differences affect classroom instruction?
4. Examine the parameters of particularity, practicality, and possibility. What challenges do you anticipate in implementing those parameters as guiding principles to your teaching? How would you address those challenges? Consider factors specific to your local context.
5. How can the ELT field transition from a conceptual and ideological discussion of postmethod pedagogy to a classroom-based application of its principles?

Resources for Further Exploration

1. Bell, D. (2003). Method and postmethod: Are they really so incompatible? *TESOL Quarterly, 37*(2), 325–336.
   In this article, David Bell emphasizes that language teachers can benefit from the "methodological coherence" (p. 334) of teaching methods while deconstructing them according to their teaching localities.

2. Islam, A. & Shuchi, I. J. (2017). Deconstruction of method-postmethod dialects in English language teaching. *Journal of Language Teaching and Research, 8*(3), pp. 539–547.
   The authors discuss the dichotomy of methods and postmethod, and how postmethod pedagogy redefines teachers' roles in their local contexts.
3. Liu, J. (2004). Methods in the post-method era: Report on an international survey on language teaching methods. *IJES, 4*(I), 137–1 52.
   In his article, Liu reports on the status of language teaching methods worldwide from a sample of 800 language teachers. One significant finding is that Grammar Translation continues to be the most widely used method despite being less favored by teachers.
4. Richards, J. C., & Rodgers, T. (2014). *Approaches and methods in language teaching (3rd edition).* Cambridge, England: Cambridge University Press.
   This book provides an overview of the history and current status of language teaching and learning methods, their theoretical underpinning, and teaching practices.

References

Akbari, R. (2008). Postmethod discourse and practice. TESOL Quarterly, 42(4), 641–652.

Allwright, R. L. (1991). *The death of the method (Working Paper #10).* The Exploratory Practice Centre, the University of Lancaster, England.

Canale, M. (1984). A communicative approach to language proficiency assessment in a minority setting. In C. Rivera (Ed.), *Communicative competence approaches to language proficiency assessment: Research and application* (pp. 107–122). Clevedon, UK: Multilingual Matters.

Canale, M., & Swain, M. (1980). Theoretical bases of communicative approaches to second language teaching and testing. *Applied Linguistics,* 1(1), 1–47.

Freeman, D. (1998). *Doing teacher research.* Boston, MA: Heinle & Heinle.

Hargreaves, A. (1994). *Changing teachers, changing times.* New York, NY: Teachers College Press.

Hazratzad, A., & Gheitanchian, M. (2009). *EFL teachers' attitude towards post method pedagogy and their students' achievement.* Proceedings of the 10th METU ELT Convention.

Huda, M. E. (2013). Post-method pedagogy and ELT in Bangladesh. *Global Journal of Human Social Science,* 13(7), 6–14.

Khany, R., & Darabi, R. (2014). ELT in Iran: Reflection of the principle-based and post-method pedagogy in language teaching. *Procedia Social and Behavioral Sciences,* 98, 908–916.

Kumaravadivelu, B. (1994). The postmethod condition: (E)merging strategies for second/foreign language teaching. *TESOL Quarterly,* 28(1), 27–48.

Kumaravadivelu, B. (2003). *Beyond methods: Macrostrategies for language teaching.* New Haven, CT: Yale University Press.

Kumaravadivelu, B. (2006a). TESOL methods: Changing tracks, challenging trends. *TESOL Quarterly,* 40(1), 59–81.

Kumaravadivelu, B. (2006b). *Understanding language teaching: From method to postmethod.* Mahwah, NJ: Lawrence Erlbaum Associates, Inc.

Mardani, M., & Moradian, E. (2016). Postmethod pedagogy perception and usage by EFL teachers and learners and its limitations, symbols, and viewpoints. *International Journal of Language Learning and Applied Linguistics World,* 11(1), 75–88.

Motlhaka, H. (2015). Exploring post-method pedagogy in teaching English as second language in South African higher education. *Mediterranean Journal of Social Sciences,* 6(1), 517–524.

Pennycook, A. (1989). The concept of method, interested knowledge, and the politics of language teaching. *TESOL Quarterly,* 23(4), 589–618.

Prabhu, N. S. (1990). There is no best method: Why? *TESOL Quarterly,* 24(2), 161–176.

Richards, J. C., & Rodgers, T. (2014). *Approaches and methods in language teaching* (3rd ed.). Cambridge, UK: Cambridge University Press.

Saengboon, S. (2013). Thai English teachers' understanding of "postmethod pedagogy": Case studies of university lecturers. *English Language Teaching,* 6(12), 156–166.

Soomro, A. F., & Almalki, M. S. (2017). Language practitioners' reflection on method-based and post-method pedagogies. *English Language Teaching,* 10(5), 234–242.

Stern, H. H. (1992). *Issues and options in language teaching.* Oxford, UK: Oxford University Press.

Van Manen, M. (1991). *The tact of teaching: The meaning of pedagogical thoughtfulness.* SUNY Press.

Course Planning in the Postmethod Era

Ideas From a Practicum Experience in Thailand

Lucas Edmond

Given Kumaravadivelu's (2003) postmethod parameters of particularity, practicality, and possibility, along with the macrostrategic framework, there is no one-size-fits-all way to design a successful language course. Particularly for new teachers, the lack of concrete direction implied here could lead to difficulties in realizing an effective curriculum. It may seem paradoxical that course design should still be systematic, organized, and ultimately beneficial to students' growth while also open-ended, holistic, and built on the individual teacher's own theories of practice.

In this case study, I discuss how I approached this apparent difficulty while developing a course in light of the postmethod framework as a novice teacher in a supervised teaching practicum at a university in Thailand. I will briefly present the process by which I planned a project-based course, a process which included negotiating my own teaching values with the students' needs and interests, critically reflecting on lessons, and most importantly, remaining flexible and in tune with students' expectations in order to help them successfully improve their language abilities and confidence. This process can easily be adapted for other teachers' particular contexts.

THE SETTING

> One day away from teaching, I'm feeling fairly uneasy about the coming course. . . . Having no concrete idea of the students' levels, nor having any textbook or target learning outcomes, I feel very lost. . . . I have a lot of theory and principles in mind, but I'm not entirely sure how I will translate them into practice. I'm thinking that I'll just learn as I go.
>
> (Personal journal entry, June 2016)

This excerpt comes from a journal I kept while teaching at the university in Isan, the northeastern region of Thailand, where I completed my graduate program's supervised teaching practicum. This entry from one day before beginning teaching succinctly captures the fears and nerves most novice teachers face when heading into a new classroom. Although armed with a multitude of theories from applied linguistics, I was apprehensive about how I would put these broad ideas into concrete action in a practical way that would meet my students' goals, needs, and expectations.

When I arrived at the university, I was assigned to teach a five-week integrated reading and writing course for ten incoming students to the university business school's international business program, an English as a medium of instruction (EMI) program designed to prepare students for a variety of professions across the business world in the ASEAN region and beyond.

I was not given any curriculum or goals; I was instead tasked with developing the course as I saw fit. Although daunting, I was excited for the opportunity to put my knowledge into practice.

DESCRIPTION OF ENGLISH LANGUAGE LEARNERS

My students were incoming first-year students, and thus my class was their first chance to interact with their new cohort as well as their first taste of university life. In addition, for most of the students, I was the first foreign teacher that they had ever had. All of the students had studied English for several years (on average 13 years) in the Thai school system, but their experiences and levels were not uniform, as they came from various high schools throughout Isan. Many students reported that their previous classes focused primarily on vocabulary and rote grammar, with few chances to engage using English. Using the Common European Framework of Reference for Language (CEFR), I estimated that most students' level fell within the A2 and B1 range. Most students had a great deal of knowledge about the language, but they did not have much experience using it in any meaningful context and lacked confidence in their skills.

PEDAGOGICAL APPLICATION AND INNOVATION: A POSTMETHOD PLANNING PROCESS

Outlining Goals and Assumptions About Language Teaching Before Planning

Before I began teaching, my practicum professor asked us to brainstorm what we viewed as the qualities of an ideal language teacher. Drawing both on my past experiences as a teacher and learner and the professional theories about language teaching I had studied in classes, I filled my paper with phrases that resonated with my teaching beliefs, such as authenticity, practicality, and atmosphere (see Appendix A). These values related not only to teaching practices but also to issues of personality and classroom dynamics.

While this is a simple exercise, it was an incredibly valuable tool that I used as a foundation for my course planning. Congruent with the parameter of practicality, a postmethod pedagogy emerges first from the individual teacher's philosophy and experience in language education. Rather than only deferring to methods and professional theories from outside, teachers must construct personal theories by drawing on expert theory in conjunction with knowledge gained from practical experience. By considering my values as an instructor, I could more clearly envision what type of class I wanted to teach as well as consider how I could adapt and negotiate these values within the specific context. Though the words I wrote may seem broad, they describe a particular type of teacher and suggest certain class practices and activities.

Of course, this does not mean that my values and beliefs did not evolve while teaching. However, clarifying these beliefs early established the baseline with which I could plan, reflect, and evaluate my practices over time.

Getting to Know the Students, Their Interests, and Their Needs

Once I had defined what I valued, I needed to negotiate how this information would help me meet my students' needs, expectations, and the particular context. Having no information beforehand, I conducted a mini-needs analysis within the first few days. In addition to standard language needs analyses, such as writing and speaking samples, I also administered a survey in which I asked open-ended questions about the students' personal interests, perceived language skills, and ranking of class activities they valued, and so on (see Appendix B). This was the first step in a dialogue between the students and me, which is an important part of the collaborative course planning process (Graves, 2008). Not all of the questions were directly relevant to language but were instead aimed at helping me understand the students' personal interests and learning histories, which also affect classroom dynamics. For example, in addition to improving their English communication, most students also explicitly mentioned doing group activities and making friends. This demonstrated that beyond studying language, the students also wanted to build bonds with their peers. As such, the goals I identified in the needs analysis were as much community-building goals as they were linguistic.

Planning, Reflecting, and Repeating

Once I had a clear picture of my own values as well as an initial idea of my students' language needs, learning styles, and personal interests, I could begin to piece together our course. Given the short duration of the course, I chose to focus mainly on building students' confidence and fluency by providing them opportunities to practice using language through interactive activities and through a class project in which they could review, share, and expand their language skills together.

I noticed early on that the students struggled with adjective use, so I decided to expand this point to a mini-unit on detail and description. Keeping in mind both the macrostrategies of activating intuitive heuristics and facilitating interaction, I started with a mix of traditional language-focused lessons and collaborative activities that ranged from sentence expansion games to simile song writing. I incorporated a mix of activities to provide students with a range of opportunities to learn and increase their communication. Then, to give the descriptive writing more context, I designed a scaffolded writing activity where students described their hometowns first with images and sensory adjectives and then worked up to writing a short paragraph about their town. As the students were interested in business and marketing, I proposed to the students that we use this descriptive writing as the first part of a running project to create a travel guide for future practicum teachers. With this, I had a foundational project to which I could tie each future unit (see Table 3.1.1 in Appendix C).

This project, which evolved over the summer, allowed students to use what they were learning in an authentic context, meeting my own goal of authenticity as well as the students' interest in communication with speakers from outside Thailand. One student, Dew, who came from a rural province in Isan, remarked, "It makes some people who doesn't know about my hometown, and they will know more, what's the favorite food, important place, and festival or something to do" (see Figure 3.1.2 in Appendix D). Aligning with the parameter of possibility, as well as the macrostrategies of raising cultural consciousness and ensuring social relevance, this project afforded students the opportunity to use English to share with a real audience about the places that they came from and their own identities. While English is often positioned as a language to access outside communities, in this case, the students could use language instead to celebrate, show off, and invite others to their hometowns.

As the summer unfolded, I continued to iteratively design the course and project through reflection and monitoring. As an action research project (Burns, 2010), I kept a journal where I recorded my observations and interpretations of my classes. Along with the help of colleagues, I systematically evaluated these notes, my students' work, and student comments. As I learned more about what the students valued, needed, and wanted, I was able to more skillfully design lessons and build our class project. This reflective process is an essential component of the postmethod parameter of particularity, as teachers must develop course materials and lessons that are effective in the specific teaching context. So although teachers start with their own set of values and beliefs, they negotiate these over time in light of the class dynamics. As no two classes unfold in the same way, teachers should strive to be well attuned to the students' progress and remain flexible in how they implement and update classroom practices.

For example, later in the session, as many students expressed interest in speaking with more English speakers, I planned an interview activity in which students wrote up questions and interviewed the other practicum teachers, who came from the United States, China, Japan, and South Korea. As with the description unit, I began by scaffolding the unit with explicit grammar instruction and an eclectic mix of activities, such as playing grammar games, watching and analyzing authentic interviews, and practicing mock interviews, during which students took turns interviewing me while the other students observed and gave feedback. This variety of activities, informed by many of the postmethod macrostrategies as well as personal theories developed through teaching in this context for several weeks, aimed to meet the students' diverse learning styles and equip them for the final teacher interviews.

To finish the unit, the students worked in small groups to interview the other practicum participants about their personal interests and experience in Thailand, an activity which became one of the most popular of the summer. One student, Noon, commented, "Before I learned this class [interview activity], I don't talk with (people from) another country, but now I talk better and I am not shy for every people." Through such opportunities to interact and work with peers and other teachers, this student's perception of her language skills and her confidence increased. Thus, as the postmethod approach espouses, the activity met not only linguistic objectives, but also allowed students to grow and strengthen their sense of self within a globalized community. Furthermore, in order to tie this activity with the class project, the students recorded the teachers' experiences in Thailand as "guest testimonials," which became a part of the final travel guide (see Figure 3.1.3 in Appendix E). As with the rest of the course, this unit activity was not planned from the beginning but instead emerged through the postmethod-informed process of reflection and collaboration.

CONCLUSION

Not only have I needed to develop lessons with an overall goal in mind, but I've also had to be flexible and willing to change. I think learning this balance must be an indicator of a good teacher, and it is something I'm still working to achieve. . . . Each new teaching setting presents its own challenges and opportunities. However, the core skills such as planning, adapting, and responding to students' needs and difficulties flexibly will be useful no matter where I go.

(Personal journal entry, July 2016)

As I have illustrated with this case study, planning within the postmethod framework is a flexible, dynamic, iterative process in which the course is constantly evaluated in light of the local context (see Figure 3.1.1). Informed by the parameters of particularity, practicality, and possibility, and the macrostrategies, teachers must consider the students' specific contexts, resources, and values to provide tailored opportunities for students to grow and develop. As with my own experience, teachers can use a variety of teaching techniques and activities to try to achieve this.

Given this eclecticism, a postmethod informed course may be realized in several ways and ultimately appear similar to other courses based on methods such as Communicative Language Teaching (CLT) or Task-based Language Teaching (TBLT). However, the key difference lies in the approach, development process, and overarching principles. Rather than taking an outside method as the starting point, teachers begin by negotiating a set of theory- and practice-derived values within the particular teaching context. Then, over time, the teacher must carefully reflect and remain flexible, constantly adapting the course activities to meet the students' needs and course goals.

As shown by my final journal entry, at the end of the course, I did not feel confident with the final outcome, and I recognized that I was still developing as a teacher, a process which is never-ending. Planning any

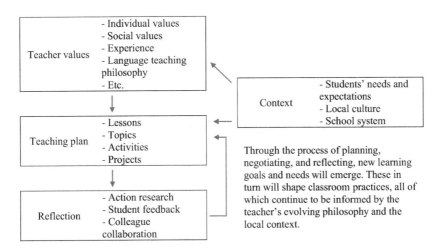

Figure 3.1.1 A model for a postmethod approach to design

Source: Lucas John Edmond

course presents a difficult task, and maintaining a postmethod approach can seem tiresome. However, by practicing the teaching skills here, such as planning, reflecting, and collaborating with students and colleagues, I was able to more effectively teach my students and grow as an instructor. The words of Belle, one student, captured well for me the outcome of the summer course. She commented:

> I feel good because I can improve my English. At first, I don't like English, and I don't know why I'm studying here, but I'm here, and I'm trying to study, and I think everybody can do it. It's not difficult.

The course not only gave her the opportunities to improve her communication skills, but her affect and interest in studying English increased as well. By following the postmethod approach, I was able to meet several personal goals and student goals. This experience continues to inspire me to refine my approach and strive to develop effective courses using the postmethod parameters and macrostrategies as guidance, a process which can be adapted by anyone for any teaching situation.

REFERENCES

Burns, A. (2010). *Doing action research in English language teaching: A guide for practitioners*. New York, NY: Routledge.
Graves, K. (2008). The language curriculum: A social contextual perspective. *Language Teaching*, 41(2), 147–181.
Kumaravadivelu, B. (2003). *Beyond methods: Macrostrategies for language teaching*. New Haven, CT: Yale University Press.

APPENDIX A
Sample Teaching Philosophy Graphic Organizer
From My First Day

Variety of Materials	- Self-made - Multimedia (when possible) - Pre-made - Textbooks - "Authentic"
Balance	- Student-teacher time - Learning styles - Students' levels and interests
Humanism	- Valuing students as individuals - Value of experience and L1 as support for L2
Focus on Authentic Communication	- Communicability with grammar as a guiding structure - "Let it pass" principle - Use of hands-on projects and tasks for learning
Enjoyable Class Atmosphere/Friendly with Students	- Relatable with stories - Activities that appeal to the interests of the students - Levity
Encouraging Output	- Writing exercises (stories, dialogues, freewriting) - Guided conversations - Creative practice with many structures - Drama and role-play - Scaffolding
Practicality	- Needs - Means - Constraints

Appendix B
Student Survey

Hello! I would like to get to know you better. Your answers will not be graded.

Name:
Preferred Name/Nickname:
Birthday: Day   Month   Year
Hometown:

Languages you speak or have studied:

First language:
Other languages:
(You don't have to be super good at these languages!)

English:
How long have you studied English?

What do you like about studying English?

What do you dislike about studying English?

Strengths:
In which areas of English do you feel strongest?
                Reading   Writing   Listening   Speaking

In which areas of English do you need to improve the most?
                Reading   Writing   Listening   Speaking

Interests:
What are your hobbies (For example, eating, karaoke, driving, organizing my room, etc.)?

What are you favorite types of books/movies (For example, comedy, romance, horror, etc.)?

What types of things do you like?

What foods do you like?

Why are you studying business? What area of business interests you (tourism, marketing, finance, etc.)?

Class:
What would you like to learn in this class?

Technology:
Do you have an email address? If you do, then please provide your address below.

Circle the resources that you have outside of class.
smartphone   laptop   desktop computer   internet connection

APPENDIX C
Final Course and Project Schedule

Table 3.1.1 Final course and project schedule

Week	Thematic focus	Language focus	Reading focus	Week's writing project
1	Introductions	Diagnostic	Skimming and Scanning	N/A
2	Writing about hometowns/favorite places	Descriptive Writing	Identifying main points	A descriptive introduction to a hometown/favorite place, along with a drawing
3	Writing anecdotes about the past	Review of Verb Tenses	Reading stories	A short narrative about time spent at hometown/favorite place
4	Interviewing visitors	Question Formation	N/A	A brief sketch of a visitor, along with a sample of interesting exchanges from the interview (testimonial)
5	Recommendations for visitors	Suggestions/Modals	N/A	A short essay giving visitors specific suggestions of places to go and things to do in the hometown/favorite place
Final Product:		A document for future practicum participants on famous places to go in Isan and beyond		

Appendix D
Project Parts 1 and 5 – Descriptive Writing and Suggestions

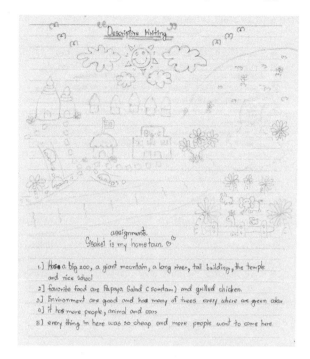

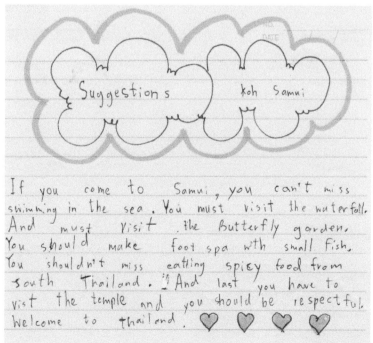

Figure 3.1.2 Project parts 1 and 5

APPENDIX E
Interview Write Up

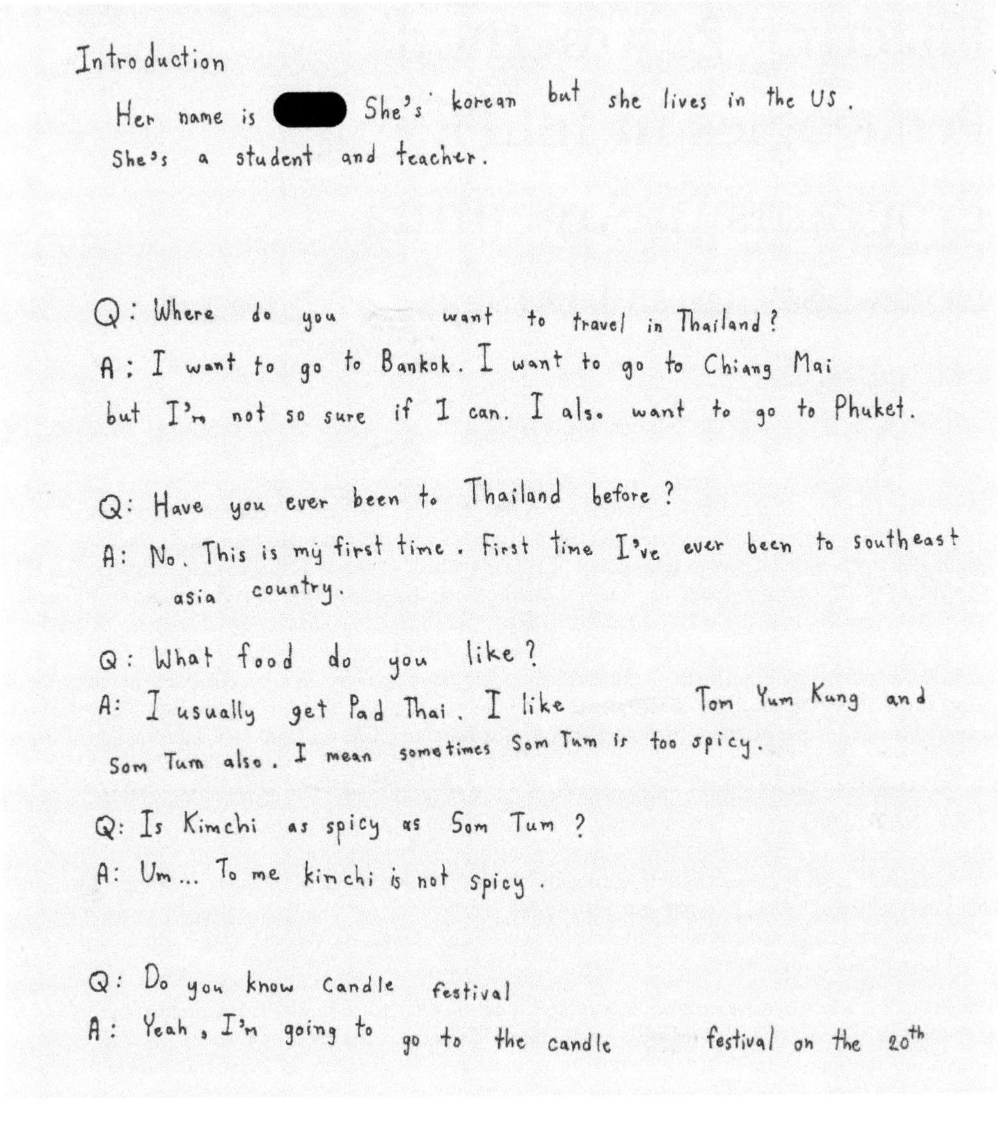

Introduction
    Her name is ⬤ She's korean but she lives in the US.
    She's a student and teacher.

Q: Where do you   want to travel in Thailand?
A: I want to go to Bankok. I want to go to Chiang Mai
but I'm not so sure if I can. I also want to go to Phuket.

Q: Have you ever been to Thailand before?
A: No. This is my first time. First time I've ever been to southeast
   asia country.

Q: What food do you like?
A: I usually get Pad Thai. I like   Tom Yum Kung and
Som Tum also. I mean sometimes Som Tum is too spicy.

Q: Is Kimchi as spicy as Som Tum?
A: Um... To me kimchi is not spicy.

Q: Do you know Candle festival
A: Yeah, I'm going to go to the candle   festival on the 20th

Figure 3.1.3 Interview write-up by a student

CASE STUDY 3.2

Enacting Postmethod Pedagogies in IELTE Programs in Argentina

Do as I Say, or as I Do?

María Alejandra Soto

Much of the discussion concerning postmethod pedagogies centers on the dichotomy between professional and personal theories or the debate over teachers as theorizers or practitioners. Enacting a postmethod curriculum, however, demands knowledge from practicing teachers other than theoretical principles and training on mechanical classroom procedures. This case study describes an Initial English Language Teacher Education (IELTE) course in foreign language didactics (*Foreign Language Didactics 1*) and analyzes the different innovations introduced to the syllabus in order to foster student-teachers' awareness of the need to develop context-sensitive pedagogies by adopting or implementing classroom practices that steer away from prescriptive, off-the-shelf methods. At the same time, this case study reflects upon the extent to which the heavy emphasis that postmethod pedagogies place on the particulars of the teaching and learning scenarios is actually mirrored in the practices of teacher educators within the IELTE program here addressed.

THE SETTING

This case study is set at the Facultad de Humanidades, Artes y Ciencias Sociales (Faculty of Humanities, Arts and Social Sciences; FHAyCS), a state-run college that is part of the Autonomous University of Entre Ríos, Argentina. Our college main building is located downtown in Paraná, the capital city of Entre Ríos, a province north of Buenos Aires.

The FHAyCS is a relatively new higher education institution, established in 2000. The number of undergraduate students taking different courses offered has been increasing exponentially since the faculty foundation, the approximate current number being close to 4,000 students. In 2019, the number of students who enrolled in our IELTE program was 143. The program lasts four years, totaling 3,392 contact hours distributed in 36 courses, most of which are taught annually from April to November. These courses aim mainly at student-teachers' development of content knowledge (CK) (38% of the curriculum load), general pedagogical knowledge (PK) (16%), and pedagogical content knowledge (PCK) (14%). Other areas included in the program relate to culture and educational policy, among a few others.

For the sake of clarity, I would like to define these concepts and relate them to the main theme of this case study. CK refers specifically to knowing the subject matter, in this case English, mainly as a system. It refers to the development of linguistic competence or instrumental content and skills in areas that are discipline-bound. On the other hand, PK and PCK are concerned with teaching itself. While PK involves knowledge of the broad principles and strategies of classroom management and organization, PCK represents an amalgam of CK and PK. In other words, PCK encompasses teachers' understanding of what makes the learning of English in the local school easy or difficult, and it includes an awareness of aspects such as the needs, attitudes, motivations, and other learner characteristics that might have an impact on learning. In this sense, PCK is relevant as it might involve adapting CK to address various needs, interests, and abilities in very specific learning contexts (For a review of PCK, see Depaepe, Verschaffel, & Kelchtermans, 2013).

Typically, learners enrolled in our program must take courses on topics such as grammar, phonetics and phonology, linguistics, and academic reading and writing. These courses are taught in English by teachers of English who have specialized in these areas. In addition, since our graduates are in a position to teach English at different levels, including in higher education, the development of PK and PCK is crucial and takes place from a very early stage in the program. Thus, as of their first year, our students must attend several compulsory subjects, including Epistemology in Year 1, Didactics and Pedagogy in Year 2, and several subjects that focus specifically on ELT in Years 3 and 4. These include Foreign Language Didactics, lesson observations, and practicum. These compulsory subjects are taught by both teachers of English and education specialists, and some are taught in English and some in Spanish.

In general, our students mainly seek to develop their CK and are initially very unsure as to whether they wish to pursue a career in teaching. Consequently, the development of PK and PCK in Foreign Language Didactics depicted in this case study poses numerous difficulties to both student-teachers and their instructors.

DESCRIPTION OF ENGLISH LANGUAGE LEARNERS

This case study focuses on *Foreign Language Didactics 1* (FLD1), a compulsory subject in Year 2 of our IELTE program. To attend this course, students must have complied with the main requirements for Year 1, which constitute the core subjects in English. FLD1 is their first encounter with content related to the development of PCK. On average, between 15 and 30 students attend the course. The students' ages vary year to year, and most can be placed in the 19–21 age range, with some students being as old as 30.

The creation of the FHAyCS in 2000 involved the disappearance of entry examinations. That development has brought about a series of challenges for our program. First, the absence of entry exams or of clearly defined benchmarks means that most students who apply to the program are admitted. As a direct consequence, classes have become increasingly larger, with as many as 35 students per group, which makes it quite challenging for teachers to differentiate instruction. Second, traditionally, students entering our program were expected to be at a minimum of intermediate level of English language proficiency. However, having no entry examinations (or any other official mechanisms or policies to gauge learners' proficiency and/or monitor and aid progress, for that matter) generally means that many Year 1 and Year 2 students who join the program have attained only a basic or elementary level of English. This can be particularly worrying for courses like FLD1, which are designed for the students at a higher proficiency level and include a theoretical component. In other words, many of the student-teachers attending the course struggle to deal with both theoretical concepts and English itself since this is the medium of instruction. This in turn causes delayed completion and high dropout rates. This situation has made it necessary for teachers to revisit their approach and practices in order to facilitate learning of student teachers and to increase student retention.

PEDAGOGICAL APPLICATION AND INNOVATION

This section analyzes the innovation introduced to the FLD1 syllabus as of 2016 in order to foster student-teachers' awareness of the need to develop context-sensitive pedagogies as well as a sense of *plausibility* in how English could best be taught in local secondary schools "by building a personal theory of teaching action based upon their own accumulated experiences – and reflection on them" (Maley, 2016).

It is important to note here that student-teachers taking FLD1 neither observe lessons *in situ* nor teach. Therefore, much of the analysis, reflection, and discussion that take place in the FLD1 classroom are based on student-teachers' recollections of their experiences as secondary school learners and on videos that I select for classwork and homework.

Introducing Changes to the FLD1 Syllabus

FLD1 was originally called *Methodology*. This course dealt with issues such as language acquisition, motivation, and learner variables. It also focused on modeling the presentation of language, strategies for the development of reading and writing, listening and speaking, and strategies for teaching grammar and vocabulary. Also, a very significant component of this subject was the study of language methods and approaches from a chronological stance. That is, students would study the progression of language teaching methods through time, beginning with Grammar Translation and moving all along the time line (i.e., Grammar Translation, the Direct Method, Audiolingualism, and so on) until the emergence of Communicative Language Teaching and other related prepackaged methods. For activities, student-teachers would usually be asked to present a method, describe its main characteristics, and follow the questions for analysis from Larsen-Freeman and Anderson (2012, p. 9). This activity would not normally include any specific assessment or discussion of issues concerning the method's suitability for schools in Argentina. In addition, it would not cover teacher preparation necessary to implement these methods.

The development of the FLD1 syllabus was primarily based on the contents of a book for student-teachers by a well-known author and publisher that has been in use by our program since the 1980s. Although this is a common practice, centering the course syllabus on only one or two such textbooks can contribute to maintaining the idea that teachers are usually mere technicians (or passive technicians in Kumaravadivelu's (2009) terms) who implement theories, practices, and materials advocated for or designed by foreign specialists (Banegas, 2014). Most importantly, perhaps, this decision to rely mainly on materials published in and particularly suited for the BANA context (as described by Holliday, 1994) seems to have a direct impact on the way English is taught at our local secondary schools, where graduate teachers also tend to rely heavily on coursebooks and other published materials for their English lessons (see Banegas, 2014; Soto, 2014). These textbook-driven practices seem to have limited relevance to our secondary school students since lessons usually focus on rigid grammar rules and make little contribution to effective language learning for more communicative purposes. This has two important connected consequences. First, learning English at local secondary schools remains highly ineffective, as secondary students frequently fail to develop a sound knowledge of the language that goes beyond mere notions of verb tenses. Second, given that it is these very same secondary students who in time become our IELTE candidates, their competencies in English are inadequate to complete a four-year teaching program successfully.

Analyzing this situation, I realized that albeit relevant to the initial education of language teachers, focusing solely on the implementation of the techniques and strategies suggested in books for teachers can also disregard IELTE as a space where aspiring teachers begin to build their teacher identities in light of their own teaching contexts. Similarly, placing a heavy emphasis on the main characteristics of a myriad of methods, many of which have not been proven effective, would not help to instill in student-teachers the idea that teaching is a situated activity that draws on teachers' own cognition. This approach also does not account for the fact that that teaching grows through collaboration and dialogue with others. Thus, I concluded that I needed to introduce changes to my syllabus that would help me and my students go beyond the mere notion of "method" in order to focus on those contextual and sociocultural factors that affect and shape teachers' situated practices and positively impact students' learning in local schools while making English a valuable component of the secondary curriculum.

The first required step was, therefore, to understand what we meant by "our local teaching context." Consequently, the first significant change introduced to the syllabus pertained to the discussion of the notion of *context*. On the premise that teachers cannot ignore contexts, cultures, and personal histories that students bring into the classroom (Kumaravadivelu, 2009; Richards, 2013), student-teachers in FLD1 are guided through a careful analysis of their teaching context – primary and secondary state schools in Entre Rios. In order to do this, I decided to incorporate Wedell and Malderez's (2013) chapter "Components of Context" into the course bibliography to help student-teachers develop a working definition of the concept. This definition describes context as made of three main components: people, place, and time. Students analyze each component in the light of visible and invisible aspects that derive from macro and micro layers, from the classroom to the world or the other way around. This initial conceptualization leads us to an exploration of our local teaching context that requires us to zoom out of the immediate particularities of each classroom and institution (the micro context) to the macro levels of the community, town, or region in the country (see Appendix A).

Thus, we begin by analyzing very concrete factors that might affect the implementation of English in the local school, such as class size, the time allotted to English lessons (usually 120 minutes a week), and the availability of resources (from classroom infrastructure to textbooks and technological devices), among other features. This usually engages students' reflection upon their own learning experience at a secondary school in order to establish whether such factors were more or less visible and the extent to which they had an impact on both what their teachers could do and what they learned. We then move on to more theoretical grounds and look at local curricular directives (including materials published by the national MoE) to contrast them with off-the-shelf published materials used locally. The purpose of this task is threefold: (1) to familiarize learners with official documents that are frequently ignored by local teachers (Soto, 2011), (2) to evaluate the relevance that the contents of published materials might have for learners in our schools, and (3) to encourage the development of context-sensitive syllabuses and teaching practices that relate to secondary school students' histories, lived experiences, and resources. Finally, we focus on more invisible variables that might impact teachers' work and students' engagement in English lessons. They include local attitudes and people's beliefs about the role of English in their community and the needs and motivations to study it.

To facilitate further understanding of the concepts, student-teachers are then asked to work in groups of two or three and watch and analyze videos showing different classroom situations. Along with this video viewing task, they produce a collaborative reflective piece in which they refer back to:

- visible aspects of a place: the school and the area of town where it is situated; the classroom, its facilities and other teaching/learning materials; the setup, electricity and internet access, any other technology available

- the visible aspects of people: the number of students, their ages, details about the teacher

- aspects concerning time: time of the day and how this affects lesson development

- other visible features present in the classroom that might be the direct consequence of invisible aspects (e.g., any learner behavior in connection to their family background, institutional culture, attitudes toward the language)

The videos selected for this assignment typically include classrooms outside of main metropolitan areas, which represent the typical context where newly graduated teachers work. They illustrate classrooms in contexts where English is mainly taught as a curricular subject in state schools (see Appendix B).

Another significant change to the FLD1 syllabus is the incorporation of a postmethod pedagogy component. To do this, we first discuss the postmethod condition and analyze how it is different from the notion of method and why it is important to go beyond it. We then explore each of Kumaravadivelu's (2009) three pedagogic parameters individually, trying to make connections to what was studied before in the course.

We begin by addressing the parameter of *particularity*, linking it to Wedell and Malderez's (2013) definition of context, and in relation to people and place, specifically. As was the case with the analysis of our teaching context, the main aim here is to try to reach that "situational understanding" that Kumaravadivelu promotes (2009, p. 171). Thus, we turn our attention to our classrooms once more, trying to identify what the particularities of English classes at the local secondary school are, for example, in terms of the goals, the contents, the materials, and the people who engage in interaction. That is, through class discussion and interaction we try to answer questions like: What are the particularities of English lessons in our schools? What characterizes teachers, learners, and institutions? What seems to facilitate or hinder the teaching and learning of English? What are the main features of the sociocultural milieu where schools are immersed? How does this impact the English class? What about teacher preparation to teach in such environment? Part of this reflective process also involves going over materials and class activities in order to determine the method underlying their selection and implementation (see Figure 3.2.1 in Appendix C & Appendix D).

The main purpose of the previously-mentioned activity is for student-teachers to assess the extent to which language teaching methods are actually implemented in the local classroom (or in the classrooms shown in the videos we watch) and to identify those factors that might make such implementation possible or not. We focus particularly on the implementation of CLT or any of the so-called communicative methods, since this is the type of approach advocated for in the official curricular documents that students must follow to design their syllabuses and plan their lessons for primary or secondary schools once in the profession. This task encompasses raising awareness of the fact that methods that are allegedly *dead* or dated are still very common in our English classrooms, as is the case of Grammar Translation or the Audiolingual Method. This in turn allows for further reflection on why it is that numerous English teachers in our context will claim that they advocate for the implementation of communicative methods and yet their actual classroom practices deviate considerably from the main tenets of CLT (see Soto, 2014), which takes us back to mainly to aspects of context and particularity (see Appendix D).

Reflections like the ones included in Appendices A–D usually lead to a consideration of the other two parameters, *practicality* and *possibility*, which represent completely new concepts to my students. However, they are less explored than particularity in my class. This could be simply attributed to time constraints, since the class runs for 28 weeks and meets in a two-hour block once a week. Yet I believe that practicality and possibility are less developed in my class, probably due to the fact that they are more theoretical in nature, and students find it more challenging to grasp their main underlying notions and implications. Additionally, the majority of students attending FLD1 have not yet taught a real lesson and thus cannot see "the whole picture" or fully internalize how such notions actually resonate in the reality of a classroom.

In a nutshell, we reflect upon how practicality involves tackling the "harmful dichotomy between theory and practice" (Kumaravadivelu, 2009, p. 172) and how it calls for informed decision making, which is the main idea I want student-teachers to come to terms with. Thus, we discuss how this parameter encompasses addressing teachers' existing knowledge and beliefs so that they can theorize their practices. In this case, we reflect upon the local secondary English class, trying to figure out what the main theories underlying teachers' practices might be and how these might connect to their actual pedagogic choices and decisions.

Similarly, I understood that the importance of addressing the parameter of *possibility*, so closely related to the main tenets undergirding critical pedagogy, could no longer be overlooked in a course for student-teachers in Latin America, where Freire strived so hard to raise issues of education, power, and dominance. Thus, I encourage students to reflect upon the reasons why, in a globalized world where English is the dominant lingua franca, it is important to offer English as part of the state school curriculum. This usually involves examining the relevance of English to the lives of our secondary school students, particularly as a gatekeeper for opportunities both locally and globally. This helps facilitate a discussion about why all students should have access to high-quality English education.

Since usually several of our student-teachers have studied English at private academies, the concept of possibility becomes clearer when they are asked to compare their experience in those schools to their experience in the secondary classroom and share it with the group. What usually makes all the difference is drawing parallelisms between both types of educational institutions regarding the purpose and motivation for attending a private school of English; the school culture/ethos; teacher's attitudes motivation, preparation; lesson frequency and duration; number of students per class; the availability of resources, and so on. On making this comparison, student-teachers usually praise their private English lessons while they tend to be very critical (even judgmental) of classes at state secondary school and in particular of teachers there. This is precisely where the changes I introduced to FLD1 seem to become relevant, since this type of reflection frequently leads itself to discussing what type of teachers they wish to become and what it would take for them to do so.

In other words, I firmly believe that, in IELTE courses like the one described in this case study, it is only once such discussions and reflections have taken place that we can start considering which method, which topics, skills, and activities, which materials and resources, and so on, are more suitable for the local English classroom. This might sound obvious, but is it?

As Giroux (1988) postulates, raising questions about relationships of power at school and in the community (margins and centers), addressing issues of identity, gender, and class, among others, are all contents that effective IELTE programs must delve into if student-teachers are to internalize the impact that broader social, economic, and political environment actually has on teaching and learning and thus bring situated changes into ELT that are not merely "cosmetic."

Postmethod Pedagogies: Do as I Say or as I Do?

It is at this juncture where I need to become critical about my own work as a teacher educator. Introducing changes into my syllabus has not been easy. Cognitions and practices are not easily modified, and this includes my own, and my colleagues'. Thus, I had to question whether my whole proposal for FLD1 was a case of *do as I say, not as I do*. In other words, enacting a postmethod curriculum demands knowledge from teachers other than theoretical principles and training on classroom procedures. Again, the enactment of postmethod pedagogies must necessarily understand teaching as a situated activity that addresses *local exigencies* and teachers' *lived experiences*. I have struggled to make this clear to my student-teachers. That is, as a teacher educator in charge of a course that is expected to delve into PCK, I have the opportunity to bring a different perspective into my syllabus and my classroom. And I have decided to take it. Still, my course is just *one* of many within an IELTE program, which also includes other subjects, perhaps reflecting more traditional perspectives.

Thus, for a long time now I have been asking myself: to what extent is my syllabus relevant? How far am I actually helping very young, inexperienced student-teachers to understand what teaching involves? Most importantly, to what extent are the concepts I want them to internalize reflected in my own practices as teacher educator within the program itself? How far are we as teacher educators providing our student-teachers with a clear, honest example of what we preach?

Enacting a postmethod pedagogy must necessarily involve redefining the nature of teacher education so that we start looking at our IELTE classrooms from the bottom up in much the same way we encourage our student-teachers to do when it comes to the primary or secondary classroom. To do this effectively, teacher educators need to begin and end with experience, grounding student-teacher learning in concrete classroom practice; we need to "get out," meaning give students' a chance to get their ideas out, before we "put in," meaning tell them what you want them to know (Malderez & Wedell, 2007, pp. 38–39) helping student-teachers explore and dig out what they already know about teaching and learning, and we can only do this if we offer adequate time for reflection and collaboration, through a dialogue-based relationship.

In this sense, FLD1 attempts to address postmethod pedagogy. First, it helps student-teachers understand local English classrooms by scrutinizing what goes on inside schools from *what they already know* given their life-long experience as students. Second, the course tries to enable students' articulation of their own cognitions through in-depth discussion while creating the necessary conditions for student-teachers to feel free to engage in a dialogic relationship with their teacher and classmates. It also encourages critical thinking and reflection, which are skills that are not usually developed in our educational culture – no matter the educational level. And, finally, it exposes students to authors that – even if difficult to tackle at this early stage in the program – will hopefully inform their pedagogic decisions in the long run so they become autonomous, reflective, and engaged professionals, not just mere practitioners.

CONCLUSION

If we truly hope for ELT to be effective in our local classrooms, it is imperative that we provide our IELTE students with clear, tangible examples of what we mean by the postmethod condition, by critical pedagogies, by being communicative in the language class. We need to create the conditions so that interdisciplinary work can occur. We need to design syllabuses ourselves that draw upon our student-teachers' resources, experiences, and lives. As Giroux (2006) suggests:

> We must get away from training teachers to be simply efficient technicians and practitioners. We need a new vision of what constitutes educational leadership so that we can educate teachers to think critically, locate themselves in their own histories, and exercise moral and public responsibility in their role as engaged critics and transformative intellectuals.
>
> (p. 4)

Adhering to the main tenets of the postmethod condition seems to indicate that an IELTE program should go beyond the sole consideration of content knowledge, pedagogical knowledge, or pedagogical content knowledge so as to encompass and foster the development of context-sensitive pedagogic knowledge.

Understanding student-teachers and supporting their learning through adequate mechanisms should help unveil their existing cognitions and establish the extent to which these are congruent with the classroom practices we expect them to engage in.

So this should be the next step in the innovation: making sure that my own practices mirror what I preach.

REFERENCES

Banegas, D. L. (2014). Of methods and postmethods: A view from Argentina. In D. L. Banegas, M. López Barrios, M. Porto, & M. A. Soto (Eds.), *English language teaching in the post-methods era: Selected papers from the 39th FAAPI conference* (pp. 15–27). Retrieved from www.faapi.org.ar/downloads/FAAPI2014.pdf

Depaepe, F., Verschaffel, L., & Kelchtermans, G. (2013). Pedagogical content knowledge: A systematic review of the way in which the concept has pervaded mathematics educational research. *Teaching and Teacher Education, 34*, 12–25. https://doi.org/10.1016/j.tate.2013.03.001

Giroux, H. A. (1988). *Teachers as intellectuals: Toward a critical pedagogy of learning.* South Hadley, MA: Bergin & Garvey Publishers, Inc.

Giroux, H. A. (2006). *America on the edge: Henry Giroux on politics, culture and education.* New York, NY: Palgrave-Macmillan.

Holliday, A. (1994). *Appropriate methodology and social context.* Cambridge, UK: Cambridge University Press.

Kumaravadivelu, B. (2009). *Understanding language teaching: From method to postmethod.* New York, NY: Routledge.

Larsen-Freeman, D., & Anderson, M. (2012). *Techniques and principles in language teaching* (3rd ed.). Oxford, UK: Oxford University Press.

Malderez, A., & Wedell, M. (2007). *Teaching teachers: Processes and practices.* London, UK: Continuum.

Maley, A. (2016). The teacher's sense of plausibility revisited. *Indonesian Journal of English Language Teaching, 11*(1), 1–29. http://dx.doi.org/10.25170%2Fijelt.v11i1.846

Richards, J. C. (2013). Curriculum approaches in language teaching: Forward, central, and backward design. *RELC Journal, 44*(1), 5–33. https://doi.org/10.1177/0033688212473293

Soto, M. A. (2011). *Teachers' beliefs and curriculum innovation uptake: Case studies of EFL teachers in Argentina* (Unpublished Masters' thesis).

Soto, M. A. (2014). Post-method pedagogy: Towards enhanced context-situated teaching methodologies. In D. L. Banegas, M. López Barrios, M. Porto, & M. A. Soto (Eds.), *English language teaching in the post-methods era: Selected papers from the 39th FAAPI conference* (pp. 39–54). Retrieved from www.faapi.org.ar/downloads/FAAPI2014.pdf

Wedell, M., & Malderez, A. (2013). *Understanding classroom contexts: The starting point for change.* London, UK: Bloomsbury.

APPENDIX A

Context and language learning

INTERACT

 Work in pairs.

1. Refer to Wedell & Malderez's (2013) components of context. Name and describe each briefly but thoroughly. You might take down notes summarizing ideas.

2. Individually, take a few minutes to think about a typical English lesson at your secondary school. You can zoom in or out of the classroom, Google fashion. Note down any characteristic that strikes you as worth mentioning.

3. Now work in pairs again to share your recollections of your secondary English class. To what extent where yours and your classmate's English lesson similar / different?

4. Identify and discuss how each of the components of context (both visible and invisible) seem to have affected the class you chose to reflect upon. Provide at least one example for each component making sure you address key concepts.

Bibliography

Wedell, M. & Malderez, A. (2013). *Understanding classroom contexts: The starting point for change.* London, England: Bloomsbury. Chapter 1.

Appendix B

Understanding English teaching contexts

Work in small groups of no more than three students to complete the tasks below.

RECYCLE

 Refer back to Wedell, M. & Malderez, A. (2013). *Understanding language classroom contexts. The starting point for change.* London: Bloomsbury. Chapter 1, pp. 7-28.

Make sure you remember and understand what the main components of context are and why it is relevant to know about them. If necessary, take a few minutes to discuss the topics again with the members of your groups. Agree on basic points.

WATCH

 Go to your online classroom.

Find the links to several videos which show different teaching and learning contexts around the world.

Watch the videos attentively and relate them to the topics in Units 1 and 2.

PUT IT ALL TOGETHER

 Once you've watched and analysed the videos do the following choose two videos.

Write a short description for each discussing how the main **components of context** (PEOPLE, PLACE, TIME) seem to affect the groups of language learners in the videos. In doing this, you might choose to zoom in / out, Google-Earth fashion.

Consider:

- ☑ PEOPLE and PLACE. What aspects are more visible in relation with these components?
- ☑ What situations / events in the videos seem to be the effect of more invisible aspects? Can you think what those aspects are / might be? (e.g. attitudes?)
- ☑ What factors might contribute to / hinder the learning process of the students involved?
- ☑ How do the teachers involved in the videos create their teaching (pedagogic) context to overcome the fact that the language is taught as a FOREIGN language and facilitate learning?

REMEMBER!

 You are expected to produce your own descriptions of the *teaching contexts* shown on the videos.

Connect your descriptions to the theory. Refer to the bibliography adequately: use citations from the texts to support your views if necessary.

Do not copy-paste information verbatim.

Bibliography

Wedell, M. & Malderez, A. (2013). *Understanding language classroom contexts. The starting point for change.* London: Bloomsbury. Chapter 1, pp. 7-28.

APPENDIX C

Language teaching methods and approaches

Work in pairs or small groups.

RECYCLE

 Refer back to Kumaravadivelu's (2009). *Understanding language teaching: From method to postmethod.* Chapter 8.

If necessary, you can also re-read the main concepts in Unit 1.

REFLECT

 Discuss the following questions:

1. How do Kumaravadivelu's ideas relate to the notion of *context,* as seen in Unit 1?

2. What are the risks of "sticking to" prescribed methods?

3. The postmethod condition tells teachers *adapt, don't adopt.* What does this mean?

4. How do questions 2 and 3 above relate to Kumaravadivelu's parameters?

Get ready to share your reflections and answers with the whole class.

WRITE

 Individually, write answers to the questions connecting the ideas studied in class. Make sure you refer back to the bibliography clearly and explicitly.

 Address the questions fully. Do not include irrelevant information.

Support your views by justifying or exemplifying what you mean clearly.

Do not copy-paste information verbatim from the sources.

Bibliography

Kumaravadivelu, B. (2009). *Understanding language teaching: From method to postmethod.* New York, USA: Routledge. Chapter 8.

Figure 3.2.1 A sample learner reflection for the task above

Source: Photo by Maria Alejandra Soto

Appendix D

Communicative Language Teaching

RECYCLE

 Refer back to the bibliography for Unit 6 *CLT and its suitability for the local English classroom*.

If necessary, you can also re-read the main concepts in Units 1, 4 and 5.

REFLECT

 Individually, take a few minutes to go back to a typical English lesson at your secondary school once more.

Consider the method / approach implemented by your teacher. Think about the following aspects:

- The lesson objective(s)
- The role of the teacher
- The role of the students
- The type of activities you engaged in
- The type of materials and resources used in the lesson
- The nature of student-teacher / student-student interaction
- The role Spanish played in the class

Take notes.

ANALYZE

 Work in small groups of three.

1. Choose **one** books below:
    - My English Trip A
    - Young Explorers 1
    - New English Adventure Starter A
    - In the Loop Starter
    - What's up? Starter
    - Solutions Elementary
    - New Headway Elementary

2. Pick **three different activities** from the book you chose.
3. Complete the table

Activity	What is does the activity focus on? (a skill? Grammar? Vocab?	What is the purpose of the activity?	What method / approach seems to underpin the activity?
1	-	-	-
2	-	-	-
3	-	-	-

CASE STUDY 3.3

Towards a Context-Sensitive Theory of Practice in Primary English Language Teaching Through Theme-Based Instruction in Serbia

Vera Savić

The postmethod pedagogy recognises the language teacher as a key factor in facilitating the process of learning. However, teachers can play this role only if they possess "the knowledge and skill, attitude, and autonomy necessary to construct their own context-sensitive theory of practice" (Kumaravadivelu, 2006, p. 173). This further requires teachers to understand and reflect on their previous experience and on what happens in the classroom, i.e. in their teaching context, and to "theorize from their practice and to practice what they theorize" (Kumaravadivelu, 2006, p. 173). This case study shows the conditions created by an in-service professional development programme that resulted in practising teachers' awareness of the need for respecting and applying the postmethod principles of particularity, practicality, and possibility in designing and teaching thematic units appropriate for their teaching contexts.

THE SETTING

This case study took place in Serbia and examined the effects of an innovative professional development (PD) programme for primary teachers of English accredited under the name *Theme-Based Instruction in Teaching English to Young Learners (TBI in TEYL)* in the 2017–2018 school year. The participants were 96 primary teachers of English from five different areas of the country, trained by accredited TBI teacher trainers in local groups (15–30 participants).

Although English has been a compulsory school subject from primary grade 1 (age 6–7) in Serbia since 2003, until 2014 there had been no PD programmes for English language teachers targeting content-based instruction at a young age. Moreover, novice teachers starting to teach young learners in Serbian schools do not get training for teaching this age group and are rarely mentored by experienced teachers. Recognising the children's need for meaningful and purposeful communication in a foreign/second/additional language (L2) learning (Shin & Crandall, 2014), the programme was designed with the aim of contributing to the effectiveness of teaching English at the primary level in Serbia by developing teachers' competence for integrating cross-curricular content and foreign language teaching. The programme focused on assisting practising teachers in developing a range of pedagogical strategies through an experiential learning process of designing and teaching a thematic unit in their actual classrooms. The PD programme activities were guided by the postmethod principles of particularity, practicality, and possibility (Kumaravadivelu, 2006) and required teachers to develop an understanding of the learners' needs and their particular local contexts.

DESCRIPTION OF ENGLISH LANGUAGE TEACHERS

Ninety-six primary English language teachers came from five geographically distant areas of Serbia. At the time of the programme, they were working in city or village state schools (or both), were fully qualified, and most of them holding bachelor's degrees in English language and literature awarded by Anglo-American departments of national universities. Several teachers had master's degrees. Most of the teachers were female, and many were in the first half of their teaching careers (0–15 years of teaching experience). Having volunteered to participate in the TBI programme, the participants were asked to identify their individual needs in reference to TBI by filling in a KWL chart. A KWL chart is a reflective activity that provides space in a chart for teachers to write down what they already know about a topic (K), what they want to know about the topic (W), and later what they learned about the topic (L). Their answers to the open-ended questions revealed that more than half of them admitted knowing nothing or very little about thematic language teaching, which was in line with an earlier study of teachers' familiarity with TBI (Savić & Shin, 2016). However, even those who claimed they understood TBI showed that their knowledge of it was vague, and only a few teachers were able to define TBI with reference to teaching English by integrating cross-curricular content connected by a theme. Nevertheless, the participants identified a comprehensive list of their PD needs in TBI. For example, they stated a desire to learn "everything" about TBI and identified a need to learn to plan a thematic unit, select materials and resources to use, integrate subject content into English lessons, and create fun and interesting activities with multimedia. Overall, they wanted to improve their teaching and learn to teach more effectively.

PEDAGOGICAL APPLICATION AND INNOVATION

The participants' K and W reflections in their KWL charts indicated their awareness of the needs for PD not only in TBI, but in general professional effectiveness and empowerment to introduce change and innovation into their regular practice. Against this background, I describe the introduction of a PD innovation, the TBI in TEYL programme, into primary teaching of English in Serbia. The programme involved the following three stages:

1. Stage One: Two-day training in theme-based instruction in autumn 2017.

2. Stage Two: Completion of a local group task that included planning of a thematic unit, designing materials and activities, and applying the plan in a TEYL class in spring 2018.

3. Stage Three: Team presentation of the thematic unit (followed by immediate self-, peer- and trainer evaluation) on the third day of the PD programme in spring 2018.

The evaluation of the programme's impact over the 2017–2018 academic year was done using the data from three sources:

1. Participants' written reflections collected at the end of Stage One (structured as the L in the KWL chart, which represented what was "Learned"

2. Content analysis of thematic unit (TU) plans created in Stage Two

3. Results of the trainer TU evaluation questionnaire and the participant programme evaluation questionnaire, both filled out in Stage Three.

The analysis of the participants' reflections on their new experiences in initial TBI training in Stage One indicated that the teachers particularly appreciated learning how to plan a TU; use stories, multimedia, and songs in TBI to focus on what children want and can do; use learners' background knowledge; integrate content and culture to develop 21st century skills; develop and sequence activities; and assess learners appropriately. Teachers' reflections also showed that the programme recognised their personal knowledge and managed to build on it.

TUs created by teachers in Stage Two of the programme showed their understanding and readiness to introduce actual change into their practice. For example, most teachers were able to include a story appropriate to the theme and the learners' language level and age (pre-A1 of CEFR, ages 7–10). This was a significant positive development in the program, since some previous studies indicated that primary teachers in Serbia rarely used authentic stories in teaching English (Savić & Shin, 2013); a great majority of the participants' groups managed to do so. Moreover, the TU's involved an extensive use of multimedia, especially video materials, and a variety of activities catering to different intelligences and learning styles of the learners, as well as to their interests (see Table 3.3.1 for sample materials and activities). These microstrategies mapped the 21st century skills (Binkley et al., 2012), like communication, collaboration, personal and social responsibility, cultural awareness and competence, creative and critical thinking, problem solving, decision making, learning to learn, computer skills, and global and local citizenship.

However, it was the Stage Three evaluation of the programme's impact that added the important parts missing in the picture of how the programme changed the Serbian teachers' practice. The trainers' evaluation of TU presentations by the teachers revealed the contextual factors that shaped the relationship between the participants' knowledge and beliefs and their actual practice (Kumaravadivelu, 2006). Some teachers had faced lack of adequate equipment, limited internet access, and other limitations that prevented their use of multimedia. Others intentionally avoided challenging themes or tasks, probably due to the lack of experience in TBI, and developed activities that were not motivating enough. In some TUs, a global perspective was missing as well as appropriate cultural content, thus limiting the pedagogical parameter of possibility.

Table 3.3.1 Sample materials and activities developed by the participants

Theme and learners' grade and age	Sample materials and sources	Sample activities
Animals (grade 4, 9–10)	Music: Camille Saint-Saëns, *The Carnival of the Animals* Story: *The Lion and the Mouse* Animated video about animals' eating habits: www.youtube.com/watch?v=3leDZ7zlwc0&feature=share	*Activity based on listening to music:* Teacher plays music and invites children to name the animals the sounds remind them of. *Activity based on the story:* Post-reading activity: Children are divided into groups, and each group is given text strips which they have to arrange in the order the text appears in the story; then, each group is given a list of adjectives (dangerous, brave, friendly, cunning, angry, strong, slow, fast, weak, scared, small, big); they are to decide which animal the adjective refers to, a lion or a mouse, and to put the adjectives into two groups; finally, they discuss the characteristics of the two animals and identify the moral of the story. *Activity based on the video:* Children work in groups to create a poster about the food chain; they can use the pictures of animals they have drawn at the beginning of the lesson or draw new ones; they are asked to write a couple of sentences describing the food chain – who eats what; the groups choose the leader who will present their work to the rest of the class. *Activity based on the video:* Teacher asks the children to identify where the animals live, to name the actions animals can do and describe their appearance, and to write it down in the form of lyrics of a rap song; the groups then create moves for the song, practice singing it and finally perform in turns.

(Continued)

Table 3.3.1 (Continued)

Theme and learners' grade and age	Sample materials and sources	Sample activities
Plants (grade 4, 9–10)	Videos: Venus flytrap, Nephentus Bloody Mary, Bladderwort, www.youtube.com/watch?v=z5fOsgrAJiU www.youtube.com/watch?v=9k0wQAVHuyg www.youtube.com/watch?v=wZcKoTxp5mc Realia: gardening tools, pots, seeds, soil, plants. Story: *Jack and the Beanstalk* Song: "Let's Plant a Garden": www.youtube.com/watch?v=XjNFgJEJp3g	*Activity based on the videos*: Teacher gives students a piece of paper and tells them to create an imaginary carnivorous plant; children should draw and colour a picture to show what their plant will look like, and then present it to the classmates; they should name an imaginary plant and tell how it will catch its prey. *Storyboard (activity based on the story)*: Divide the class into teams; give children a copy of the storyboard pictures and a set of the storyboard sentences, and ask them to cut up the sentences strips and place them under the correct pictures. *The Giant's Chant (activity based on the story)*: Teacher mimes actions and tells children, "This is the way the giant . . . (smells his lunch, falls asleep . . .)"; children are encouraged to copy the actions; teacher then divides the class into 4 teams, each team gets a different verse; as the 1st team chants verse 1, the others do the actions; the 2nd team chants verse 2, the others do the actions, and so on. *Activity based on the song*: The pupils are divided in groups of 3 or 4 students and are given pieces of paper in colour; on the yellow ones they should write the names of the gardening tools and on the green ones the activities in the garden; during the activity, the song is played and when the teacher stops it, the groups should stick their yellow pieces of paper on the board; then the teacher starts the song again, and the students write on the green pieces of paper; the teacher stops the music and they stick the green pieces of paper on the board; the winner is the group with the most correct answers. *Activity based on the song*: The pupils are divided into groups of 4 and are given pots with soil and seeds. Each student is given a piece of paper on which it is written which tool they should take and what activity they should perform. They perform the activities and say what they are doing and what their friends are doing.
Food (grade 3, 8–9)	Video: healthy eating: www.youtube.com/watch?v=mMHVEFWNLMc Role-play: Conversation about food www.youtube.com/watch?v=k-besF9yuHY Video: School lunches you've probably never heard about: www.youtube.com/watch?v=-7YBTX7vnVc Story: *I Will Never Not Ever Eat a Tomato*, by Lauren Child.	*Activity based on Healthy Eating and School Lunches Around the World videos*: The teacher hands out cut-out paper plates to children and gives them instructions to "prepare" their own healthy meal. They can use food cut-outs or they can draw their own food and then colour it. They have 20 minutes to do this activity and are free to walk around the class and exchange ideas with their friends. The teacher walks around the classroom giving any support they might need. After 20 minutes they present their meals, saying what food is on their plate and why it is healthy. *Role-play* (based on the YouTube presentation): Children use food cut-outs to talk about their preferences in relation to food. *Activity based on the School lunches video*: In groups, children create posters with pictures of local healthy food they would like to have in their school lunch; each food category should be represented appropriately. *Activity based on the book*: Role-play of the closing dialogue between Lola and Charlie. Children repeat the dialogue in pairs, substituting "tomato" with any vegetable they personally do not like eating.

Traffic (grade 4, 9–10)	Animated video: Transport for kids – Means and Modes www.youtube.com/watch?v=rPL4B1keV10 Worksheets: Imperatives www.slideshare.net/monicaruizgutierrez/imperatives-commands-sentences Animated video: Asking the way www.youtube.com/watch?v=AgTkKGM0TWE Story: *This Is the Way We Go to School* by Edith Baer – A book about children around the world: www.youtube.com/watch?v=1eBZAh1lN2E Pictures: Children going to school in different parts of the world – 25 of the most dangerous and unusual journeys to school in the world, by Julija Neje: www.boredpanda.com/dangerous-journey-to-school/ Song: "This Is the Way We Go to School": www.youtube.com/watch?v=fsIb5L0_pGY Online maps	Play Pictionary using transportation vocabulary. Pupils are divided into 3 groups. Each group gets 3 words. One member of the group draws and the other pupils guess what it is. Use traffic lights to illustrate imperative. Write imperative next to the lights: Red-Stop! Don't go! Yellow-Get ready! Don't rush! Green-Go! Don't wait! Pupils look at the pictures and fill in with the appropriate verb of movement. Pupils look at the map and explain the way one should take in order to get to the hotel, bank, library, and the museum. *Role-play*: One pupil asks the other for the way to the library. The pupil answers by using verbs of movement and imperative. Pupils listen to the story *This Is the Way We Go to School* by Edith Baer. Then they talk about the story and tell how children go to school. Pupils look at the pictures of children going to school and discuss them in pairs. Then they draw themselves going to school. Finally, the class bar graph created with pictures showing different ways of going to school is displayed on the board. Pupils survey the means of transport they use for going to school and name the most usual one.

In spite of the constraints in some local contexts, the programme was successful in introducing change in many of them. The TU evaluation questionnaires completed by the trainers (two trainers worked independently on assessing each TU presentation) evaluated highly the contents of the thematic units and acknowledged the teachers' engagement and the effectiveness of TBI in a particular teaching context. The TBI trainers praised the development of themes into individual lessons; the choice and variety of activities; the level of challenge posed to English language learners; the choice of subject content integrated; the involvement of learners in decision making; the choice and integration of stories, songs, video materials, and visuals; the use of ICT by the learners; and solutions that were truly context-sensitive. Some of these solutions included adapting the activities to a child with special educational needs, teaching a TU on sports outside the classroom, using a range of realia in teaching, using appropriate online activities instead of printed/coursebook materials, using competitive activities/games, including a global aspect of a theme and raising international culture awareness, teaching grammar in context, integrating peer support and peer-assessment, providing real-life experiences to ELLs, and motivating ELLs to use books from the school library. The trainers also observed successful collaboration of the teachers in TU planning and teaching and collaboration between English language teachers and subject teachers. For example, an art teacher created illustrations for a storytelling TBI lesson, and the English language teacher utilised the pictures with great success to introduce and practice new vocabulary related to free-time activities, like the unusual ones such as going rock climbing and scuba diving, or some more frequently practised in Serbia, like rollerblading, playing chess, going fishing, or doing karate. Both teachers used a lot of imagination to adapt and illustrate the well-known fable *The Ant and the Grasshopper* (see Figures 3.3.1 and 3.3.2 in Appendix A), while the children's familiarity with the original story in their mother tongue contributed greatly to their achievement in the storytelling lesson. An effective contextualisation of new language taught in the *Free Time* thematic unit was thus accomplished through collaborative efforts of the teachers of English and art. The trainers' comments in the questionnaire gave evidence of microstrategies incorporated in this teacher development programme, relating to macrostrategies of maximising learning opportunities, facilitating negotiated interaction, fostering language awareness, contextualising linguistic input, integrating language skills, promoting learner autonomy, ensuring social relevance, and raising cultural consciousness (Kumaravadivelu, 2006).

This is further supported with the results obtained through the programme evaluation questionnaire completed by the teachers. In this questionnaire, the teachers were asked to reflect on the areas of pedagogical innovation introduced through TBI experience. The teachers saw three aspects of TBI as highly innovative:

1. Productive collaboration in team TU planning that allowed the teachers to share ideas and learn from and support each other;

2. The link between new TBI knowledge and practical application in the classroom; and

3. Development of new teaching strategies and techniques that enhanced the teachers' motivation to participate in the TBI activities and helped improve the quality of their teaching.

Both the trainers' and teachers' comments spoke to the TBI programme's adaptability to a local context through a series of microstrategies.

CONCLUSION

The TBI in TEYL in Serbia programme aimed to foster primary L2 teachers' capacity to develop context-sensitive, situation-specific ideas within macrostrategic theoretical framework and microstrategic realisation of classroom procedures, through collaborative thematic planning and reflective approach to classroom practice and its effectiveness. The pedagogic parameters of particularity, practicality, and possibility were taken into account when designing and carrying out the programme, and the participants were encouraged to "theorize from their practice and to practice what they theorize" (Kumaravadivelu, 2006, p. 184). The focus in the PD programme was to engage L2 teachers in new applications of existing knowledge and TEYL experience and to develop new knowledge and TBI teaching strategies in collaborative work. This makes the PD programme potentially adaptable to other teaching contexts worldwide.

ACKNOWLEDGEMENT

The TBI in TEYL programme was originally designed as a collaboration between Joan Kang Shin (George Mason University, USA) and myself (University of Kragujevac, Serbia) for training practising English language teachers in Serbian primary schools. It was supported by the US Embassy in Serbia.

REFERENCES

Binkley, M., Erstad, O., Herman, J., Raizen, S., Ripley, M., Miller-Ricci, M., & Rumble, M. (2012). Defining twenty-first century skills. In P. Griffin et al. (Eds.), *Assessment and teaching of 21st century skills* (pp. 17–66). Dordrecht, Germany: Springer.

Kumaravadivelu, B. (2006). *Understanding language teaching: From method to postmethod.* Mahwah, NJ: Lawrence Erlbaum Associates, Publishers.

Savić, V., & Shin, J. K. (2013). Contextualising language learning through stories in Serbia. *Teaching Innovations, 26*(1), 62–83.

Savić, V., & Shin, J. K. (2016). Improving quality of primary English language teaching in Serbia through theme-based instruction. In J. Teodorović (Ed.), *Improving quality of elementary education* (pp. 328–338). Jagodina, Serbia: Faculty of Education.

Shin, J. K., & Crandall, J. (2014). *Teaching young learners English: From theory to practice.* Boston, MA: National Geographic Learning/Cengage Learning.

APPENDIX A
Activity Based on the Story *The Ant and the Grasshopper*

This is a story created by adapting the fable *The Ant and the Grasshopper*. The illustrations and worksheets for the Free Time Activities lesson are based on the story. The materials were created by Dragana Stankovic (English language teacher) and Nemanja Arsic (art teacher), at the Dositej Obradovic primary school located in the village of Vranovo, Serbia, and presented at the TBI seminar in Smederevo, Serbia, on March 19, 2018.

THE ANT AND THE GRASSHOPPER
....

The Ant and the Grasshopper are best friends. They live in the same field. They go to the same school. It's Monday.

Grasshopper: I'm bored. Let's do something.

Ant: You are bored! Why don't you study? Do you know we have a Maths test on Friday?

Grasshopper: Maths test! Oh, no! I don't like Maths. I know nothing about Maths. I hate Maths.

Ant: I can help you. I like Maths. We can study together today.

Grasshopper: Today? Oh, I can't study today. Today is Monday. On Mondays I go rock climbing. Why don't you come with me? It will be fun!

Ant: I can't. I must study for the test.

Grasshopper: Oh, don't be silly. The week is long. We can study tomorrow.

Next day after school.

Grasshopper: Hey, Antie! Let's play.

Ant: Play? But we have to study! You know . . . the test!

Grasshopper: Today? I can't today. It's Tuesday. On Tuesdays I go scuba diving.

Ant: What about tomorrow?

Grasshopper: Tomorrow? Oh, no. It's Wednesday. I do karate on Wednesdays. And on Thursdays I play chess with my friend Bumblebee.

Ant: And on Fridays you go fishing?!

Grasshopper: No, I go rollerblading on Fridays.

Ant: What about the test? When do you plan to study?

Grasshopper: Oh, my friend. All you do is study, study, study. Relax. Be more like me. Enjoy.
So Friday comes. The Ant and the Grasshopper are going back home from school. The Ant is happy, he gets an A. The Grasshopper is sad. There is an F on his paper.

Grasshopper: I know. Next time no rock climbing, no scuba diving, no chess, karate. . . . Next time I will study.

Figure 3.3.1 Illustrations for *The Ant and the Grasshopper*

Source: Drawings by Nemanja Arsić, Art Teacher, Serbia

Figure 3.3.1 (Continued)

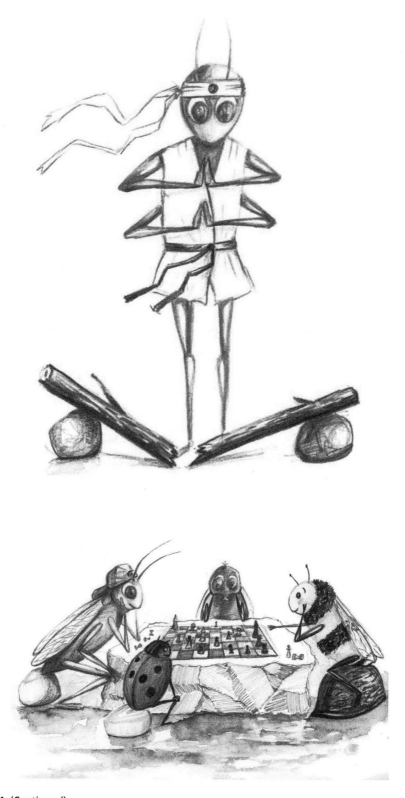

Figure 3.3.1 (Continued)

Figure 3.3.1 (Continued)

Figure 3.3.1 (Continued)

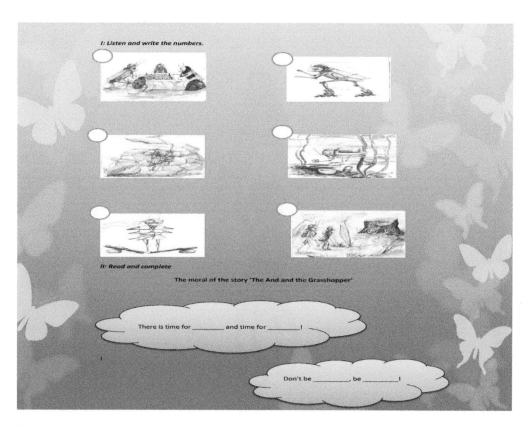

Figure 3.3.2 Sample worksheet for *The Ant and the Grasshopper*

Source: Worksheet Developed by Dragana Stanković, Primary EFL Teacher, Serbia

UNIT 4
Culturally Responsive Pedagogy in ELT

CHAPTER 4

Culturally Responsive Pedagogy in TESOL

M'Balia Thomas and Marta Carvajal-Regidor

FRAMING THE ISSUE

Culturally Responsive Pedagogy (CRP) is an instructional stance toward the schooling of youth and adult populations who are culturally, linguistically, sociopolitically, and/or economically marginalized. It highlights the interplay between identity, language, and learning in schooling. CRP has historic ties to Multicultural Education (Banks, 2009) and is concerned with the systemic inequities in educational attainment and experiences borne by marginalized populations. Like Multicultural Education, CRP attends to the impact of deficit thinking in educational spaces toward the cultural, linguistic, and literacy practices of these students and their home communities (Paris, 2012). CRP reframes these students' cultural and linguistic resources by seeing them less as obstacles that hinder learning and more as assets that facilitate the acquisition of new knowledge.

Using the term "Culturally Relevant Pedagogy," Ladson-Billings (2009) advocates for pedagogy that embraces the lived experiences and cultural identities that racial/ethnic minority students bring to the classroom. In her seminal work, *The Dreamkeepers: Successful Teachers of African American Children*, Ladson-Billings (2009) documents the culturally relevant techniques of teachers noted for their successes in producing academic achievement among African American students – a group historically marginalized within the United States. She calls these teachers "dreamkeepers" (p. 157) in recognition of the instructional methods they adopt that are grounded in their students' cultural ways of being and experiencing the world. These culturally centered practices (1) foster students' ability to navigate the cultural gaps between school and home knowledge (their cultural competence), (2) promote academic success even while maintaining students' cultural and linguistic identity, and (3) empower students to serve as sociopolitical agents with the capacity to critique the deficit discourses they encounter in school talk and texts (Ladson-Billings, 1995).

Sharing Ladson-Billings's concern for students' cultural competence, success, and empowerment, Gay (2018) addresses the impact of deficit pedagogies embedded within the interpretation and delivery of U.S. curriculum. In *Culturally Responsive Teaching* (Gay, 2018), she writes in support of pedagogy that embraces the cultural and linguistic pluralism within modern U.S. classrooms. She advocates for an affirming and caring attitude toward students and the diverse languages, communication styles, and literacy practices they bring to class, as well as "a critical consciousness surrounding issues of race, difference, inequality, and equity" (Gay, 2018, p. 143). A critical consciousness awakens educators to the ways curriculum (the official curriculum consisting of textbooks, fictional books, and the national and state standards as well as the internet, mass media, and video resources) can be selected, interpreted, and made meaningful across culturally and linguistically diverse groups of students (see Fredricks, 2012; Kesler, 2011; Lee, 2014).

The names Ladson-Billings and Gay are synonymous with CRP. Their work aims to dismantle the deficit pedagogies that mark the education of marginalized students in the United States and simultaneously promote instruction that educates students "*through their own cultural filters*" (Gay, 2013, p. 50, italics in original). Moreover, their work has given rise to research that takes up these original ideas and applies them in ways that are culturally sustaining (Paris, 2012) and culturally revitalizing (McCarty & Lee, 2014); ways that speak to the unique lived experiences of culturally and linguistically diverse communities outside the United

States (Fredricks, 2012; Lee, 2014; Marshall, 2010). CRP researchers and practitioners in contexts outside the United States often direct their attention to the socioeconomic and political hegemony, and the cultural and linguistic marginalization, encountered by learners and users of English across the globe. Their concern is for English language education (ELE) and the ways it (1) reinforces and highlights unequal access and privilege in countries, (2) reflects imposed knowledge and standardized instructional and assessment practices, and (3) introduces identity-erasing texts and instructional methods. Given the concern for academic equity and cultural and linguistic inclusion, the ideology, stances, and pedagogical techniques of CRP hold significant value for ELE and the Teaching of English to Speakers of Other Languages (TESOL).

The present chapter examines the concept of CRP and the implications it holds for ELE. Building upon the historical framing established in the introduction, we outline five stances that mark a culturally responsive pedagogy. We examine the implications these five stances hold for different contexts of English language education: K-12 and Adult English as an Additional/Second Language (EAL or ESL) in Anglophone settings, Postsecondary/Higher Educational settings in Anglophone countries, as well as non-Anglophone countries where English serves as a medium of instruction (EMI), and K-12 and Adult English as a Foreign Language (EFL) in non-Anglophone settings. The chapter concludes with a discussion of the future direction of culturally responsive practice in two areas of English language education – language policy and distance education.

CONCEPTS AND THEORETICAL CONSIDERATIONS

As a stance against deficit pedagogies, CRP takes aim at the gaps between the knowledge, discourses, and literacy practices cultivated within a student's home and community setting and those taught in school. Culturally responsive educators create active and collaborative spaces in which students can use those assets or knowledge resources to dialogue with, resist, interrogate, and compare the official or sanctioned curriculum of school (Moje et al., 2004). In these culturally responsive spaces, five stances guide teacher activity: Pedagogy as (1) a sociocultural phenomenon, (2) sustaining and revitalizing, (3) participatory, (4) supportive of students' linguistic rights, and (5) caring. A description of these five pedagogical stances follows.

Pedagogy as a Sociocultural Phenomenon

A culturally responsive stance toward pedagogy recognizes that teaching and learning are sociocultural acts inseparable from the larger sociopolitical contexts in which they occur. Moreover, teaching and learning are mediated by the prior knowledge and symbolic tools at one's disposal, such as home and community language, prior schooling experiences, and community values and folklore around learning (Gay, 2018). Therefore, to foster student learning, teachers should be well informed about their students' lived experiences and positionality within their homes and communities and about the ways in which these experiences differ from their own (Lee, 2014). Additionally, teachers should make pedagogical adjustments that capitalize upon the symbolic resources students bring from home. They should adopt instructional techniques that facilitate dialogue so that, in interaction with others, students can address, respond to, and engage with curricular texts and the larger social discourses embedded within them (Gay, 2013). The school knowledge acquired through such a pedagogical stance is contextually situated, collaboratively negotiated, and personally tied to the lived realities of students.

Pedagogy as Sustaining and Revitalizing

A culturally responsive stance toward pedagogy approaches instruction and curriculum in ways that are culturally sustaining (Paris, 2012) and culturally revitalizing (McCarty & Lee, 2014). A culturally sustaining stance treats students' lived experiences, including the home and community cultural and linguistic knowledge upon which these experiences are derived, as valuable assets. These assets can be taken up as "dynamic, shifting, and ever changing" (Paris, 2012, p. 95) cultural and linguistic resources that both students and teachers can draw upon to facilitate acquisition of official school knowledge and to sustain, affirm, and contribute to the revitalization of home and community knowledge. The work to sustain and revitalize home and community knowledge is crucial in settings where educational sovereignty – a community's right to self-determine and govern their children's educational goals and curricular content – has been limited. For example, referencing the systematic and historic erasure of Native American and First Nations peoples in the Americas, McCarty and Lee (2014) champion culturally revitalizing practices that adopt a return to local ways of knowing, Native languages, and educational philosophies and pedagogies. Such practices enable Indigenous peoples to recapture tribal and educational sovereignty and enable educators to support the cultural and linguistic identities of Native and First Nations students (McCarty & Lee, 2014).

Pedagogy as Participatory

A culturally responsive stance toward pedagogy is participatory in its pursuit of democratic teaching. This is teaching that decenters the official school curriculum from a place of privilege and resituates it around the knowledge, experiences and artifacts that students possess (Lee, 2014). It is participatory in that it is developed, implemented, and evolves through student input, teacher "critical reflection," and "collective action" (Auerbach, 2000, p. 145). Kesler (2011) provides an example of a participatory stance toward pedagogy. He presents a critical reflection on three pedagogical tasks assigned to students and his reevaluation of those tasks in light of his students' lived experiences. For example, in one assignment students were tasked with creating a "Family Tree." However, the gendered and hierarchical organization of the "Family Tree" highlighted the absent family members and differently organized familial structures of one of Kesler's students, an adoptee. With the help of her adoptive mother, the student reconceptualized the hierarchical structure of the family tree as a non-hierarchical "Family Flower" (Kesler, 2011, p. 420). The visual representation of the flower, with the student as the center of various nodes of familial relations, more accurately represented the makeup of the student's adopted family. The adapted assignment supported the student's identity as an adoptee. Moreover, it allowed her to participate successfully in the task, and it initiated a classroom conversation about differences in family structures.

Pedagogy as Supportive of Students' Linguistic Rights

A culturally responsive stance toward pedagogy is supportive of students' rights to their home and community languages. These languages include dialects, vernaculars, and heritage-informed speech strategies, such as translanguaging (see Ch. 5 of this volume), code-switching, code-meshing, lexical borrowing, and other languaging practices (Li, 2018). They also include community-informed discourse styles, such as call and response (a participatory and interactive discourse between speaker and audience) and "talk-story" or "co-narration" (the collaborative and joint engagement in a communicative task) (Gay, 2018, p. 119–120). Communication styles are closely tied with group identity, membership, and personal values. However, within educational spaces, language can be officially regulated through local, state, and federal educational policies as well as unofficially monitored by peers and family. This has an impact on students' sense of self and agency. Driven by a desire to foster sociolinguistic justice for these students, Bucholtz, Casillas, and Lee (2017) educate bilingual Spanish-English secondary students to draw upon their home and community languages in official school settings. By providing a pedagogical space for students to articulate their linguistic autobiography, these "researcher-activists" (Bucholtz et al., 2017, p. 48) helped students to recognize the breadth and legitimacy of their language skills, not only as markers of their personal and social identities but also as legitimate aspects of a diverse linguistic repertoire.

Pedagogy as Caring

A culturally responsive stance toward pedagogy reflects a concern for "the implications [one's] work [has on] students' lives, the welfare of the community, and [the] unjust social arrangements" (Ladson-Billings, 1995, p. 474) in which students may find themselves. This is "caring for instead of about the personal well-being and academic success of ethnically diverse students" (Gay, 2018, p. 58, italics in original). For Gay, this distinction places the emphasis of care on actions that support the educational needs, interests, and desires of students rather than engaging in "an emotionality without intentionality and purposeful action" (p. 58). This support is expressed through pedagogical actions that foster student "competence, agency, autonomy, efficacy, and empowerment" (Gay, 2018, p. 58). These attributes are developed through instructional methods that accommodate cultural and linguistic differences in learning styles, manners of self-expression, and expressions of support, encouragement, and recognition. Dialogue between teachers and students takes on an importance in a pedagogically caring space as teachers work to empower youth and adult populations whose cultural and linguistic practices are marginalized in educational settings (Gay, 2018).

These five stances toward pedagogy as a sociocultural phenomenon, as culturally sustaining and revitalizing, as participatory and supportive of students' linguistic rights, and as demonstrating care underlie a culturally responsive approach toward the education of culturally and linguistically marginalized youth and adults. Although CRP is typically associated with responsive pedagogy in the struggle against deficit pedagogies in the United States and their impact on educational equity and racial, ethnic, and linguistic inequality in this setting, the next section will examine the implications for and implementation of culturally responsive pedagogy across English language educational contexts.

IMPLICATIONS FOR ENGLISH LANGUAGE EDUCATION

Despite its roots in U.S. educational inequity and racial/ethnic inequality, CRP holds important implications for English language education (ELE) across Anglophone and non-Anglophone contexts. CRP can empower educators and students to address the hegemonic aspects of English instruction. These include the place English language instruction takes, often at the expense of local or other national languages being taught, the inequities in access to such instruction, and the differences in motivation and value that ELE represents for newly arrived immigrant groups and historically marginalized groups.

In the section that follows, we consider the implications of CRP across contexts of ELE. We examine cases where CRP has been implemented in Anglophone contexts where English is taught as an additional or second language (EAL and ESL) at the K-12 level and in an adult content language setting (a citizenship course). We examine instances of CRP in an Anglophone higher education setting, as well as non-Anglophone settings where English serves as the Medium of Instruction (EMI). Lastly, we examine non-Anglophone contexts where English is taught as a Foreign Language (EFL) at the secondary and adult education settings. In all, the goal is to demonstrate the affordances CRP holds for ELE.

English as an Additional Language

EAL refers to the teaching of English in Anglophone countries. Much of this English instruction is a result of accommodating newly arrived migrants, refugees, and immigrants from non-Anglophone countries or from Anglophone countries with culturally diverse, pluralistic societies and local educational practices. For students who enter Anglophone countries as refugees, formal schooling may have been an interrupted process. The multiplicity of languages, the varied lived experiences, and diverse socialized schooling practices these students bring to educational settings can pose enormous challenges for educators. These challenges are particularly significant for educators who are monolingual or have grown up in homogenous cultural environments and do not share cultural or linguistic backgrounds with their students. Nonetheless, CRP provides a pedagogical guide for ELE in EAL contexts. This approach to pedagogy challenges EAL educators to first reimagine students' cultural and linguistic resources as assets (rather than deficits) to be drawn upon and repurposed in the pursuit of acquiring the English language and academic content.

Adopting an assets pedagogy approach (Paris, 2012) within the context of K-12 EAL, Herrera, Holmes, and Kavimandan (2012) have developed *Biography-Driven Instruction* (BDI). This theoretically grounded instructional approach for multilingual and multicultural classrooms adopts a three-step instructional process whereby teachers activate, connect, and affirm student home and community knowledge as part of the process of students acquiring content or classroom knowledge. In the activation phase, the instructor plans activities that can prompt sociocultural, linguistic, cognitive, and academic biographical knowledge about the students. Students can use whatever language they wish to communicate this information, and they can work solely or in cooperative groups with peers. The teacher observes and writes down this biographical information which is then incorporated into the upcoming instructional activity. The teacher facilitates connection-making between students' current knowledge and new knowledge. This connection is made by the teacher revoicing – "reporting, repeating, rephrasing, or expanding upon" (Herrera et al., 2012, p. 6) – what was heard from students. The teacher then asks students to confirm or disconfirm the accuracy of the teacher's interpretation. Finally, "authentic assessments" (Herrera et al., 2012, p. 7) are developed during the affirmation phase. Assessments are adapted from students' work and used to benchmark, measure, and reflect on student achievement. BDI's three-step process encourages a culturally sustaining, participatory, and caring approach to K-12 EAL in a multilingual and multicultural classroom setting.

Like their K-12 counterparts, adult EALs are acquiring English as an additional language. They are often educated in Content and Language Integrated Learning (CLIL) settings, where they develop academic literacy or some content area knowledge. These classrooms are often multilingual and multicultural environments consisting of students with varied levels of formal schooling. CRP provides a point of departure for addressing how learners' prior educational socialization can shape their present instructional needs. For example, Altherr Flores's (2018) research with adult emergent readers in U.S. citizenship classes provides examples of socialization issues that CRP can take up. In many ways, these classes are CLIL settings where English instruction accompanies the learning of citizenship content. However, the study materials provided for these courses are filled with culturally specific literacy structures that can pose challenges for EALs with emergent literacy or those socialized with different literacy practices. One pedagogical structure upon which the test relies is the 'adjacency pair' – a visual and organizing structural design of test questions and answers (Altherr Flores, 2018, p. 26). In the English language, this design is recognizable by the "?" and "." punctuation marks that accompany such pairs (Altherr Flores, 2018). Instead of relying on direct instruction and memorization to help learners negotiate these structures, a CRP approach might relate linguistic structures like the adjacency pair to cultural resources students already possess, such as call-response (Gay, 2018), a communication strategy that superficially mirrors the structure of an adjacency pair. Such an approach empowers students by providing them with new literacy skills to decode and read the cultural literacy clues embedded within text structures rather than leave them to rely on memory.

English Medium Instruction

CRP has particular implications for English medium instructional sites (EMIs). EMIs traditionally refer to institutions of higher education located in non-Anglophone countries. In these contexts, many of which may be multilingual, multicultural, and multiethnic, English serves as the academic lingua franca and its speakers "form part of the Expanding Circle of Speakers of English" (Doiz, Lasagabaster, & Sierra, 2011, p. 347). In these settings, questions of linguistic competence (particularly in the content area), equity of access, and language competition are at issue (Doiz et al., 2011). The challenge of addressing these three factors can be seen in Spain's Basque Autonomous Community where English-medium content courses offered at the postsecondary level as part of a Multilingualism Programme (MP) compete with content courses provided in the Basque (local) and Spanish (national) languages (Doiz et al., 2011). In a study conducted at the University of the Basque Country, perceived competition between English and the revitalized Basque language was cited as one reason the MP had difficulty attracting teachers; while fear of performing less well academically in these courses was given by students for not enrolling (Doiz et al., 2011). Yet incorporating into the MP culturally responsive pedagogical practices that are both culturally sustaining (Paris, 2012) and culturally revitalizing (McCarty & Lee, 2014) could attend to teacher concerns and student fears. Adopting practices such as pedagogical translanguaging (Li, 2018) could reaffirm students' identities as competent multilingual users where English is simply one "additional option" (Doiz et al., 2011, p. 356) in their linguistic repertoire.

EMIs also include postsecondary institutions located in Anglophone countries where enrollees consist of culturally and linguistically diverse international students and "home-grown" or local students from multilingual and multiethnic households (Marshall, 2010). The challenge for both categories of students is that each is often faced with enrolling in required intermediary English classes, either through Intensive English Programs (IEPs) for international students or remedial English classes for local students. Marshall (2010) writes about the latter group, the children of immigrants in Canada who attend local secondary schools, but test-in to an academic literacy course as a required part of their University enrollment. These students struggle with the deficit ideologies that mark their English verbal or written skills as not living up to the idealized native speaker even though they bring "complex repertoires of languages, identities, and social practices" (Marshall, 2010, p. 42) to the classroom. Marshall highlights the struggle for identity that underlies this experience and explains why it can impact student retention in the University. He documents the reflective, discursive, transitional, and recursive processes by which these students must "re-embrace" and "re-become ESL" (p. 46) in order to move forward in empowered ways as learners. Here, a culturally responsive and sustaining way forward involves teaching students to embrace their multilingual identities and linguistic repertoires and to use these skills in the acquisition of knowledge across all content and subject areas.

English as a Foreign Language

In EFL contexts, culturally responsive pedagogy can attend to the need for English language teaching to be sensitive to the situated historical, sociopolitical, and socioeconomic factors that give rise to English as an International Language (EIL). Traditionally, EFL teaching is marked by notions of linguistic imperialism given that in order for English to be taught, other often minoritized languages are not taught. Additionally, English language instruction becomes an issue of access and prestige that further entrenches local inequalities. These are issues that can impact motivation and self-perceptions in ELE and lead to disempowerment for youth and adult populations historically and newly marginalized in non-Anglophone settings. CRP can work to address issues of marginalization, affirm identity, and empower learners to confront the hegemony of EL education in their lives. For that, teachers need to learn to include the students' sociocultural realities in their teaching and use activities that facilitate development of students' sociocultural consciousness (Ladson-Billings, 1995).

An example of CRP enacted in an EFL context that is designed to be relevant, responsive, and sustaining for a population of students who are locally marginalized is seen in Lee's (2014) work with North Korean refugee students in South Korea. These students often experience disenfranchisement from both instruction and the curriculum. Not only do these students have to adjust to different instructional methods but also face implicit discrimination as the curriculum revolves around lived experiences that are different from their own. To address this disenfranchisement and deficit mentality toward North Korean refugee students, Lee (2014) created an after-school program with a curriculum designed to increase English language literacy among North Korean refugee students. The program's curriculum was organized around students' interests and funds of knowledge as well as topics that more closely mirrored "the students' concerns and expectations" (Lee, 2014, p. 4). Lee drew upon classroom observations, teacher/student interviews, and student surveys to gain knowledge about the students' English learning histories. She noted their desires to learn English but observed lack of motivation due to the content and instructional practices used in South Korean classrooms. In response, Lee used children's books in English and designed participatory lessons that involved explorations of "themes such as identity, peace, friendship, honesty, courage, and racism" (p. 4). This approach created space for the students to make connections between these themes and the lived experiences of displacement and discrimination the students were facing. This participatory approach was an empowering cultural response to the lived experiences and educational realities of a locally marginalized group of learners within an EFL context.

Another example of CRP in an EFL setting comes from Fredricks's (2012) work with English language learners in Tajikistan. In an effort to move beyond the imposed Anglophone themes, values, and images often found in English texts adopted in EFL classrooms, Fredricks selected English language texts whose characters and themes were drawn from various cultures and countries in Central Asia. Culturally responsive texts, rather than Western texts that make up the traditional English literary canon, were selected at the students' behest, as they wished to "compare the context of these . . . texts with their own social and political contexts" (Fredricks, 2012, p. 494). The discussion of these texts took place in critical literature circles (CLCs) that encouraged student comprehension and voice by emphasizing their personal responses to the "depictions of events, communities, characters, and themes and . . . relate them to pertinent issues in their lives" (Fredricks, 2012, p. 495). The act of asking students to select and discuss readings with cultural and literary significance to themselves fosters a culturally responsive instructional environment. Thus, through the texts and critical discussions in English, the students engaged with the ways people in other cultures in their geographical region deal with the social and political issues of their everyday lives and analyzed beliefs and values reflected in these texts (Fredricks, 2012). As the students engaged in these discussions with the content and themes relevant to them, they became more confident users and learners of English.

FUTURE DIRECTIONS

In this chapter, we presented CRP, its key stances, and the implications it holds for English language education globally. In closing, we address two areas in ELE where we anticipate further strides being made to pedagogical practice in culturally relevant, responsive, sustaining, and revitalizing ways. These include language-in-education policies and distance learning/online education.

Language-in-education policies mandate the language stances teachers are likely to enforce, authorize, and legitimize in the classroom. Given their relative power to interpret and enforce language policies, teachers should be prepared to advocate for students' linguistic rights and to act as change agents for culturally responsive pedagogies (Michener, Sengupta-Irving, Proctor, & Silverman, 2015). As change agents, teachers can support instructional approaches that build English fluency and literacy while working to sustain and revitalize home languages, cultural practices, and community identities. Additionally, they might adopt alternative and supplemental texts, draw upon students' varied perspectives, extend wait time to answer in English, and use "whole-class discussions to regulate and model a more equitable share of participation across students" (Michener et al., 2015, p. 214).

Distance learning or online education necessitates that attention is paid to the linguistic and cultural elements of online instructional design. The design of these platforms should incorporate and respond to the cultural, educational, and linguistic resources that diverse students bring to online learning. While online educational programs have potential to democratize English language education by increasing access to instruction and language learning resources, they may unwittingly reflect an Anglo-European cultural bias in their preference for specific instructional, curricular, and assessment techniques (Smith & Ayers, 2006). Cultural bias may be reflected in the online program's instructional design (e.g., the semiotic and spatial organization of information online), curricular content (e.g., what knowledge is deemed relevant for students to acquire), and pedagogical approach to instruction (e.g., ways of working collaboratively or providing feedback to another classmate). A culturally relevant stance toward online education is responsive to the culturally shaped literacy practices (Altherr Flores, 2018), the socialized academic structures in which students were primarily educated (Marshall, 2010), and the "cognitive and psychological ethos" (Smith & Ayers, 2006, p. 402) learners bring to the space.

In closing, CRP fosters a democratic, equitable, and inclusive stance toward the education of students in a culturally and linguistically diverse world. On local and global levels, it helps learners of English as it supports the development of a sociopolitical consciousness, one that empowers students and teachers to take aim at the deficit pedagogies and linguistic and cultural hegemony that perpetuates social inequalities. CRP also reaffirms a cultural linguistic identity, seeing and promoting (a) the benefits of plurality and multilingualism in society and within educational spaces, and (b) the links these have to learners' identities. In essence, CRP represents a pedagogic shift that has the potential to empower learners, lead to their educational success and attainment, and contribute on a personal level to the sustaining of student identity, agency, and belonging as learners.

Discussion Questions

1. A culturally responsive approach to pedagogy highlights the relationship between identity, language, and learning (specifically educational attainment) and the growing impact of pluralism in educational spaces. In your own words, describe how this works. Why is it important? What does CRP accomplish for the institution/educator, students, and their community?

2. A culturally responsive approach to pedagogy sustains and revitalizes the cultural products, practices, and ways of knowing of students' homes and communities. Bucholtz et al. (2017) and Herrera et al. (2012) identify student (auto-) biographies as one way of accessing student knowledge. What activities or tasks might you assign to students that creates a space for them to dialogue around or showcase the cultural products, practices, and ways of knowing that are significant to their families or larger communities?

3. A culturally responsive approach adopts a participatory stance to pedagogy. In keeping with Auerbach (2000), we use the term "participatory" rather than "student-centered." How does a participatory stance toward pedagogy differ from a student-centered one? How might such a stance reflect student-centered practices?

4. A culturally responsive approach to pedagogy supports students' rights to their home languages and communication styles. However, these rights are sometimes in conflict with national, state, and local educational policies. What are some of the language-in-education policies (see Michener et al., 2015) that shape local efforts to engage in culturally responsive participatory and language practices in your setting? What action steps might you or other stakeholders (family and community members) take to attend to these obstacles?

5. A culturally responsive approach to pedagogy should extend to instruction that takes place in online and mediated learning environments. Imagine you have the opportunity to plan an eight-week online course on English language literature and that this course would be comprised of students across the Anglophone and non-Anglophone world. Consider the approaches taken by Fredricks (2012) and Lee (2014). What English language literary texts – novels, short stories, or poems – might you collaboratively select with students to reflect the diversity of languages, dialects, and users across the English-speaking world? How might you facilitate this collaboration online? According to the principles of CRP, how does a diverse reading list contribute to the educational attainment and experience of all students?

Resources for Further Exploration

1. González, N., Moll, L., & Amanti, C. (Eds.). (2005). *Funds of knowledge: Theorizing practices in households, communities and classrooms*. Mahwah, NJ: Erlbaum.
   This seminal reader provides a methodological guide for unearthing the home and community knowledge students possess and which can be capitalized upon in the classroom.
2. Hammond, Z. (2014). *Culturally responsive teaching and the brain: Promoting authentic engagement and rigor among culturally and linguistically diverse students*. Thousand Oaks, CA: Corwin.
   The text examines brain-based research behind and support for engaging in culturally responsive curricular and instructional practices.
   Hammond's blog (online at https://crtandthebrain.com/blog/) provides audio and video clips that delve into the principles behind the book.
3. Meshake, R., & Montero, K. (2013, April 25). *Songide'ewin Art Exhibit: Aboriginal Narratives* [Video file]. www.youtube.com/watch?v=Tk5tTtVM2jQ
   This resource presents interviews and visual images of culturally revitalizing and identity affirming paintings and poems created by students at the Sir John A. Macdonald Secondary School (Ontario, Canada). The texts and their public display at the *Art Gallery of Hamilton* were designed to foster dialogue and encourage truth and reconciliation between Indigenous and non-Indigenous communities. Meshake and Montero provide firsthand evidence of culturally sustaining and revitalizing practices, as well as the power of public exhibition, on student creative expression, personal and community identity, and community involvement.
4. Nieto, S. (2013). *Finding joy in teaching students of diverse backgrounds: Culturally responsive and socially just practices in U.S. schools*. Portsmouth, NH: Heinemann.
   Although the focus of the book is educators within a U.S. setting, this excellent work delves into the CRP and Social Justice inspired pedagogical practices of individual and communities of practicing teachers.
5. Paris, D., & Alim, S. (Eds.). (2017). *Culturally sustaining pedagogies: Teaching and learning for justice in a changing world*. New York, NY: Teachers College Press.
   Paris and Alim's edited volume is significant in that it brings together important scholarly voices on the nature and implementation of Culturally Sustaining Pedagogy.

References

Altherr Flores, J. A. (2018). Decoding citizenship in USCIS naturalization test materials: A critical social semiotic analysis. *Critical Multilingualism Studies*, 6(1), 22–50.

Auerbach, E. R. (2000). Creating participatory learning communities: Paradoxes and possibilities. In J. K. Hall & W. Eggington (Eds.), *The sociopolitics of English language teaching* (pp. 143–163). Clevedon, England: Multilingual Matters.

Banks, J. A. (2009). Multicultural education: Dimensions and paradigms. In J. Banks (Ed.), *The Routledge international companion to multicultural education* (pp. 9–32). New York, NY: Routledge.

Bucholtz, M., Casillas, D. I., & Lee, J. S. (2017). Language and culture as sustenance. In D. Paris & S. Alim (Eds.), *Culturally sustaining pedagogies: Teaching and learning for justice in a changing world* (pp. 43–59). New York, NY: Teachers College Press.

Doiz, A., Lasagabaster, D., & Sierra, J. M. (2011). Internationalisation, multilingualism and English-medium instruction. *World Englishes*, 20(3), 345–359.

Fredricks, L. (2012). The benefits and challenges of culturally responsive EFL critical literature circles. *Journal of Adolescent & Adult Literacy*, 55(6), 494–504.

Gay, G. (2013). Teaching to and through cultural diversity. *Curriculum Inquiry*, 43(1), 48–69.

Gay, G. (2018). *Culturally responsive teaching: Theory, research, and practice* (3rd ed.). New York, NY: Teachers College Press.

Herrera, S. G., Holmes, M. A., & Kavimandan, S. K. (2012). Bringing theory to life: Strategies that make culturally responsive pedagogy a reality in diverse secondary classrooms. *International Journal of Multicultural Education*, 14(3), 1–19.

Kesler, T. (2011). Teachers' texts in culturally responsive teaching. *Language Arts*, 88(6), 419–428.

Ladson-Billings, G. (1995). Toward a theory of culturally relevant pedagogy. *American Educational Research Journal*, 32(3), 465–491.

Ladson-Billings, G. (2009). *The dreamkeepers: Successful teachers of African American children* (2nd ed.). San Francisco, CA: Jossey-Bass.

Lee, M. W. (2014). A participatory EFL curriculum for the marginalized: The case of North Korean refugee students in South Korea. *System*, 44, 1–11.

Li, W. (2018). Translanguaging as a practical theory of language. *Applied Linguistics*, 39(1), 9–30.

Marshall, S. (2010). Re-becoming ESL: Multilingual university students and a deficit identity. *Language and Education*, 24(1), 41–56.

McCarty, T. L., & Lee, T. S. (2014). Critical culturally sustaining/revitalizing pedagogy and Indigenous education sovereignty. *Harvard Educational Review*, 84(1), 101–124.

Michener, C. J., Sengupta-Irving, T., Proctor, C. P., & Silverman, R. (2015). Culturally sustaining pedagogy within monolingual language policy: Variability in instruction. *Language Policy*, 14, 199–220.

Moje, E. B., Ciechanowski, K. M., Kramer, K., Ellis, L., Carrillo, R., & Collazo, T. (2004). Working toward third space in content area literacy: An examination of everyday funds of knowledge and discourse. *Reading Research Quarterly*, 39(1), 38–70.

Paris, D. (2012). Culturally sustaining pedagogy: A needed change in stance, terminology, and practice. *Educational Researcher*, 41(3), 93–97.

Smith, D. R., & Ayers, D. F. (2006). Culturally responsive pedagogy and online learning: Implications for the globalized community college. *Community College Journal of Research and Practice*, 30(5–6), 401–415.

Why Are There So Many Immigrants Here?

Problem-Posing With Middle Schoolers in Hawai'i

Gordon Blaine West

In this case study, I recount the process of guiding students in a summer ESL program through a problem-posing pedagogy (Freire, 2000) that was informed by their questions and used materials that they researched and produced or that were curated for them. Richards, Brown, and Forde (2007) offer ten key principles for a culturally relevant pedagogy: recognize individual differences and similarities with students; use materials that represent students; teach about diversity; promote equity and respect; use valid means of assessment; build relationships with students, families, and communities; motivate students to be active participants in learning; encourage critical thinking; set high expectations; and help students develop social and political consciousness. We followed these through centering the class on answering questions the students raised and addressing problems they faced as recent immigrants. Through this process, students were able to learn more about the diversity and history of their new home in Hawai'i, find and assert their place in this new context, and promote equity and respect while developing the students' social and political consciousness.

THE SETTING

This case study describes a class I taught in a private secondary school in Hawai'i during an intensive summer ESL program for mainly incoming and some continuing international students. The program met for six weeks, five days a week, from 8:00 a.m. to 12:00 p.m. As a summer program, it was considered a remedial course for students whose English language proficiency scores on a placement exam showed their need for more support in order to perform at the level of their non-ESL peers.

A basic curriculum was given by the program director, and it consisted of a novel, *The House on Mango Street* by Sandra Cisneros, and two textbooks, one focused on reading and writing, and the other on listening and speaking. Both textbooks featured a heavy focus on grammar and vocabulary, with online homework, quizzes, and culminating tests that were to be given on the final day of the program. In the textbooks, the chapters were organized thematically with little connection between chapters. Language was presented as sets of decontextualized discrete grammar and vocabulary items that were only loosely connected to students' lives through awkward (as my teaching notes from the time describe them) turn-to-your-partner activities to discuss their friends or dating habits using the prescribed grammar and vocabulary.

Besides using the novel and textbooks, with the unit quizzes and cumulative tests serving as assessment measures, the only other curricular requirement was to use iPads during class. The school had a one-to-one iPad program and teachers were required to use them in class to support learning in lessons, although the amount and scope was up to the individual teachers.

DESCRIPTION OF ENGLISH LANGUAGE LEARNERS

There were ten students in my class for the summer program. Seven were from Japan, two from China, and one from Russia. Four of the Japanese students were continuing students at the school, with one entering 9th grade in the fall. All the other students were entering 8th grade in the fall. The six newly arrived students were living mostly with host families, although at least one boy was living at a hotel with his mother during the program. The students seemed to have come from privileged backgrounds. Although I never asked for specifics about their parents, one volunteered that his father was the CEO of a large corporation, and another wrote of flying to Hawai'i on his father's private jet.

Although these students came from positions of privilege, they were nonetheless subject to new positionalities as ESL students in Hawai'i. Vandrick (2015) writes of the types of challenges and discrimination that ESL students face, although some have more or less resources and ability than others to face these challenges depending on gender, race, ethnicity, social class, sexual identity, religion, language, and immigration status. Their new positionality in Hawai'i may have been one of relative privilege to other immigrant students at public schools, and to scholarship students from Samoa and other Pacific Islanders at their own school who had less economic means or social status. In other ways, by being placed in remedial ESL programs and isolated from the rest of the school, especially during summer programs, they were less privileged than peers from Hawai'i or the mainland United States who had the option of summer enrichment classes or sports camps instead of remedial classes. As they adjusted to life in Hawai'i, the students were having to navigate new positionalities based on race, ethnicity, language, and gender, while still having to deal with positionalities within their immigrant groups that they brought with them. An example of this was one Japanese boy from a rural area being made fun of and positioned by other Japanese students as less cosmopolitan and sophisticated than those from large urban areas. Positionalities of the students in this context were complex and also dynamic, shifting as they adjusted to their new home.

PEDAGOGICAL APPLICATION AND INNOVATION

To enact a culturally and linguistically relevant, critical pedagogy with students in this space, I used a problem-posing pedagogy (Freire, 2000) that evolved over time to help students not only address equity issues related to their positioning as ESL students but also to, at times, interrogate their privileges (Vandrick, 1995, 2009). The first day of our program focused on exercises to get to know each other and start to build trust. For that, I introduced the idea of negotiating the syllabus (Crookes, 2013). On the second day, we began negotiating the course, focusing on developing a big question that students wanted to answer during our time together. As newcomers, the students all mentioned initially being shocked to be able to speak to many people in their home language in Hawai'i. The main question they came to was: "Why are there so many immigrants here?"

We discussed the given curriculum and required outcomes and assessments, as well as how to use the iPads in class, and they decided that they would like to learn how to make movies and produce a film. We spent between an hour to two hours each day on readings, assignments, and tasks required by the curriculum. The rest of the class time was largely focused on student-led research projects, presentations of their findings, and learning the process of filmmaking. Their research was largely conducted in their home languages on the iPads. In my role as a facilitator and guide, I also curated resources in English to provide a range of perspectives on immigration to Hawai'i by people from different countries and eras. Additionally, I asked questions to help them think in more historical terms about their research. For the first two weeks, we focused on learning the history of immigration to Hawai'i together, and as a culminating activity, we toured the Hawai'i Plantation Village, which shows historically preserved and recreated buildings built by native Hawaiians and different groups that immigrated to Hawai'i to work in sugar cane plantations (see Figure 4.1.1). The students then wrote reflections on what they had learned from their research and our trip.

Through another round of negotiations and discussion, the students became curious about why people were emigrating to the United States more generally. This corresponded to their curiosity about the novel we were assigned. They were even more curious about contemporary immigrant experiences and especially about

Figure 4.1.1 Restored and replica buildings, including houses built by various ethnic groups that lived and worked on the plantations

Source: Photo by April-Joyce Labrador

experiences of other young people. They began research on young immigrants on the U.S. mainland, while I once again helped to curate resources. We also watched and discussed a documentary called *Chicago: Little Mexico* (Marzynski, 2006) from the U.S. TV news series from PBS, *Frontline*, that helped to answer questions they had about immigration in Chicago from their novel. We also watched and discussed *The Harvest (La Cosecha)* (Romano, O'Connor, Longoria, & Romano, 2010), a documentary about Latinx child immigrants, around the same age as the students, doing agricultural work in the United States. At the same time as the students were researching their questions about youth immigration, we were learning about the process of producing a film, including how to write a script, do character sketches, write treatments, and make storyboards. We completed work on this stage of the course after about two and a half weeks.

The students decided that they wanted to write short fictional stories about immigrants – this time to share what they had learned. Initially, these short stories were planned to feed into the film scripting process, but the students later decided they did not want to produce a fictional film, and so these stories were a separate activity. The themes and story lines, some about young people from positions similar to their own interacting with Latinx farm workers, showed that they understood the injustices faced by immigrants and were in some cases interrogating their own positions and identities as immigrants. They also drew connections in some cases between the historical positions of Japanese and Chinese agricultural workers in Hawai'i in the past and current Latinx agricultural workers on the mainland United States. One student wrote a story about herself as if she'd been born into a family of plantation workers in Hawai'i. In the story, she writes about the hard work of cutting the sugar cane, which we'd learned about during our field trip, and she writes about the poverty and having to miss school due to her working in the fields, similar to the children shown in the documentary we watched. Another student wrote a story about an immigrant newly arrived in the United States and the difficulty of making friends when they had to work all day in the fields. Through stories like this, students demonstrated an understanding of their own positions as immigrants and an empathy for others in different circumstances that helped to lead into the final project.

After yet another round of negotiation and discussion, the students shared their own feelings of being lost and feeling intimidated navigating their new school and neighborhoods in Hawai'i. They felt segregated from the rest of the students since they were all placed in ESL for the summer, without any interaction with local students at the school who were involved in summer enrichment programs (rather than remedial programs). They decided to make a video that would be a resource for new international students who would be placed in the ESL program. The class broke into different groups, and we discussed how to divide responsibilities based on what we knew about the filmmaking process at that point.

Students began scripting and developing storyboards. They also did a neighborhood and campus mapping project to help them identify places that were important, useful, or interesting to them. They mapped things like the people in the administration office who were helpful and approachable, their favorite grocery shops and restaurants with food from their home countries, parks to play soccer, and their favorite beaches. At the same time, they began researching other similar videos for inspiration. They first found campus tour videos produced by UCLA and Yale but then also found other student-made school tour videos from high schools in the United States, an elementary school in South Korea, and schools in both China and Japan. The videos they found were in multiple languages, although they decided to make theirs in simple English since they agreed that they wouldn't know what country the new students might come from.

The students used the community mapping project and their research of other videos to complete storyboards and scripts. We reserved time for filming during the class, using their iPads, and students also filmed some footage after school. When it came time to edit, we got a school technology coordinator to run a workshop on editing, and the students learned things like adding voice-overs and putting transitions in their videos. They worked in teams to edit their own segments and then to put them together in coherent ten-minute video guides to life in Hawai'i and at the school for newcomers.

To comply with documentation and accountability practices at the school, I took what we had negotiated and wrote it up into a project description, and we created a set of requirements for the project (i.e., minimum length, all group members participate, and so on; see Appendix A). I created a simple viewing guide to help discuss the videos when we watched them together (Appendix B). Creating these official documents helped give the students a voice in the accountability process, and while we did conform to some extent in providing this sort of rigid, formal documentation, the process of creating it allowed for their input and their ideas to prevail over some of the regular top-down practices. At the end of the program, they shared the video with the ESL director and had a short viewing party with the other classes on the second-to-last day of the program.

Throughout the program, we focused on language, learning how to use multiple languages to conduct research, learning how to present findings in various genres and registers in English, and acquiring the technical vocabulary and ways of speaking in filmmaking.

CONCLUSION

Approaching the class from a problem-posing stance, we were able to open a space for a more culturally and linguistically relevant pedagogy. We didn't totally ignore the given curriculum but worked to find ways to minimize it and supplement it with more meaningful work. The students were able to choose the questions they wanted to focus on, to find answers to those questions, and in the process, to interrogate their own privilege relative to other immigrants and develop a political consciousness around immigration issues. In the end, they worked to produce a video as a response to their own experiences that could help other students who might be in similar positions in the future. This class does, however, still represent a privileged example, both in student population and in program structure. I would argue, though, that even in privileged contexts, culturally and linguistically relevant pedagogy is needed to address equity issues and interrogate privilege.

References

Crookes, G. V. (2013). *Critical ELT in action: Foundations, promises, praxis*. New York, NY: Routledge.

Freire, P. (2000). *Pedagogy of the oppressed*. New York, NY: Continuum.

Marzynski, M. (Reporter). (2006, October 31). Chicago: Little Mexico [Television broadcast]. In M. Marzynski (Producer), *Frontline*. US: Public Broadcasting System.

Richards, H. V., Brown, A. F., & Forde, T. B. (2007). Addressing diversity in schools: Culturally responsive pedagogy. *Teaching Exceptional Children*, 39(3), 64–68.

Romano, U. R., O'Connor, R., & Longoria, E. (Producers), & Romano, U. R. (Director). (2010). *The Harvest/La Cosecha* [Motion picture]. Globalvision & Shine Global, US.

Vandrick, S. (1995). Privileged ESL university students. *TESOL Quarterly*, 29(2), 375–381.

Vandrick, S. (2009). *Interrogating privilege: Reflections of a second language educator*. Ann Arbor, MI: University of Michigan Press.

Vandrick, S. (2015). No "knapsack of invisible privilege" for ESL university students. *Journal of Language, Identity & Education*, 14(1), 54–59.

Appendix A
Campus Tour Movie Project Description

(Drafted together with students during the project planning process)

Campus Tour Movie

....

Purpose: The purpose of this project is to practice English through filmmaking, to get to know the school better, and to make something that will be useful to other ESL students who are coming to the school for the first time.

Directions: You will make a short video showing several places on campus. For each place, you should have one member of the group film, and one member of the group either in the film or reading a script on a voice-over. **Each member must speak in the video** (either on or off camera). For each place you show on your tour, you should give at least the follow information:

- The name of the place

- What is used for or what happens there

- Why it is important for students to know about

- Who is there usually (names of teachers and staff – i.e., librarians, secretaries, etc., grades of classes – i.e., 7–8th grade, elementary grades, etc.)

- Information about the building – when it was built, who it is named after *if you can find this information – a good way is to ask people who work there

The video tour should be about 5 minutes long. We will work on editing in class, and you will have time to film around campus during class time. **You may not leave campus for any reason during filming**.

Appendix B
Video Viewing Guide

(Created by the author as a way to stimulate initial discussion of videos during shared viewing)

Campus Tour Videos

. . . .

Name: _____

Video 1

Whose video?

Where did they go?

1.

2.

3.

4.

5.

6.

7.

8.

9.

10.

Write what they said about two of the places.

What was the most interesting thing about the video?

CASE STUDY 4.2

Teaching ESL Through Social Justice Themes in China

Developing a Critical Consciousness

Hetal Patel

When I taught ESL in a public school in the United States, culturally responsive pedagogy was something regularly discussed. When I moved to China, a few months into teaching, I knew that my students were just accepting my curriculum and were not actually engaging with the curriculum. It dawned on me that culturally relevant pedagogy is just as necessary in China as it is in the United States. I began by making small changes to a presentation unit. I still taught the language skills that I was expected to teach, such as public speaking skills and MLA citations; however, I changed the content of the presentation to social justice themes. This case study discusses an example of integrating social justice themes within the constraints of a preset language curriculum.

THE SETTING

This case study took place at a private international high school in Suzhou, China. Suzhou is a prospering, well-developed city not far from Shanghai. The school serves about 800 Chinese students, most of whom are transferring in from Chinese middle schools. About 70% of the students are boarding students, including students who board just for the week and students who board for the entire term. The majority of teaching staff and school administration are from the United Kingdom or other countries where English is spoken as a first language. Generally, students and parents have chosen this school because they are aiming to attend a reputable university in either the United States or the United Kingdom. Like many similar schools in the area, there is a strict English-only policy in classrooms. However, in practice, many teachers allow students to use Mandarin Chinese for short periods of time if it is for an academic purpose.

Most courses at the school use International General Certificate of Secondary Education (IGCSE) and A-level curriculum. Students are required to take English classes every year, and in grades 9 and 10, the school provides an IGCSE ESL curriculum. This case study takes place in an 11th grade English class. The course is focused on developing academic English with thematic units and a variety of language-based assessments, including speeches and essays.

DESCRIPTION OF ENGLISH LANGUAGE LEARNERS

Nearly all of the students who attend this school are English learners; however, they enter school with varying degrees of English proficiency. As English is a compulsory subject in Chinese schools, all students have the common experience of the national English curriculum. Additionally, many students previously attended after-school English lessons and some have even studied abroad for various lengths of time. In terms of the Common European Framework of Reference (CEFR), the average student's English level ranges from a B1 to B2 level, or intermediate to upper intermediate user of English.

As the students are mostly local, Mandarin Chinese is the first language of the majority of students. However, many students also are proficient in the local Suzhou language, which is a dialect of the Wu language and not mutually intelligible with standard Mandarin Chinese.

Generally, the students are motivated to learn English because they realize that in just a few years they will need to use English both academically and socially. Additionally, the external pressure of achieving a high score on standardized English proficiency exams like TOEFL or IELTS is a cause of great stress for some students. For many students, the difference in which university they are able to go to hinges on one of these test scores. The result of these two factors is an English curriculum that focuses on increasing academic language proficiency with an emphasis in the skills students will need for success in college.

PEDAGOGICAL APPLICATION AND INNOVATION

In the 11th grade English curriculum, there is a predetermined set of skills, i.e., emphasis and word stress, with a set type of final assessment, i.e., a speech. However, the teachers on that grade level team are free to adjust the content to fit with student needs. Despite the fact that when I taught refugees and immigrants back in the United States, I taught with culturally responsive teaching at the forefront of my mind, when I first arrived to China, culturally responsive teaching fell to the bottom of my list. I found my students to be quite unresponsive to my teaching. I realized that in the United States, often when I taught an irrelevant lesson, I found that students were quite vocal in communicating that the lesson was irrelevant. At this school, I found that my students were equally disengaged, but it was easier to ignore, and so it was easy to continue teaching in an unengaging way. At some point, in the middle of another dull, dry lesson, it dawned on me that I needed the culturally responsive teaching here in China as much as I needed it in an urban school in the United States.

I began by making some changes to the unit that would end in an informative speech. The original assessment asked students to speak about a war and present the two perspectives involved. Keeping with the idea of perspectives, I decided that I would ask students in groups to pick a social justice issue in the West and present their perspectives on that issue.

I introduced the unit by including activities investigating stereotypes and an open discussion on how the students imagine their identity may impact their life abroad. I used *Poll Everywhere* (www.polleverywhere.com/) to collect anonymous responses from students answering the question, "What is a stereotype I have heard before?" Before collecting these, it was very important that I established the purpose of this activity. It was to see what stereotypes we as a group have encountered that we are not assuming that anyone else believes. I began our discussion by posting examples on the lighter side that have impacted me personally such as women are bad drivers. I noticed that many of my students seemed to be impacted by the same stereotypes that many of my Asian students faced in America. After I had a list of stereotypes that impacted students, as a class, we chose a stereotype and discussed the possible harm that this stereotype might cause. An important step in this process is highlighting to students the possible harm caused by even a "good" stereotype such as Chinese students are good at math. Following a class discussion, I asked students to have the same discussion in groups with a different stereotype. Finally, I asked students to reflect on the question, "What social problems or injustices can happen if people believe a stereotype to be true?" I concluded class by giving my students the vocabulary list (Appendix A) for their reference. I asked my students to keep this list and take notes on it as different words came up in class.

After this, for the next several lessons, the students examined a variety of highly engaging texts that represented different perspectives on social justice issues, including texts such as Beyoncé and Chimamanda Adichie's song "Flawless," (Beyonce, Jay-Z, Drake, Adichie, & Ocean, 2013) the film "Hidden Figures," (Melfi et al., 2017) and Native Americans in sports logos like the Cleveland Indians. Looking at various sample texts allowed my students to build empathy, and have "Aha!" moments as they realized things like why people find the Cleveland Indians sports logo to be offensive. Students also brought texts to class to share and analyze. One of my students had recently watched the film *Straight Outta Compton* (Gray et al., 2015) and was able to find some relevant facts based on the film to share with the class. Interspersed with these social justice oriented lessons, I also included lessons focused on presentation skills. This continued until students had a taste of a wide variety of social justice issues as well as sufficient instruction on presentation skills.

The culmination of the unit was an informative speech. Due to the variety of interesting examples and the range of student experience, each group in the class was easily able to choose a unique topic with ample evidence to draw from. The task sheet and rubric (see Table 4.2.1 in Appendix B) provided students with a scaffold for topic construction as well as a structure for their presentation. The class produced a wide range of high-quality presentation topics ranging from the portrayal of women in superhero movies to the treatment of African Americans by the police. I found this unit to be the most successful presentation-based unit I had ever taught. The students were genuinely excited to share their perspectives with their peers. It also made for a pleasant assessment experience for everyone.

Overall, I felt a high level of engagement from my students because they felt that the issues were relevant to their lives. In a survey at the end of the year, students reported that they found this unit to be highly engaging and the most useful unit of the year. Many students commented that this unit particularly interested them because they felt that when they go abroad, they may face this type of discrimination and through this unit they learned more about how to handle it. I found this to be incredibly interesting because we never explicitly discussed how to deal with discrimination, but when given the space, students within themselves were able to develop in their ability to work through a situation where someone may be experiencing injustice.

CONCLUSION

Through this unit, my students both expressed themselves and developed their "critical consciousness" to challenge stances on various social justice issues with which they will soon find themselves face to face (Ladson-Billings, 1995, p. 160). While working through this unit and sharing my ideas with others, I found that many educators operate based on an assumption that their Asian students are too meek and obedient to care about social justice issues. CRP is a pedagogy and a mindset that is both possible and essential in a global context. It requires teachers and students to shift thinking to the belief that all students can go to any country around the globe and elevate their voices to recognize and challenge oppression.

REFERENCES

Beyonce, Jay-Z, Drake, Adichie, C. N., & Ocean, F. (2013, January). Flawless: On beyonce [MP3]. Parkwood, Columbia.

Gray, F. G. (Director), Cube, I., Woods-Wright, T., Alvarez, M., Berstein, S., & Dre, D. (Producers), Herman, J., & Berloff, A. (Writers). (2015). Straight Outta Compton [Video file]. Universal, US.

Ladson-Billings, G. (1995). But that's just good teaching! The case for culturally relevant pedagogy. Theory Into Practice, 34(3), 159–165. doi:10.1080/00405849509543675

Melfi, T. (Director), Melfi, T., Williams, P., Chernin, P., Gigliotti, D., Topping, J. . . . Schroeder, A. (Writers). (2017). Hidden figures [Motion picture on DVD]. TSG Entertainment, Fox 2000 Pictures, Chernin Entertainment, Levantine Films, USA.

Appendix A
Social Justice Issues Vocabulary List

Through this unit you will need to know some new vocabulary related to social justice issues. The following is a list of words to help get you started.

- society (n) /societal (adj)
- portray (v)
- feminism (n)
- subtle (adj)
- stereotype (n)
- discrimination (n)
- submissive (adj)
- dominant (adj)
- bias (n)
- feminine/masculine (adj)
- gender (n)
- race (n)
- minority (n or adj)
- ethnicity (n)/ethnic (adj)
- scapegoat (n)
- mascot (n)
- indigenous (adj)
- community (n)

APPENDIX B
Presentation Task Sheet

Choose a social justice issue.

Use your critical thinking skills and background knowledge to choose a specific, narrow context to study. The context does not necessarily have to be a geographical place. You could study for example, *gender equality in Korean dramas*.

EXAMPLE TOPIC

Indigenous equality in sports mascot logos in America.

Group Members Names:

_____ _____ _____

Topic: _____

- Does your topic have a lens (does it focus on the perspective of a group experiencing a social justice issue)?

- Does your topic have a narrow context?

 Teacher Signature of Approval _____

Presentation Structure – Assign Roles: Who Will Do What?

- Introduction
    - o Capture the audience's attention in an interesting but focused way
    - o Share the outline for the presentation

- Describe the social justice issue and the lenses involved
    - o Give background on your context
    - o What do other researchers or experts say?

- Analysis
    - o What kind of conflict does your issue exemplify?
    - o What are the lenses of the different groups involved?
    - o In your opinion, why is this issue important? What is the impact?

- Conclusion
    - o Leave the audience with something to think about
    - o References in MLA style – please include this, but don't read it out loud

Table 4.2.1 Presentation task grading rubric

1 = poor 5 = excellent	Speaker 1:	Speaker 2:	Speaker 3:

Presentation skills

Volume and Tone

- Are you loud enough to hear the whole time?
- Is there a variation in your tone?

Eye Contact and Body Language

- Did you look at the audience for most of the time?
- Did you stand up straight and face the audience confidently?

Evidence of Rehearsal

- Did you clearly practice what you were going to say?
- Did you pronounce all of the words correctly?
- Did your speech finish in the time frame?

Content

Organization

- Do you have an interesting, relevant introduction?
- Have you presented your outline?
- Did you use transitions to make your content flow logically from one idea to the next?
- Do you have an interesting, relevant conclusion?

Explanation of lens and context

- Do you clearly explain your social justice issue and the lenses involved?
- Do you describe your context in an accurate and easy to understand way?

Analysis

- Does your analysis show evidence of critical thinking?
- Does your analysis use several methods of reasoning? (anecdotes, evidence, etc.)

Format

- Do visuals aid or support the content/help the audience understand the concept presented?
- Is the font, color, etc. readable even from the back of the room?
- Is the layout interesting to look at?

References

- Is there a citation slide at the end in MLA formatting for all sources?

Total Marks out of 40

Time: _____ 8min to 10min

Applying Culturally Responsive Pedagogy to Engage With Cultural Differences in an ESL Composition Course in the U.S.

Zhenjie Weng, Mark McGuire, and Tamara Mae Roose

Culturally responsive pedagogy (CRP) is centered on "building upon, appreciating, and sustaining students' cultural difference in one's teaching practice" (Warren, 2018, p. 170). More specifically, this approach views "cultural differences as assets," so teachers apply CRP to their classrooms by "using the cultural knowledge, prior experiences, frames of reference, and performance styles of ethnically diverse students to make learning encounters more relevant to and effective for them" (Gay, 2010, p. 31). A culturally responsive teacher views students' cultural knowledge as an instrumental resource that directly shapes what happens in the classroom (Gay, 2010). By knowing about the lives of their students, teachers can design their instruction to build upon what students already know to give them access to new learning (Villegas & Lucas, 2002).

CRP provides a powerful framework for working with culturally and linguistically diverse students; yet, as English as a Second Language (ESL) instructors, the authors found that in the existing literature on CRP, the focus is on the U.S. multicultural education of African American, Hispanic, and Native American students in K-12 contexts with minimal attention to international student populations in the United States. This leaves a potentially significant niche for this pedagogical case study.

THE SETTING

This case study describes an ESL composition class taught at a large land-grant university in the Midwestern United States, considered to be highly diverse and among the most popular schools for international students. In 2017, a total of 6,412 international students on the main campus made up around 11% of the total student population ("Enrollment Report", 2018). International students at the university came from more than 49 countries, but the leading home country for international students was China, at 75% of the international population. India was the second, at around 13%, with 12% from South Korea and elsewhere. Among the international student population, 3,650 of them were undergraduates, predominantly majoring in business, engineering, social sciences, biomedical and biological sciences, mathematics, and statistics (Office of International Affairs, 2018).

The ESL Composition class was designed to prepare international students with necessary skills for successful writing in college courses. The course focused on the integration of sources into academic research papers and appropriate formatting and documentation styles. As a result, the students in the class were regularly required to read beyond their textbook, which solely taught writing skills such as finding, evaluating, and summarizing sources. Supplementary reading materials selected by ESL composition instructors varied in theme and genre. For example, some instructors chose news articles, while others chose academic articles.

DESCRIPTION OF ENGLISH LANGUAGE LEARNERS

In this case study, we discuss an ESL composition class taught by Medwin (pseudonym) across three semesters, Fall 2017 through Fall 2018. He had been teaching at Chinese universities prior to his teaching position at this institution. Each term, there were 18 international students in Medwin's class, all of whom were from China, except for one student from Malaysia in Fall 2017 and one from South Korea in Spring 2018. The population for each term was roughly divided in half between male and female students. Their ages ranged from 18 to 21.

Most students had just left their home country or prior university and tested directly into Medwin's course. For some, it was their second semester at the university as they had completed their prerequisite ESL courses and then continued into the ESL composition course Medwin taught. Beyond these general categorizations, students in this class came from diverse educational and linguistic backgrounds. For example, informal conversations with students revealed that some had attended international schools in their home countries while others had graduated from high schools in English-speaking countries. Although many students from mainland China referred to themselves simply as "Chinese", there were various ethnic, linguistic, socio-economic, religious, and regional identities among them.

PEDAGOGICAL APPLICATION AND INNOVATION

When CRP is applied to ESL contexts, teachers often exclusively attend to language differences of students or their linguistic needs by providing language learning strategies, often at the expense of addressing their cultural and social needs (Yoon, 2008). Despite this common tendency of language teachers, Medwin not only recognized the cultural differences and identity conflicts within the classroom, both those of the teacher and of the students, but also legitimized the existence of those tensions as representing conflicts among valid perspectives.

Because of the range of backgrounds, each individual student from Medwin's class carried unique social and cultural attributes and needs to the classroom, which posed a challenge for Medwin if he was to engage all the students in class. These social and cultural needs included, but were not limited to, maintaining their cultural identities, embracing new, culturally hybrid identities, and engaging in socialization into the culture of higher education. For example, in some student writing and class discussion, there was uncertainty about the value of their identity as Chinese in the United States. Medwin was sympathetic to this tension because he also had to reconcile his identities as an American who was socialized into mainstream U.S. classrooms with Western teaching methods and who then taught in China for several years before returning to the United States. Introducing students to Western cultural norms while sustaining their own cultural identities was hard to balance in the curriculum design. Knowing that his class should help prepare students for their future courses in the United States, Medwin's teaching methods at the beginning of the semester demonstrated the construction of a classroom culture in which active participation was a form of educational socialization to prepare students for later courses. However, his effort was challenged by his students' consistent silence in classroom discussions.

Reflecting on the dilemma, Medwin realized students' silence may not necessarily have been because of their spoken English proficiency but rather because the reading materials used for class discussions were not contextualized according to the students' social and cultural backgrounds. Medwin drew from his experience teaching in China, informal conversations with students, and in-class surveys to revise his reading materials. Acting on his students' preferences, he affirmed student agency while seeking to better incorporate students' cultural identities. He did this, specifically, when selecting reading materials. Medwin presented the concept of social issues, and then asked the class for examples they thought were compelling while he wrote them as a list. Then, according to that list, he selected and arranged articles for the course and made them available to students for use in their writing assignments. The revised reading list was more culturally relevant and meaningful to the students, focusing on social issues chosen by the students themselves. The readings were then discussed in class, encouraging the students to engage with the social problems mentioned and to reconcile the perspectives of the authors and of their classmates with their own. When Medwin asked students questions, he would recontextualize his questions according to the cultural backgrounds the students were from. For example, when they talked about contemporary issues of marriage in the United States, Medwin would ask for students' perspectives about marriage, including perspectives drawn from expectations in their home countries. As a result, students were more interactive in sharing their perceptions, which not only facilitated their language development but also increased their willingness to participate in conversation and class discussions. This resolved the initial dilemma of student silence through application of a CRP strategy and facilitated the co-construction of a relevant and meaningful classroom community by engaging the students in social issues they chose, rather than presenting topics solely focused on the United States.

In order to support the students' maintenance of their own cultural identities, Medwin endeavored to create a multilingual and multicultural classroom. He explicitly talked about his own studies in England and teaching experiences in China and showed the students his appreciation of different music, art, and literature from other countries, including their own. For example, when students were doing group work, he always played background music from different countries. With the music in the background, students were less self-conscious and felt more comfortable when talking to their peers in their L1 or L2. For each song he played in class, Medwin would write down the name of the musician and music on the board in its original language. Once, as he tried to write down a Japanese band's name on the board, the students were excited to see his effort and insistence to write in Japanese. They were even taking pictures of the board after he finished. Medwin was not especially fluent in writing the characters, but he used that lack of fluency to model humility and persistence in language learning, demonstrating that the classroom was an acceptable place to make mistakes in the interest of mutual cultural exchange. In interviews with students, some of them said they sent the pictures of Medwin writing the names of Chinese bands to their friends, who then felt that Medwin was a considerate and caring teacher. The students also reported they felt a sense of belonging in the class because the instructor maintained and modeled authentic interest in other languages and cultures, including those of his students.

The innovation in this course relates to Medwin's integration of CRP with social construction theory. Social construction refers to the concept that "what we take to be the truth about the world importantly depends on the social relationships of which we are a part" (Gergen, 2015, p. 3). This theory provided Medwin with a lens to understand, contextualize, and reflect on cultural tensions in a respectful and collaborative way with his students. Otherwise, the tensions of culture and identity that occurred among them would have been resolved according to assumed power structures between teachers and students. Whether classroom tension was about academic conventions or about broader social issues, social construction made it possible to interpret them as conflicting relative norms rather than casting one view or another, particularly that of the instructor, as being "right."

This innovation was threefold: (1) the promotion of student agency, like selecting course materials with students, (2) the encouragement of multiple perspectives, mainly reflected in the writing assignments which asked students to write about a social issue of their choice and to argue a position (later assignments asked them to take a contrary position to their earlier papers, prompting them to explore another perspective), and (3) the cultivation of a safe classroom space for students to explore multiple identities. Vitally, none of these were dictated by the instructor. As students discussed racism, poverty, LGBT rights, feminism, religion, language politics, and so on, Medwin elaborated on how each person occupies multiple identities negotiated in the context of the culture and openly shared the challenging stereotypes he encountered as a result of cultural tension surrounding his own identities. His critical openness encouraged students to share and be more critical as well. The students began questioning familiar labels like "Asian," "rich," and "non-native speaker," which are often problematic and over-essentializing terms placed on them. Students questioned and resisted these labels in the process of examining their identities. In particular, class discussion and reflection led to rejecting the term "non-native speaker" (Ortega, 2013), and repositioning themselves as "users" rather than "learners" of English (Cook, 1999).

Based upon the class discussions, Medwin would further reinforce students' critical thinking by posting online writing assignments (Appendix A), which "pushed students to consider critical perspectives on policies and practices that may have direct impact on their lives" (Ladson-Billings, 2014, p. 78). This integration of CRP and social construction enabled students to learn not only the principles of writing and language but also how (via their own agency) they could reconcile themselves with the world around them.

CONCLUSION

This case study has focused on how the teacher's culture, the different cultures of the students, and the expectations of the cultural context affected classroom dynamics and how innovative CRP increased understanding between the teacher and the students. The case study revealed that CRP in ESL contexts could be more individually inclusive and heuristic for students. The following are pedagogical recommendations for English language teachers.

(1) Allow students agency in course content design by presenting them with options for various discussion topics, and be attentive to their interests and stated needs.

(2) Provide students with opportunities to talk about their social and cultural concerns and needs in the new environment through writing or discussion, according to the context and comfort level of the students.

(3) Transition between large-scale and small-scale questions with a real-life focus as much as possible. For example, start with "How does poverty affect people's lives? Does it differ across cultures?" to "Describe a time when you could not get something you needed in an unfamiliar country. How did you adapt to overcome that problem?" Likewise, begin with "What does the culture expect of young adults? How do cultural expectations vary?" and move toward "Describe a time when someone had unfair expectations of you. Is it possible that it was because they had a different culture, a different age, or a different social class?"

(4) Show solidarity and respect toward students' differences to build rapport with them so that they can be more open about their needs. This can be accomplished by the instructor asking genuine questions and taking sincere interest in each student's experience, rather than asking students to appeal to the interest of others by displaying or representing their culture.

(5) Model how they can negotiate their own often complex and conflicting identities. This could include tensions between national and regional identities, linguistic identities, or identities of lifestyle such as religion or sexual orientation.

These pedagogical applications reinforce that not only students' linguistic but also their social and cultural needs should be taken into consideration in curriculum design.

REFERENCES

Cook, V. (1999). Going beyond the native speaker in language teaching. *TESOL Quarterly*, 33(2), 185–209.

Enrollment Report. (2018). Retrieved from http://enrollmentservices.osu.edu/report.pdf

Gay, G. (2010). *Culturally responsive teaching: Theory, research, and practice* (2nd ed.). New York, NY: Teachers College Press.

Gergen, K. J. (2015). *An invitation to social construction*. Thousand Oaks, CA: Sage.

Ladson-Billings, G. (2014). Culturally relevant pedagogy 2.0: a.k.a. the remix. *Harvard Educational Review*, 84(1), 74–84.

Office of International Affairs. (2018). Ohio State ranked in top 20 for education abroad and international students. Retrieved from https://oia.osu.edu/global-gateways/4389-ohio-state-ranked-in-top-20-for-education-abroad-and-international-students.html

Ortega, L. (2013). Ways forward for a bi/multilingual turn in SLA. In S. May (Ed.), *The multilingual turn: Implications for SLA, TESOL, and bilingual education* (pp. 32–52). New York, NY: Routledge.

Villegas, A. M., & Lucas, T. (2002). Preparing culturally responsive teachers: Rethinking the curriculum. *Journal of Teacher Education*, 53(1), 20–32.

Warren, C. A. (2018). Empathy, teacher dispositions, and preparation for culturally responsive pedagogy. *Journal of Teacher Education*, 69(2), 169–183.

Yoon, B. (2008). Uninvited guests: The influence of teachers' roles and pedagogies on the positioning of English language learners in the regular classroom. *American Educational Research Journal*, 45(2), 495–522.

Appendix A

Here are some writing prompts that the teacher, Medwin, has used in his class to encourage students to think critically on social and identity issues.

Writing Prompt One

- What kind of story do you think people imagine when they see you? Do you think they may believe wrong or misleading stereotypes?
- How do different parts of your identity intersect (come together) in unique ways?
- How would you prefer to be seen by others?
- How would others prefer to be seen by you?

Writing Prompt Two

Intersection of identities is the idea that a person has multiple identities at the same time and that they mix together to affect their circumstances and the socially constructed rules of those circumstances. For example, during the Civil Rights Movement and the feminist movements around the same time, Black women were awkwardly positioned in silence because White women did not want them involved in feminist movements, and Black men did not want them involved in seeking racial justice. Likewise, being gay and Asian is a very different experience from being gay and White. Each of those identities contribute to their experiences.

Discuss this idea and how your experiences might reflect that reality. Reflect on discrimination that you have experienced or witnessed. It does not have to be big, but something that seemed unfair to you. It can be in relation to race, economic class, orientation, language, etc. Write a paragraph or two generally about these questions.

UNIT 5
Translingualism in TESOL

CHAPTER 5

Translingualism in the Teaching of English
Theoretical Considerations and Pedagogical Implications

Eunjeong Lee

FRAMING THE ISSUE

Song runs a Korean restaurant in a rapidly growing mid-size town in a Southwest state of the United States. As a migrant from South Korea, she grew up only speaking Korean. But while she established her life in the United States, she learned to communicate with her employees, customers, and other merchants outside her restaurant in Spanish, Chinese characters, and English. Whenever she enters the kitchen where some of her staff members speak Spanish, they seamlessly engage in a conversation like this (in this short dialogue, Korean is italicized, Spanish underlined to indicate translanguaging):

Employee: "*Unni*, pulpo *upseo*."
(Unni, we don't have octopus; unni is a Korean address term for Korean females to refer to older fellow Korean females)

Song: "Pulpo no mas? Okay, *unni* will buy more at the Restaurant Depot later."

(No more octopus? Unni will buy more at the Restaurant Depot later)

Song then walks out of the kitchen and checks on her customers in the dining hall. She had learned that her customers expect her to engage in small talk with them – a communicative norm that shows Southern hospitality. "Was everything okay, ma'am and sir?" Song asks. Looking closely, she notices that the customers were members of her church, and she changes her tone, "Oh my God! So good to see you!"

Like Song, many people engage in communicative practices that cross linguistic, cultural, and other boundaries every day. Particularly in the backdrop of accelerated mobility, advanced technology, transcultural flows, and transnational activities (Dovchin & Lee, 2019), we continue to see and hear complex ways people learn, use, and develop relationships with many other languages and related practices in meaning making – or what Blommaert (2010) calls "mobile resources." This way, our language and literacy practices are always constituted by multiple communicative resources (e.g., named languages, different modalities, understanding of particular communicative genres) we develop across different contexts (both physical and virtual) and timescales. This view toward language as a constantly evolving, emergent, and dynamic meaning-making practice across different named languages and modalities has been theorized under the umbrella term, *translingualism*.

As a new orientation to language, the advancement of translingualism has not only challenged the way language is conceptualized but has complicated what it means to make meaning in an ever more globalized world. Accordingly, the shift in the view toward language generates important questions in teaching English: What does it mean to teach English in an increasingly multilingual world? What knowledge is relevant and legitimate in learning and teaching English? And what should/could teaching English look like and achieve? These questions have crucial implications in our work as a researcher and teacher of English learning and teaching, challenging us to reimagine what English language education can look like.

This chapter aims to review the recent development and discussion of translingualism in teaching English as an additional language. While translingualism has been studied in various disciplines such as Sociolinguistics, Bilingual Education, Applied Linguistics, Literacy Studies, and Cultural Studies, this chapter focuses on the understanding and applications of translingualism as relevant to English language and literacy education. I first review the ascendency of translingualism and its theoretical framework. I focus in particular on how it problematizes the monolingual ideology and structuralist perspective that undergird our understanding of fundamental notions such as language, language learning, competence, and proficiency. Then the chapter discusses what implications such reconceptualization has on teachers and teacher education programs. Finally, I conclude with a discussion on future directions in research on translingualism and pedagogical considerations and end with key questions to think about for teachers interested in a translingual pedagogy.

CONCEPTS AND THEORETICAL CONSIDERATIONS

From Monolingualism to "Multilingual Turn" in Language and Literacy Education: Translingualism as a New Orientation to Language

Originally coined by a Welsh education scholar, Cen Williams (1996), the term translanguaging (originally termed trawsieithu or "translinguifying"), was first understood as a pedagogical approach in Welsh-English bilingual school contexts. The idea was for teachers to provide "input" in one language, and elicit students' "output" in another for the purpose of increasing proficiency in both languages. Since then, the term has been adopted by scholars from different fields such as Education, Applied Linguistics, and Composition and Rhetoric to name a few, generating a series of related terms such as translanguaging (García, 2009; García & Li, 2014), translingual practice (Canagarajah, 2013), translingual approach (Horner, Lu, Royster, & Trimbur, 2011), or more recently, translingualism, as a theoretical and pedagogical framework with a particular orientation to language and literacy.

While evolved in different disciplines with affinities to different terms, the basic principle of translingualism lies in its attempt to understand language from a multilingual, rather than a monolingual perspective. Monolingualism maps out language relations by viewing language as a discrete and static entity with clear boundaries. Even discussions on bi-/multilingualism, despite the focus on language diversity, maintain the same monolingual view toward language. Heller (1999) describes the monolingually oriented understanding of bi-/multilingualism with the term "parallel monolingualism." Simply put, "parallel monolingualism" refers to the approach to understanding multilingual realities as consisting of multiple monolingualism where each language exists independently of other languages. In contrast, translingualism views boundaries of language more fluid and sees language relations as dynamic, "treating languages as always in contact and mutually influencing each other, with emergent meanings and grammars" (Canagarajah, 2013, p. 41). From this perspective, language difference is a natural part of social realities and human interactions – be it difference across various named languages or a subtler difference within a variety of language. In a similar sense, translingualism views language norms as negotiable and emergent in a communicative situation, rather than fixed and stable. The change in the way we view our social realities from a multilingual perspective then makes it imperative to reconceptualize our teaching and research practices.

As well documented, the teaching and learning of English has historically operated under a monolingual (i.e., one language for one nation – namely English in the U.S. context) and monoglossic ideology (i.e., standardized English as the single most important language in our society) (Canagarajah, 2013; García & Li, 2014). And these ideologies have not only reified English as reducible sets of features and forms, but also constructed the myth of "Standard English," creating a false dichotomy between "school" (or white, middle-class English) and "home" language (Seltzer, 2019). Additionally, as recent work on raciolinguistics has shown, the monolingual and monoglossic ideologies are used to racialize language-minoritized students, constructing them as linguistically "deficient" (Flores & Rosa, 2015). Defying the English-only, monolingual ideology, translingualism views bi-/multilinguals' fluid language practices from their own rights, away from an external, monolingual perspective (Otheguy, García, & Reid, 2015).

A translingual perspective is particularly timely in the current multilingual realities that are often characterized with transnational movement of people and various ways of making meaning. Scholars in Second Language Acquisition have also recognized the multilingual and multimodal nature of communication more recently, and therefore, the need to understand language from such a perspective. For example, Ortega (2014) pointed out the monolingual bias in Second Language Acquisition studies where language learning is measured based on language learners' production of a "correct" language form. Ortega then argued for a change of a perspective that views language learners as language users in their own rights rather than against the monolingual-oriented perspective that focuses on the native speaker norms and standards. Calling for a "multilingual turn," May (2014) also expressed the need to understand our social reality that is constantly in flux, evolving, and therefore dynamic and complex.

Indeed, the shift in the orientation to language is well shown in the definition of translanguaging. García (2009) defines translanguaging as "*multiple discursive practices* in which bilinguals engage in order to *make sense of their bilingual worlds*" (p. 45, emphasis in original). These discursive practices, García and Li (2014) explain, include those practices of drawing on multiple named languages, moving "between systems that have been described as separate, and beyond them" (i.e., other visual resources, sounds, gestures) (p. 42). This way, translingualism challenges a monolingual approach to bilingualism such as additive bilingualism that still views bilingual students' language resources operating in separate, independent language systems ([cf.] "parallel monolingualism"). Recognizing the fluid nature of multilinguals' language practices, translanguaging promotes a dynamic model of bilingualism, which views multilinguals' discursive practices emerging from one integrated linguistic repertoire (García & Li, 2014). In doing so, translingualism empowers multilingual students by acknowledging their entire repertoire as crucial for their meaning making rather than as a source of deficit that inhibits their acquisition or practice of English.

Beyond Language Norms: Language as Negotiated, Performative, and Multimodal Meaning-Making Practice

The shift in the orientation to language – from a discrete, separate, independent system to a more dynamic and integrated one, and from monolingual-oriented to multilingual-oriented – challenges the structuralist conceptualization of language. In the Saussurean approach, language was understood as a self-contained system of structure. This view disregards the way language functions and shapes individuals' lives, leading to a narrow focus on skills and forms, stripped of the lived experiences of individual speakers. Translingualism, in contrast, is grounded in the view of language as a negotiated and performative meaning-making *practice* (Canagarajah, 2013). The translingual orientation to language and literacy recognizes the socially and ideologically constructed language boundaries and literacies, as briefly discussed earlier. And therefore, translingualism also sees that individuals are able to negotiate the language norms to empower their own identity and voice (and thereby language and literacy as *performative*) (Creese & Blackledge, 2015). In this regard, a translingual approach emphasizes processes and practices of individuals in negotiating power, ideology, and meaning across multiple languages and literacies.

It is in this sense that translanguaging is distinguished from code-switching. While code-switching also deals with how multilinguals utilize more than one named language in a given utterance, the concept differs from translanguaging in its assumption and orientation toward language. Rooted in the traditional notion and myth of linguistic purity and monolingualism, code-switching starts with an assumption that languages should be kept as separate and discrete entities. Foregrounding multilinguals' discursive practices to make sense of their bi-/multi-/translingual lives, translingual approaches attempt to move beyond the structuralist focus on language form and norms and the monolingual ideology that also supports such focus (García & Li, 2014).

Translingualism also recognizes the multimodal nature of communication. As opposed to the traditional logocentric view of language that prioritizes alphabet-based text over other signs, translingualism recognizes that individuals draw on a variety of communicative resources such as gesture, posture, gaze, drawing, or any other multimodal resources to make meaning. Canagarajah (2013) emphasizes that the prefix "trans" does not just signal going across different languages but also includes different semiotic resources such as different modalities (e.g., visual, aural, gestural) and rhetorical strategies as part of meaning-making practices. García and Li (2014) have similarly noted that translanguaging "signals a trans-semiotic system with many meaning-making signs, primarily linguistic ones, that combine to make up a person's semiotic repertoire. Languages then are not autonomous and closed linguistic and semiotic systems" (p. 42). Thus, every communication situation is translingual, as people may draw on a variety of named languages and related practices in the process even if a product may not include multiple named languages. By examining the way individuals draw on various semiotic resources in their communicative repertoire, translingualism provides a useful framework in challenging assumptions about what counts as meaning-making practices.

Reconceptualizing Language Practice, Competence, and Proficiency From a Translingual Perspective

The efforts to examine multilinguals' language practices from a holistic perspective – that is, language as an integrated, coherent system, as García and Li (2014) describe – have directed scholars' attention to language learning beyond the traditional focus on acquisition of language forms. Research on second language acquisition has traditionally focused on, and continues to focus on, how closely a language learner produces a particular form of a named language (Ortega, 2014). Scholars have contended that instead of focusing on language users' acquisition of language norms, or deviation from the norms, researchers and teachers should pay attention to what individuals *do* with multiple languages and how language difference functions in a given communicative situation (Horner et al., 2011). To this end, Canagarajah (2013) has argued that multilinguals' language practices and processes need to be centralized in studying multilingual communication beyond what language or what form is used.

With the understanding of language practices as an act of drawing from a variety of linguistic and other resources, translingualism argues for a different conceptualization of language competence and proficiency. Particularly considering increasingly multilingual realities, the understanding of language competence and proficiency needs to reflect this complexity and dynamicity of multilinguals' language practice. More specifically, scholars have argued that individuals' ability to draw on available resources to respond to a given communicative situation is equally, if not more, important to one's grammatical knowledge (Canagarajah, 2013; García, 2009). Along similar lines, proficiency is not conceptualized for each language separately; instead, it is viewed as a way one makes meaning across different named languages and literacy practices.

Canagarajah (2013) calls such ability of multilinguals Performative Competence. This concept highlights translingual practices that multilinguals draw on in communication, not just the knowledge of grammar for each language, as is often emphasized in the monolingual, form-focused model. Or as Canagarajah (2013) explains, it is about *how* multilinguals communicate, not *what* they communicate. As the focus of performative competence is on how one responds to a communicative situation using all available resources, the concept also recognizes the importance of one's willingness and ability to negotiate multiple languages and other resources. To this, scholars have noted the importance of translingual dispositions that guide individuals' translingual practices, and therefore, the need to recognize this as a significant aspect of multilinguals' competence (Lee & Canagarajah, 2019).

With its challenge to many core concepts in language and literacy, and the monolingual ideology in general, translingualism poses some important questions for English language educators to consider: What would English language teaching look like when it is translingually oriented? How could the field of English language and literacy education reinvent its practice? What challenges and opportunities does such teaching entail? In the next section, I discuss these questions and explore the implications of translingualism for English language teaching.

IMPLICATIONS FOR ENGLISH LANGUAGE EDUCATION

As translingualism emphasizes a new way to understand language relations in multilingual realities where language difference is a norm rather than a deficit, a translingual pedagogy fundamentally challenges how English should be learned and taught. Indeed, an increasing number of publications have begun to discuss implications of translingualism in the teaching of English, including what a pedagogy reflective of translingual orientations may look like and what such pedagogy can achieve. García, Johnson, and Seltzer (2017) have particularly emphasized the potential of a translanguaging pedagogy in working toward equitable education for language-minoritized students. They argue that the primary goal of a translanguaging pedagogy is "ensuring that bilingual students, especially those who come from language minority groups, are instructed and assessed in ways that provide them with equal educational opportunity" (p. ix). And doing so requires teachers to not only understand students' linguistic and cultural history and backgrounds but to also value and leverage these resources, fully aware of and maximizing *translanguaging corriente* – the "flow of students' dynamic bilingualism that runs through our classrooms and schools" (García et al., 2017, p. 21).

Implications for Classroom Language Practices

Emerging work shows how teachers can encourage students to use all of their languages as crucial communicative resources in working against the English-only ideology. And particularly, studies have shown how a translingual pedagogy promotes students' learning both English and academic content via their translingual practices. Lin (2013) reports a few pedagogical practices adopted in secondary schools in Hong Kong that actively cultivate students' use of both Cantonese and English as well as their multimodal practices. For instance, instructors used a bilingual note to students where instructional materials are presented both in Cantonese and English side by side so students can practice academic literacies in both languages. In addition, Lin discusses how encouraging students to draw on their L1 and multimodal resources in their science journal (e.g., pictures and drawings) helped scaffold students' learning of the content. Probyn (2015) discusses eight teachers' systematic use of students' home language, isiXhosa, along with English, the official language of instruction, in Grade 8 science classrooms in South Africa. While the majority of the teachers in the study utilized isiXhosa as a way to clarify students' potential misunderstanding of the content, one teacher showed a systemic a purposeful shuttling between everyday language and scientific terms in isiXhosa to build on students' learning of academic discourse.

While the examples demonstrate active use of multiple named languages, a translingual pedagogy can be conceived as a dynamic manifestation of teachers' orientation to language. For instance, a translingual approach can also show in teachers' mundane yet "extraordinary" labor of reading, discussing, and evaluating language and language difference, including their students' and their own (Alvarez & Lee, 2019). Translingual work begins with teachers' own listening and reading practices in the classroom that can have a material consequence in students' lives. And those practices can cultivate the very condition that can help either maintain or disrupt the monolingual ideology. Rather than assuming language difference as an error, translingual scholars have argued, teachers need to consider how the language difference contributes to the meaning that students are trying to make in their communicative situation. As Horner et al. (2011) argue, such assumption should be the last resort in a translingual approach to students' language practice.

Conceiving a translingual pedagogy of an enactment of translingual disposition is particularly helpful when teachers may not share the same language background as students'. I, together with Canagarajah (see Lee & Canagarajah, 2019), have examined one such instance in an ESL writing classroom where the "native" English-speaking instructor, Daphne, enacts her translingual disposition in various aspects of her pedagogy. In particular, Daphne shows her translingual reading of student work by focusing on the rhetorical function and practice behind the students' accented writing, rather than evaluating the writing purely based on their language use. Daphne's case shows that the core of a translingual pedagogy lies in the instructor's dispositions and the pedagogical work that emerges from such dispositions. The everyday work of translingualism can cultivate a culture of and attitudes toward linguistic pluralism in the classroom – a welcoming pedagogical gesture toward students' translingual practice.

Implications for the Curriculum and Assessment for English Language Teaching

Translingualism's view of communication as multilingual and multimodal has also implications for the English language curriculum. To embrace translingualism, the language and literacy classroom must invite students to explore and inquire about the translingual nature of language and literacy practices as they learn English. Particularly, many have suggested language and cultural difference can serve as a topic of inquiry in the classroom. For instance, de los Ríos and Seltzer's (2017) study examines two teachers' translanguaging pedagogies in the United States, one in an 11th and 12th grade Chicanx/Latinx studies course and another in a high school English classroom, with Latinx students as dominant populations in both settings. These teachers had students analyze their own language practices and explore how their language practices are entangled within language hierarchies. In one such activity, the students read a Mexican literary genre, *corridos*, which explores Mexican people's border conflicts and social justice issues. Building on their understanding of how language intersects with one's identity and ideology, the students then engaged in a spoken-word performance where they explored their own experience of the relations between identity, language varieties, and language hierarchies. The authors report these translanguaging pedagogies were able to help students to question the dominant English-only ideology in the United States and school context and helped students to see how their cultural and linguistic practices also contribute to their academic performance.

In addition, the significance of multimodality in communication also requires reconceptualization of what and how we teach and assess in our classes. As briefly discussed earlier, our students engage in multilingual and multimodal practices as part of their everyday literacy practice. Students' familiarity and interests in digital media consumption and production can be a good starting point for educators to discuss and further develop their multimodal meaning-making practices through assignments such as digital storytelling, composing a photo essay or other multimodal composition, and creating an online portfolio. To facilitate students' competence in multimodal communication, teacher education programs also need to place multiliteracies as a core curricular objective so teachers are prepared for designing, implementing, and assessing multimodal projects in their classes (Lin, 2013). And as teachers and students engage in translanguaging, how students' language practices can be also assessed from a translingual perspective requires serious consideration both in terms of what is assessed (cf.) "performative competence") and how it is assessed.

In assessing students' language practices, teachers may need to discern the "mistakes" – nonsystematic, eclectic language use – from "errors" – systematic "deviance" from the language conventions – to better understand students' meaning making and help raise students' sensitivity to their language choice (Canagarajah, 2013). Similarly, teaching with translingual dispositions would require teachers to teach English not against the yardstick of the native speaker norms but toward students' own evolving understanding of their multilingual world to help them to position themselves as a language user, not a forever language learner. This means assessing what students can do with English rather than how closely to the norms of the "native" English speakers they can produce English (Hall, 2014).

Implications for English Language Teacher Development and Education

Translingualism challenges the assumptions behind the current knowledge base of language teachers that are largely shaped by the monolingual ideology. And yet all of the pedagogical enactments should begin with critical reflections on teachers' own identity and ideology toward the translingual and transmodal nature of communication. Research has shown the significance of teachers' identities and lived experience in enacting translingual pedagogy productively and ethically (Motha, Jain, & Tecle, 2012). Even those teachers who may not identify themselves as emergent bilinguals or multilinguals can reflect on how they are in fact surrounded by subtler and less obvious language differences such as different registers and regional varieties. The teachers can further explore what values toward language they bring to the classroom by questioning what different lived experiences might have shaped their values toward language and literacy (Lee & Canagarajah, 2019). By critically examining their socialization into different language practices and communities, and values and ideologies embedded in these spaces, teachers, including those who may not identify as multilingual, can better understand the monolingual and monoglossic ideology and how such ideology positions students.

Particularly in a setting where teachers do not share the same language as the students, teachers need to be willing to learn and actively draw on students' expertise in their sociocultural, linguistic, or other semiotic practices, and learn from and along with their students about a variety of language practices that the students engage in. García (2017) suggests teacher education programs can prepare teachers to better understand the multilingual landscape that our students navigate through a project where they examine multilingual students' daily language practice by means of interviews and further investigating their engagement with literacies and other language resources. To that end, teachers' self and collaborative inquiry needs to be an important agenda in teacher education programs. Teachers' ongoing learning of students' language practices will be essential in understanding and building on students' full range of language practice. And through the inquiry project, teachers can better understand the sociolinguistic reality that their students navigate and the knowledge and experiences that these students often bring to school that are not always visible (García et al., 2017).

Finally, teacher educators have to learn along with their teachers in reconceptualizing what is the legitimate knowledge in preparing to teach in the multilingual realities. Translingualism is built upon the recognition of always changing language, and therefore, language practices, while acknowledging the still dominant monolingual ideology. This means that teacher educators should also recognize the evolving nature of knowledge toward language and language practices along with their teacher candidates. While the notion of language as a social practice has been widely acknowledged, the negotiated and performative nature of language needs to be further highlighted, as much of pedagogical work is guided by asset-based pedagogy that separates "school" language (i.e., English) from "home" language (i.e., languages other than English) (Flores & Aneja, 2016; García, 2009). Focusing on questions of language varieties, language ideology, social inequality, and social justice in teacher education agendas can help realize the transformative potential of a translanguaging pedagogy toward the goal of educational equity.

FUTURE DIRECTIONS

As shown in this chapter, with its implications in pedagogy and policy, research on translingualism still has a great deal of work to be done. While more and more scholarship reports the pedagogical benefits of translanguaging, relatively little has been reported in how translanguaging pedagogy can be adopted in language teacher education programs. Flores and Aneja (2016), for instance, report how centering translingualism in their graduate TESOL program helped expand the teachers' conceptualization of language and recognize their multilingual identity as an asset. Taking up a translingual pedagogy begins with understanding how the monolingual and monoglossic ideologies shape the way we understand and evaluate language and literacy, or in Flores and Rosa's (2015) term, the way we listen as a "white listening subject." However, changing teachers' long-held beliefs, values, attitudes, and history toward language and literacies is not an easy task – it requires a sustained engagement and inquiry. In this sense, research needs to further examine what successful translanguaging-focused teacher education curriculum consists of and how such knowledge and beliefs are translated into actual practices as well as what issues beginning teachers encounter in adopting translanguaging pedagogy in their development as teachers.

Given that the monolingual, English-only ideology is still strongly present, even among English language learners, teachers, and teacher educators, translanguaging may be met with more resistance from various stakeholders in English language education. Teachers can start discussions by questioning how they understand "error" in student writing, and how such conception influences their reading and assessment of student writing. More specifically, teachers can bring discussions on the ideological nature of language and literacy, and what is perceived as error more specifically, with their students. In such space, students and teachers can both not only question the dominant monolingual ideology and its role in their language learning and practice in English but extend such critique to other language practices that they draw on in their day-to-day communication. Also, importantly, finding and creating such pedagogical space also requires teachers' willingness to negotiate with the various structural constraints in their teaching. In this regard, longitudinal studies would provide more insights as to how teachers learn to enact a translanguaging pedagogy while negotiating different constraints in their local settings.

Equally important, as briefly noted, is to help those teachers who may not consider themselves as multilingual to enact translingual dispositions in a sustainable manner. Even those who may not claim a "multilingual" status must work to develop their translingual dispositions and enact translingual pedagogies. As Lee and Canagarajah's (2019) study shows, one's orientation to (cross-)language relations is at the crux of translingualism, and teachers can promote this orientation in their pedagogy in various ways. While multilingual teachers bring firsthand experience of varying degrees of translanguaging, enacting translingual pedagogy requires both dispositional and other pedagogical labor regardless of their language experiences. After all, enacting translingual pedagogy starts from recognizing how the current practices of English language teaching is built on the monolingual and monoglossic idea of language learning and teaching.

In carrying out a translanguaging pedagogy, we also need more research on translanguage in a wider range of contexts. So far, most research reporting translanguaging emerges from the U.S. or Western European contexts, and relatively little is shared from Latin America, Asian, or African contexts. There are many factors that can influence the degrees and shapes of a translanguaging pedagogy in a given school ecology. These factors include, but are not limited to, the language of learning and instruction in school, the teacher's familiarity with language and literacy practices of students, students' linguistic and cultural backgrounds, life experiences, the school's existing language policy and attitudes toward multilingualism, teacher development, assessment requirements, and the status of the language(s) that are being translanguaged. Particularly, in a context where English serves as a medium of instruction (EMI), more research is needed on how to apply translanguaging pedagogy where a monolingual ideology prevails.

While changing our reading and listening practices for students' language away from such monolingual and monoglossic ideology is a good start, without a change in actual assessment practices the work may be only half done. Ultimately, it is the testing practice, among many other structures that maintain the monolingual bias, that makes actual and lasting material consequences in students' life. To this end, there have been promising efforts to evaluate students' language use with the process- and practice-based understanding of language such as dynamic assessment where students' ability to complete a task with additional resources present is evaluated, and labor-based or contract-based grading that evaluates students' work by focusing on the amount of labor that was performed (Inoue, 2015). Yet assessment practices that incorporate translanguaging in the test design itself (i.e., instructions and learners' responses) are still very few. Even those teachers who attempted to integrate translanguaging in assessment practices still have reported tension around the monolingual force in evaluating students' language learning (Schissel, De Korne, & López-Gopar, 2018). To move forward, we need more concrete examples of how assessment can be designed from a translingual perspective that aligns with pedagogical translanguaging.

Finally, the field of ELT needs to continue to engage in self-reflexivity in our own practices and discourses to challenge the prevailing monolingual and monoglossic ideology in teaching and learning English. There have been emerging concerns that translingualism or other progressive discourses popular in Applied Linguistics and language studies inadvertently supports neoliberal agenda of higher education. While attention to reflexivity seems to be more visibly present in publication, conferences, and other knowledge construction domains, we still hear of unequal hiring and assessment practices that show that the monolingual and monoglossic ideology is quite alive. We need to continue to unpack our own assumptions toward language and literacy to better study different forces of English and how we ourselves are contributing to or disrupting the discourse of the separatist ideology and promoting educational equity and social justice. To this end, Lin (2013) poses important questions:

> What can initiate change in monolingual TESOL methodologies and testing practices? What resources and strategies can local actors mobilize to create conditions that affirm students' linguistic and cultural resources and identities while at the same time helping them gain access to global resources?

> (p. 539)

With its theoretical tenet centering around equitable education, translanguaging is not just a matter concerned about how English should be taught and how we should understand the way we make meaning. Moving forward, translingualism can help our field to move matters beyond the walls of our classroom and raise its voice about unequal social spaces and how our view toward language participates in disrupting or maintaining social inequality in those spaces.

Discussion Questions

1. What challenge do you see in experiencing or recognizing the translanguaging *corriente*?
2. How would you strategically enact a translanguage pedagogy in a setting where you do not share the same language resources with your students? What should go into pedagogical planning?
3. How could you design classroom assessment in a way that prioritizes co-construction and negotiation of language diversity and students' ability to draw on their entire linguistic repertoire?

4. Imagine you are teaching an English test preparation course with a large number of students. In what ways could you enact translingual pedagogy in such context?
5. Reflect on your current assessment practices. How do your current assessment practices reflect translingual pedagogy or dispositions?

Resources for Further Exploration

1. Ascenzi-Moreno, L. (2018). Translanguaging and responsive assessment adaptations: Emergent bilingual readers through the lens of possibility. *Language Arts, 95*(6), 355–369. This article provides a good example of how teachers can adopt tenets of translingualism in their classroom assessment through a study on a teacher's formative assessment of students' reading abilities that invites students to draw on all of their multilingual language resources.
2. City University of New York-New York State Initiative on Emergent Bilinguals (CUNY-NYSIEB) research team. (2019). CUNY-NYSIEB. Retrieved from www.cuny-nysieb.org/. This is a website established by the research team of CUNY-NYSIEB, where teachers can find both their research on translanguaging pedagogies and resources in the form of webinars, classroom videos, sample curricular units, lesson plans and activity guides, and other helpful resources for teachers in planning and designing translingual pedagogies.
3. Early, M., Kendrick, M., & Potts, D. (Eds.). (2015). Multimodality: Out from the margins of English language teaching [Special issue]. *TESOL Quarterly, 49*(3), 447–622. *https://doi. org/10.1002/tesq.246*. This special issue of *TESOL Quarterly* on multimodality in teaching of English will help teachers to better grasp the concept of multimodality as defined and researched in relation to language and literacy education. Additionally, the special issue accompanies various pedagogical approaches, examples, and issues concerning multimodality as understood and enacted in conjunction with efforts to promote students' plurilingual resources.
4. Lee, J.W., & Dovchin, S. (Eds.) (2019). *Translinguistics: Negotiating innovation and ordinariness*. New York, NY: Routledge. This edited collection provides detailed accounts of ubiquity of multi-/translinguality across a variety of contexts where English is used, learned, and taught (e.g., U.S., Korea, Australia, Italy, Puerto Rico; both physical and virtual spaces), based on which educators can shape their curriculum and classroom practices.
5. Macedo, D. (Ed.) (2019). Decolonizing foreign language education: The misteaching of English and other colonial languages. New York, NY: Routledge. This book will be useful for teachers and researchers who would like to further explore the topic of the politics of language and language education, in the discussions of which translingualism is situated and has been contributing.

REFERENCES

Alvarez, S. P., & Lee, E. (2019). Ordinary difference, extraordinary dispositions: Sustaining multilingualism in the writing classroom. In J.W. Lee and S. Dovchin (Eds.), *Translinguistics: Negotiating Innovation and Ordinariness* (pp. 61–72). New York: Routledge.

Blommaert, J. (2010). *The sociolinguistics of globalization*. Cambridge, UK: Cambridge University Press.

Canagarajah, A. S. (2013). *Translingual practice*. London, UK: Routledge.

Creese, A., & Blackledge, A. (2015). Translanguaging and identity in educational settings. *Annual Review of Applied Linguistics, 35*, 20–35.

de los Ríos, C.V., & Seltzer, K. (2017). Translanguaging, coloniality, and English classrooms: An exploration of two bicoastal urban classrooms. *Research in the Teaching of English, 52*(1), 55–76.

Dovchin, S., & Lee, J. W. (2019). Introduction to special issue: The ordinariness of translinguistics. *International Journal of Multilingualism*, 16(2), 105–111.

Flores, N., & Aneja, G. (2016). "Why needs hiding?": Translingual (re)orientations in TESOL teacher education. *Research in the Teaching of English*, 51(4), 441–463.

Flores, N., & Rosa, J. (2015). Undoing appropriateness: Raciolinguistic ideologies and language diversity in education. *Harvard Educational Review*, 85(2), 149–301.

García, O. (2009). *Bilingual education in the 21st century*. Oxford, UK: Wiley-Blackwell.

García, O., Johnson, S. I., & Seltzer, K. (2017). *The translanguaging classroom: Leveraging student bilingualism for learning*. Philadelphia, PA: Caslon.

García, O., & Li, W. (2014). *Translanguaging: Language, bilingualism and education*. Basingstoke, UK: Palgrave Macmillan.

Hall, C. (2014). Moving beyond accuracy: From tests of English to tests of "englishing". *ELT Journal*, 68(4), 376–385.

Heller, M. (1999). *Linguistic minorities and modernity: A sociolinguistic ethnography*. London, UK: Longman.

Horner. B., Lu, M. Z., Royster, J. J., & Trimbur, J. (2011). Language difference in writing: Toward a translingual approach. *College English*, 73, 303–321.

Inoue, A. (2015). *Antiracist writing assessment ecologies: Teaching and assessing writing for a socially just future*. Fort Collins, CO and Anderson, SC: WAC Clearinghouse and Parlor Press.

Lee, E., & Canagarajah, A. S. (2019). Beyond native and nonnative: Translingual dispositions in language and literacy education. *Journal of Language, Identity, and Education*, 18(6), 352–363. https://doi.org/10.1080/15348458.2019.1674148

Lin, A. (2013). Toward paradigmatic change in TESOL methodologies: Building plurilingual pedagogies from the ground up. *TESOL Quarterly*, 47(3), 521–545.

May, S. (2014). Introducing the "multilingual turn". In S. May (Ed.), *The multilingual turn: Implications for SLA, TESOL, and bilingual education* (pp. 1–6). New York, NY: Routledge.

Motha, S., Jain, R., & Tecle, T. (2012). Translinguistic identity-as-pedagogy: Implications for language teacher education. *International Journal of Innovation in English Language Teaching and Research*, 1, 13–28.

Ortega, L. (2014). Ways forward for a bi/multilingual turn in SLA. In S. May (Ed.), *The multilingual turn: Implications for SLA, TESOL, and bilingual education* (pp. 32–53). New York, NY: Routledge.

Otheguy, R., García, O., & Reid, W. (2015). Clarifying translanguaging and deconstructing named languages: A perspective from linguistics. *Applied Linguistics Review*, 6, 281–307. https://doi.org/10.1515/applirev-2015-0014

Probyn, M. (2015). Pedagogical translanguaging: Bridging discourses in South African science classrooms. *Language and Education*, 29(3), 218–234.

Schissel, J. L., De Korne, K., & López-Gopar, M. (2018). Grappling with translanguaging for teaching and assessment in culturally and linguistically diverse contexts: Teacher perspectives from Oaxaca, Mexico. *International Journal of Bilingual Education and Bilingualism*. doi:10.1080/13670050.2018.1463965

Seltzer, K. (2019). Reconceptualizing "home" and "school" language: Taking a critical translingual approach in the English classroom. *TESOL Quarterly*, 53(4), 986–1007. https://doi.org/10.1002/tesq.530

Williams, C. (1996). Secondary education: Teaching in the bilingual situation. In C. Williams, G. Lewis, & C. Baker (Eds.), *The language policy: Taking stock* (Vol. 12, No. 2, pp. 193–211). Llangefni, Wales: CAI

CASE STUDY 5.1

Leveraging Translanguaging in Role-Plays in a U.S. University

Katja Davidoff and Zhongfeng Tian

This case study discusses a class project that provides an example of the tenets of translanguaging. This project took place in an intensive higher-education English language class in early spring of 2018. Students were encouraged to choose and research a character of historical and social importance in their own culture and language. The students could do their research and collaborate with peers using any language and were asked to present their findings in English using interactive scenarios. The students had the freedom to research and prepare for this project in both their native and a second language. This gave them the opportunity to experience language in a fluid sense rather than being asked to compartmentalize their knowledge and communication in separate languages. As the students explored new content in two languages, they further developed English language skills and experienced language holistically while acquiring new content knowledge.

THE SETTING

This case study took place at the English language center of an urban university in the Northeast region of the United States. The center is located on campus and students are a mix of English language learners of various levels, conditionally admitted students planning to matriculate into academic programs, and professionals who want to study English for specific purposes. Students take classes and participate in activities in the center in addition to general university activities on campus. The center offers courses with an academic, cultural, and professional focus. Students generally take required core courses that integrate the four language skills with academic focus and orient them to U.S. culture. One of the goals is to acclimate students to life and academic work in the United States before they fully matriculate to academic programs that offered them their conditional admission. Students also take elective courses aligned with the areas of personal interest. In addition, the center offers an intensive program in English for specific purposes. Those students may already be professionals in their fields but need language support in their chosen career areas. When students enter the programs, they take online and in-person placement tests to determine their levels. The advanced level is for students who have been deemed ready to take the TOEFL exam according to the program standards and/or may be conditionally admitted to the university. The top level students are fluent in English with few or minimal errors.

ENGLISH LANGUAGE LEARNERS

Students in this case study are young adult international students. The students are predominantly 17–22 years old, mostly undergraduates, and have come to the United States for an intensive English course that focuses on improving integrated language skills. The students are also interested in exploring and learning more about culture in the United States. The setting for the case study is an intensive English class, called *Spring Boost Intensive English*, which meets for three hours per day over four weeks in the Spring semester. Some students have an additional afternoon class for two hours. Students are primarily from Japan, with about 10%

from China. The students are at a low-to-intermediate level of English language proficiency, though their speaking levels are more reflective of lower-level students. They come from schooling where they have not been given much opportunity to speak and express their opinions in class and have been heavily corrected for making errors when speaking in English; hence their willingness to speak is limited. The students are in an integrated class that focuses on oral/aural, reading, writing, and listening skills with the use of an ESL textbook for support. They are given individual and group projects on issues related to academic topics in the textbook and are asked to do presentations in addition to basic vocabulary quizzes. The classes tend to be student-centered with small bits of information and vocabulary presented by the instructor and then filtered into projects and interactive tasks for students to use in groups. The course offers an opportunity for students to study topics with facilitation and support given by the instructor and integrates cultural lessons focused on weekly field trips.

PEDAGOGICAL APPLICATION AND INNOVATION

In the past, students have come to the center with a reluctance to speak freely and to let go of the boundaries of their identity. What this means more specifically is that when students arrive and must function in a second language, the resulting discomfort sometimes causes them to feel that relaxing their personal boundaries is somehow equivalent to giving up one's principles or morals. The result is that students sometimes start class with preconceived notions of who they will and will not work with, what kind of subjects they will discuss, and/or which activities they will participate in. In other words, before they even start class, they have expectations of what learning should look like and how it will take place. Often those ideas are very different from how we are trained to teach our classes: to be more interactive and student centered. The posturing and rigid stance of students does not help to create a comfortable rapport in class, which is necessary for language learning to take place. In addition, it makes arranging a student-centered class and facilitating interactive lessons more difficult. Students have also on occasion inadvertently offended other students when cultural misunderstandings occurred.

In this case study, the first author, Katja Davidoff, has devised a number of role-play projects (Davidoff, 2020) to encourage interaction between students and to provide students with the freedom to express themselves in character, thereby increasing their tolerance for ambiguity through a sense of acting and imagination and encouraging fluency. Furthermore, the allowance of students to choose a character of historical significance in their home culture or history provides the students a sense of pride in their identity and the opportunity to share that with others during the role-play.

This particular project combines role-play with cultural value to students, as they have a personal interest in identifying with and sharing a figure of historical importance they admire. In this role-play, the students are asked to choose a historical character of significance to them. They are then required to learn a set of facts about the historical character using parameters identified by the instructor to enhance collaboration between students. Finding out these historical facts allows the students to better understand the historical setting and context of the characters and provides a common base for the students to communicate during their role-plays. The students have the flexibility of researching and preparing for their presentation in their home languages in addition to helping others in whichever language is most comfortable and useful to them. The option for the students to choose how to use language when completing their research and preparing for the role-play facilitates their translanguaging, adds comfort to their research process, and helps students to fully anticipate what will be needed for the presentation. By taking away the focus on English only at the research stage, the impetus to secretly use translation aids and the level of anxiety is lowered in students. The students spontaneously communicate, in both their native or home language and in English, to research and obtain the information needed. There is no distinct separation between which language is used and when, leading to a more holistic experience, thereby supporting the concept of translanguaging. Since students have the freedom to use their own language, their language use is more natural and less stinted.

A common problem faced by English language teachers is what some instructors call "accidental plagiarism." This happens when a student has limited ways to express certain concepts or ideas and/or does not know how to adequately paraphrase or summarize information. When a student learns another language, often their use of certain commonly accepted ways to express themselves is limited. This limited repertoire can make expressing oneself in the target language, without using language that closely matches the language of the source, extremely challenging. The allowance and purposeful use of translanguaging in projects or language lessons helps to minimize accidental plagiarism by allowing the students the freedom to not be restricted by the phrases present in their target language repertoire. Furthermore, the use of home language in the process of researching and preparing the assignment changes the affective perception of the project, also reducing the stigma or resistance to presenting in the second or new language.

The instructor will gauge how much time is needed for students to research their characters and prepare for the presentation. After the students have had ample time to conduct research, they prepare to meet the other historical figures. During the final part of the project, the historical figures come together and discover information about others via role-play and dialogue. The presentation then involves the historical characters meeting each other and engaging in a conversation. Lower-level students conduct interviews that are simpler in structure. For higher-level students, the historical characters come together at a historical dinner party during which all of the characters get to circulate and meet each other. To facilitate this interactive play, the teacher gives the students a list of interview questions. The purpose of using teacher-generated questions is to provide scaffolding for the students who might need additional help. It also creates a scenario that guides the students toward a respectful engagement with possible cultural and ideological differences. Having a list of interview questions provided by the teacher helps to address two areas of difficulty – differences of opinions and interpretations of history that can potentially create conflict and the need for additional support for lower-level students.

When a class demonstrates a higher level of fluency and appears to have bonded, the instructor allows more flexibility with the project and more opportunities for the conversation to take different directions. Once students understand how the beginning of the project is structured, they are free to meet and interview who they like at a historical dinner party of sorts. The instructor only steps in to facilitate with anyone who seems stuck. Students are expected to interact with other students in their historical characters and interview them. The questions and the types of information are established in previous classes via suggestions from the students. The teacher helps to fine-tune questions or modify anything that may seem inappropriate. The interviews are video recorded and assessed with a rubric. Students have the opportunity to watch other students' interviews and their own recordings with feedback from the instructor. First students receive feedback from other students and after the project is completed, the students are given a filled-out rubric addressing the content and presentational aspects they were required to use during the interaction.

In these projects, students were encouraged to use their home languages and personal knowledge of culture and history to research their historical figures, help others, and prepare for their interviews. Students enjoyed being able to play a role and demonstrated more active participation than in previous activities and classes. Providing students with an opportunity for autonomy in choosing what is meaningful to them, researching, and collaborating with others who share their languages, and using content knowledge in their home languages to support the interactions in the second language coincides with the establishment of a translanguaging space (Li, 2011). In this translanguaging space, the students were encouraged to use their full linguistic repertoire in their home languages and in English for the research and preparation of the project.

The students engage in translingual practices at the final stage of the projects as they carefully prepare and plan to engage in role-plays in class. They use their home languages and English to develop and perform the characters as well as accessing their internal semantic representation of the importance and impact these characters had on humans in history during the interaction. The students' linguistic expression and mental representation of the characters will be affected by their inner mental associations with those characters. Those associations will be characterized by how the students unconsciously and cognitively decide to draw meaning of the characters' importance and effect on society and history. Sometimes the inner representations cannot find adequate expression in the second language or cannot be translated and maintain the original message the interlocutor wants to convey. The use of translanguaging in this part of the activity provides an opportunity for the students to keep their original semantic definitions intact. Once the students are ready with their own definitions of the importance and role of the characters, they move to the interaction and performance step.

In class, they perform their historical characters based on multilingual research they have done as they "meet" each other and interact in English. The comfort and ease of the interactions between students as evidenced by body language and increased fluency in their conversations represents the success of using translanguaging to attain knowledge about their characters and to prepare for the interaction. These students did not solely rely on the list of preapproved questions; they smiled, laughed, and greatly seemed to enjoy the interactions. The permission to use native or home languages and English at all preparation stages appeared to give students a more complete sense of learning where language development happened hand-in-hand with the acquisition of historical knowledge. This holistic learning is an important tenet of translanguaging.

The meeting between historical characters sometimes took on an unexpected development as the students would suddenly decide to do something humorous or deviate from the teacher-provided questions. In such cases, the instructor intervened only if students appeared to need help. On occasion, historical characters would create a funny chicken and egg scenario where one would state that they could not have existed without the other and vice versa. This was amusing to watch and seemed to create fun situations for the students. On occasion, a student would really enjoy getting fully into character proclaiming all the ways in which they have changed the world with the expected aplomb. This required other students to think on their feet to respond. These were situations where the time spent on research in any language and engagement in translanguaging prepared the students to respond and react appropriately to improvisations.

The deviations from the suggested script provided impetus for future projects. This is the reason behind our use of historic role-plays to further develop internal knowledge of history in home and second languages. The role-plays provide a productive translingual space where linguistic constraints are reduced and the students can express themselves without feeling that their home languages and cultures are disregarded or ignored. In addition, the chance for students to help each other with their projects using home languages and English is another example of engaging in translingual practice. It relaxes the constraints of the pressure to speak English that the students often feel in ESL classes.

CONCLUSION

This case study features a role-play activity designed to incorporate translanguaging to help university-level ESL students develop interactive presentation skills. In this activity, the students were asked to embody culturally relevant historical figures of their choice and interact with each other. The students were encouraged to use their native and home languages and engage in translanguaging during their research and preparation stages. In this class, we observed fewer instances of unintentional plagiarism and reduced reliance on smart phone applications for translation purposes – a significant difference from classes where the use of English only is emphasized. We also observed an increase in our students' spontaneous speaking, writing, and overall fluency in using English. We found that the creation of a translanguaging space significantly increased learner comprehension and comfort level with using English.

One of the most crucial aspects of establishing a translingual space is instructor and student buy-in of the idea. Sometimes students come to class with the belief that language development and exposure should only be done in the target language or it does not constitute valid learning. It is important to help students to understand how translingual practice and activities that facilitate it can enhance and support language learning. Another important aspect is to create a comfortable and productive learning environment in which students can use their home languages as a resource for knowledge development. Translanguaging situates English language learners as resourceful multilingual speakers with rich linguistic and cultural resources and abilities for successful communication and not as deficient non-native speakers as can be perceived from a monolingual view (Kleyn & García, 2019). Validating and leveraging students' full linguistic repertoires helps them to live their thoughts, engage in research, and increase their confidence and speaking skills.

REFERENCES

Davidoff, K. (2020). *Intercultural role plays for the classroom.* Cochin, India: Kalapurakkal House Publishing.

Kleyn, T., & García, O. (2019). Translanguaging as an act of transformation: Restructuring teaching and learning for emergent bilingual students. In L. C. de Oliveira (Ed.), *The handbook of TESOL in K-12* (pp. 69–82). Hoboken, NJ: Wiley-Blackwell.

Li, W. (2011). Moment analysis and translanguaging space: Discursive construction of identities by multilingual Chinese youth in Britain. *Journal of Pragmatics, 43*(5), 1222–1235.

CASE STUDY 5.2

Translingual Practices in an Adult ESL Literacy Class in the U.S.

Sarah Young Knowles

This case study focuses on the translingual use of adult learners' L1 Spanish and L2 English in their development of English language and literacy practices. In teacher-fronted, English-only literacy instruction, students are often positioned as passive recipients of L2 knowledge and skills. Instructional materials focus on bottom-up processes, often in isolation, that are designed to develop decoding, vocabulary, and comprehension skills. However, this approach neglects the metalinguistic assets and multilingual resources that emergent readers and writers bring to their literacy development. These resources can be drawn upon in an ESL literacy class through the use of the learners' L1 in translingual board work, note-taking, language awareness activities, and reflection.

THE SETTING

The educational context for this case study is a large urban adult ESL program in the United States. This program offers supplementary ESL literacy classes for learners who struggle with reading and writing in their mainstream ESL class, often due to previously limited or interrupted schooling. These 30-minute supplementary classes use the basal readers *Sam and Pat* (Hartel, Lowry, & Hendon, 2005) and *Talk of the Block* (Haffner, 2009), which focus on phonics, vocabulary, decoding, reading comprehension, and word- or sentence-level writing skills. The combination of mainstream ESL classroom instruction with the supplementary literacy classes is meant to provide targeted and structured support for students who are most in need of these services, while raising their awareness of, motivation for, and confidence in their literacy skills.

In my previous experiences as a teacher and observer in these classes, I noted how these 30-minute classes would pass quickly with a series of basic literacy tasks, with little time for discussion about the learning process itself, and no opportunity for engaging with "the entirety of the learner's linguistic repertoire" (Li, 2018, p. 16). Although students often whispered insights to one another in their L1 Spanish, these contributions were kept on the periphery with the primary focus being on English literacy. The rich translingual notes that the learners wrote to themselves in their notebooks as they navigated the literacy materials tended to go unnoticed and unexamined by their teachers.

DESCRIPTION OF ENGLISH LANGUAGE LEARNERS

Participants in these ESL literacy classes are initially identified by their classroom teachers, often through observation of behaviors such as struggling to (1) grip a pencil or manipulate print materials properly, (2) form letters or numbers, (3) locate specific text on a page, (4) write or read level-appropriate vocabulary words, (5) copy text from the board or from paper, or (6) interpret drawings, charts, maps, or graphic organizers used in class (Spiegel & Sunderland, 2006). Other behavioral clues that may occur during classroom reading activities include looking at the teacher or other students rather than the printed text, paraphrasing or "reading from memory" rather than reading from the text itself, and becoming withdrawn or disruptive.

Each supplementary ESL literacy class is capped at six students, with most groups having two to four members who consistently attend. The majority of students who attend the literacy classes tend to be native Spanish speakers from Central and South America, ranging in age from 20–70 years old. Some may be recent arrivals in the United States, while others may have lived here for much of their adult lives. Most students have six or fewer years of formal education in their home countries. Students generally have a low level of oral proficiency, but some students have developed stronger oral skills as a result of living and working in the United States for many years. Students in these classes tend to express strong motivation and commitment to developing their English language and literacy skills, despite common feelings of frustration, confusion, or anxiety.

PEDAGOGICAL APPLICATION AND INNOVATION

In my experience, the opening of a translingual space in an adult ESL literacy setting is rare. There is the belief that there is just too much to do, too many "building blocks" of English literacy to provide, to have the time to incorporate and draw on learners' other languages. When these learners with limited schooling and L1 literacy levels come to an ESL class, the approach tends to be teacher-centered and remedial in nature, with the focus on the learners receiving information about English language and literacy rather than co-constructing it with the teacher and their classmates. It emphasizes bottom-up learning by building word families from vowel sounds, by narrowing language exposure to a tightly controlled script, and by prioritizing fictional content over the students' personal needs for literacy use. Even if ESL literacy teachers are proficient in their learners' L1s, the existing materials do not seem to allow for or encourage any use of the L1.

What happens when ESL literacy teachers start drawing on the L1 resources of their students? In particular, how can teachers and students "do literacy" in English while intentionally *reflecting* on their learning in the L1? I found that by engaging learners in metalinguistic discussions in Spanish before and after they completed a literacy task in English, we constructed a much stronger understanding of how their languages were working for them. We opened an ongoing conversation *about* language that had been neglected by the textbook. Given the English proficiency level of these learners, this conversation could only be done by using their L1, which positioned both languages as valuable for us.

A common ESL literacy task in the class is reading a short text aloud. For example, the first few lines of one of the short texts in Haffner (2009) begin, "This is Bob. Bob is in bed. Bob is sick in bed" (p. 15). If the students can accurately decode the words while reading aloud and answer text-based comprehension questions such as "Where is Bob? How does Bob feel?", the task is assumed to be complete. However, by pausing to use their L1 to describe what the reading process was like for them, I learned that one of my students was actively using both of her languages while reading:

> Como aquí, yo voy pensando, 'This is Bob." Como "Quién es esa persona?" así como en español. Pero al mismo tiempo como es, para practicarlo en inglés. Y como pensando, lo que está pensando en eso momento, de "Bob is in bed." Como pensar "Oh él está enfermo, está en la cama." Así, eh. Bob is sick in bed. Bob is in bed. Él está en la cama. Como pensando como en el español, pero a transmitirlo en inglés.

> *Like here I'm thinking, "This is Bob," like "Who is this person?" in Spanish. But at the same time, I'm practicing it in English. And I'm thinking that in this moment, Bob is in bed. Like, Oh, he's sick. He's in bed. Like that. Bob is sick in bed. Bob is in bed. He's in bed. Like thinking about what it is in Spanish but changing it to English.*

As a result of using the learners' Spanish L1 to elicit their metalinguistic reflections about the L2 learning process, I began to change my approach to ESL literacy instruction. After they completed each decoding and reading activity in English, I asked learners to tell me in their L1 what they were thinking when they completed the activity:

- How did you complete the activity?

- What was easy for you about the activity? Why?

- What was difficult for you about the activity? Why?
- What could help you do this activity better?
- Could I do something differently to help you?
- How does this activity help you learn English?

The students were naturally able to express much more knowledge, understanding, and nuanced language use when we made more explicit efforts at translanguaging in class. The following chart (Table 5.2.1) provides examples of how ESL literacy instructors can take a translanguaging approach with adult English language learners.

Table 5.2.1 Contrasting a "traditional" approach to ESL literacy instruction with a translanguaging approach

	'Traditional' approach to ESL literacy instruction	Translanguaging approach to ESL literacy instruction
Board work	Teachers elicit student responses to English literacy tasks and write their answers on the board, correcting their students' errors as they write. The target forms are modeled implicitly by only writing "correct" language on the board.	Invite students to come to the board to write their answers themselves. Use a combination of L1 and L2 to discuss the language students produce and what changes might need to be made.
Constructing meaning	Students work through the literacy tasks under the guidance of the teacher. Class works together to produce the correct answers in English.	Students discuss answers to literacy tasks in the L1 before working together to construct a response in the L2. Students use the L1 to actively discuss the strategies they are using to make sense of the literacy tasks, and evaluate these strategies based on their effectiveness in constructing meaning in the L2.
Personal note-taking	Literacy students tend to take note-taking very seriously, often indiscriminately copying text from the board into their notebooks. They also make notes to themselves that appear "incorrect" at a glance, such as phonetic spellings of English words based on their L1. Teachers may encourage students to keep organized or "clean" study notes in their notebooks, but otherwise do not review the notes except to check the accuracy of exercises.	Students periodically share whatever translingual notes or transcriptions they were making for themselves in their notebooks with the teacher or classmates. The class uses the L1 to discuss what students write down in their notebooks and why, shedding light on their understanding of English literacy as well as their own metalinguistic awareness.
Choice of instructional texts	Basal readers using fictional stories are used to build learners' literacy skills in phonics, decoding, spelling, sight words, reading comprehension, punctuation, and so on.	The Language Experience Approach (Vinogradov, 2010) utilizes learner-generated stories about their lives to elicit and produce language for building learners' literacy skills in phonics, decoding, spelling, sight words, reading comprehension, punctuation, and so on.
Metalinguistic knowledge and awareness	Teachers use metalanguage to present English literacy tasks to students. For example, the class distinguishes between "long" and "short" vowels, generates word families based on selected phonemes (e.g., pat-cat-mat-hat), and practices spelling words provided by the instructional text. The language focus resides in the carefully scripted instructional materials provided.	Teachers take a Language Awareness approach to ESL literacy development, which involves "paying motivated attention to language in use, and which enables language learners to gradually gain insights into how languages work" (Bolitho et al., 2003, p. 251). The learners' own linguistic environments are brought into the classroom to generate questions and discoveries about the relationships between the L1 and the L2.

Source: Sarah Knowles

CONCLUSION

This case study proposes a translingual approach to working with emerging readers and writers that can change our perspectives of the linguistic resources that these learners bring to the ESL literacy classroom. Many teachers rarely take the opportunity to elicit rich descriptions of language and L2 learning from the very students who may struggle the most to express themselves and who, consequently, most need to be asked. An English-only approach to basic literacy instruction means that the students' metalinguistic awareness can only be demonstrated to the extent that they understand and can respond to their teachers' utterances, and their teachers understand and can respond to the students' utterances. At a fundamental level, this innovation requires shifting our perspective and categorization of these learners from "low-literate" to multicompetent, emerging multilinguals (e.g., Cook, 1992). It should be noted that ESL teachers who can communicate in the learners' L1 have an advantage in this approach, but students can engage in many of these practices in their L1 even if their teachers are not able to do so themselves.

REFERENCES

Bolitho, R., Carter, R., Hughes, R., Ivanic, R., Masuhara, H., & Tomlinson, B. (2003). Ten questions about language awareness. *ELT Journal*, 57(3), 251–259.

Cook, V. (1992). Evidence for multicompetence. *Language Learning*, 42(4), 557–591.

Haffner, A. (2009). *Talk of the block: Health. Short vowels.* Syracuse, NY: New Readers Press.

Hartel, J., Lowry, B., & Hendon, W. (2005). *Sam and pat.* Boston, MA: Thompson/Heinle.

Li, W. (2018). Translanguaging as a practical theory of language. *Applied Linguistics*, 39(1), 9–30.

Spiegel, M., & Sunderland, H. (2006). *Teaching basic literacy to ESOL learners.* London, UK: LLU.

Vinogradov, P. (2010). Balancing top and bottom: Learner-generated texts for teaching phonics. In T. Wall & M. Leong (Eds.), *Low-educated second language and literacy acquisition: Proceedings of the 5th symposium* (pp. 3–14). Retrieved from https://drive.google.com/drive/folders/1ra07ww_PnwMMu0CI81hS2IJaG8awHFDW

CASE STUDY 5.3

Koryoin (고려인/КОРЁ САРАМ) Children's Translingual Practices for Learning English

A Case Study of Russian-Korean Children in South Korea

Youngjoo Yi and Jinsil Jang

This case study explores ways in which teachers can enact a translingual pedagogy based on the findings from our research on Koryoin children's engagement in translingual practices while learning English as an additional language in South Korea. One of our main findings shows that our participants, Koryoin children (ethnic Koreans who have migrated from the post-Soviet states to South Korea), voluntarily engaged in translingual practices in the contexts of home and community. They developed their own translingual and multimodal strategies in order to facilitate their learning of both English and Korean, as well as to promote content learning. In this chapter, *translingual practices* refer to dynamic, spontaneous, and hybrid literacy practices that traverse across languages and negotiate/orchestrate diverse semiotic resources (e.g., speech, writing, pictures) for meaning-making (Canagarajah, 2013; Horner, Lu, Royster, & Trimbur, 2011). In the subsequent sections, we will first describe the setting and participants and then suggest specific pedagogical implications related to enacting a translingual pedagogy in the classroom.

THE SETTING

In order to examine Koryoin children's English language learning and translingual practices, we located children and families in one of the fastest-growing Russian-Korean communities in South Korea, known as "Koryo-chon" (pseudonym). With approximately 2,000 Russian-Korean residents, Koryo-chon is located in a rural city with a population of about 80,000 people in the southwest part of South Korea. Although "Koryoin" ("고려인" in Korean and "Корё сарам" in Russian) is the term that ethnic Koreans living in the post-Soviet states (e.g., Kazakhstan, Russia, and Uzbekistan) use to refer to themselves, it also refers to ethnic Koreans who have migrated from the post-Soviet states to South Korea (in this chapter, we use the term as the latter meaning). With a large influx of Koryoin families to South Korea, a growing body of research has found that many Koryoin children tend to lack Korean language proficiency, and their low Korean proficiency has been a serious obstacle for their academic achievement and their socialization with other Korean peers (Kim, 2018). Unlike many other bilinguals, these Koryoin students need to use and navigate all three languages as they learn English. As many may know, EFL teachers in Korean classrooms, especially in elementary classrooms, heavily use the Korean language to teach English. Thus, Koryoin children should learn Korean in order to learn English, and we cannot overlook their Korean learning when we discuss their English learning. Their use of all three languages (Russian, Korean, English) is almost natural and imperative in their daily lives.

DESCRIPTION OF ENGLISH LANGUAGE LEARNERS: KORYOIN CHILDREN

The focal participants in our qualitative case study were four Koryoin children (two groups of siblings) in the rural Russian-Korean community, "Koryo-chon." Artur (Grade 6) and Mikhail (Grade 4) are brothers; Ludmila (Grade 8) and Stepan (Grade 6) are siblings. When they started participating in this research in Spring 2018, Artur/Mikhail and Ludmila/Stepan had lived in Korea for one year and three-and-a-half years, respectively. All four are friends and live in the same apartment complex in "Koryo-chon" where they mostly use Russian except when communicating with monolingual-Korean speakers. They were all born in Uzbekistan and have a high proficiency in their L1 – Russian. However, they came to Korea with different language learning experiences and histories. In Uzbekistan, Artur's English learning experience began in his fifth year of Uzbekistani elementary school, whereas Mikhail didn't receive any English education in or out of school. In contrast, Ludmila started to learn English as a foreign language in third grade while Stepan learned the English alphabet and basic English words in a private institute in Uzbekistan.

Before migrating to Korea, Artur and Mikhail had private Korean lessons for a year in preparation for living in Korea, while Ludmila and Stepan did not receive any Korean language education in Uzbekistan. They found English much easier to acquire than Korean. With more confidence in English, they tend to be more motivated to learn English as an L2 and to more frequently use English via their social networking sites.

PEDAGOGICAL APPLICATION AND INNOVATION

From the exploration of the four Koryoin children's translingual practices, we have found that Koryoin children have developed their own *translingual strategies* in order to facilitate their language learning and to promote content learning. They voluntarily engage in translingual practices across varied contexts, especially at home and in the community, which suggests that it is critical for teachers to design a classroom context where English learners (ELs) feel that their translingual practices are respected and valued. In order to design such a context and enact a translingual pedagogy, we suggest specific pedagogical implications.

First, teachers need to constantly encourage their students to use their full linguistic repertoires and non-linguistic semiotic resources (e.g., images) for learning English and subject matter. For instance, in a summer computer-coding class where English and Korean both were used for instruction, two Koryoin children were paired up to complete a task written in English and Korean (two L2s) and with many visuals while discussing and solving problems in L1 (Russian) as seen in Figure 5.3.1. Although this scene was observed in a content classroom, ESL/EFL teachers can certainly design a translingual context where ELs are encouraged to use multiple semiotic resources.

Second, teachers can purposefully design activities and assignments that require students to engage in translingual practices (e.g., *translating* their writing, producing *bilingual texts*) (read the three specific examples presented after Figure 5.3.5).

Third, teachers can choose texts that have multilingual versions so that students can read and/or listen to multilingual texts and take notes in multiple languages. For instance, one of the participants, Stepan (a beginning EL) was a huge fan of a Japanese manga series, *One Piece*, which is available in multiple languages (e.g., English, Korean, and Russian). Stepan read the Russian version several times when he lived in Uzbekistan, and later he read the Korean and English versions since he moved to Korea. Interestingly, while reading the English version, he kept the lexical notebook to record some useful expressions and unfamiliar English words while using all three languages. After reading the English and Korean versions, he drew a comic strip to capture one interesting storyline using Korean, English, and images as seen in Figure 5.3.2.

Fourth, creating multilingual and multimodal Word Walls can be an effective resource in a translingual classroom. Teachers can create and post a list of basic "school vocabulary" (see Figure 5.3.3) in English, Korean, and Russian to have Koryoin students frequently exposed to previously learned English words with Korean and Russian translations.

Figure 5.3.1 Koryoin children utilize three languages and non-linguistic resources

Source: Photo by Jinsil Jang

Figure 5.3.2 Stepan's drawing of a comic strip after reading multiple versions of texts

Source: Photo by Jinsil Jang

Figure 5.3.3 The school vocabulary chart in English, Korean, and Russian displayed in the classroom

Source: Photo by Jinsil Jang

Lastly, when teachers try to enact a translingual pedagogy in their classroom, they should not overlook the importance of explicit instruction on *how to engage in translingual practices*. Even if teachers encourage students to use multiple languages in their classroom, students might not feel that it is appropriate or desirable to use their first, home, or heritage languages in the classroom. Also, they might not know what it means to take advantage of their full linguistic repertoires. Thus, teachers should explicitly teach students how to use their multiple languages and literacies for learning. For example, our trilingual participants have developed their own translingual strategies for learning their L2s (English and Korean) outside school, which gives us insights into translingual strategies instruction. For instance, when Artur (6th grade male) tried to solve multiple-choice reading comprehension questions on Roman public bathrooms (as seen in Figure 5.3.4), he understood the reading passage in English and even drew the image of Roman public bathrooms after reading the passage, but unfortunately, he couldn't understand the question written in Korean. Because of this, he had to look up the meaning of the Korean vocabulary. At that point, he tried to use different online sources/dictionaries and search engines (e.g., English-based *Google Translate*, Korean-based *Naver*, a Korean

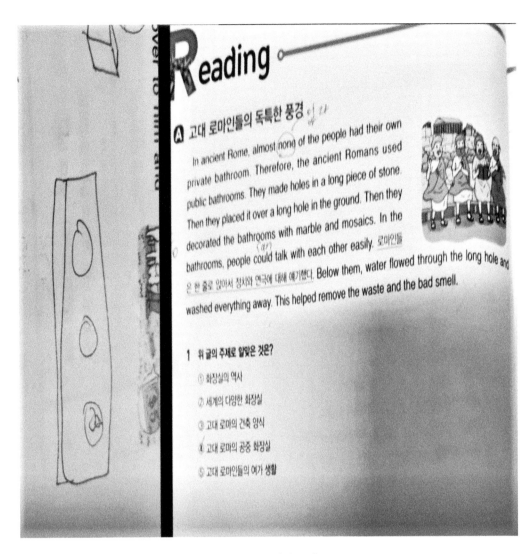

Figure 5.3.4 Artur's reading workbook written in English and Korean

Source: Photo by Jinsil Jang

website), but he came to learn that (a) the direct translation to and from Russian and Korean did not always give him the most accurate meaning, (b) an English-based *Google Translate* search served him better for translation to and from "Russian and English," and (c) a Korean-based *Naver* (Korean website) search served him better for translation to and from "English and Korean." Thus, he often first used *Google Translate* to translate to and from Russian and English and then used *Naver* to translate English to Korean instead of directly translating to and from Russian and Korean.

Given Artur's translingual practice, we recommend that teachers offer explicit translingual strategies instruction (e.g., how to use different online sources in multiple languages and images). For instance, they can explicitly teach students how to conduct an image search for a word (drawing on a non-linguistic semiotic resource) so that students can check if their understanding of a word is accurate. When students read about Roman public bathrooms, their image search can lead them to the image like the one in Figure 5.3.5, which can facilitate their comprehension of the reading passage.

Figure 5.3.5 Image from the search for words 'Roman public bathrooms'

Source: "Ostia Antica Latrines" by A Road Retraveled is licensed under CC BY-ND 2.0

Based on our work with Koryoin children, we would like to introduce three specific translingual activities, "Everyday Literacy Project," producing "Bilingual Identity Texts," and a "Bilingual Speech Contest," which can be implemented in EFL/ESL classrooms.

An "Everyday Literacy Project" can be a powerful way to connect our ELs' out-of-school literacies to in-class practices. ELs first identify and investigate language/literacy practices around their everyday lives across various contexts. For instance, they can gather everyday texts (local ethnic magazines, newspapers, signs) in multiple languages (e.g., Russian, Korean, English) and examine how languages are used beyond their classroom (e.g., in a public library, a local church, a community center, or on social networking sites) (see Figures 5.3.6 and 5.3.7 for a sign post and a bus map written in multiple languages). Then, students can write a brief report in which they examine the languages and cultures present in their everyday texts and compare it with a study of the languages and cultures in their academic literacy practices.

Figure 5.3.6 Signpost explaining recycling in six languages

Source: Photo by Jinsil Jang

Another activity we recommend is creating bi- and multilingual texts, which can be an empowering translingual activity. For instance, producing "bilingual identity texts" (detailed by Cummins, Hu, Markus, & Kristiina Montero, 2015) through translingual practice allows students to express their ideas and identities more freely. Beginning-level ELs can design digital stories about themselves or their interests/hobbies in the multiple languages they use in their daily lives (visit http://digitalstorytelling.coe.uh.edu/ to learn more about educational uses of digital storytelling). With more advanced ELs, they can engage in a role-play through which they argue for or against the use of translingual practices in the classroom from the positions of different stakeholders (e.g., teachers, administrators, policy makers). Then, students write an opinion essay individually or collaboratively. Such translingual activities can be a powerful way to validate students' identity, voice, and agency.

The last activity we recommend is a "Bilingual Speech Contest" which can be another compelling way to involve students in translingual practices. For instance, our student, Artur (Grade 6), participated in the contest. He wrote two versions of a speech script in his L1 (Russian) and Korean and then delivered a speech

Figure 5.3.7 Bus map written in multiple languages

Source: Photo by Jinsil Jang

in both languages (Korean speech first and Russian later). While preparing for the speech contest, he constantly used all three languages to make sense of his script and speech.

CONCLUSION

Many ELs engage in translingual practices for language learning and everyday communication. Yet teachers may not know their students' rich and meaningful engagement in translingual practices. Thus, at varying degrees, students' translingual competence may not be acknowledged in the classroom. While implementing translingual practices into classroom instruction (e.g., assessment issues of how to evaluate translingual texts) is a daunting task (Gevers, 2018), we hope that teachers will be able to develop a translingual perspective of language teaching and learning to enact a translingual pedagogy. Furthermore, teacher educators should engage pre- and in-service teachers to problematize the dominant monolingual ideology and rethink their pedagogical practices with children who already engage in translingual and multimodal practices in their everyday lives.

REFERENCES

Canagarajah, A. S. (Ed.). (2013). *Literacy as translingual practice: Between communities and classrooms.* New York: Routledge.

Cummins, J., Hu, S., Markus, P., & Kristiina Montero, M. (2015). Identity texts and academic achievement: Connecting the dots in multilingual school contexts. *TESOL Quarterly, 49*(3), 555–581.

Gevers, J. (2018). Translingualism revisited: Language difference and hybridity in L2 writing. *Journal of Second Language Writing, 40,* 73–83.

Horner, B., Lu, M. Z., Royster, J. J., & Trimbur, J. (2011). Language difference in writing: Toward a translingual approach. *College English, 73*(3), 303–321.

Kim, K. (2018). Children's experiences of international migration with particular references to Koreyin children in Gwangju metropolitan. *The Institute for Cross-Cultural Studies Seoul, 24*(2), 61–103.

UNIT 6
Multiliteracies in TESOL

CHAPTER 6

A Pedagogy of Multiliteracies and Its Role in English Language Education

Shakina Rajendram

FRAMING THE ISSUE

The digital age has reshaped our communication landscape by changing the way language is used and creating new communication forms and functions. As societies become more globally interconnected through digital technologies, a wider and more complex range of communication modes is needed to disseminate and exchange knowledge. Against this backdrop, individuals have simultaneously become consumers and creators of digitally mediated communication (Lotherington & Jenson, 2011). The communication practices of our learners today are intrinsically multimodal, as they naturally draw on multiple semiotic modes such as text, images, video, and sound to express their ideas, consume information, and create new content on social media, photo- and video-sharing websites, videogaming, podcasts, vlogs, blogs, and so on. The evolving and dynamic nature of communication in the 21st century calls for an expanded understanding of what it means to be literate. Whereas traditional notions of literacy were confined to the acquisition of language skills, new communication modes now necessitate learners developing literacies beyond the linguistic (e.g., digital literacy, information literacy, visual literacy, media literacy, data literacy). However, this does not mean sidestepping the teaching of language skills. It is critically important for learners to develop an integrated repertoire of multimodal literacies as well as competencies in reading, writing, listening, and speaking in order to successfully navigate their academic, social, digital, and workplace environments.

A growing body of research on first language (L1) literacy has responded to this need by exploring the affordances of digital and multimodal literacy practices to enrich traditional print-based L1 literacy teaching (Yi, 2014). However, these new literacy practices have not received as much attention in second language (L2) contexts, and there is still a pull back toward more conventional, pen-and-paper English language teaching (ELT) approaches (Kiss & Mizusawa, 2018). The studies that do address new literacies in L2 classrooms focus more on the use of digital technologies and less on the intricate intersections between the diverse modalities and literacies making up a learner's communicative repertoire (Lotherington & Jenson, 2011; Ntelioglou, 2012). Lankshear, Snyder, and Green (2000) argue that digital technologies tend to have an add-on nature in the classroom because teachers often try to fit technology into their existing teaching approaches, for example, by getting learners to type up a story on their computer rather than handwrite it on paper. Lankshear et al. refer to this add-on approach as a "digital makeover" (p. 102) and caution that simply adding new technologies or a multimodal element to existing approaches does not automatically constitute effective pedagogy. Teachers instead need to reinvent their ELT pedagogy by incorporating technology and multimodality into language learning in more symbiotic ways. This involves designing lessons that are informed from the very onset by learners' diverse and intersecting literacies. The evolving global communication landscape calls for more integrative ELT approaches that embed language learning with the multimodal literacies learners need to "comprehend, manage, create and communicate knowledge in our technologically sophisticated, multilingual, culturally diverse globalized societies" (Taylor, Bernhard, Garg, & Cummins, 2008, p. 275). The multiliteracies pedagogy is an example of such an approach.

Concepts and Theoretical Considerations

Background and Rationale for the Multiliteracies Pedagogy

The multiliteracies pedagogy was introduced in 1996 by the New London Group (NLG) as an approach to literacy pedagogy that would be receptive to the changing cultural, linguistic, and communicative realities of increasingly globalized societies. In developing the multiliteracies pedagogy, the NLG aimed to broaden existing understandings of literacy to account for the multiplicity of discourses present in the emerging global order. The term multiliteracies encapsulated two foundational ideas regarding this multiplicity: (1) the scope of literacy pedagogy needed to be expanded in response to the multiple interrelated cultures and languages in society, and (2) literacy pedagogy needed to incorporate the multiple modalities and text forms associated with new technologies (New London Group, 1996). At the time of the introduction of multiliteracies, the rapid widespread use of the internet had led to the burgeoning of new forms of communication which integrated textual and linguistic modalities of meaning-making with audio, visual, spatial, and behavioural modalities (Cope & Kalantzis, 2000). Helping learners to navigate this new multimodal world of communication required teaching them a new multimodal literacy. However, traditional literacy pedagogy, or what the NLG termed "mere literacy", was dominated by linguistic modalities centered on the teaching of reading and writing (New London Group, 1996, p. 64). Furthermore, despite the existence of multiple Englishes in culturally and linguistically diverse modern communities, the successful outcome of traditional literacy instruction was still conceived as the mastery of a single, standardized form of English. Given that the proliferation of new technologies, and the growing local diversity and global connectedness of societies were reshaping the way that language was used, the NLG believed that teaching only textual and linguistic modes in a single formal written language was insufficient. Literacy pedagogy needed to change to be responsive to social change.

To address the fundamental question of "what" this new literacy pedagogy should be, the NLG developed the concept of Design. Underlying the notion of Design is the belief that literacy educators and learners are "both inheritors of patterns and conventions of meaning and at the same time active designers of meaning" (p. 65). Meaning is not seen as something that resides passively in texts but as something that is actively derived through a dynamic process of Designing (Warner & Dupuy, 2018). The Designing process involves drawing on Available Designs (the various meaning-making resources available at a learner's disposal) to transform existing meanings into new Redesigned meanings. The NLG propose that during the Designing process, learners can draw on six available design elements or modes of meaning-making:

1. linguistic (e.g. learner's home and school languages, dialects, rhetorical structures)

2. visual (e.g. images, colours)

3. audio (e.g. music, sound effects)

4. gestural (e.g. movement)

5. spatial (e.g. positioning of objects)

6. multimodal (i.e. a combination of modes).

Explaining the multimodal interconnectivity and integration between the different design elements, the NLG drew attention to the concepts of hybridity and intertextuality. Hybridity refers to the creative combination of established meaning-making modes such as in popular music where cultural forms and traditions are combined with new audio electronics to create hybrid musical genres. Intertextuality refers to the complex ways that meaning is established through their relationships with other texts, narratives, and modes of meaning, An example of intertextuality is when viewers of a movie come to understand its meaning by making connections between the various roles, scenes, and narratives in the movie or when they make connections between the movie they are watching and other movies or texts.

Key Components of the Multiliteracies Pedagogy

The NLG proposed that a multiliteracies pedagogy based on the concept of multimodal, hybrid, and intertextual designing could be enacted by educators through four components: Situated Practice, Overt Instruction, Critical Framing, and Transformed Practice. These four components were later renamed by

Kalantzis and Cope (2008) as Experiencing, Conceptualising, Analysing and Applying. Situated Practice or Experiencing is concerned with immersing a community of learners in meaningful and authentic opportunities for them to reflect on and tap into their lived experiences, interests, and ways of understanding the world (Ntelioglou, 2012). Situated Practice involves considering the affective and sociocultural identities and needs of their learners, and creating secure spaces where learners can take risks and trust their peers and teachers to guide them. Overt Instruction or Conceptualising focuses on scaffolding learning activities by building on what learners already know and giving them explicit information to guide their learning. Here, the NLG cautions that Overt Instruction does not imply the direct transmission of information, rote memorization, or drills. Rather, the aim of this stage should be to provide instruction that helps learners to gain conscious awareness and control of their own learning (Vinogradova, 2017).

In the Critical Framing or Analysing component of the multiliteracies pedagogy, learners explore, analyse, and constructively critique texts in relation to the "historical, social, cultural, political, ideological, and value-centered relations of particular systems of knowledge and social practice" (New London Group, 1996, p. 86). The goal of this critical practice is to distance themselves personally and theoretically from what they have already learned and mastered so that they can find ways to innovate creatively. This forms the basis for the fourth component of the pedagogy, Transformed Practice or Applying Creatively. This step affords learners the opportunity to apply what they have learned from their critical reflection and newly learned literacy practices to innovate new texts, which are embedded within their own contexts and inspired by their own goals and values. Transformed Practice usually involves learners creating hybrid, intertextual multimodal texts which combine various design elements to transform the meaning of existing texts. Examples of these texts include comics, graphic novels, brochures, digital stories, animations, short films, web pages, slideshows, and music videos.

Although the four-component framework of the multiliteracies pedagogy has been critiqued as leading to a linear and bounded approach to understanding literacy engagement (Leander & Boldt, 2013), these components were not intended to be hierarchical or linear. Kalantzis and Cope (2008) describe "the process of moving backward and forward across and between these different pedagogical moves as 'weaving'" (p. 28). When the four components of the pedagogy are "woven" together, each is improved and transformed by the others. For example, when Overt Instruction is founded on learners' interests and real-life experiences, as uncovered during Situated Practice, the role of the teacher during instruction would be to co-construct knowledge with learners and scaffold their learning rather than just transmit information to them. In the same way, when Critical Framing is linked to Transformed Practice, learners' critical reflection will lead to practical action grounded in authentic contexts and purposes.

Connections Between Multiliteracies and Other Theories

Considering multiliteracies and pedagogical approaches that emphasize their importance, it is critical to recognize that new pedagogies do not exist in isolation or dismiss approaches developed earlier. For example, Cope and Kalantzis (2000) emphasize that it is important for existing literacy teaching approaches to build on each other instead of working in isolation or opposition to one another. Pointing out the similarities between multiliteracies and other language teaching approaches, they explain that the multiliteracies pedagogy aims to supplement current teaching practices rather than to replace or negate what teachers already do in the classroom. Accordingly, Cole and Pullen (2010) posit that the characteristic of the multiliteracies pedagogy that best aligns with contemporary education is its ability to integrate with and extend other educational theories and pedagogies. Multiliteracies has been tied to several other theories, such as Cummins' (2001) Academic Expertise Framework, which focuses on the importance of building on learners' prior knowledge, critical inquiry, and active self-regulated learning.

The notion of Situated Practice, where teachers draw on learners' identities, interests, lived experiences, and social positioning is also consistent with key concepts in critical pedagogy, critical race theory, and postcolonial, post-structural, and feminist theories (Ntelioglou, 2012). Multiliteracies has also informed the work of New Literacy Studies and "new literacies" scholars (Coiro, Knobel, Lankshear, & Leu, 2008) who address social inequities by challenging traditional print-based approaches to literacy and arguing for new literacies to be included in schooling practices. Examples of these new literacies include digital literacy, which refers to the ability to use and work with digital tools such as computers; and information literacy, which refers to the ability to find, understand, evaluate, create, and disseminate information in various formats.

In the field of second language acquisition, the multiliteracies pedagogy has been used to resist the mainstream view of language acquisition as primarily a cognitive and individual process. The multiliteracies pedagogy is compatible with more critical and sociocultural approaches to second language education because of the value it places on learners' multilingualism and multiculturalism. This has important implications for English language education, especially in linguistically and culturally diverse contexts.

Implications for English Language Education

In recent decades, multiliteracies has informed the practices of teachers in classrooms around the world. However, despite the far-reaching influence of the NLG's ideas in mainstream education, in many L2 classrooms, language is still taught as a set of productive (speaking and writing) and receptive (listening and reading) skills, without consideration for the socially constructed, multimodal features of language (Lotherington & Jenson, 2011). Kiss and Mizusawa (2018) argue that language teaching, specifically the teaching of writing, seems to exist in a sociocultural vacuum, governed by prescriptive standards and structures instead of social realities. In contrast to this, the multiliteracies pedagogy in the context of ELT sees language as dynamic, multidimensional and multimodal, involving different communication forms which are dependent on social context, audience, participants, and purpose. To help students develop the richness and complexity of communication practices which are evident in the communities of practice students participate in, teachers need to design pedagogical practices that themselves are rich, complex, and reflective of society. Multiliteracies engage learners in rich and highly contextualised language learning by expanding their literacy repertoires to include the fuller range of communicational forms used in society (e.g. linguistic, visual, audio, gestural, tactile, and digital).

Making Provision for Different Learning Styles and Abilities

The multiliteracies pedagogy in ELT is inclusive, as it makes provision for learners with different learning styles and abilities as well as learners who struggle with conventional literacy skills. Kiss and Mizusawa (2018) remind us that learners' language ability is never a measure of their cognitive ability. If teachers restrict their learners to use only oral or written language to express what they know, teachers may not get an accurate representation of learners' background knowledge, their diverse literacy strengths, or their mastery of classroom content. The multiliteracies pedagogy allows learners with lower levels of English proficiency to leverage modes such as art, drama, music, and video to help them express their thoughts and ideas. When learners are able to demonstrate their knowledge, contribute to class discussions, and complete tasks through these modes of communication, it will make them feel more confident in their own ability and instill a sense of accomplishment in them (Burke & Hardware, 2015). Teachers can turn this into valuable opportunities for language learning by planning their language instruction around the knowledge and ideas learners have demonstrated multimodally and providing the necessary scaffolding to broaden learners' knowledge. The more learners' academic self-concept is nurtured, the more academically engaged and emotionally invested they will be. Teachers have used the multiliteracies pedagogy to engage English Learners (ELs) cognitively while also affirming their individual and group identities, such as through creating multimodal and multilingual identity texts representing learners' lived experiences, languages, and cultures (Giampapa, 2010); composing intertextual graphic stories depicting learner's family stories and immigration experiences (Danzak, 2011); and recording digital podcasts to express different aspects of their identities (Wilson, Chavez, & Anders, 2012).

Developing Critical Literacy

Traditionally, language instruction was based only on teaching the four skills and did not leave much room for the development of critical thinking. As societies become more and more diverse and globalized, the English language classroom needs to be a space that not only promotes the development of language skills but also empowers ELs to be contributing members of society. ELT pedagogy based on multiliteracies moves English language learning beyond just the acquisition of language skills, and supports the development of critical literacy. For example, in Danzak's (2011) graphic story writing project, ELs in a middle school English for Speakers of

Other Languages (ESOL) class in the United States created multimodal graphic stories to explain their families' motivation for leaving their home country, to describe their emigration journeys, and to compare and contrast their experiences in their home country and in their current home. Besides affirming their identities, this multimodal composing activity also helped students to become more critically literate, as it prompted them to critically examine their social and cultural contexts and address issues such as racism, anti-immigration discourses, gender equality, and social justice in their graphic stories. Similarly, in Wilson et al.'s (2012) digital podcast project which was carried out among eight ELs in a Grade 8 English Language Development class in southern Arizona, students exercised critical literacy by analysing and interpreting images and texts and reflecting on significant events that shaped their identities. Similarly, in a digital storytelling and video book report project conducted among Grade 8 English as a Second Language (ESL) students in an urban school in Newfoundland and Labrador, Canada, the students examined controversial issues such as religion and death in a novel by situating their understanding of the novel within their own lived experiences and sociocultural viewpoints (Burke & Hardware, 2015). The activities and projects presented help learners to develop literacy as an integrated set of linguistic, sociocultural, and cognitive skills within a critical framework rather than as a set of productive and receptive skills within a sociocultural void.

Promoting Interdisciplinary Learning

In addition to making learners more critically literate, language learning activities based on the multiliteracies pedagogy also promote interdisciplinary learning and language acquisition across the curriculum. For example, in Danzak's (2011) project, the multiliteracies pedagogy was integrated with academic English language instruction to support the language learning of students across content areas. As students composed their stories using different modalities, including graphic organizers, journals, and technology, they were motivated to learn new academic words and phrases such as "ancestors", "legend", "leading figure", and "national hero" to make their narratives more compelling (Danzak, 2011, p. 192). Through the multimodal composing activity, students also learned how to use skills such as sequencing, describing, explaining, and comparing and contrasting to fulfil different communicative functions. Practising these functions in the context of a meaningful project helped them to build skills that could be transferable to other content-areas. Thus, using the multiliteracies pedagogy enables teachers to bridge their students' language learning with their academic development.

Building on Learners' Linguistic and Cultural Diversity

Another contribution the multiliteracies pedagogy makes in English language education is that it brings linguistic and cultural diversity into the language classroom. The starting point for L2 learning based on the multiliteracies pedagogy is learners' funds of knowledge, which encompasses the skills, knowledge, lived experiences, and rich linguistic and cultural resources they bring to the classroom. This is consistent with plurilingual and translanguaging pedagogies which view the diversity of languages and cultural experiences of learners as resources for effective learning. Teachers using a translanguaging approach pedagogy would design instructional units, lesson plans, and assessments that are informed by learners' diverse language practices, semiotic resources, and ways of knowing (García, Johnson, & Seltzer, 2017). Curiel (2017) proposes a "translanguaging multiliteracies" pedagogy, where learners are encouraged to draw from all their linguistic resources to design, produce, and distribute multimodal and multilingual texts and make intertextual connections within and across different content areas such as language arts, science, and social studies. Because of the value the multiliteracies pedagogy places on learners' linguistic and cultural diversity, it has been effective in schools where there are learners of different ethnicities and linguistic backgrounds. For example, in a dual language multimodal identity text project carried out among 27 kindergarten ELs in a highly diverse suburban elementary school in Toronto, Canada, learners' home languages were incorporated into the identity texts and combined with visual, written, and oral modes (Taylor et al., 2008). The emphasis placed on learners' L1s in the creation of the texts positioned them as "experts in their cultural and linguistic funds of knowledge" (p. 277).

Encouraging Student Engagement and Agency

By drawing on ELs' cultural and linguistic repertoires as valuable resources in the classroom, teachers can make English learning more relatable, thereby transforming learners who are resistant to learning English into engaged learners who are active participants in their learning. Yi's (2014) review of empirical research on multimodal literacy practices in ELT showed that participation in multimodal projects improved the attendance of at-risk students and created a more positive and highly visible school presence for students who had been treated as deficit or delinquent before. Consistent with Yi, Rajendram's (2015) review of studies using the multiliteracies pedagogy with ELs at the elementary, secondary, and tertiary levels indicated that it promoted student engagement by enabling all students to actively participate in their own learning instead of merely receiving instruction from the teacher. Students in Rajendram's review also demonstrated agency and leadership by offering their expertise to peers and taking turns to lead different stages of the creation process. Likewise, Kajee's (2011) study which took place in an undergraduate English as an Additional Language (EAL) classroom in Johannesburg, South Africa, found that by combining multiple semiotic resources with learners' linguistic and cultural funds of knowledge such as African praise poems which are sung to show respect to important people, the multiliteracies pedagogy enabled learners to "reconstruct, remake and reshape their own social identities as subjective agents of change" (p. 250). The findings of these various studies are consistent with the NLG's suggestion that learners can actively shape their own social futures by creating new social and literacy practices that impact their community, workplace, and public futures.

The multiliteracies pedagogy has significant benefits for English language education. Firstly, it expands learners' linguistic repertoire to include a range of linguistic, visual, audio, tactile, and digital communication forms. Secondly, it is more inclusive of learners with diverse abilities, learning styles, and levels of proficiency, as it allows them to leverage alternative modes of expression (e.g. visuals, drama, music) to express what they know. Thirdly, learners develop critical literacy as they examine and analyze the sociocultural and political contexts and issues surrounding the multimodal texts they use or produce. Fourthly, the multiliteracies pedagogy infuses language with content, thereby promoting learning across the curriculum and building interdisciplinary knowledge. Fifthly, this pedagogy is linguistically and culturally responsive, as it draws on the lived experiences and home languages and cultures of multilingual ELs. Finally, multiliteracies promotes student engagement and encourages learners to take ownership over their own learning. The following section discusses the challenges of implementing the multiliteracies pedagogy in English language education and provides recommendations for future directions.

FUTURE DIRECTIONS

Although the benefits of the multiliteracies pedagogy for English language education are undeniable, there are several challenges which need to be addressed before the pedagogy can be effectively implemented in classrooms. One obstacle to the successful implementation of the multiliteracies pedagogy is that it is not typically included as a core component of pre- and in-service language teacher education (Burke & Hardware, 2015). Even when a multiliteracies component is included, it is usually only completed as an add-on component rather than as a main part of the teacher education curriculum (Rowsell, Kosnik, & Beck, 2008). If teachers do not have adequate preparation for designing and enacting the pedagogy in their classrooms, they will not be able to harness its full potential for language learning. Without relevant preservice teacher education courses and in-service professional development opportunities, teachers may also be unsure about how to evaluate learning based on multiliteracies. The multiliteracies pedagogy requires different forms of assessment than regular language teaching methods, as the emphasis of the approach is on developing critical self-reflection, engaging in constructive criticism of texts, recognizing intertextual connections, and designing hybrid, multimodal, and multilingual texts. Thus, teachers need to integrate more holistic, formative assessments that capture what learners are doing throughout the different components of the multiliteracies pedagogy rather than only evaluating their finished products. McClay and Mackey (2009) also recommend using distributive assessment models where teachers collaborate with their students on what they need to assess. This includes peer-to-peer assessments which give students the chance to collaborate and assist each other and sideshadowing protocols where students reflect on and appraise their works-in-progress during the different stages of development with the help of the teacher. In examination-oriented programs, it may be harder for teachers to move away altogether from the focus on measurable learning outcomes. Teachers in those contexts would benefit greatly from research on how to bridge the gap between the conventional language assessments needed to prepare students for high-stakes standardized tests and the more holistic measures needed to assess students' learning within the multiliteracies pedagogy.

Another challenge in implementing the multiliteracies pedagogy in English language classes may be the lack of access to multimodal ELT resources in some contexts. In general, ELT textbooks have become less text-heavy and more visual, and ELT publishers are integrating multimodal and digital elements into their materials much more than before. Examples of these materials include the National Geographic Learning's Keynote textbook series which includes TED Talks, a mobile application, and website resources, and Cambridge University Press's Collaborate textbook series which includes documentaries, videos, audio, digital workbooks, and activities for interactive whiteboards. Thus, teachers have a greater variety of multimodal and digital ELT textbooks and materials that they can select from. Teachers can also augment their existing ELT books and materials with multimodal resources such as blogs, memes, film, videos, podcasts, slam poetry, music, and social media, integrating these resources in lessons in a seamless way. However, in contexts where teachers may not have access to multimodal resources or digital technologies in the classroom, learners could contribute artifacts from their own lives, for example by bringing in posters, brochures, and flyers from their neighbourhood, collecting food labels, taking pictures of the different languages they see on buildings in their communities, and interviewing family members and neighbours. Teachers in collaborative communities of practice can compile these resources into a shared database. Since language is socially situated, using resources from outside the classroom can contextualize learners' understanding of language and engage them in communication as it exists in their social worlds (Lotherington & Jenson, 2011). To develop learners' critical literacy, teachers can also plan activities for learners to engage critically with these authentic resources by analysing, discussing, and redesigning them. In contexts where authentic resources in English are not easily available, learners could create simple multimodal resources themselves, such as comics, picture books, brochures, newsletters, and posters. Including learner-selected and learner-created resources in the classroom can encourage more agentive and participatory learning, extend students' language learning beyond the walls of the classroom, and connect their in-school language learning with their out-of-school lifeworlds, thereby making language learning more meaningful, relevant, and engaging.

Discussion Questions

1. How can you use the multiliteracies pedagogy to support the English language learning of your students while developing their interdisciplinary knowledge?
2. In the Critical Framing/Analysing step of the multiliteracies pedagogy, learners critically explore, analyse, interpret, and critique texts. What are some questions learners can ask about their textbooks to practise their critical thinking?
3. Reflect on the linguistic and cultural diversity of your community. Think about a multiliteracies project that could draw on the diverse linguistic and cultural resources in your community.
4. What are some ways you can incorporate the multiliteracies pedagogy in your classroom if you have limited or no access to technology?
5. The multiliteracies pedagogy requires using more holistic forms of assessment. What criteria would you use to assess the multimodal texts that your learners create?

Resources for Further Exploration

1. Cope, B., & Kalantzis, M. (Eds.). (2015). *A pedagogy of multiliteracies: Learning by design*. New York, NY: Palgrave Macmillan.
   This book, edited by two of the original members of the New London Group, describes the implementation of multiliteracies pedagogy through new, digital media platforms in a variety of countries, including Australia, Canada, Greece, Italy, Japan, South Africa, and the United States.

2. Kalantzis, M., Cope, B., Chan, E., & Dalley-Trim, L. (2016). *Literacies* (2nd ed.). Melbourne, Australia: Cambridge University Press.

   This book provides a comprehensive introduction to the use of new literacies within a rapidly changing media environment, with a focus on designing learning experiences that combine reading, writing, oral, visual, audio, gestural, spatial, and tactile modes of communication.

3. Lotherington, H. (2007) From literacy to multiliteracies in ELT. In J. Cummins & C. Davison (Eds.). *International handbook of English language teaching.* (pp. 891–905). New York, NY: Springer.

   This book chapter examines the evolution of literacy into multiliteracies in English language teaching and discusses the implications of this epistemological shift for digitally, pedagogically, and ecologically responsive English language teaching and learning practices.

4. New Learning Online: http://newlearningonline.com/

   This website provides information on Mary Kalantzis's and Bill Cope's latest research in literacies, multiliteracies, New Learning, Learning by Design, and e-learning ecologies and contains a wide-ranging collection of articles, videos, lectures, and other resources in these areas.

5. Paesani, K., Allen, H. W., & Dupuy, B. (2016). *A multiliteracies framework for collegiate foreign language teaching.* Upper Saddle River, NJ: Pearson.

   This handbook is a valuable resource for foreign language educators who would like to use multiliteracies pedagogy in their language curriculum, instruction, and assessments, as the book provides educators with sample learning activities, lesson plans, and assessment materials.

REFERENCES

Burke, A., & Hardware, S. (2015). Honouring ESL students' lived experiences in school learning with multiliteracies pedagogy. *Language, Culture and Curriculum, 28*(2), 143–157.

Coiro, J., Knobel, M., Lankshear, C., & Leu, D. J. (Eds.). (2008). *Handbook of research on new literacies.* New York, NY: Routledge.

Cole, D. R., & Pullen, D. L. (2010). *Multiliteracies in motion: Current theory and practice.* New York, NY: Routledge.

Cope, B., & Kalantzis, M. (2000). Introduction: Multiliteracies: The beginnings of an idea. In B. Cope & M. Kalantzis (Eds.), *Multiliteracies: Literacy learning and the design of social futures* (pp. 3–8). London, UK: Routledge.

Cummins, J. (2001). *Negotiating identities: Education for empowerment in a diverse society.* Los Angeles, CA: California Association for Bilingual Education.

Curiel, L. C. (2017). *Texturing with multimodal texts across content areas: A translanguaging multiliteracies approach to teaching and learning* (Doctoral dissertation). The University of Texas at Austin, Austin, Texas.

Danzak, R. L. (2011). Defining identities through multiliteracies: EL teens narrate their immigration experiences as graphic stories. *Journal of Adolescent & Adult Literacy, 55*(3), 187–196.

García, O., Johnson, S., & Seltzer, K. (2017). *The translanguaging classroom: Leveraging student bilingualism for learning.* Philadelphia: Caslon.

Giampapa, F. (2010). Multiliteracies, pedagogy and identities: Teacher and student voices from a Toronto elementary school. *Canadian Journal of Education, 33*(2), 407–431.

Kajee, L. (2011). Multimodal representations of identity in the English-as-an-additional-language classroom in South Africa. *Language, Culture and Curriculum, 24*(3), 241–252.

Kalantzis, M., & Cope, B. (2008). Digital communications, multimodality and diversity: Towards a pedagogy of multiliteracies. *Scientia Paedagogica Experimentalis, 45*(1), 15–50.

Kiss, T., & Mizusawa, K. (2018). Revisiting the pedagogy of multiliteracies: Writing instruction in a multicultural context. *Changing English, 25*(1), 59–68.

Lankshear, C., Snyder, I., & Green, B. (2000). *Teachers and techno-Literacy: Managing literacy, technology and learning in schools.* Sydney, AU: Allen & Unwin.

Leander, K., & Boldt, G. (2013). Rereading "a pedagogy of multiliteracies": Bodies, texts, and emergence. *Journal of Literacy Research*, 45(1), 22–46.

Lotherington, H., & Jenson, J. (2011). Teaching multimodal and digital literacy in L2 settings: New literacies, new basics, new pedagogies. *Annual Review of Applied Linguistics*, 31, 226–246.

McClay, J. K., & Mackey, M. (2009). Distributed assessment in our space: This is not a rubric. In A. Burke & R. F. Hammett (Eds.), *Assessing new literacies: Perspectives from the new classroom* (pp. 113–132). New York, NY: Peter Lang.

New London Group. (1996). A pedagogy of multiliteracies: Designing social futures. *Harvard Educational Review*, 66(1), 60–92.

Ntelioglou, M. B. Y. (2012). *Drama pedagogies, multiliteracies and embodied learning: Urban teachers and linguistically diverse students make meaning* (Unpublished doctoral dissertation). Ontario Institute for Studies in Education, University of Toronto, Toronto.

Rajendram, S. (2015). Potentials of the multiliteracies pedagogy for teaching English language learners (ELLs): A review of the literature. *Critical Intersections in Education*, 3, 1–18.

Rowsell, J., Kosnik, C., & Beck, C. (2008). Fostering mulitiliteracies pedagogy through pre-service teacher education. *Teaching Education*, 19(2), 109–122.

Taylor, L. K., Bernhard, J. K., Garg, S., & Cummins, J. (2008). Affirming plural belonging: Building on students' family-based cultural and linguistic capital through multiliteracies pedagogy. *Journal of Early Childhood Literacy*, 8(3), 269–294.

Vinogradova, P. (2017). Teaching with digital stories for student empowerment and engagement. In M. Carrier, R. M. Damerow, & K. M. Bailey (Eds.), *Digital language learning and teaching: Research, theory, and practice* (pp. 127–140). New York, NY: Routledge & TIRF.

Warner, C., & Dupuy, B. (2018). Moving toward multiliteracies in foreign language teaching: Past and present perspectives . . . and beyond. *Foreign Language Annals*, 51(1), 116–128. http://doi.org/10.1111/flan.12316

Wilson, A. A., Chavez, K., & Anders, P. L. (2012). "From the Koran and family guy": The expressions of identity in English language learners' digital podcasts. *Journal of Adolescent and Adult Literacy*, 55(5), 374–384.

Yi, Y. (2014). Possibilities and challenges of multimodal literacy practices in teaching and learning English as an additional language. *Language and Linguistics Compass*, 8(4), 158–169.

CASE STUDY 6.1

Using Art to Spark Conversation With Recently Arrived Immigrant English Language Learners in the U.S.

Brian Tauzel

Through a year of arts-based discussion at the Metropolitan Museum of Art (the Met) in New York City (USA), my class of 12th grade English language learners (ELLs) and I collaborated in a dynamic process of multimodal, multilingual meaning-making. Our four class visits to the museum supported my students' language development and particularly their confidence in academic discussions. More importantly, it empowered them to comment on complex political, economic, and social issues. The core principles of a multiliteracies pedagogy ran as threads through our sessions at the museum. A series of "snapshots" or noteworthy moments from three of our lessons is discussed here, illustrating how core elements of a multiliteracies approach coalesced to support students' linguistic and intellectual growth. In my reflection on the outcomes of this approach, I consider its capacity for fostering educational equity and social justice-focused teaching and learning for ELL students.

THE SETTING

In the 2015–2016 school year, my students and I took part in the Astor Educators Initiative, a transformational professional learning community at the Met. The initiative was supported by a grant from the Brooke Astor Fund, and it aimed to connect educators from New York City public schools that serve student populations traditionally underserved by U.S. schools, which in my case meant ELLs and immigrant-origin youth. The program enhanced educators' capacity to design and deliver arts-based lessons using the museum's resources. Student outcomes included: (a) increasing young people's access to the Met's world-renowned art collection, (b) engaging students in collaborative meaning-making through visual inquiry and interpretation, and (c) expanding students' ability to tap into social-emotional learning and critical thinking skills.

During that time, I was teaching 12th grade social studies and ESL classes in a school with an exceptionally diverse student population. Our 350 students came from more than 50 countries and spoke more than 25 different home languages. This school belongs to the Internationals Network for Public Schools (http://internationalsnps.org/), a collective of specialized high schools and middle schools which share a mission of providing high-quality education and advocacy for immigrant ELL students. As of 2020, the network comprised 28 schools and academies across the United States.

By their senior year, my students were already familiar with our school's pedagogical approach of highly collaborative, student-centered, project-based learning. This instructional model encourages continual cross-cultural negotiation and constant translanguaging, a process of multilingual meaning-making (see García,

Sylvan, & Witt, 2011). Thus, our school's instructional approach and the goals of the Astor Educators Initiative were closely aligned with a pedagogy of multiliteracies, which supports participants in collaborative, multimodal, multilingual meaning-making (Cope & Kalantzis, 2009).

DESCRIPTION OF ENGLISH LANGUAGE LEARNERS

The 17 students I took to the museum came from Bangladesh, China, the Dominican Republic, Ecuador, Egypt, Ivory Coast, and Yemen. They brought a wide array of skills, insights, and experiences to our classes. While some drew on extensive formal education in their home countries, others' prior schooling had been interrupted or severely impacted. As a result, students had differing levels of academic literacy, both in English and in other languages. For example, upon entering our school as 9th graders, some students were able to rely on academic writing skills from prior schooling, while others were encountering basic literacy skills for the first time. Students also came from a variety of educational paradigms. At times this resulted in competing assumptions about the relationship between teacher and students, the roles of student participation in class, and beliefs about how knowledge is created and shared between people.

PEDAGOGICAL APPLICATION AND INNOVATION

As an ESL and social studies teacher, I was concerned not only with my students' language development but also with their political socialization. Specifically, I was considering how my students could participate as fully, actively, and critically as possible in our democratic society following graduation. Beyond understanding the U.S. political system and formal pathways of civic engagement (e.g., voting rights, congressional representation, running for a political office), I wanted my students to participate in debate and dialogue and to self-advocate by raising their voices in matters important to them and their communities. I hoped our work at the Met would enhance students' engagement with ideas of power and agency. This manifested even through the simple act of visiting the museum. Museums are places for public learning, but awe-inspiring spaces like the Met can seem to some people intimidating or exclusive. As I watched my students on our first visit, their cautious body language and comments signaled their apprehensiveness. Over the course of our visits, I reminded students that our visits were designed purely for them to explore the museum. During one lesson, the program facilitators had cordoned off gallery space for us, so I told the students playfully that we had reached VIP status. That got some students to laugh and relax a little. By our final visit, students entered and moved through the galleries with confidence. They knew they had the right to be in the space for their own enjoyment and edification.

Keeping in mind the curricular goals outlined above, our discussions in the museum were a catalyst for "a pedagogy for active citizenship, centered on learners as agents in their own knowledge processes, capable of contributing their own as well as negotiating the differences between one community and the next" (Cope & Kalantzis, 2009, p. 172). Centering "visual texts" such as paintings, in our lessons provided an important step toward equity. It afforded all students an opportunity to interrogate complex ideas and contribute to the construction of knowledge, regardless of their literacy skills or ability to access academic writing.

The four core principles of a pedagogy of multiliteracies – situated practice, overt instruction, critical framing, and transformed practice (New London Group, 2000) – ran through all aspects of our program in the museum. And while language development was a critical outcome of our lessons at the Met, the multiliteracies approach also holistically addressed the interplay between linguistic, cultural, and social meaning-making.

Situated Practice – The Known and the New

The first principle of a multiliteracies pedagogy, *situated practice*, permeated all our visits to the Met. In the museum, our core instructional strategy was a group discussion technique called *Pyramid of Inquiry*, developed by our program leader and arts educator, Nicola Giardina (see Giardina, 2018). This approach employs tiers of increasingly complex questions. It starts by eliciting students' prior knowledge and then builds upon their foundational understandings to prompt higher-order thinking and the integration of new ideas through deep conversation among students.

I began each lesson with an invitational round of observation-based questions about an art piece. For example, I would ask, "What do you see or notice?" I typically asked students to jot down their observations, do a "turn and talk" with a partner, or participate in a whole group "whip-around" so that everyone could share a quick initial remark. Students were welcome to respond using complex sentences, short phrases, or even single words. Starting with low-risk questions encouraged everyone to participate, which reinforced students' confidence in their ability to discuss art. This round of observations also generated a collective language bank that students could use to describe the artwork. The ideas they shared could be recorded on poster paper or in notebooks and referenced by students at later points in the lesson.

The next step in the pyramid of inquiry included questions to support inferencing about the artwork. For example, when looking at Winslow Homer's *Dressing for the Carnival* (Figure 6.1.1). I said, "Some of you shared that the people in this picture are celebrating. What makes you say that?" I pushed students to call in the visual evidence that backed their interpretation. This move also served as a bridge between academic writing techniques and discussion techniques. In our classroom, when the students were writing position papers, they had learned linguistic structures that linked their claims to evidence from texts. In the galleries, they practiced linking their claims to visual evidence, underscoring how familiar meaning-making strategies could be applied in new contexts.

At times I had my students tackle inferential questions such as, "What do you think is going on in this picture?" in pairs or small groups. Students then looked more closely at the visual text. This also entailed a negotiation of meaning between students. For example, when guessing the profession of Elijah Boardman, a man in an 18th century portrait (Figure 6.1.2), students pointed out the ornate clothes, accessories, ledgers, and quill pens to support their guesses that he might be a nobleman, banker, scholar, or writer. One student, drawing on prior knowledge from global history courses, said he looked like "a French absolute ruler." The bolts of fabric visible through a doorway behind him eventually helped us understand his vocation as a textiles merchant.

Before the final round of questions, I typically added new information about the artwork or artist. Sometimes I gave a five-minute mini-lecture or provided a paragraph or a page of text, which provided context and

Figure 6.1.1 Winslow Homer, *Dressing for the Carnival*, 1877, Metropolitan Museum of Art

Figure 6.1.2 Ralph Earl, *Elijah Boardman*, 1789, Metropolitan Museum of Art

background information about the artist and their world. For example, I might point out that the vibrantly colored paints used by an artist were incredibly expensive to produce or that the social mores of the artist's world differed in some significant way from ours.

The final questions in the pyramid of inquiry prompted students to integrate this new knowledge by revisiting their initial interpretations of the art. For example, I might ask them:

- Now that you know this information, why do you think the artist made the choice to do X and not Y?

- What do you think the artist was trying to say to us about the world they lived in?

- Do you think this art still matters to people's lives today?

In the process of addressing these more abstract questions, students considered how artists communicate complex meaning to viewers through visual media instead of, or in combination with, alphabetic representations of meaning.

To highlight the other three tenets of a multiliteracies pedagogy – overt instruction, critical framing, and transformed practice – I will zoom in on specific moments from three of our museum visits. Each moment revolves around a different work of art and serves as a "snapshot" of our practice, illustrating how a pedagogy of multiliteracies supported learning in the museum.

Overt Instruction – Tables for Ladies

The principle of overt instruction supports students in sense-making by helping them focus on, name, and organize their learning process. During one lesson, I asked students to interpret a painting by Edward Hopper, *Tables for Ladies* (Figure 6.1.3), which depicts women taking on new roles in the 1930's U.S. workforce. The focus was an intersection of socioeconomic class and gender in the U.S. (see Appendix B for activity details). This lesson also functioned as an example of how different media – visual texts or written texts – can be used as vehicles to express meaning. Throughout the lesson, overt instruction was provided to help students develop their own conceptualizations of work.

Figure 6.1.3 Edward Hopper, *Tables for Ladies*, 1930, Metropolitan Museum of Art

Source: © 2020 Heirs of Josephine N. Hopper/Licensed by Artists Rights Society (ARS), NY

To start the lesson, I asked students to notice the central figure in the painting – a woman, perhaps a waitress in a restaurant, wearing a white apron – and to imagine her work life. They jotted their ideas in journals. What did this woman do at work each day? Did she have a good job? Did they imagine she enjoyed her job?

I knew that many students worked outside of school, often in restaurants or service jobs. In class, students shared stories of working late nights and weekends, being paid under the table, chasing hourly wages, and feeling the satisfaction of a paycheck. Tapping into situated practice, I asked students to draw on their own firsthand knowledge of work, socioeconomic status, and labor exploitation while analyzing Hopper's painting. Some students made connections with workplace gender dynamics in the United States and in their home countries. Others brought up workplace politics, suggesting a hierarchical relationship between the central figure in the painting, the woman in white, and the woman in black at the cash register, permitted to handle money. One student imagined the woman in white as trapped in her job, working so many hours to survive that she was unable to hone new skills that would advance her career. The subsequent conversation centered on distinctions between having a job, done primarily for monetary gain, and having a career, aimed at lifelong stability, professional advancement, or personal fulfilment.

I asked the students to record their initial interpretations in their notebooks and then provided them with new contextual information shared through overt instruction. A decade before this painting was completed, women in America won the right to vote all across the country. Within the intervening decade, the 1920s, gender roles changed dramatically in American society. We focused on the significance of the title of the work, *Tables for Ladies*, and reflected on things we take for granted – joining the workforce, earning your own money, spending it however you wanted (even just by going to a restaurant) – as representations of a radical social transformation for many American women. Financial independence led to many other possible new freedoms.

We then did a collective reading of the poem "New Freedom," by Carla Cherry (Cherry, 2015), one of the teachers in my Astor Educators Initiative cohort. Her poem (reproduced here with permission of the author) was inspired by Hopper's painting (Figure 6.1.3). I added an in-text gloss with synonyms and short definitions to help my students with challenging vocabulary.

New Freedom

This couple is here every Thursday night
He hangs her coat, her hat; his coat, his hat
They order the meatloaf special
Leave a dime after the bill

Every night there are bottles of sparkling water
adorning this buffet table
grapefruit arranged in a line
fruit basket in the middle with a sole pineapple, oranges, apples
surrounded by heads of lettuce.
I serve plate after plate, balanced adroitly on tray against bosom

Do they ever think about the burn in my back
from ferrying fruit and meals from kitchen to table
or how my waist itches
from tying this apron's bow as tight as my smile?

That new cashier complains
about her aching feet. She stands in the same spot.
Taps out figures and gives back change all day, into night, as
I pocket my clinking tips each trip from table to kitchen.

We women got the vote.
Cut our hair and hemlines
Swung our hips to the beat and smoked in public.
I went from scrubbing floors in my mama's kitchen
and ironing my father's shirts
to this new burn in my back

As a final step, I asked students to compare their initial interpretations of Hopper's painting, recorded in their notebook, to Cherry's poetic vision of the painting. Finally, I passed out sentence frames excerpted from Cherry's poem. Students used them to craft their own poems, inspired by other paintings in the gallery, all depicting people at work. Their poems integrated stylistic elements from Cherry's model text, personal knowledge from their own work experience, and contextual knowledge gleaned from the lesson. In this process, students also created a set of artifacts that provided them with an overview of their own evolving conceptualizations of work.

Critical Framing – Patterns of Power

Arts-based discussions opened our class dialogue to questions of power – including *who* and *what* gets portrayed, *how* those subjects are portrayed, and *whose* portrayal gets privileged (i.e., whose work is shown in the museum). These critical reflections on patterns of power and representation linked back to classroom lessons on dominant narratives in history.

While studying *Juan de Pareja*, the portrait by Diego Velázquez (Figure 6.1.4), I asked the students to decipher the inscrutable expression on the subject's face (see Appendix C for activity details). I handed out illustrated word banks which showed vocabulary terms for different emotions or moods. Each vocabulary term was illustrated with a facial expression. Students picked a fascinating range of responses to describe this man's expression. Some said he was relaxed, confident, powerful, or proud. Others said he was cautious, prudish,

Figure 6.1.4 Diego Rodríguez de Silva y Velázquez, *Juan de Pareja*, 1650, Metropolitan Museum of Art

or obstinate. Some students predicted that Juan de Pareja might have been a nobleman based on his posture, attire, and the simple fact that his portrait was shown in the museum.

I revealed the disquieting relationship between the artist and subject, who were master and slave. I asked students to revisit their initial responses to this portrait, modifying or confirming their original answers about what the sitter might be thinking or feeling. As students attended to one another's different interpretations, they recognized the plausibility of divergent answers. By surfacing the range of beliefs in our class, students discovered that they could persuade others or be provoked into new ways of seeing. One student said that it had changed her perception:

> cause I thought he was, like, powerful . . . but after knowing he's a slave, I don't know. I don't know what to think! Just, I'm getting shocked. I cannot see him anymore [as] a powerful person. When I see his eyes, it's like fire in them.

Through the lesson, I posed complicated questions for my students to wrestle with:

- What were the possible dynamics at play between the painter and this subject?
- What did it mean that Velázquez captured de Pareja's likeness in the style of Spanish nobility?
- What did it mean that this specific portrait, a study for a papal portrait, won Velázquez wide critical acclaim?
- Did Velázquez's eventual manumission of de Pareja alter this story or not?

After de Pareja was freed, he also became a renowned artist. While in the gallery, I passed out reproductions of one of de Pareja's paintings, *La Vocación de San Mateo*, which shows his exceptional artistic technique. We compared it to a scene painted by Velázquez, *Las Meninas*, and noticed that both artists painted themselves into the bottom left corner of the scene. What did these parallel details suggest? (See Appendix A for URLs to the images of these paintings.)

As students grappled with these questions, testing out various explanations for this knotty story, I heard them continually revising their impressions. Once power and privilege started calling our attention, they seemed to crop up everywhere we looked. Suddenly our perceptions about the world were more malleable. In the expansive gallery space, students had space to consider narratives not often inscribed in textbooks. Their growing critical consciousness animated deeper conversations on race, religion, class, and gender. These moments also compelled me to listen to my students closely. Pushing my students to elaborate on their thinking surfaced fascinating ways in which they were viewing the world and power dynamics that I might not have predicted.

While teaching this lesson, I was conscious of my identity as a white educator and that my students were being racialized as people of color within the U.S. social paradigm. They were confronting new labels, very different from the ones applied to them in other countries. Part of this process included grappling with the brutality and hegemony underpinning racial constructs, both in the United States and globally. At the same time, I wanted my students to recognize individual agency and complexity in human relationships. Ending our critical inquiry and accepting the broadest brushstrokes of dominant historical narratives – including those about race – would risk obscuring the richness, nuance, and compelling humanity of any person's life.

Transformed Practice – Art for Self-Advocacy

In the spring of 2016, several students helped spearhead our final museum trip, enacting skills they had learned during our prior visits. These students stepped into the role of facilitators, replicating our multiliteracies approach as a form of self-advocacy and peer education. Students were aware of the Islamophobic and xenophobic rhetoric being churned out of the 2016 U.S. election cycle. Within months they would be leaving our school for the next chapter in their lives, and I wondered how I could support them beyond the walls of our school. With this in mind, I invited students to lead our final trip to the museum as an exercise in self-determination.

Four Muslim students from different countries volunteered to choose pieces from the Met's Islamic Art collection and develop lessons around them. They researched the artwork on the Met's website, drew on their own cultural and religious experiences, and read texts in Arabic and English to develop their discussion questions. On our last visit to the museum, these students facilitated the discussion activities they had prepared for their classmates using our Pyramid of Inquiry model. Their funds of knowledge shone through in their lesson design, such as when they translated various Arabic terms into English for their multilingual classmates. One group picked a *Tughra*, an ornate, highly stylized signature from a 16th Century Sultan (Figure 6.1.5) to highlight the precious status of calligraphy and the divinity of written word within their cultural heritage.

All of us enjoyed the activities and gained new insights that day. One Christian student was surprised at the many parallels between her religion and her classmates' religion. The students who facilitated the discussions saw how melding their personal knowledge with discussions of art could become an act of agency. They led the same kind of activities they had previously experienced as participants. This time though, they were the experts, helping their classmates explore issues of pride, religious identity, and the corrosive impacts of stereotyping. In other words, they were engaging in transformed practice. Almost a year after guiding her classmates in this discussion, one student facilitator reflected on the experience this way:

> We cannot just depend [on] knowledge [of] the things we take in classes. We have to use other strategies to feed ourselves with more knowledge, which I can say that by going to the museum, I got to express something new that I never got to think about before.

Figure 6.1.5 *Tughra (Insignia) of Sultan Süleiman the Magnificent*, 1555–1560, Metropolitan Museum of Art

This student's articulation of "other strategies to feed ourselves with knowledge" is a testament to her expanded awareness. She was underscoring the variety of ways we can build an understanding of our world. In this case, arts-based discussion was a vehicle for the *exploration* of new ideas and the *expression* of new ideas, a means of self-knowledge and self-representation.

CONCLUSION

During our visits to the Met, my class of 12th grade ELLs engaged in generative, compelling conversations on complex sociopolitical and historical themes. Our discussions expanded students' understanding of literacy practices beyond the boundaries of written text.

A multiliteracies approach ran through all aspects of the Astor Educators Initiative. The resulting opportunities for multimodal engagement fostered educational equity by enabling *all* my students to participate in rich academic discussions. Students who might have been stymied by a strict adherence to text-based expression gained confidence in expressing their ideas through arts-based discussion, regardless of their academic English literacy proficiency. Their engagement was facilitated by four principles of a multiliteracies pedagogy – situated practice, overt instruction, critical framing, and transformed practice.

The enactment of a multiliteracies approach at the Met validated the voices and experiences of my ELL students. It also opened new possibilities for lessons that merged language development with a discussion of topics that are of central importance to many young adult immigrant ELL students and which are crucial in teaching for social justice. These topics included social constructs of gender, class, power, privilege, race, and religion in the United States.

REFERENCES

Cherry, C. M. (2015). New freedom. *New York City Writing Project*. Retrieved November 1, 2018, from http://nycwritingproject.org/2015/05/nycwp-voices-new-freedom-by-carla-cherry/

Cope, B., & Kalantzis, M. (2009). "Multiliteracies": New literacies, new learning. *Pedagogies: An International Journal*, 4(3), 164–195.

García, O., Sylvan, C. E., & Witt, D. (2011). Pedagogies and practices in multilingual classrooms: Singularities in pluralities. *Modern Language Journal*, 95(3), 385–400.

Giardina, N. (2018). *The more we look, the deeper it gets: Transforming the curriculum through art*. Lanham, MD: Rowman & Littlefield.

New London Group. (2000). Introduction: Multiliteracies: The beginnings of an idea. In B. Cope & M. Kalantzis (Eds.), *Multiliteracies: Literacy learning and the design of social futures* (pp. 3–8). London, UK: Routledge.

Appendix A
Art Used in the Social Studies Class
(in Order of Appearance in the Case Study)

Artist: Winslow Homer

Name of the Piece: *Dressing for the Carnival*

Display Location: The Metropolitan Museum, Accession Number: 22.220

URL: www.metmuseum.org/toah/works-of-art/22.220/

Artist: Ralph Earl

Name of the Piece: *Elijah Boardman*

Display Location: The Metropolitan Museum, Accession Number:1979.395

URL: www.metmuseum.org/art/collection/search/10830

Artist: Edward Hopper

Name of the Piece: *Tables for Ladies*

Display Location: The Metropolitan Museum, Accession Number: 31.62

URL: www.metmuseum.org/toah/works-of-art/31.62/

Artist: Diego Rodríguez de Silva y Velázquez

Name of the Piece: *Juan de Pareja*

Display Location: The Metropolitan Museum, Accession Number: 1971.86

URL: www.metmuseum.org/toah/works-of-art/1971.86/

Artist: Juan de Pareja

Name of the Piece: *La Vocación de San Mateo*

Display Location: Museo del Prado, Inventory Number: P001041

URL: www.museodelprado.es/en/the-collection/art-work/the-calling-of-saint-matthew/
34917e11–611e-451d-84df-a0efb1ac6381

Artist: Diego Rodríguez de Silva y Velázquez

Name of the Piece: *Las Meninas*

Display Location: Museo del Prado, INventory Number: P001174

URL: www.museodelprado.es/en/the-collection/art-work/las-meninas/
9fdc7800–9ade-48b0-ab8b-edee94ea877f

Artist: Court Artists and Illuminators

Name of the Piece: *Tughra (Insignia) of Sultan Süleiman the Magnificent*

Display Location: The Metropolitan Museum, Accession Number: 38.149.1

URL: www.metmuseum.org/art/collection/search/449533

Appendix B
Overt Instruction Activity

This is an excerpted activity from a lesson at the Metropolitan Museum of Art focusing on overt instruction.

Lesson Rationale

This lesson preceded a career fair we organized for our school's 12th graders. Since our students were nearing the end of their senior year, we wanted to help them explore different career paths, with the idea that it could inform their choices following high school. Our staff invited panels of professionals from a variety of fields to our school where they would be interviewed by students. This lesson served as a preview to that career fair, providing students with a chance to surface their thinking about jobs and professions. By asking questions about the workers portrayed in this painting, students were prompted to start considering what they might value and aspire to in their own professional lives. In addition, this lesson was designed to lead into an instructional unit on economic systems, labor politics, and socioeconomics.

Tables for Ladies (see Figure 6.1.3. for image)

Artist: Edward Hopper (American, Nyack, New York 1882–1967 New York)

Date: 1930

Medium: Oil on canvas

Classification: Paintings

Credit Line: George A. Hearn Fund, 1931

Accession Number: 31.62

Question Sequence in the Pyramid of Inquiry Model

Observation questions for this work of art:

• What do you notice in this image?

Inference/evidence questions for this work of art:

• Would you ever see this same kind of restaurant scene, walking down the street in NYC today?

   o What would be different/similar today?

• Look at this woman with the blond hair. In your notebook, write down,

   o 1) What does she have to do in her job?

   o 2) Do you think this woman has a good job?

   o 3) Do you think this woman likes doing her job?

Teacher shares – at the time this was painted, in 1930, America was going through some of the biggest social changes it has ever seen. During the decade before this, the 1920s, women got the right to vote all across the country for the first time in American history. The roles they played and freedoms they demanded in society changed dramatically after that. Teacher explains significance of title of the work, *Tables for Ladies*, then explains that the simple fact of joining the workforce to earn their own money, then spending it however they wanted – even just by going to a restaurant by themselves – represented a radical social transformation. Financial independence led to many other possible new freedoms.

Interpretation question for this work of art:

- Now I'm going to share with you a poem called "New Freedom" by this phenomenal American poet named Carla Cherry. She saw this painting and something about it struck her so deeply that she was compelled to imagine the life of this woman and write a poem about her.
  - Teacher reads the poem aloud, then has students reread the poem in pairs. The poem is modified with an in-text gloss for vocabulary terms students may not be immediately familiar with.
- What does Carla Cherry imagine about this woman's life? What words in the title or the poem give you that idea?
- Is Carla Cherry's interpretation of this woman's work similar or different from your own?

APPENDIX C
Critical Framing Activity – Patterns of Power

This is an excerpted activity from a lesson at the Metropolitan Museum of Art focusing on critical framing and patterns of power.

LESSON RATIONALE

Students have been studying the idea of race as a social construct and the fallacy of biologically based foundations for race. They also explored why the system of racial categorization developed the way it did in the early United States and what impact it had on U.S. politics and policy as well as individual lives in the United States. By investigating depictions of race in Western art, students will consider how art mirrors life and how it can be seen as a vehicle for understanding the social context it was created in.

Juan de Pareja (see Figure 6.1.4. for image)

Artist: Diego Rodríguez de Silva y Velázquez (Spanish, Seville 1599–1660 Madrid)

Date: 1650

Medium: Oil on canvas

Classification: Paintings

Accession Number: 1971.86

QUESTION SEQUENCE IN THE PYRAMID OF INQUIRY MODEL

Observation questions for this work of art:

- Just like on our last visit, today we're going to start with a portrait.

  o What do you notice about this painting?

Inference/Evidence questions for this work of art:

- What could the sitter's clothes and body language tell us about him?

- Come look closely at his face; can you tell how he's feeling based on his face? What mood do you think he's in? Teacher passes out vocab list of feelings words – Let's do a 2–4–6 on this one (strategy to have students form small groups; first they find a partner and share their responses, then each pair finds another pair and forms a group of 4. Teacher sets a timer for 6 minutes. Pairs and small groups talk continuously for the entire 6 minutes.)

Interpretation question for this work of art:

- I'm going to ask you to turn to a partner, and stare at them, without talking or giggling, just stare at their face. Study it and try to notice every detail you can without looking away or talking. (Teacher times students for 30 seconds or so). I only asked you to sit for 30 seconds. . . . How did it feel?

- Teacher says: To paint a picture like this takes hours and hours sitting together quietly in the same room; what do you think the relationship might have been like between this painter and the subject?

  o What makes you say that?

The teacher then tells background info: That Diego Velázquez was one of the most famous European painters in the mid-1600s and that Juan de Pareja and his family were owned as slaves by Velázquez and his family.

• Teacher asks students: Thinking about your answers to the previous questions – would you go back and revise any of your answers knowing what you know now?

   o For more processing time, the teacher may recommend that students write prompts in their notebooks, using the sentence frame "At first I thought . . . but now I think . . . "

Teacher adds more background info, explaining that Diego Velázquez painted Juan de Pareja in this portrait as a practice run for his portrait of Pope Innocent X, the most important religious/political leader in the Christian world, and that, after painting this portrait, Velázquez not only showed it in an exhibition but he won critical acclaim for it, and several years later he manumitted (freed) de Pareja.

• Teacher asks students once again how their ideas have changed or been confirmed in light of this new information.

Finally, the teacher explains that de Pareja, now considered a free person, went on to become a successful painter in his own right and that some of his paintings are found in the Prado Museum, one of the most famous museums in the world. Teacher passes out images of de Pareja's *The Vocation of Saint Matthew* as well as images of Velázquez's *Las Meninas*.

• What similarities do you notice in these two paintings? How does looking at this art affect your ideas about the relationship between Velázquez and de Pareja?

The teacher may point out the stylistic parallels, such as the similar method that both artists employed of including self-portraits in their works.

CASE STUDY 6.2

Exploring Places and Spaces of Migration and Immigration Using Google Earth

A Multiliteracies Approach for English Learners in the U.S.

Natalia A. Ward and Amber N. Warren

This case study illustrates the use of a pedagogy of multiliteracies (Cope & Kalantzis, 2009; New London Group, 1996) by demonstrating how one English as a second language (ESL) teacher utilized this approach to design and implement project-based learning. A multiliteracies pedagogy provides a map for creating learning opportunities for all students. In its original form, it consisted of four dimensions: situated practice, overt instruction, critical framing, and transformed practice. These four dimensions were reframed by Cope and Kalantzis (2009) to reflect "more immediately recognizable pedagogical acts or knowledge processes" (p. 184). The four dimensions are articulated as: (1) *experiencing* the new and the known by reflecting on personal experiences and immersing oneself in unfamiliar situations, (2) *conceptualizing* by developing concepts and building mental models and schema, (3) *analyzing* the perspectives of oneself and others, and (4) *applying* what has been learned and creatively transferring knowledge from one setting to another (Cope & Kalantzis, 2009). We illustrate these dimensions through the case study presented here, highlighting how each of these dimensions are visible in the teachers' and students' actions.

THE SETTING

In a suburban classroom in the Southeastern United States, seven multilingual students aged 9 to 11 years old gather. They come from South and Central America, Asia, and the Indian subcontinent. For an hour each day, they go to their pull-out English as a second language (ESL) classroom to work with their English language teacher. The purpose of these lessons is to scaffold learning in the content areas, supporting students and preparing them for the content that will be encountered in their grade-level classrooms. Their ESL teacher knows that to support her learners academically, she needs to design lessons that encourage them to make connections between the academic content, the English language, and the extensive cultural and linguistic capital they bring to the classroom. Around the room, small groups of students are working together on their latest project: exploring places and spaces of migration and immigration through Google Earth (www.google.com/earth/). Armed with scaffolding handouts designed to guide students' attention to different locations, students discuss and pose more questions than answers through their engagement with technology and content. The room is abuzz with multiple languages, laughter, and conversations, as students try to make sense of what they notice and write down in their notes. Today they are historians, and part of being a historian is being able to share what you know with others in the way they can understand. The teacher circulates around the room asking students to catch her up on their progress.

DESCRIPTION OF ENGLISH LANGUAGE LEARNERS

The students in this classroom are fourth and fifth graders (ages 9–11). In the Southeastern state where they attend school, their English language acquisition levels are measured based on the state English language proficiency assessment. Students in ESL are provided with content-based instruction from their ESL teacher designed to support the development of linguistic and academic content knowledge. The students' levels range from low-intermediate to intermediate-advanced. There are seven boys and girls currently in the fourth-fifth grade class. Josie and John are U.S.-born siblings whose parents emigrated from Mexico. Daniela arrived in the United States from Mexico when she was six years old. Josie, John, and Daniela speak almost exclusively Spanish at home and are proud of their family heritage. Sadie and Devan came to the United States from India and speak Gujarati. Bishr and Rasul came to the United States from Iraq two years ago. Most students are literate in their home language, are proud to showcase their skills in the classroom, and are always encouraged by their teacher to draw on their linguistic knowledge to broker new understandings of English and academic content. For this case study, we zoom in on one group of students working together on their project: Josie, Daniela, and Devan. To protect the identity of the young students, all names used in this case study are pseudonyms.

PEDAGOGICAL APPLICATION AND INNOVATION

Overview of the Unit

In this classroom, the teacher uses a pedagogy of multiliteracies (New London Group, 1996) as a framework for engaging students. She invites students to use multiple modes of expression, including drawing, designing, and composing using both traditional (textbooks, notebooks, paper, pencils, and markers) and digital (online) means (e-books, wikis, websites). These modalities afford students opportunities for multiple means of expression as they work to connect the known with the new, analyze, conceptualize, and transfer knowledge from one mode to another, following a pedagogy of multiliteracies framework. She also encourages students to draw on their personal experiences and connect these to classroom discussions. Students' personal funds of knowledge are understood to be valuable resources for making sense of academic content (Gonzalez, Moll, & Amanti, 2005). To support her learners' content knowledge and language development, she intertwines history/social studies curricula and English language learning goals throughout her unit.

For this unit, students are exploring topics related to migration and immigration around the globe. This topic requires approaching the learning objectives with a critical eye to build on students' wealth of experience, broadening the topic to situate it within a more global perspective of migration and immigration patterns throughout history. The teacher chooses not to shy away from the complex topic of colonization, including U.S. westward movement and the treatment of the land and the people living there. By employing a pedagogy of multiliteracies framework, she creates opportunities for her students to think like historians and to draw conclusions based on their research and discussions.

Innovation-in-Action

To begin the unit, the teacher invites students to share their own journeys. The children are encouraged to build on their own personal experiences and background knowledge and bring the richness of their wealth of experiences to the forefront. Daniela tells her group about her journey from Mexico, Devan shares that he is from India. Josie is at first confused, because she was born in the United States and insists that there is nothing for her to share. The teacher reminds them that a journey does not have to include immigrating from one country to another, adding that each of us has a story to tell. Josie tells her group about living in a bigger city before coming to the district where their current school is located. Alongside this discussion of personal journeys, students begin to explore texts related to migration and immigration through teacher read-alouds and small group work. To investigate the historical experiences of migrants and immigrants, students use a mix of primary documents, written texts, trade books, and websites, such as https://kids. nationalgeographic.com; www.dkfindout.com/us/; https://kids.britannica.com. Students read books like *How I Learned Geography* by Uri Shulevitz (2008) and *If Your Name Was Changed at Ellis Island* by Ellen Levine (1994).

They analyze historical and modern images of immigrant and migrant children. They search online and take notes, while comparing their experiences to those of others.

Students record their own stories in the format of a journal entry, following the example of the primary documents of journals kept by various historical figures they encounter in the classroom. Daniela writes:

> Today is the date I left my country. It is almost night and my family and I are leaving for the United States of America tomorrow! I'm feeling kind of sad and also happy, because I will see new things. We are going to live in the city. This city is probably different from the country from where we are moving and that is Mexico. My parents decided to come to America because they needed a job and money. We left many things behind in Mexico. Our family, friends, pets, and house. Two things I will miss very much are my pets and my family.

At this stage students also begin to explore the power of media and tools, like Google Earth and wikis. Students almost immediately choose to search their home locations on Google Earth, using street view close ups to showcase the places and spaces that mean "home." Josie grows excited as she "flies" around the 3D globe to locate the hometown of her family and trace her personal journey across the United States using Google Earth. Devan shouts, "Can we fly to my country next?" Students quickly realize that they have much to learn about the parts of the world from which their classmates came from. Because students want to share that information with other classes as well, the teacher prompts them to collaboratively create wikis that would contain information, images, videos, personal anecdotes, and maps related to their families' home countries. Students use Google Sites as a structured wiki platform that provides a user-friendly interface intuitive enough to be used even by the youngest students. Inspired by the students' interest, the creation of wikis becomes the focal point of several lessons, and students bring artifacts and notes from home on which family members write names of important places and information for students to include. Students from several ESL classes collaboratively develop the wikis and then enthusiastically share them with each other. Telling these informative, personal, and often emotional stories helps bring a meaningful connection to the historical contexts students are beginning to study, as they start to recognize that history is made up of individual stories, just like theirs.

After sharing personal journeys and reading about the experiences of immigrants, students journey deeper into U.S. history. Using the dimension of *experiencing* from a pedagogy of multiliteracies (Cope & Kalantzis, 2009), the teacher invites her students to connect their personal experiences and perspectives (experiencing the known), as they begin to immerse themselves in the worlds of the historical figures they study next (experiencing the new). For example, after reading parts of *Westward Expansion* (2010), a nonfiction text by Teresa Domnauer, Josie began to wonder about the people who lived in the lands that were being explored and taken over by European Americans. She was troubled by the act of taking land that already belongs to someone else. To investigate this further, Josie, Daniela, and Devan decide their group would explore Lewis and Clark's journey from the perspective of one of the Native American tribes they encountered. Next, the teacher implements the dimension of *conceptualizing* to help them draw distinctions between various ideas related to migration (within the United States and across the globe) and develop concepts and "transferable disciplinary schemas" (Cope & Kalantzis, 2009, p. 185). That is, through linking personal experiences of immigration to descriptions of migration and immigration encountered in texts, students are provided with an opportunity to generalize and link concepts of historical migration patterns to form theories about migration, immigration, colonization, and expansion as historical and current issues. The students read additional books like *Into the West: Causes and Effects of U.S. Westward Expansion* by Terry Collins (2013). They step into the shoes of historical immigrants and record what they are learning in notebooks. Students learn that often historians, like explorers of new lands, keep a journal with their notes, discoveries, questions, and maps. They research online and ask their school librarian for other resources. The students take notes and are eager to share what they are learning with others.

Through ongoing discussions, questioning, and research through traditional and digital texts, students are *analyzing* what they are learning to develop a critical capacity to evaluate different perspectives, interests, and motives both of themselves and others (Cope & Kalantzis, 2009). As they piece together the stories of past immigrants and the effects that this migration had on the Native Americans and others already living on those lands, students record their findings onto new Google Earth maps. They upload drawings, journal entries, and notes with facts to their growing Google Earth tours.

In this way, they *apply* their knowledge – the last dimension described in a pedagogy of multiliteracies approach – by transferring what they have learned into a digitally rendered journey, combining English language writing practices with their new knowledge of U.S. history, geography and mapping skills.

To share the growing understanding with their classmates, the students create a Google Earth tour with journal entries that are typed or handwritten and scanned, and descriptions of various locations of interest. They add placemarks to important locations on the map and indicate their importance by typing comments. They change pushpin icons to their own scanned drawings. After creating placemarks, they connect them to create a tour and record it for further viewing (See Figures 6.2.1 and 6.2.2). Students finally present their tour to other groups and are ready to apply the knowledge and skills they learned through this unit in other content areas classes and within new units of study.

Figure 6.2.1 Google Earth tour created by a student

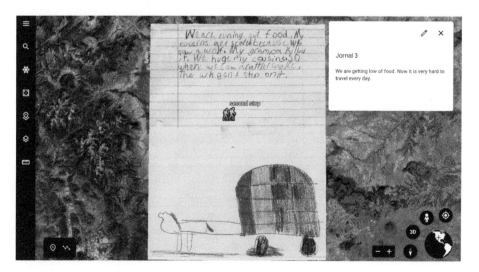

Figure 6.2.2 Student journal entry uploaded to Google Earth tour

Throughout the unit, the teacher and her students navigated the various dimensions of a pedagogy of multiliteracies. They began with *experiencing* the new and the known by connecting their own stories to the stories of immigrants throughout history. Through this, they *conceptualized* new ideas about patterns of migration, immigration, and colonization and *analyzed* new information through their developing schema. Finally, they *applied* their new understandings to create a complete digital project. This unit encapsulates how a pedagogy of multiliteracies, with its multiple dimensions and considerations, can serve as a useful framework for navigating the complex academic and linguistic terrain of a classroom.

CONCLUSION

This case study illustrates how English language development, history/social studies curricula, and learning goals were integrated through a mix of traditional and digital media, culminating in the creation of immigration and migration journeys with Google Earth. The pedagogy of multiliteracies provided the teacher with a comprehensive framework to explore important topics and texts from various angles and points of view, to offer students a creative choice, and to capitalize on the potential of digital literacies in a social studies unit. The interactive nature of the project-based activities infused with technology, particularly Google Earth, engaged students and validated their rich cultural resources and experiences. By making connections between events from students' home lives and the academic content and language of schooling, the teacher helped students see relevance in the content they were studying.

REFERENCES

Cope, B., & Kalantzis, M. (2009). "Multiliteracies": New literacies, new learning. *Pedagogies: An International Journal, 4*, 164–195. doi:10.1080/15544800903076044

Gonzalez, N., Moll, L. C., & Amanti, C. (Eds.). (2005). *Funds of knowledge: Theorizing practices in household, communities, and classrooms.* Mahwah, NJ: Erlbaum.

The New London Group. (1996). A pedagogy of multiliteracies: Designing social futures. *Harvard Educational Review, 66*(1), 60–93.

Children's Books Mentioned

Collins, T. (2013). *Into the west: Causes and effects of U.S. westward expansion.* New York, NY: Scholastic.

Domnauer, T. (2010). *Westward expansion.* New York, NY: Scholastic.

Levine, E. (1994). *If your name was changed at Ellis Island.* New York, NY: Scholastic.

Shulevitz, U. (2008). *How I learned geography.* New York, NY: Farrar, Strauss, & Giroux.

Appendix A
Books and Websites to Use With Students

Table 6.2.1 Books and websites to use with students

Resource	Description	Grade Level
Johmann, C.A., & Kline, M.P. (2002). *The Lewis and Clark expedition: Join the corps of discovery to explore uncharted territory.* Charlotte, VT: Williamson Publishing.	This nonfiction book focuses on the history of the expedition and the main players and then follows their journey to the Pacific.	Grades 3–4
American legends: The life of Sacagawea. (2013). Ann Arbor, MI: Charles River Editors.	Includes passages from primary texts, images, and describes Sacagawea's role in Lewis and Clark's expedition.	Non-graded
Levine, E. (1992). *If you traveled west in a covered wagon.* New York, NY: Scholastic.	Written as a series of questions and answers, this informative text can be a great classroom resource when questions about transcontinental journeys arise.	Grades 3–5
MacCarald, C. (2018). *Perspectives on European colonization of America (Perspectives on U.S. history).* Mankato, MN: 12-Story Library.	Provides different views on groups of colonial European settlers. Focus on how different people were affected by waves of European settlement during this time period.	Grades 4–6
Erickson, P. (1997). *Daily life in a covered wagon.* New York, NY: Puffin Books.	Filled with photos of the actual artifacts from the past, this book explores what the daily life was like on the wagon train.	Grades 3–4
Watling, J. (1993). *Los hijos de la Tierra y el Cielo/Children of the Earth and Sky.* New York, NY: Scholastic.	Spanish language text that shares stories of five Native American children from five North American tribes.	Grades K-5
Friedman, M. (2010). *The Oregon Trail: A true book.* New York, NY: Scholastic.	True Books are an excellent nonfiction book choice for studying a variety of topics. This particular book offers main points about the Oregon Trail.	Grades 3–4
Saylor Academy (2012, April 16). *Native American land losses.* Retrieved from https://youtu.be/ZZCvUroBpaE	Seventeen-second video that shows Native American land losses from 1784 to present day.	All grades
Trinklein, M., & Boettcher, S. (2012). *The Oregon Trail.* Retrieved from http://oregontrail101.com	This Oregon Trail site has a plethora of fun facts, maps, and information. The texts can sometimes be complex; therefore, teacher scaffolding or guidance is advised.	Grades 4–6

CASE STUDY 6.3

Rappin' on Campus
Multiliteracies in Action in Japan

David Dalsky and Jueyun Su

This case study exemplifies how creating a multimodal educational rap video that showcases academic contents can be an engaging way to implement multiliteracies pedagogy in an EFL classroom. More specifically, we demonstrate how the pedagogical application of this project involves Learning by Design (Kalantzis & Cope, 2005) and Team Learning (Stewart, Dalsky, & Tajino, 2018). The procedure featured a wide range of learning activities informed by several knowledge processes (i.e., experiencing, conceptualizing, analyzing, and applying) with English as the primary language of communication. The project resulted in a pedagogically innovative video *Nurture or Nature* featuring a rap song with academic lyrics and hip-hop dance moves uploaded to Kyoto University's OpenCourseWare YouTube website (Dalsky, 2013).

THE SETTING

The educational rap video *Nurture or Nature* (Dalsky, 2013) described in this case study was produced from late June, 2012, and finally published in January, 2013, on the campus of Kyoto University (KU) in Japan. One of the key features of the KU undergraduate program is its Liberal Arts and General Education curriculum, which includes an English-based component from an English for General Academic Purposes (EGAP) framework (see Maswana, Smith, & Tajino, 2010). When this project was undertaken, the first two years of the four-year curriculum were designed to provide students with the foundation for advancing as international scholars. At the same time, all KU students were required to complete *English W1* academic writing and the *English R1* reading courses. The curriculum was reformed after the project described in the present case study took place (see Katsurayama et al., 2018).

Students who volunteered to participate in the academic rap video project mostly came from one of the first-year academic writing classes taught by the first author (the instructor) in 2012–2013. The class met weekly for 90 minutes (15 weeks/semester) to practice academic skills related to the topics arranged in the book, *Writing for Academic Purposes* (Tajino, Stewart, & Dalsky, 2010). In the class, a process approach to academic writing was used. During the course, students were expected to work on several revisions of a 2,000-word research paper about an academic topic related to their major, and students were encouraged to focus on ideas, arguments, structure, and features of academic writing, such as citations, and engage in peer feedback activities.

In the *English W1* academic writing class, the instructor occasionally played U.S. background music to create a relaxing learning atmosphere. One day, after class, a student approached the instructor and expressed his desire to write original academic rap music. The instructor, who enjoys rap music, was inspired by the student and asked the students in the class to volunteer to join an extracurricular project focused on writing rap music. Four other students volunteered to take part. The instructor also found some students outside of the class who were interested in joining the project: a male U.S. exchange student from the Massachusetts Institute of Technology and a female Japanese graduate student from KU.

The instructor used funds from a teaching budget to commission an avant-garde jazz/jazz fusion trumpeter to create original beats, and a renowned academic rapper to lead in the production of the rap song. The instructor also coordinated with the KU OpenCourseWare project at the university's Media Center to access video recording equipment, and a platform on YouTube (the KU OpenCourseWare channel). In the end, a total of seven students, an instructor, an academic rapper, a musical composer, and two KU OpenCourseWare project members collaborated to realize the production and publication of the academic rap video.

DESCRIPTION OF ENGLISH LANGUAGE LEARNERS

The five Japanese students (three female students and two male students) from the English writing class who volunteered to participate in the project were around 20 years old. They were all highly motivated and attended most of the writing classes during the semester. The students' major was Integrated Human Studies, a unique major at KU that aims to integrate humanities, social sciences, and natural sciences into an interdisciplinary field. The purposes of the English class were to improve academic writing skills and to learn academic vocabulary. The Japanese graduate student's major was cognitive science. She and the U.S. exchange student took part in this project out of interest and curiosity.

The six Japanese learners' English level was around elementary-intermediate. They were able to understand frequently used expressions in familiar matters, describe basic opinions and plans, and communicate in daily situations. They were interested in American pop culture and had experiences with a variety of media such as movies, television, YouTube, and Twitter. They all had access to computers and the internet.

PEDAGOGICAL APPLICATION AND INNOVATION

Description of Academic Rap Video Project

The purpose of the academic rap video project was to offer an opportunity for the learners to share their understandings of an academic topic to a broad audience online in English (and also their native language to a lesser extent) through video production. The instructor made it clear to the students from the beginning of the project that the final video product would be uploaded to YouTube through the KU OpenCourseWare channel, and all of the students consented. The ten-week project was organized in approximately the following way and the production team met mostly during 50-minute lunchtime meetings:

- *Week 1: Preparation.* The instructor provided a list of academic topics related to the students' major with a brief introduction. The students then discussed and decided on one academic topic of interest.

- *Week 2: Introduction of the academic topic in English.* The learners read the learning materials related to the academic topic prepared by the instructor (i.e., the nurture and nature debate in psychology). The definitions of academic concepts that were frequently used for the topic (e.g., genes, traits, DNA) were discussed by the group using academic dictionaries (e.g., Kyoto University Academic Vocabulary Research Group and Kenkyusha, 2009).

- *Week 3: Introduction to academic rap music.* An academic rapper was invited to explain basic concepts in rap music: the structure (i.e., verse, chorus, intro/outro, after/before the chorus, and bridge) and the rhymes. The students watched some sample educational rap videos on websites (e.g., *Science with Tom*, n.d., and *Flocabulary*, n.d.) and analyzed one rap video's lyrics in a group.

- *Week 4–6: Songwriting.* First, the learners brainstormed with the instructor and decided on the subtopics that were presented in an introductory psychology textbook published in English (i.e., selective breeding, twin studies, and molecular genetics), which composed the verses of the song. The academic rapper and the instructor guided the students in writing the lyrics using a textbook (Rappaport & Thomas, 2009). During the rhyme writing, the students were also encouraged to use their native language in lyrics to express their ideas and feelings.

- *Week 7–10: Production of the video.* The students watched some rap videos and summarized the features of the meaning-making process together (e.g., gestures, dance moves). One Japanese student in the group emerged as the student leader, who arranged and recorded video scenes to complement the rhymes in the song. Another student edited the video and added subtitles. Finally, the KU OpenCourseWare project members published the academic rap video on YouTube.

Multiliteracy Pedagogical Innovation

This case study demonstrates multiliteracy pedagogical innovation in several ways. It is a multimodal academic rap video. It includes knowledge-sharing using technology, language play, team learning, and application of the Learning by Design approach (Kalantzis & Cope, 2005). We discuss each of these aspects in detail.

MULTIMODAL ACADEMIC RAP VIDEO

The academic rap video was inherently multimodal because students were challenged to integrate linguistic (English and Japanese), visual (video), auditory (music), and gestural (hip-hop dance moves) modes. Through the process of writing lyrics, the learners used the target language (English) and their native language (Japanese) to express ideas and emotions. Both English and Japanese served as resources for meaning-making (e.g., nature and nurture are *gocha gocha* [*messy*]). Linguistic competence, in this case, is seen as a component of symbolic competence proposed by Kramsch (2006), and the learners are thus seen as legitimate users of English and whole persons rather than simply "still-not-good-enough learners." The learners had to engage in referee design and adjust the presentation according to the imaginary audience on the digital media.

The hip-hop dance video as an artifact, compared to mere writing or speaking production, proved to be a richer source of information that heightened the teacher's awareness of (1) how the learners view the target language, (2) what attitudes they have toward language learning and language use, (3) how they understand and interpret target language-related culture, and (4) how they negotiate their identities and beliefs with the discourse community.

KNOWLEDGE-SHARING USING TECHNOLOGY

The resulting visual and audio learning/teaching material made use of a relatively new communication technology to share knowledge (i.e., YouTube). The pedagogy of multiliteracies is expected to fulfill the mission of education which is "to ensure that all students benefit from learning in ways that allow them to participate fully in public, community, and economic life" (New London Group, 2000, p. 9). By sharing knowledge with the world through the internet, the learners recognized and extended their roles as social participants and global citizens, which in turn promoted their motivation to learn and communicate in English. This can also be seen as a way of learning by teaching, which is beneficial to retaining knowledge.

LANGUAGE PLAY

The text (see Appendix A) was popular and involved language play, as it was generated through beats and rhymes at the formal level. It consisted of imaginary scenes at the semantic level and attitudes toward psychology expressed in a humorous way at the pragmatic level (see Cook, 2000). Indeed, language play and creativity are connected, and "creativity functions to give pleasure, to establish both harmony and convergence as well as disruption and critique, to express identities and to evoke alternative fictional worlds which are recreational and which recreate the familiar world in new ways" (Carter, 2015, p. 82).

For example, in the chorus of the song, words that rhyme with the word *nature* were listed first, and the learners then used their imagination to choose and link the words with other words to express their ideas and feelings (i.e., *sure, lecture, mixture, torture*). The figurative usage of the word *torture* in "We'll do this in English because we like torture!" showed that even though English is hard to learn, they are willing to learn it and created humor which might resonate with the other English language learners.

TEAM LEARNING

The endeavor was fundamentally collaborative, as it involved learners, a psychology content specialist (teacher), a jazz musician, and a biology content specialist (rapper-teacher), in an intercultural social learning blend. To be sure, this social learning structure could be viewed as one example of team learning (see Stewart et al., 2018).

APPLICATION OF THE LEARNING BY DESIGN APPROACH

Both the teacher and the learners were engaged in Learning by Design (Kalantzis & Cope, 2005; Cope & Kalantzis, 2015). The teacher created an authentic learning environment by connecting the learners with the outside world as a designer. During the process of going beyond the classroom, the learners were able to notice the skill and knowledge they lack for using English in everyday life, as there are not enough opportunities for the learners to use English in an EFL context. Likewise, the learners *as designers* decided what they needed to learn, what they wanted to learn, and how they wanted to learn it. They were also constructing knowledge and externalizing thinking by writing the lyrics and, of course, collaborating to make the rap video.

CONCLUSION

This project demonstrated how Japanese students were able to share their English creation on an internet platform as legitimate users of English. With a little musical inspiration, learning an additional language can be interesting and enjoyable, as well as effective. For example, by taking an active role in songwriting, vocabulary is no longer something out there waiting to be learned; it is instead something in the head desiring to be expressed. This hands-on learning practice supported by both an English instructor and an academic rapper allowed students to become active participants and contributors in the meaningful construction of knowledge. The rhymes and figurative language in songwriting also opened the doors to the beauty of language. This case study demonstrated that by engaging our students in a creative project using multiliteracies, the use of additional languages in daily life has legitimate potential for the expression of the creative and emotional aspects – in this case, "rappin' on campus."

ACKNOWLEDGMENTS

We would like to express our sincere gratitude to academic rapper, Tom McFadden, avant-garde jazz/jazz fusion trumpeter, Toshinori Kondo (alumnus of KU, 1967), the KU OpenCourseWare project members, and all of the students who participated. The success of the project would not have been possible without their inspiration and devotion.

REFERENCES

Carter, R. (2015). *Language and creativity: The art of common talk.* New York, NY: Routledge.

Cook, G. (2000). *Language play, language learning.* Oxford, UK: Oxford University Press.

Cope, B., & Kalantzis, M. (2015). *A pedagogy of multiliteracies: Learning by design.* New York, NY: Palgrave Macmillan.

Dalsky, D. (2013). *Nurture or nature.* Kyoto University Academic Hip Hop: Introduction to Psychology Lunchtime Seminar: 2012–2013. Retrieved October 22, 2018, from www.youtube.com/watch?v=xq6MrP6Qu-I&feature=youtube

Flocabulary: Educational Hip-Hop. (n.d.). Retrieved October 22, 2018, from www.flocabulary.com

Kalantzis, M., & Cope, B. (2005). *Learning by design.* Melbourne, AU: Common Ground.

Katsurayama, K., Takahashi, S., Kanamaru, T., Sasao, Y., Stewart, T., Dalsky, D., & Tajino, A. (2018). English education in the liberal arts and general education at Kyoto University: A focus on the English writing-listening course. *Kyoto University Institute for Liberal Arts and Sciences Bulletin, 1,* 111–121 (in Japanese).

Kramsch, C. (2006). From communicative competence to symbolic competence. *The Modern Language Journal, 90*(2), 249–252.

Kyoto University Academic Vocabulary Research Group and Kenkyusha. (2009). *Kyoto University data-based academic vocabulary: Basic English words 1110* [京大・学術語彙データベース 基本英単語 1110]. Tokyo, Japan: Kenkyusha.

Maswana, S., Smith, C., & Tajino, A. (2010). The primary features of academic writing. In A. Tajino, T. Stewart, & D. Dalsky (Eds.), *Writing for academic purposes: Eisakubun wo sostugyoshite eigoronbun wo kaku* (pp. 9–17). Tokyo, Japan: Hituzi Syobo Publishing.

New London Group. (2000). A pedagogy of multiliteracies designing social futures. In B. Cope & M. Kalantzis (Eds.), *Multiliteracies: Literacy learning and the design of social futures* (pp. 9–36). New York, NY: Routledge.

Rappaport, A., & Thomas, D. (2009). *Writing academic rhymes: Developing higher-order thinking skills through high-interest writing: Teacher resource book.* New York, NY: Flocabulary.

Science with Tom. (n.d.). Retrieved October 22, 2018, from www.youtube.com/channel/UC3gFS6DINL-JBj5kd6hm9Ng

Stewart, T., Dalsky, D., & Tajino, A. (2018). Team learning potential for TESOL practice. *TESOL Journal, 10*(3). https://doi.org/10.1002/tesj.426

Tajino, A., Stewart, T., & Dalsky, D. (2010). *Writing for academic purposes.* Tokyo, Japan: Hituzi Syobo Publishing.

Appendix A
Song Lyrics

Nurture or Nature

We're on a quest to understand nurture and nature.
It's kinda complicated and we'd like to make sure
to explore both in this little lecture.
Because in the end, it's always a mixture.

Intro
So many ways to answer this question.
So here's a few methods we like to mention.

Selective Breeding

Is dog excitability influenced by "nature"?
Take the most excited and mate 'em together.
If over generations they're getting crazier
genes are influencing this dog's behavior.
Selective breeding works well in mice
over time we can make them more wise.
shou chu shocchu nomu chu[1]
sake ni necchu kodomo mo auruchu.[2]
With animals, breeding's a great way to know
but how about humans? *Ningen wa dou*[3]?

Twin Studies

We can't just breed them like *shibaken*[4]
so we turn to natural experiments.
Like twins – take a look at what they share
like a lot of DNA and the color of their hair.
But if they share environment it might get sloppy
so we study those who have been adopted.
And as they age, it becomes apparent
they act more like their biological parents.
On certain tests – like the IQ
But don't quit your efforts. *Sokyu*[5]!
(PAUSE)
But don't quit your efforts. *Sokyu*!

We're on a quest to understand nurture and nature.
It's kinda complicated and we'd like to make sure
to explore both in this little lecture.
Because in the end, it's always a mixture.

We're on a quest to understand nurture and nature.
It's kinda complicated and we'd like to make sure
to explore both in this little lecture
We'll do this in English because we like torture!

Molecular Genetics

Now to the DNA in your hair follicles.
How do we link one trait to one molecule?
Look in a family with different fates,

we can see how genes might influence traits.
Behavior from brain from transmitters from genes
For example, the receptor for dopamine.
Have the D4? Like novelty seeking?
Then do *kosupure* at *sotsugyo shiki*[6]!
I know gene stories are pretty fun,
but their relationships with traits is rarely one-to-one.
So before you blame everything on genetics
remember the case of the diabetics.
If one twin gets it the other might not
Environmental factors matter a lot.
Yes genes might influence the trait
But it's far more likely if you're overweight.
Remember: It's like we told ya.
Nature and nurture are *gocha gocha*.[7]
(PAUSE)
Nature and nurture are *gocha gocha*.

We're on a quest to understand nurture and nature.
It's kinda complicated and we'd like to make sure
to explore both in this little lecture.
Because in the end, it's always a mixture.

We're on a quest to understand nurture and nature.
It's kinda complicated and we'd like to make sure
to explore both in this little lecture.
We'll do this in English because we like torture!

NOTES ON SONG LYRICS

1 [焼酎しょっちゅう飲むチュチュ] On the other hand, often drinking *shouchu* (a strong Japanese distilled spirit) while making the sound *chuchu* (a sound used to describe the sound of drinking).
2 [酒に熱中 子どももアル中] will make the children become obsessed with alcohol; the children will be addicted to alcohol.
3 [人間はどう] How about humans.
4 [柴犬] a Japanese dog breed.
5 [即急] Quickly.
6 [Then do コスプレ at 卒業式] Then do cosplay at the graduation ceremony.
7 [ごちゃごちゃ] messy.

UNIT 7
Collaborative Technologies and TESOL

CHAPTER 7
Teaching With Collaborative Technologies Across Borders

Ilka Kostka

With the widespread use of the internet and mobile devices, there is tremendous potential for technology to support English language learning. In this chapter, I first discuss the theoretical underpinnings of educational technology, collaborative writing, and the synergy of the two for learning ESL and EFL language learning. Then I examine the implications for using technology to support English language instruction and share some insights for future scholarship.

FRAMING THE ISSUE

Modern technology has profoundly changed the way students communicate, access information, and learn in such that it is difficult to imagine second language (L2) learning without it. Learners can live in Brazil and interact with other English learners across the globe through social media sites. English teachers can teach students in Japan from the comfort of their homes in Canada. Learners within the same on-ground class can work together online to complete projects, give each other feedback, and extend classroom discussions. Mobile devices also allow learners to read and listen to English at home, on the beach, in a bus or train, in a café or restaurant, or library at any time of the day or night. All of these developments have transformed the ways in which English is learned and taught in a wide range of settings.

On one hand, technology can support individualized second language learning. For instance, technology can create opportunities for learners to easily access authentic language input, enhance their learning strategies, and customize tools and technological resources to fit their needs (Chapelle & Jamieson, 2008). Similarly, Larsen-Freeman and Anderson (2011) describe how programs can provide individualized feedback and opportunities for practice in the target language that are appropriate for learners' particular proficiency levels. More recently, proponents of the flipped learning approach have argued that using technology to deliver course content outside of class gives English language learners more time to learn and work at their own pace (e.g., Voss & Kostka, 2019). With computer-mediated support, learners can take more control of their own learning and work toward their personal learning goals in ways that can surpass traditional ways of learning in a classroom.

On the other hand, there is great potential for technology to facilitate collaborative learning among L2 learners. With the emergence of Web 2.0 in the early 2000s, opportunities for communication, interaction, sharing, and networking in the form of blogs, wikis, and social networking sites have exploded (Reinhardt, 2019). In fact, Lomicka and Lord (2019) state that the use of technology for social purposes is one of the defining elements of the past decade. They note that Generation Z learners, which refers to digital natives who have grown up with technology, "have become accustomed to how easy it is to communicate and collaborate across the globe, allowing them to be known as a generation without boundaries" (p. 14). Storch (2019) states that the scholarly interest that has accompanied these developments is likely due to the necessity for professionals to co-produce written texts in the workplace and the developments in Web 2.0 that have made co-authoring easier and more efficient, illustrating how these online activities have real-world applications.

When considering the impact of technology on learners, we also need to consider the ways in which it has affected teachers. To a certain extent, technology has made the types of activities and tasks that teachers do easier to manage. For instance, learning management systems and cloud-based platforms such as Google Classroom allow teachers to efficiently organize material, deliver content to students, and extend discussions and group work beyond the four walls of the classroom. There are also tools that can help teachers and stakeholders conduct formative and summative assessments of students' learning and provide feedback on their work, in addition to widespread commercial exams such as the internet-based Test of English as a Foreign Language (TOEFL iBT). Finally, technology has affected how teachers connect to each other and remain current in their fields, as new opportunities have risen for teacher education, networking, and professional development.

There is no doubt that technology can serve as a tremendous resource for English language learners. In the following section, I discuss the theoretical considerations for using technology to support English language learning, focusing on collaborative learning and calling attention to its benefits and challenges. Next, I discuss the implications for technology in English language education, focusing on best practices, professional development for teachers, support for students, accessibility, and assessment and feedback. I conclude the chapter by highlighting future trends and areas that are likely to continue garnering attention.

CONCEPTS AND THEORETICAL CONSIDERATIONS

Theorizing Educational Technology

Educational technology can be simply defined as electronic tools and applications that support and facilitate learning by providing content, enhancing learners' performance, or organizing learning materials. With the aim of operationalizing the term *technology* in this chapter, I consider a wide range of resources to encompass technology, such as the internet, laptop and desktop computers, word processing programs (e.g., Microsoft Office, Google Docs), cloud-computing software used for data storage and sharing (e.g., Apple iCloud), mobile devices (e.g., smartphones, tablets), whiteboards, telecommunications software (e.g., Skype), videoconferencing software (e.g., BlueJeans), and learning management systems (e.g., Blackboard Learn, Moodle). All of these are currently used in a variety of settings to support English language learning.

The area of language teaching that has aligned most closely with instructional technology is Computer-Assisted Language Learning (CALL), which includes the fields of English as a Second Language (ESL), English as a Foreign Language (EFL), and foreign language instruction. In their review of literature on technology in applied linguistics, Lomicka and Lord (2019) trace the development of CALL from its birth in the 1960s to its current state, which is primarily characterized by the use of technology for social purposes, including mobile learning, gaming, and social media. The authors also discuss a study they conducted with foreign language teachers and undergraduate and graduate students majoring in foreign languages at various universities across the United States. Their objective was to examine participants' perspectives about the role of technology for language teaching. One key finding that emerged is that despite the significant attention on technology to teach languages, its implementation in language classrooms is not as widely used prominent as one may think. They conclude that language educators are "at a stage of primarily superficial use of technology in our classes" (p. 18). Although their review focuses on foreign language instruction, their findings align with the views of others who have stated that technology is not always maximized for English language instruction due to a lack of effective training for teachers and students (e.g., Healey et al., 2008). These findings highlight the mismatch that may occur between potential technology use and its actual use for supporting teaching and learning and have implications for advancing teacher development.

Nevertheless, the areas of CALL and second and foreign language teaching and learning have come together to explore the potential of technology for second language (L2) learning. A likely reason is the natural alignment of socially oriented theoretical frameworks with the affordances of Web 2.0 technologies for interaction, participation, and networking (Reinhardt, 2019). Principles of collaborative learning also parallel social views of second language learning that emphasize learning and knowledge construction as processes that occur among people. One particular example of this alignment is collaborative writing, which Storch (2019) notes has been informed primarily by sociocultural and activity theories that conceptualize language as a tool for mediation and learning. These theoretical frameworks are not new to the field; however, technology affords a different and perhaps more engaging platform for social interaction and meaning-making to occur.

Linking Collaborative Learning and Technology

The Eberly Center for Teaching Excellence and Educational Innovation at Carnegie Mellon University (n.d.) defines collaborative learning as "people working together to solve a problem, create a product, or derive meaning from a body of material. A central question or problem serves to organize and drive activities and encourage application, analysis, and synthesis of course material." Jacobs (2004) defines key principles of collaborative learning as ensuring that students have the skills needed to collaborate; encouraging group autonomy, peer interaction, and individual accountability; promoting equal participation among members; and fostering positive relationships among students so they consider the group as one unit. As the author notes, these principles can help collaborative activities run smoothly.

For the past few decades, scholars in the field of English language teaching have examined the role of technology in fostering learning of the four skills (i.e., reading, writing, listening, and speaking), as well as grammar and vocabulary. Table 7.1 provides examples of common applications that can support collaborative English language teaching and learning in a wide range of educational settings (e.g., K-12 or postsecondary settings) and in both ESL and EFL contexts.

Table 7.1 Overview of selected tools to support collaborative English language learning

Purpose	Examples of tools and software	Description	Collaborative feature(s)	Link
Collaborative knowledge construction	bubbl.us	Web-based tool for creating mind maps and brainstorming ideas	Simultaneous editing	https://bubbl.us/
	Google Classroom	Offers multiple different tools to organize materials, foster collaborative learning, and conduct assessments	Google Docs, Google Sheets, and Google Slides	http://classroom.google.com
	Padlet	Virtual bulletin-board for creating an unlimited amount of short text boxes	Knowledge creation and idea sharing with video, text, or images	https://padlet.com/
Publishing tools	Wix	Web-based platform for designing websites	Option is available to add other contributors to websites	www.wix.com
	WeVideo	Cloud-based platform for creating digital stories	Collaborative video creation and editing	www.wevideo.com/
Assessment	KAHOOT!	Game-based software that provides either teacher-created or existing multiple-choice quizzes	Offers either individual or team play	https://kahoot.com
	Quizlet	Electronic vocabulary flashcards that either already exist or are created by Quizlet users	Interactive study material and games and shared flashcards used among students	https://quizlet.com/

Source: Ilka Kostka

Among the four skills, writing has received considerable attention because many technological tools provide convenient ways for writers to work together. Storch (2019) defines collaborative writing as "an activity that requires the co-authors to be involved in all stages of the writing process, sharing the responsibility for and the ownership of the entire text produced" (p. 40). In an earlier study of 23 adult ESL learners working either alone or in pairs on texts, Storch (2005) found that participants who worked together wrote more linguistically accurate and complex texts and held mostly positive views on collaborative writing in terms of improving their language skills, sharing ideas about writing, receiving feedback from peers, and enjoying the writing process. As this early study indicated, there is great potential for using technology to support collaborative writing.

More recently, Reinhardt (2019) categorized empirical research on collaborative writing technologies into three major areas: blogs, wikis, and social networking platforms. He identified the many benefits of collaborative writing that have emerged from empirical research, including increased audience awareness and autonomy, the development of intercultural exchange among writers, and literacy development (Reinhardt, 2019). In another recent article, Storch (2019) created a time line of empirical research on collaborative writing over the past 25 years, beginning with a 1994 study examining learner talk during writing to research published in the late 2000s that began to explore the role of technology to support collaborative writing in particular. A conclusion that can be drawn from both her review and Reinhardt's (2019) analysis is that scholarship on collaborative second language writing has remained stable and is likely to continue in the near future whether there is a technology focus or not.

Despite these positive outcomes, challenges can arise as well. For instance, in Kessler's (2009) study of 40 preservice ESL teachers in Mexico, findings indicate that learners may focus more on meaning and content and neglect grammatical accuracy. Other work has highlighted the affective factors that may negatively impact the success of collaborative writing tasks. Storch's (2005) study described indicated that some participants reported lacking confidence in their language skills in order to provide constructive feedback to their peers, and two participants felt that writing with others was distracting. In addition, students may also be resistant to using the personal social media platforms for academic use (Godwin-Jones, 2018; Shih, 2011). These studies remind us that successful collaboration should not be assumed, as students come to writing classes with ideas about the writing process, bring different learning styles, and have varying learning experiences, all of which have implications for instruction.

IMPLICATIONS FOR ENGLISH LANGUAGE EDUCATION

There is general consensus that students' learning outcomes should be prioritized before considering the technology that would support those learning goals (Chun, Kern, & Smith, 2016; Egbert, 2005). In other words, using technology solely to incorporate or experiment with new tools and applications should not be the pedagogical goal. It is important for teachers to view technology as a resource that should support learning rather than drive it. Larsen-Freeman and Anderson (2011) also state that technology "should be integrated into the curriculum and not just added in because it is new" (p. 201). Their assertion reiterates the importance of planning carefully for technology use and keeping learning at the forefront. In this section, I discuss key implications for technology use in supporting English language learning that stem from this overarching implication, focusing on best practices, teacher and student training, and assessment and feedback.

Drawing From Best Practices and Standards

Keeping up with developments in technology is critical, as tools and applications constantly and rapidly change. Nevertheless, teachers can draw from established best practices for guidance. To provide an example, Egbert (2005) described key principles for CALL that are still relevant to English language teachers today, such as placing the focus on language learning (and not technology), meeting students' individual needs, and drawing from theory and practice to inform instruction. Egbert's guidelines can ensure quality implementation of technology no matter which tool teachers use, and they can help teachers create ideal environments in which technology supports instruction. Chun et al. (2016) also acknowledge the pace and degree to which technology develops and provide a series of guiding questions that language teachers can ask themselves when considering technology use. Their questions revolve around what students' learning goals are; what linguistic, cultural, and institutional resources are currently available; how these resources can be leveraged to support students' goals; and how teachers assess the success of students' use of these resources to achieve their goals (p. 70). These fundamental principles and questions can provide a foundation for teachers to draw from when designing activities, assignments, and learning objectives.

Teachers can also consult established standards and frameworks to inform their use of technology. In 2008, TESOL International Association, in collaboration with several experts and practitioners in the field, published a set of standards to guide the implementation of technology in English language classrooms (Healey et al., 2008). Additionally, Stockwell and Hubbard (2013) draw from scholarship in CALL, mobile learning, and mobile-assisted learning to provide ten considerations for teachers that are focused specifically on using mobile technologies to support language learning. Beyond the field of English language teaching, the International Society for Technology in Education (ISTE, n.d.) developed standards and resources for K-12 educators in all disciplines to guide digital instruction. While these standards are not geared specifically toward English language teaching, language teachers can still "enhance them to fit the specific requirements of language teaching" (Hubbard, 2008, p. 180). ISTE members are located all over the world, and the organization provides numerous resources for professional development, including published reports, online communities, podcasts, and blogs.

Facilitating Teacher Development

Perhaps ironically, technology can be leveraged in both formal and informal ways to deliver professional development about the latest developments in technology. Formal resources for professional development include resources provided by TESOL International Association such as online certificates, virtual seminars, and online courses that are available both in teacher-facilitated and self-study formats. In addition, online open-access journals, such as The Electronic Journal for English as a Second Language (TESL-EJ), regularly publish reviews and articles about internet and media tools in addition to peer-reviewed research articles. These articles can be accessed anywhere in the world, and all former issues are currently archived. Teachers can also make use of multimodal resources, such as videos in reputable YouTube channels geared toward English language teachers (e.g., SmrtEnglish), newsletters and blogs, and online discussion groups to provide content to students and to find ideas for teaching. Finally, training is needed to ensure that teachers are equipped to integrate new software into their curricula and address technical issues that may arise when using varying technological tools. Numerous technology-based resources provide video tutorials and written guidelines to help users, in addition to information for technical support.

Training Students

A critical point to keep in mind is that although students may have access to digital resources, they may not know how to use them for language learning (Chapelle & Jamieson, 2008). Therefore, they would benefit from explicit training on how to use technology for learning (Li & Zhu, 2013). Hubbard (2013) refers to this strand of scholarship as "learner training," which focuses on helping students use technology more effectively to achieve learning goals than they would without technology. Hubbard's views are similar to those of flipped learning experts, who state that teachers should show students how to interact with videos and other instructional content outside of class to maximize their learning (Bergmann & Sams, 2012). Training students is especially important when flipped learning is implemented, as students engage with course content outside of class and without the support of their teacher. Voss and Kostka (2019) assert that teachers should provide clear instructions and expectations for work completed outside of class students in order to facilitate learning and prepare them for learning in class. In flipped approaches and all others, students should not be left on their own to figure out how to use their technological resources to learn.

Ensuring Accessibility

Accessibility is a key concept in technology-supported instruction, yet training students to use technology operates on the underlying assumption that students have access to it. If students cannot readily access the tools needed to work on course assignments, learning cannot take place. In the *TESOL Technology Standards*, Healey et al. (2008) address the issue of accessibility by instead using the term "available technology" (p. 7). The authors suggest that considering teaching and learning first shifts the focus from the tool to possibilities for its adaptation and use. Once teachers know what purpose they would like technology to serve, they can begin to consider which tools will help them achieve their learning goals.

Bergmann and Sams (2012) discuss availability within the context of flipped learning and how teachers can support students' learning outside of class when technology is either limited or unavailable. As they assert, a "lack of equitable access is not an insurmountable obstacle and can be overcome with a little creativity and resourcefulness" (p. 97). For example, they describe how K-12 teachers can share videos in different ways (e.g., loading material onto flash drives or students' devices) and encourage teachers to write grants to obtain funding for resources that can support learning. In addition, teachers can do a little research to identify which resources are already available in their teaching settings by consulting with administrators, staff, instructional designers, and colleagues. For instance, there may be tools that schools or universities have licenses for but are not widely used. Similarly, there may be features of currently used tools that teachers are unaware of, especially as software is continuously updated and improved.

Egbert (2005) discusses another element of accessibility, which is the importance of accommodating different learning styles and intelligences. She goes on to say that an ideal technology-enhanced activity would be one for which students can choose the mode in which information is presented (e.g., visual images or written text). She states that giving students a choice can help meet their needs, as the advantage of using multimodal technologies is that choices are indeed available. For instance, if teachers would like students to learn content outside of class by watching a video, they could also give students a transcript to support comprehension. They could also show students how to enable closed-captioning, which may also facilitate comprehension. In this way, the focus remains on achieving learning goals and not struggling with learning new technologies.

Finally, teachers should prepare a backup plan in case technology fails or becomes unavailable. For instance, a common task in reading and writing classes is for students to work together to create mind maps of a text they have read. While electronic tools can help them work efficiently and easily edit their work, slow internet connectivity on the day of class may interfere with students' productivity. Should that be the case, teachers could bring large sheets of butcher paper to class on which students can create a mind map; they could also ask students to work at the blackboard or on a whiteboard. If students were to analyze and edit the structure of a paragraph in a Google doc but internet connectivity fails, the instructor could project a handout of the paragraph and ask students to write their revisions on paper. Planning for limited or failed access to the internet and technology tools can ensure that a lesson will run smoothly (and learning will take place) if resources become unavailable or limited. In this way, the focus also remains on learning.

Providing Assessment and Feedback

When considering the affordances of technology for learning, we must also think about how technology can measure whether learning objectives are achieved. In their review of 20 years of scholarship in assessment and technology in the journal *Language Teaching and Technology*, Chapelle and Voss (2016) discuss the major ways in which technology has impacted second language assessment. First, they describe how computer-adaptive testing adjusts the test to each unique learner and provides teachers with data about learners' performance and time spent on the test. Next, they discuss innovative testing methods that can provide opportunities for learners to learn from both the test and the process of completing the test. These developments have implications for collaborative learning, as students' work can be recorded and stored for further analysis and assessment later.

Technology can also be used to provide formative assessment. For example, polling software KAHOOT! is a free game-based tool that teachers can use to assess learning, teach new concepts, and review previously learned material. To play, students answer multiple choice questions either on the web-based platform or on the KAHOOT! mobile app. Teachers can either create their own quizzes or use existing quizzes that are publicly available and share their quizzes with other teachers at their schools. Voss and Kostka (2019) describe how teachers who implement flipped learning can use KAHOOT! to measure students' understanding of content they learned outside of the classroom. KAHOOT! can be used with English language learners in a variety of settings, such as in middle schools, high schools, and with adult learners, and in ESL or EFL contexts. Students can play KAHOOT! games using an iPad, computer, or smartphone, and teachers can opt to create either individual or team games.

Teachers may also find ways to repurpose existing software to provide feedback. For instance, Li and Li (2018) conducted a study with 13 undergraduate ESL students at a university in the United States to examine the potential of matched text detection software Turnitin for facilitating peer review online. The authors found that Turnitin helped students shift their focus from local to more global aspects of each other's papers, allowed them to provide comments more efficiently, and helped teachers manage the learning process. Shih (2011) conducted a study of 23 English learners at a university in Taiwan to examine their use of Facebook to provide peer feedback. Results show that using Facebook can lead to gains in writing skills, increased opportunities for students to learn about writing from each other, and improved collaboration among students. As these findings illustrate, traditional collaborative writing activities were made easier and more efficient with the use of software.

FUTURE DIRECTIONS

Collaboration, interaction, knowledge construction, and learning via technological mediums have become a necessary and common part of modern life. In fact, Chun et al. (2016) assert that technology "is so pervasive and so interwoven with human activity that to teach language without some form of technology would create a very limited and artificial learning environment – if it were even possible at all" (p. 65). Mobile devices, web-based tools, and social media platforms continue to become more sophisticated and more prevalent. Thus, the English language community will benefit from staying abreast of the wide range of available technologies to enhance learning and support both teachers and students in its implementation and use.

Perhaps the most promising affordance is the potential for English teachers to extend and cultivate both individual and collaborative learning in non-traditional settings and in non-traditional ways. With the ubiquitous nature of technology and its increased access in many educational settings, there is great potential for collaborative learning beyond the four walls of a traditional classroom setting in both ESL and EFL environments. Individualization and portability are thus likely to be critical features of the next stage of development with both Web 3.0 technologies (Chun et al., 2016) and English language teaching and learning more broadly. These developments may even lead to a reconceptualization of technology-supported learning. As Reinhardt (2019) notes, future research should examine how learning anytime in any place "blurs the increasingly archaic and perhaps irrelevant borders between formal and informal learning" (p. 31). Learning without borders is indeed a common thread that runs through this chapter and the three case studies presented in this unit, and it is worthy of scholarly attention.

In addition, instructional approaches that incorporate the best features of varying technology-facilitated learning approaches are likely to continue to impact English language learning in the future. For instance, flipped learning continues to garner interest in the field of TESOL, as the approach gives English learners more opportunities to work together in class on cognitively demanding tasks, receive more exposure to authentic language, and increase time spent on learning English (Voss & Kostka, 2019). Tomlinson (2013) argues that blended learning, which combines face-to-face and online learning, can optimize second language learning by providing more individualized feedback and exposure to English, offering flexibility for students and teachers, and delivering cost-effective instruction. The author states that blended learning can also address some of the challenges inherent to teaching academic English, such as addressing varying individual needs and proficiency levels in one course, large class sizes, and a lack of time to provide sufficient exposure and feedback. Both flipped and blended learning approaches can leverage technology to create collaborative and student-centered learning environments.

As noted in this chapter, opportunities and challenges are part and parcel of innovation and change. Nonetheless, the future of technology-supported English language instruction is promising. As technological tools continue to emerge, develop, and improve, approaches to using them to support English language learning will develop as well. With these developments will also come enhanced theoretical frameworks and methodologies to support implementation and research, which will in turn continue to advance English language teaching. Teachers and students who are prepared to embrace these opportunities and address these challenges will undoubtedly make the most of the affordances of technology for English language teaching and learning and continue to make a positive impact on students' learning trajectories and on the field.

Discussion Questions

1. Consider your role as a teacher, program administrator, teacher educator, and/or other stakeholder. How do you ensure that technology is effectively implemented to support learning?
2. Think about the setting in which you teach. What technological resources are available? How would you leverage them to support English language learning?
3. How do you foster successful collaboration among your students? What are the considerations you keep in mind when designing collaborative activities?
4. While technology offers many affordances for teaching and learning English, there are also drawbacks. Which challenges are the most pressing? How do you address problems that arise with your students?
5. Think about the pedagogical principles for implementing technology that are discussed in this chapter. Which do you adhere to? Which would you incorporate more effectively into your teaching?

Resources for Further Exploration

1. Chapelle, C., & Sauro, S. (Eds.). (2017). *The handbook of technology and second language teaching and learning*. Oxford: Wiley-Blackwell.
   This handbook is a collection of chapters written by experts in the field of technology and language teaching and covers topics such as teaching specific language skills, assessment, and research methods.
2. The Computer-Assisted Language Instruction Consortium (n.d.). Retrieved from https://calico.org/.
   CALICO is a professional organization that brings together language teachers who are interested in using technology to support instruction. On the organization's website, readers can find information about the annual conference and links to sister organizations.
3. Edutopia (n.d.). Retrieved from www.edutopia.org/technology-integration.
   Edutopia is a resource geared toward K-12 teachers. However, the *Technology Integration* section of this website includes informative articles and videos that are applicable to English language teachers.
4. Perren, J., Kelch, K., Byun, J., Cervantes, S., Safavi, S. (Eds.). (2017). *Applications of CALL theory in ESL and EFL environments*. Hershey, PA: IGI Global.
   This edited volume includes chapters that discuss a wide range of CALL topics, including collaborative writing, idiomaticity in CALL, flipped learning, blended learning, theoretical conceptualizations of CALL topics, and portfolio assessment.
5. The Electronic Journal for English as a Second Language (n.d.). Retrieved from www.tesl-ej.org/wordpress/.
   TESL-EJ is an open access journal that publishes four annual issues on ESL/EFL research. One section of the journal, *On the Internet*, features articles about technology tools and software that teachers can use to support learning.

REFERENCES

Bergmann, J., & Sams, A. (2012). *Flip your classroom: Reach every student in every class every day*. Alexandria, VA: ASCD.

Chapelle, C., & Jamieson, J. (2008). *Tips for teaching with CALL: Practice approaches to computer-assisted language learning*. White Plains, NY: Pearson.

Chapelle, C. A., & Voss, E. (2016). Twenty years of technology and language assessment in language learning & technology. *Language Learning & Technology, 20*(2), 116–128. doi:10125/44464

Chun, D., Kern, R., & Smith, B. (2016). Technology in language use, language teaching, and language learning. *The Modern Language Journal, 100*, 64–80.

Eberly Center for Teaching Excellence and Educational Innovation. (n.d.). Retrieved from www.cmu.edu/teaching/technology/collaborationtools.html

Egbert, J. (2005). *CALL essentials: Principles and practice in CALL classrooms*. Alexandria, VA: TESOL Press.

Godwin-Jones, R. (2018). Second language writing online: An update. *Language Learning & Technology, 22*(1), 1–15.

Healey, D., Hanson-Smith, E., Hubbard, P., Ioannou-Georgiou, S., Kessler, G., & Ware, P. (2008). *TESOL technology standards: Description, implementation, integration*. Alexandria, VA: TESOL.

Hubbard, P. (2008). CALL and the future of language teacher education. *CALICO Journal, 25*(2), 175–188.

Hubbard, P. (2013). Making a case for learner training in technology enhanced language learning environments. *CALICO Journal, 30*(2), 163–178.

International Society for Technology in Education. (n.d.). Retrieved from www.iste.org/

Jacobs, G. M. (2004, September). *Cooperative learning: Theory, principles, and techniques*. Paper presented at the First International Online Conference on Second and Foreign Language Teaching and Research.

Kessler, G. (2009). Student initiated attention to form in autonomous wiki based collaborative writing. *Language Learning & Technology, 13*(1), 79–95.

Larsen-Freeman, D., & Anderson, M. (2011). *Techniques and principles in language teaching* (3rd ed.). Oxford: Oxford University Press.

Li, J., & Li, M. (2018). Turnitin and peer review in ESL academic writing classrooms. *Language Learning & Technology, 22*(1), 27–41.

Li, M., & Zhu, W. (2013). Patterns of computer-mediated interaction in small writing groups using wikis. *Language Learning and Technology, 16*(1), 91–109.

Lomicka, L., & Lord, G. (2019). Reframing technology's role in language teaching: A retrospective report. *Annual Review of Applied Linguistics, 39*, 8–23.

Reinhardt, J. (2019). Social media in second and foreign language teaching and learning: Blogs, wikis, and social networking. *Language Teaching, 52*(1), 1–39.

Shih, R. (2011). Can Web 2.0 technology assist college students in learning English writing? Integrating Facebook and peer assessment with blended learning. *Australasian Journal of Educational Technology, 27*(5), 829–845.

Stockwell, G., & Hubbard, P. (2013). *Some emerging principles for mobile-assisted language learning*. Monterey, CA: The International Research Foundation for English Language Education.

Storch, N. (2005). Collaborative writing: Product, process, and students' reflections. *Journal of Second Language Writing, 14*, 153–173.

Storch, N. (2019). Collaborative writing. *Language Teaching, 52*(1), 40–59.

Tomlinson, B. (2013). Comments on part 1. In B. Tomlinson & C. Whittaker (Eds.), *Blended learning in English language teaching: Course design and implementation* (pp. 61–62). London: British Council.

Voss, E., & Kostka, I. (2019). *Flipping academic English language learning: Experiences from an American university*. Singapore: Springer Nature.

CASE STUDY 7.1

Developing Skills for Independent L2 Writers in Hawai'i

Democratic Participation in Classroom Assessment

Mitsuko Suzuki

To become effective 21st-century writers, L2 learners need to develop a range of knowledge and skills beyond formulaic writing structure, including critical thinking, metacognitive awareness, cross-cultural competence, technology literacy, and communication skills (Binkley et al., 2012). Recognizing the powerful role technology can play in promoting these skills, this case study used Google Docs and online editing tools to implement student-created rubric, peer-assessment, and self-editing into a college writing course. These simple, yet powerful online tools facilitated students' collaboration and discussion about the cultural differences in writing style and provided them opportunities to practice constructive communication and metacognitive skills in L2.

THE SETTING

Intermediate Academic Writing 3 (IAW3; pseudonym) is a semester-long academic writing course offered by a Hawaiian public university. The course is required for English as an additional language (EAL) learners, both undergraduate and graduate school students, who do not meet the exemption criteria (i.e., TOEFL paper-based test score 600) and had demonstrated intermediate-level proficiency on the placement test. While this course aims to develop students' writing fluency and discourse skills in both academic and personal writings, the course also aims to empower students as independent writers who can assess and improve their writing in English.

Held twice a week for a 15-week term, IAW3 adopts a process-oriented approach, which guides students to focus on the "procedures for identifying and solving problems, discovering novel ideas, expressing them in writing, and revising emergent texts" (Ferris & Hedgcock, 2014, p. 65). The course introduces essential writing skills (e.g., writing effective introduction and conclusions, summarizing, quoting) through three paper assignments: a personal reflection on one's defining moment in life, a response to written arguments, and an argument paper. For each of these paper assignments, students are required to hand in three drafts, receive feedback from their peers in class, and have at least one individual conference with the teacher. Hence, IAW3 provides students with opportunities to develop their writing skills through multiple drafting and revising.

Description of English Language Learners

In Fall 2017, IAW3 had a range of students aged from 19 to 26 enrolled with different academic goals. Seven of them were undergraduate exchange students staying for one or two semesters. They were sophomores and juniors at their home university, aiming to improve their general English language skills. Others were full-time students: two at undergraduate and six at graduate level. While these full-time students were all in need of developing their English academic writing skills, in the pre-course survey, the undergraduates were concerned with their writing at surface level (i.e., sentence structure, citation styles), whereas the graduate students were more interested in improving their writing at the discourse level. The students' majors varied, including science, geography, literature, tourism management, and business. Regardless of their backgrounds, though, it was their first time to enroll in an American university course.

The students had academic writing experiences in their first language (i.e., Chinese, Korean, Japanese, and Thai), but not necessarily in English. Most of the exchange students had previous exposure to vocabulary and grammar through reading but less experience in writing English beyond a paragraph level. On the other hand, the full-time students' previous experience in English writing was mostly through their preparation for standardized tests, such as Test of English as a Foreign Language (TOEFL) and Graduate Record Examinations (GRE).

Pedagogical Application and Innovation

The class was divided into three approximately three-week cycles. Each cycle focused on different types of text to gradually develop students' English writing and critical thinking skills. In their first cycle, students were instructed to reflect on their defining moment in life, providing reasons and evidence to illustrate the significance of the event. The second cycle's focus was a response paper, where students analyzed and evaluated the claims made in an article. For their last writing, an argument paper, students had to synthesize and logically organize different sources to support a point of view. Apart from regular class activities such as free writing, for each cycle, the students engaged in rubric making, peer assessment, and self-editing. As explained next, each of these activities covered various aspects of 21st-century skills.

The Use of Google Docs

As it was the most accessible and familiar application for the IAW3 students, Google Docs was used as the main in-class collaboration tool. Google Docs is a free word processor in which users can create, edit, and save their documents online. This web-based application lends itself to collaborative classroom activities, as documents can be shared and edited with multiple users in real-time. In IAW3, Google Docs provided a platform for the students to brainstorm ideas in small groups, initiate classroom discussions, and refine their ideas throughout the activities. These interactions, in turn, co-created their mutual understanding of "good writing" and improved their cross-cultural competence, computer skills, and communication skills in English.

Student-Created Rubric

Co-constructing the rubric for their paper assignment helps students not only discover the important aspects of writing (e.g., Becker, 2016) but also hone their communication and collaboration skills in English. For each cycle, the students first began by comparing two sample essays: one well written and one poorly written. In small groups, students were tasked to identify the well-written essay and list some characteristics of effective and ineffective writing on a shared Google doc. Their ideas led to a classroom discussion on the organization, development of ideas, and the cultural aspects of writing. As an example, in the Excerpt 1, a question related to thesis statements also encompassed cross-cultural understandings of good writing styles:

Excerpt 1

Student A: I have a question. Do you always need a thesis statement in an essay?

Teacher: Mmhh. . . . That's a good question. Any thoughts?

Student B: . . . I learned that in English you always have to.

Student A: Oh, okay . . .

Teacher: In English. . . . How about in Chinese essays? Do you need it?

This conversation further invited other students to share the writing style in their first language. The teacher then explained the purpose of thesis statements and how some English essays do not necessarily require it.

After familiarizing students with the basic structure and requirement of the essay with another round of this activity, students co-created the rubric together in class. For this activity, students opened a shared Google doc with a blank rubric with criteria categories (e.g., organization, use of language) and three levels of rating (Appendix 7.1.A). Each group was assigned to write the performance descriptions for one of these criteria. Once the groups completed this task, they examined what the other groups wrote in their assigned criteria. If the group had suggestions or questions, they added those comments in the rubric using a different color. Based on these student comments, the teacher facilitated the consensus of rubric terms. For instance, when a group wrote "Almost no grammar mistakes" for the highest level of performance under mechanics, another group suggested a stricter criterion (i.e., "No grammar mistakes"). This comment opened up a classroom discussion about their own goals as English writers, as well as that of the audience of the paper. As students agreed that comprehensibility is the most important goal to achieve, this criterion was rewritten to "No grammar mistakes that make reading difficult" and "No use of long, complex sentences that are hard to read."

Peer Assessment and Self-Editing

The peer assessment and self-editing phase encouraged students to use their metacognitive skills by giving them the opportunity to read and give feedback to each other's papers and revise their own drafts using online sources. In their first cycle, a brief introduction to a peer feedback session was held to familiarize the students with the activity. The teacher handed out a short sample essay and its feedback from two students (Appendix 7.1.B). After reading these samples, students discussed in groups which feedback was more helpful and listed their reasons on a shared Google doc. Based on this list, the class further came up with their own rules for their peer feedback session:

1. Be polite and respect the author, (Use words like "you could . . ." and "it would be even better if . . .").

2. Encouragement first. Start with compliments.

3. Clarify "why" the author needs to make improvements and give specific solutions,

4. Write more than just "good." Add explanation.

5. Do not deny the author's opinion.

These rules were always reviewed before their peer feedback sessions in other cycles.

After this feedback introduction, the students got in pairs and commented on each other's drafts using the feedback form (Appendix 7.1.C). This form was based on the criteria that corresponded to those of the rubric students co-created. As some of the students found it difficult to focus on all these criteria at the same time, students were required to specify the area that they especially wanted feedback on (see Step 1 of Appendix C). For a post-activity, students wrote a short thank you note to their peer reviewer, highlighting what they learned from their session:

"Your advice was helpful. I will work on the thesis statement."

"I think your organization is good. It showed me a good example."

"When I read your paper, I realized that my citation style was wrong."

As these comments from their thank you notes demonstrate, the students seemed to benefit not only from the feedback itself but also from reading others' pieces of writing.

The students also improved their papers by exploring and utilizing different online sources. Before submitting their second drafts, the teacher introduced several online sources (e.g., Grammarly, PaperRater) that students could use to check their grammar mistakes and plagiarism. While identifying and correcting one's grammatical errors are not always easy, these sites highlight errors and suggest a possible correction, along with an explanation associated with that grammar point. For homework, the students self-edited their drafts using one of these sites. The students kept records of the types of errors they made and focused on improving those points in their other drafts. In addition, while self-editing, the students evaluated the usefulness of the site based on its user-friendliness and the extent to which it helped them realize and revise their common errors. In class, the students exchanged their evaluations, sharing tips on how to best utilize these online tools. These tips were shared in Google Docs as a guideline for their future self-editing.

CONCLUSION

While the writing assignments in IAW3 required the employment of critical thinking, the activities embedded other 21st-century skills to scaffold these writings. The creation of a collaborative rubric encouraged learners to co-discover features of writing in different texts and cultures. In peer-assessment, students engaged in constructive communication, helping each other reflect on weaknesses and strengths. Their metacognitive awareness was further improved through online self-editing tools. Moreover, as demonstrated in a student's reflection, these 21st century skills promoted their sense of ownership (Norton, 1997) or pride in their own way of using L2 as multilingual writers:

> In my country, I learned how to get good scores on English tests. . . . But in this class, I had a lot of opportunities to share my opinions with my classmates. . . . I was ashamed with sharing my opinion with other classmates at first, but now I enjoy. Now I feel writing in English is officially one of my skills to show and express my thought or emotions.

REFERENCES

Becker, A. (2016). Student-generated scoring rubrics: Examining their formative value for improving ESL students' writing performance. *Assessing Writing*, 29, 15–24.

Binkley, M., Erstad, O., Herman, J., Raizen, S., Ripley, M., Miller-Ricci, M., & Rumble, M. (2012). Defining twenty-first century skills. In P. Griffin, B. McGaw, & E. Care (Eds.), *Assessment and teaching of 21st century skills* (pp. 17–66). Dordrecht, Netherlands: Springer.

Ferris, D., & Hedgcock, J. (2014). *Teaching L2 composition: Purpose, process, and practice* (3rd ed.). New York, NY: Routledge.

Norton, B. (1997). Language, identity, and the ownership of English. *TESOL Quarterly*, 31(3), 409–429. doi:10.2307/3587831

Borderless Learning Using Online Writing and Videoconferencing

A Case of Agriculture Students in Indonesia

Mushoffan Prasetianto

This case study illustrates how university students in Indonesia engage in an online cultural writing exchange project with university students in Japan. In this process, Indonesian students for whom English is a required subject in their university studies in Agroecotechnology collaborate on writing assignments and online discussions with their counterparts in Japan using a Moodle-based online collaborative writing space and videoconferencing.

THE SETTING

This case study describes collaboration between undergraduate students majoring in Agroecotechnology, Faculty of Agriculture, at a university in Malang, Indonesia, as they collaborated with undergraduate students at a university in Japan. For Indonesian students, English was a compulsory three-credit course and consisted of a lecture (two credit hours) and practicum (one credit hour). The English course met twice a week – one meeting for lecture and the other meeting for practicum. Each class meeting lasted one hour and 40 minutes. The course was focused on the development of the four skills – reading, writing, speaking, and listening. By the end of this course, the students were expected to be able to (1) read agriculture-related texts to inform and support their study and composition of an undergraduate thesis, (2) write reports and descriptive and expository essays, (3) orally present agriculture-scientific articles at conferences and seminars, and (4) engage in a conversation on their topic of study. The lecture format of the class focused on meeting the first two objectives, and the practicum focused on the other two. The course discussed in this case study included an online cultural exchange writing component in collaboration with a similar class for agriculture majors in Japan. The purpose of this component was to provide the students with an additional opportunity to work on their writing and reading, to develop further awareness and appreciation for cultural diversity, and to practice communicating agriculture-related issues in their local area to their collaboration partners.

DESCRIPTION OF ENGLISH LANGUAGE LEARNERS

The English language learners described in this case study were 26 first-year and five second-year undergraduate students. All students came from various ethnic and cultural groups in Indonesia and were bilingual in Bahasa Indonesia and various native languages: Papuan (1), Jakartan (4), Lampungese (1), Sundanese (9), Javanese (13), and Batak (3). Nine students were male and 22 students were female. They were 18–21 years old. On an English language proficiency test similar to TOEFL PBT (paper-based) conducted at the beginning of the course, the average score was 434 out of 677. This score corresponds to the low intermediate to intermediate English language proficiency level.

As these students were majoring in Agroecotechnology, their future professional possibilities included becoming field managers, agricultural planners, consultants, communicators, agro-entrepreneurs, government workers, researchers, and educators in agricultural and environmental sciences (Fakultas Pertanian, 2017). These students would need English in their professional careers to communicate with international clients, read contracts and partnership agreements, and write for research and academic publications.

PEDAGOGICAL APPLICATION AND INNOVATION

The English language class discussed here incorporated blended learning, using online writing activities and videoconferencing between the students in Indonesia and Japan. Blended learning in this class combined online and face-to-face modalities where the students collaborated and engaged in online tasks outside of the classroom for six weeks. In class, the students were guided in the development of their academic writing skills starting from how to write a clear sentence to how to write an academic essay.

The online collaborative writing component was a part of the Online Culture Exchange Program (OCEP) – a Moodle-based collaborative writing space run by the Language Education Center and Center for Animal Disease Control at the University of Miyazaki, Japan (https://ocep.vss.miyazaki-u.ac.jp/esp/).

Online Writing Exchange Structure

The online writing exchange aimed to improve the students' writing skills and increase intercultural knowledge. The students were expected to work on their expository and descriptive writing on the topics of nature, culture, global environment, and local agriculture-related issues. Language-wise, the students worked on using present, past, and present perfect tenses, adjective clauses, passive voice, and various question structures. Each student was paired with a writing partner from Japan and had to complete some assignments in collaboration with this partner.

The writing exchange required the students to write one initial post of at least 100 words in response to a discussion prompt developed by the instructors. The students needed to respond to the post of their writing partner and to the posts of two other students from Japan in at least 20 words. The students were encouraged to ask questions, request clarifications, and state their own opinions on the topic. They also had to respond to all comments and questions made to their initial posts. This created space to establish initial interactions and connections between the writing exchange participants.

The writing exchange was organized in four stages that corresponded to four topics of discussion and inquiry.

1. Stage One: Introductions
   The students were asked to introduce themselves and write about places important to them, such as their campus and hometown, in order to get to know each other.

2. Stage Two: Nature and culture
   The students could choose between the topics of nature and culture and were asked to describe one species of plants or animals or discuss a cultural practice.

3. Stage Three: Environmental issues
   Three videos on global environmental issues with transcripts were uploaded on the OCEP platform. The students needed to select and watch one of the videos and discuss/express their opinions on the topics and issues raised in the video.

4. Stage Four: Agricultural issues
   The students chose an agricultural problem or challenging issue in their surroundings. They needed to explain the issue and give some solutions. They were encouraged to support their opinions with some data (e.g., by inserting relevant tables and figures).

Preparation for Collaboration

Both course instructors in Indonesia and Japan collaborated to set up the course. Together, they defined learning objectives, identified the structure and topics of online discussions, and ensured that all components of the online collaboration aligned with the students' field of study and language learning objectives of the two courses. They also developed the time line for the online discussion, set up a videoconference between the two classes, and assigned study buddies. The study buddy system was used for the students to have a regular collaboration partner in order to bring some interaction predictability to the project, maximize student interactions across the two classes, and create a system of mutual support and accountability.

Online Collaborative Work

The students mainly used the internet browser on their smartphones to access the OCEP website, make initial posts, and respond to their partners. With excellent Wi-Fi connection on campus and relatively good internet connectivity in the city (4G networks), using smartphones worked well and eliminated the need for the students to bring their laptops just for the purpose of the exchange. The students could access their discussions and the OCEP website in various locations and whenever they had time.

Collaborating with a "buddy" from Japan and discussing the topics, the students could also upload images related to the topic to complement or visualize what they have written (see Figure 7.2.1). The students engaged in a series of posts responding to initial posts, asking questions, and commenting on their buddy's answers. From this post-reply activity, the students were able to exchange knowledge through questions and answers on the topic of the respective collaboration stage. They were encouraged to ask questions about the initial posts to deepen their understanding of the topic and their partner's perspectives. This activity generated various language production from the students such as simple present, simple past, and present

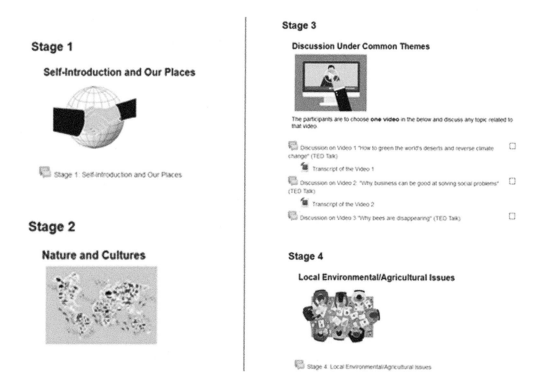

Figure 7.2.1 Examples of student's topic discussions on the OCEP platform

Source: Mushoffan Prasetianto

Credit: Tamao Araki, organizer of the program

perfect tenses; noun and adjective clauses; and Why and Yes/No questions while providing a setting for the students to get to know each other better. As a result of this online writing exchange, Indonesian students deepened their knowledge about the culture of Japan, its nature, and agriculture-related issues.

In the Classroom

Students prepared for their online collaborative work and reported on it during in-class meetings. In class, at the beginning of the online exchange program, the students were organized in groups of four. The groups stayed the same for the duration of the online writing exchange, and the instructor assigned the groups based on students' levels of English language proficiency. The instructor looked at the results of proficiency tests, quizzes, and assignments to ensure that a variety of language levels were present in each group to facilitate peer learning.

Before the students wrote their initial posts at every stage of the exchange, they shared and discussed their drafts with the group. In these group discussions, the students gave feedback, discussed content, and checked grammar accuracy and offered corrective feedback. After that, the students revised their drafts and shared revised posts with the group, which led to another round of feedback and revisions. This share-check-revise activity aimed to prepare the students to post online and provide an opportunity for peer learning and feedback while focusing on the use of grammar tenses, passive voice, and adjective clauses. The instructor monitored group discussions and was ready to assist when needed.

Through observations of students' group work and while reading the online posts, the instructor took note of frequent grammar mistakes and addressed them later in class. This provided another opportunity for the students to work on certain grammatical elements that were challenging to them and improve their writing.

The assessment of the online writing exchange was based on two components: active interaction with the exchange partner through their posts and the content and accuracy of their initial posts. To assess the students' active interaction, the instructor looked at the level of participation and engagement in online discussions. If a student made one initial post of at least 100 words at every stage of the writing exchange, they would get 25 points. If a student gave three replies – one to a post by their exchange buddy and two to the posts of other Japanese students, they would get 15 points. If students responded to a reply written by a Japanese student to their initial post, they would get 10 points. The assessment component of initial posts evaluated grammatical features (e.g., tenses, passive vs active voice, adjective clauses) and the originality of the post. If students used the correct tenses and adjective clauses, they got 25 points. If students wrote original posts, they got 25 points.

Videoconference

During the collaboration, students got a chance to talk to their Japanese counterparts using Skype as a videoconferencing tool (see Figure 7.2.2). This provided them with an additional opportunity to interact with their collaboration buddies and also practice listening and speaking skills. Videoconferences were conducted twice, during the fourth and sixth weeks of the program. The instructors in Indonesia and Japan identified the times for videoconferences, prepared with assistance from IT staff all necessary equipment (cameras, microphones, LCD projectors, and screens), and tested the internet connection.

During videoconferences, the students in both countries asked each other questions about life on their campuses, their field of study, and cultural aspects and brought up other topics from their online discussions. As they prepared questions in advance, they focused on question structures and were encouraged to use images and gestures to facilitate communication and comprehension.

Students were highly enthusiastic about videoconferences, as they were excited to interact with students from a different country and see their online partners. And it was a new experience for them. They were eager to ask questions, even though they occasionally needed recasts and clarifications to facilitate their comprehension. In both conference days they requested to extend the length of the videoconference and to add another conference day.

Both instructors were present in class during videoconferences and helped out when students needed additional language support and clarifications. In addition, the instructors acted as moderators during the video sessions to ensure that the interactions moved along and that everyone got a chance to participate.

Figure 7.2.2 A videoconference in progress

Source: Mushoffan Prasetianto

Both videoconferences were video-recorded, and the recordings were used to assess students' speaking and overall participation in the activity. In speaking assessment, the instructors focused on the students' ability to ask clear and grammatically correct questions and appropriately answer the questions addressed to them.

CONCLUSION

Telecollaboration between two university-level English language classes in Indonesia and Japan used a Moodle-based online collaborative writing space and videoconferencing to facilitate the development of integrated language skills, content knowledge, and cultural learning. Students engaged in peer-learning through a series of online posts on personal and professional topics and got a chance to meet each other virtually and engage in oral interactions via Skype during in-class videoconferencing sessions. Thus, the use of telecollaborative technology facilitated students' engagement in English while further mastering their oral and written command of the target language.

REFERENCE

Fakultas Pertanian. (2017). *Study program specification, bachelor program: Agroecotechnology study program*. Unpublished Program Standards. Malang, Indonesia: Universitas Brawijaya.

Implementing Flipped Classrooms in Uzbek and Karakalpak EFL Teacher Education

Gena Bennett, Aybolgan Borasheva, and Dilnoza Ruzmatova

A flipped classroom (FC) is an alternative instructional model to traditional lecture-based instruction in which lectures are removed from class time and delivered to students via technology; for example, via video recordings and other online learning materials (Bergman & Sams, 2012; Brinks Lockwood, 2014) like PDFs, recorded sounds, and websites (Ozdamli & Aşıksoy, 2016). Then, based on students' understanding of the material received outside of class, time in class is spent in workshop fashion, raising questions and engaging in activities such as group work, discussions, and projects. This case study describes the use of Google Classroom and the text messaging app Telegram for implementation of FC in tertiary institutions in Uzbekistan in order to increase students' English proficiency by providing more opportunities for use of the language, participation in class, an increase in confidence, and overall enthusiasm for learning.

THE SETTING

Uzbekistan is a country in Central Asia with a population of 32 million. The official language of the country is Uzbek, but as a former state of the USSR, Russian is spoken at all levels of life. Given its importance as an international language, English has also become important to education in Uzbekistan and is now required at primary, secondary, and tertiary levels. This case study involves institutions of higher education, both of which train future teachers, in two regions of Uzbekistan – the capital Tashkent and the autonomous Republic of Karakalpakstan. The Uzbekistan State World Languages University (UzSWLU) in Tashkent is the leading university for teaching foreign languages, and its graduates typically work as English translators/ interpreters or teach English in educational institutions at all levels. Nukus State Pedagogical Institute (NSPI) in Karakalpakstan is an institute aimed at training specialists in many areas of public education. Before leaving NSPI, each student has a contract with the primary or secondary school where they will work after graduation. Like many countries where English is not used regularly outside of the classroom, the overall English proficiency of Uzbek citizens, including many English teachers, is low.

Like many developing countries, the number of mobile phone users in Uzbekistan exceeds the number of internet users – 25 million to 15 million, respectively (Hootsuite, 2018). The cloud-based instant messaging and voice over IP service Telegram is the most popular messenger app in Uzbekistan, which actually leads the world in the number of users of Telegram (Sevitt, 2017). In fact, mobile companies provide extra megabytes for Telegram so users can download or watch videos, as the authors of this chapter know from their own mobile phone accounts.

As a way to better prepare future teachers to learn and use English, we started implementing a FC model in our teacher-training classes.

DESCRIPTION OF ENGLISH LANGUAGE LEARNERS

Most students at both UzSWLU and NSPI are bilingual in Uzbek and Russian, and many of them are multilingual and speak an additional ethnic language such as Karakalpak, Tajik, or Turkmen. Students in this case study are typical college-age, 18–25 years old, though there is one 45-year-old student who was returning to school for a second career in English language education. In this case study, we focus on second-year students since they were already familiar with campus life and the challenges of being a student and may respond with enthusiasm to an innovation like FC. Like many who study and teach foreign languages in Uzbekistan, all but one of the students are female. At NSPI, students mainly take their courses in Russian, Karakalpak, or Uzbek, and English levels may vary from A1 to B1 on the Common European Framework of Reference for Languages scale (CEFRL). English is the main language of classroom instruction at UzSWLU, so the level is higher, typically B1 to B2, on the CEFRL scale. Because neither institution has placement exams, there is a range of levels in each class, and the instructors must determine current students' levels and adjust input accordingly.

PEDAGOGICAL APPLICATION AND INNOVATION

In traditional lecture-based classrooms, teachers present course content through a lecture format in which students are passive receivers of knowledge. Students are then expected to apply this knowledge through home tasks, and in the next class session the teacher reviews materials and proceeds to the next lecture. With this instructional model, teachers rarely have the chance to interact with students or encourage students to interact with one another. Thus, teachers have been looking for ways to change this class dynamic and also to incorporate technology into their classrooms to create better learning opportunities for their students (Koehler, Mishra, Hershey, & Peruski, 2004). In FCs, lectures are removed from class time and delivered to students through pre-class input using various technology applications. Then, time in class is spent in workshop fashion, raising questions and engaging in class activities such as group work, discussions, and projects (Halili & Zainuddin, 2015; Lee & Wallace, 2018; Milman, 2012; Oki, 2016). With FCs, students actively participate in learning via constructive processes as they become more autonomous learners. In addition, FC provides a more flexible learning environment as learning is not limited to the four walls of schools anymore and can happen at any point in time outside of class (Köruğlu & Çakir, 2017).

FCs are still an innovative methodology today, but in our context, they are, literally, unheard of. The benefits of FC, particularly increased willingness to communicate and an increase in the use of the target language, seemed alluring for our foreign language environment where we regularly face such challenges as lack of student participation, limited opportunities for interaction and authentic communication, and diminished motivation. As two of us completed our first blended course, with the third author as the instructor, and experienced the benefits of FC firsthand, we were eager to try this model with our own students.

The first consideration for implementing FC in Uzbekistan was access to and reliability of internet access. We were unsure if FC required the use of technology or if a mere "flipping" of lecture and homework activities was enough. An investigation into the literature showed that while FCs are generally tied to the use of technology, this does not always have to be the case (Brinks Lockwood, 2014; Lee & Wallace, 2018). Students can study various types of materials (e.g., readings from a textbook or worksheets developed by the teacher) on their own outside of class in order to grasp the meaning of the content. The most important consideration for FC is this access to content outside of class in order to free up in-class time for workshop activities based on this content. The second consideration, then, was how to deliver the pre-course content. Since authors work in two different universities, there was an opportunity to implement two models. At one university, a Google Classroom was set up with course materials and opportunities for discussion (Figures 7.3.1 and 7.3.2), and students could access the Google Classroom at home, or they could access the Classroom at the university's computer lab. Although this still put the content inside the school walls, the students could access it at any time outside of their face-to-face class and still had to be prepared for in-class activities and projects. At the second university, the teacher emailed students copies of materials and also set up a binder of materials in an office accessible to students. Again, students may have accessed the materials in the school, but in-class time was reserved for applications, activities, discussions, and projects.

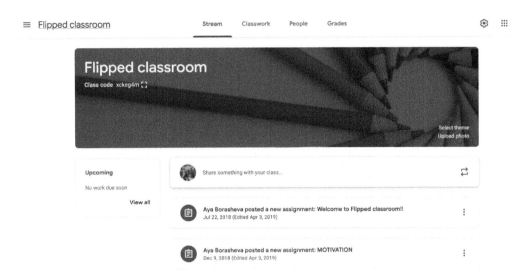

Figure 7.3.1 Google Classroom setting

Source: Google and the Google logo are registered trademarks of Google LLC, used with permission

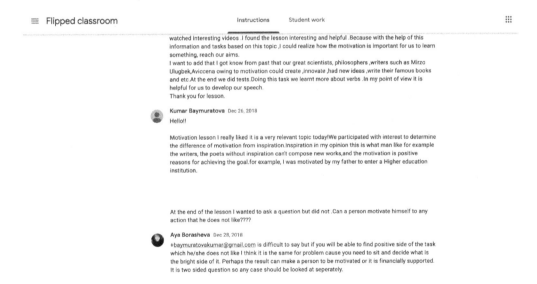

Figure 7.3.2 A glance at Google Classroom process

Source: Google and the Google logo are registered trademarks of Google LLC, used with permission

Soon after starting to follow the FC model, we had an additional idea. Considering the ubiquitous use of the messaging app Telegram, we decided to engage students at both universities via Telegram. First, a Telegram channel was created as a source for materials (Figure 7.3.3A). After that, a group chat was established where students could ask questions or discuss anything concerning FC (Figure 7.3.3B). Although students were allowed to participate in any language in which they felt comfortable, the group chat was led in English, and many students participated in English. Students also began sharing interesting materials on the group chat, taking ownership of the activity (Figure 7.3.3C).

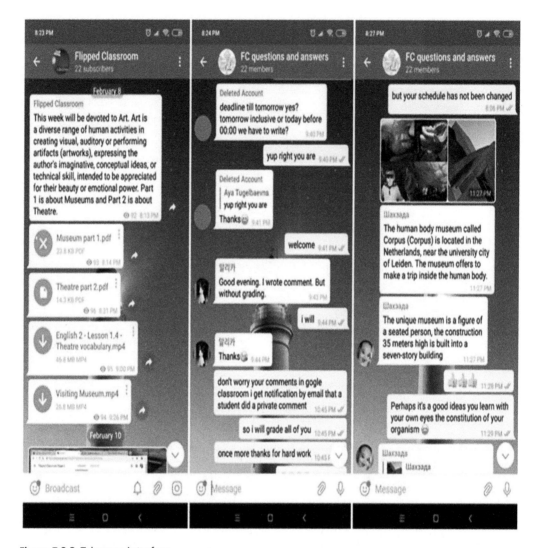

Figure 7.3.3 Telegram interface
Source: Creative Commons Licensing

The use of Telegram to deliver FC materials was innovative and allowed students access to materials outside of school, in any place, at any time, further allowing us to implement one of the core characteristics of FC. For example, the students reported that they were able to access the materials on Telegram on their way to or from school.

Another consideration in implementing FC in our context was dealing with the students' apprehension toward working with materials online, as this was completely new to them. Anticipating questions from the students, we had discussions to ensure that the students fully understood the tenets and purposes of FC and that we addressed any outstanding questions. For example, when students first heard about FC, their concern was that it would affect their marks because they wouldn't have the bandwidth to download videos. The use of Telegram eased this concern because many mobile companies provide extra megabytes to download from Telegram. Instructors also shared and discussed Bloom's taxonomy (as cited in Halili & Zainuddin, 2015, p. 315) with students to demonstrate the advantages of FC compared to a traditional classroom. In this discussion, students were presented with an example scenario. We asked them to imagine two situations: when a student knows the course materials before class and is then able to answer questions during class versus when a student hasn't seen the course materials beforehand and therefore cannot answer teacher questions in class; which one is better? Moreover, students were told that they had their teachers as guides and could approach us at any time to request help or ask questions. These meetings were very productive and addressed the students' fears. An email from one student demonstrates this clearly.

Nov 19, 2018

Hello!

At first, it [FC] seemed too hard for me. Then after preparing to class works at home, I could understand the lesson.

I like this method because it helps us to study deeper. We have enough time to learn and prepare for the materials, also we discuss it with the teacher all lesson, in which we can ask unknown things and have an answer to them.

A final consideration in implementing a FC was the workload of the teacher. To get all the materials available to students outside of class, the teachers had to do more work ahead of time. The teacher also had to spend more time looking for and creating online materials that students could access. Furthermore, the teachers had to be well prepared for class, as students arrived ready to engage and discuss. It was not enough to just lead the students through exercises in the textbook. During class, students asked more questions not only about course topics, but also about other information they had found outside of class. This indicated another benefit of FC – an increase in student autonomy

After our first semester using FC, we saw an increase in willingness to communicate, use of English in and outside of the classroom, enthusiasm for learning, as well as an increase in overall satisfaction with the FC instructional model. For example, based on three in-class observations, students in the FC made more than twice as many contributions in class (e.g., asking or answering questions, giving presentations, having conversation) as students concurrently enrolled in a traditional class. Furthermore, we have observed that the students in the FC were more willing to use the target language after participating in FC than students in the concurrent traditional class. In addition, after participating in the FC, 87% of students felt that their English had improved. The following post from a student in Google Classroom illustrates students' overall impression of using FC:

Thanks for giving the opportunity to participate in this experiment. Together with FC and you my English has noticeably improved. All your topics are super cool 👍 The most favorite thing to me is that we learned English not with boring learning of grammar, but with useful exercises, video, listening, reading. Thank you very much you tried to make all the topics clear to us. I would really like to continue FC in the next term.

(Comment from Google Classroom. N.N. 8:45 PM)

CONCLUSION

Implementing FC in tertiary institutions that prepare teachers in Uzbekistan has offered an innovative model in Central Asia to increase students' English engagement. The use of technology to conduct a FC provided students with more opportunities to use English, participate in class, increase confidence, and overall become more enthusiastic about English language learning. Students and teachers alike enjoyed the FC format, as it created conditions to increase engagement, and English language use thus improves English performance and brings liveliness to the learning atmosphere of the classroom. On the post-course survey, 100% of students in the FC indicated that they wanted to participate in FC learning in the future! As a result, we are currently working on developing and implementing more flipped learning English language classrooms throughout our region.

References

Bergmann, J., & Sams, A. (2012). *Flip your classroom: Reach every student in every class every day*. Washington, DC: International Society for Technology in Education.

Brinks Lockwood, R. (2014). *Flip it! Strategies for the ESL classroom*. Ann Arbor, MI: University of Michigan Press.

Halili, S. H., & Zainuddin, Z. (2015). Flipping the classroom: What we know and what we don't. *The Online Journal of Distance Education and E-Learning*, 3(1), 28–35.

Hootsuite. (2018). *Digital 2018: Uzbekistan* [PowerPoint slides]. Retrieved from www.slideshare.net/DataReportal/digital-2018-uzbekistan-january-2018

Koehler, M. J., Mishra, P., Hershey, K., & Peruski, L. (2004). With a little help from your students: A new model for faculty development and online course design. *Journal of Technology and Teacher Education*, 12(1), 25–55.

Köruğlu, Z. C., & Çakir, A. (2017). Implementation of flipped instruction in language classrooms: An alternative way to develop speaking skills of pre-service English language teachers. *International Journal of Education and Development Using Information and Communication Technology*, 13(2), 42–55.

Lee, G., & Wallace, A. (2018). Flipped learning in English as a foreign language classroom: Outcomes and perceptions. *TESOL Quarterly*, 52(1), 62–84.

Milman, N. (2012). The flipped classroom strategy: What is it and how can it best be used? *Distance Learning*, 9(3), 85–87.

Oki, Y. (2016). Flipping a content-based ESL course: An action research report. *Hawai'i Pacific University TESOL Working Paper Series*, 14, 62–75.

Ozdamli, F., & Aşıksoy, G. (2016). Flipped classroom approach. *World Journal on Educational Technology*, 8(2), 98–105.

Sevitt, D. (2017, February 27). *The most popular messaging apps by country*. Retrieved from www.similarweb.com/blog/popular-messaging-apps-by-country

UNIT 8
Digital Literacy and TESOL

English Language Education and Digital Literacy in the 21st Century

Richmond Dzekoe

FRAMING THE ISSUE

Literacy, traditionally understood as the ability to read and write, is important in teaching language and culture because it is "intimately tied to the sociocultural practices of language use in a given society" (Kern, 2000, p. 25). The relationship between literacy and language learning is evident in the plethora of research and other scholarly works on how to develop literacy through language education. Various ways of theorizing literacy influence the development of different language learning theories and pedagogies. The traditional notion of literacy informs pedagogical practices in language education that focus mainly on helping students develop text-based (alphabetic) literacy, such as competence in speaking, listening, reading, and writing. Underlying the text-based literacy approach in language education is the understanding that knowledge about the world is derived primarily through reading and writing, and the belief that language learning should help students acquire knowledge about linguistic and cultural systems for communication (Hafner, Chik, & Jones, 2015).

The early parts of the 20th century saw a major shift in the traditional notion of literacy. Works in literacy studies, such as John Debes's (1969) article "The Loom of Visual Literacy" and Rudolf Arnheim's (1969) book *Visual Thinking*, began to call for a definition of literacy that goes beyond the traditional meaning. Specifically, these scholars argue that to be literate, one has to have both text-based literacy and visual literacy, which "refers to a group of vision competencies a human being can develop by seeing and at the same time having and integrating other sensory experiences" (Debes, 1969, p. 27). These competencies include the ability to comprehend, interpret, and create messages in visual formats. To some extent, this idea of visual thinking initiated the sensory turn in literacy theory with a central argument that the ability to use the senses and sensory experiences is an authentic source of knowledge about the world. Sensory knowledge is an essential component of literacy because each of the senses has a vital role to play in the acquisition of knowledge about the world. In second language education, this new shift in the notion of literacy influenced theories and pedagogical practices that began to emphasize the use of visual aids (e.g., the audio-lingual and communicative language teaching methods) and gestures (e.g., total physical response). The notion of visual literacy also guided a rich body of research on how skills in visual and text-based (alphabetic) literacy might enhance performance in each other.

Research in literacy studies, applied linguistics, and English language education in the 1980s and 1990s continued to call attention to the importance of visual literacy and the need to explore the impact of technological advancement on literacy practices (Mills, 2016). This era saw the development of new notions of literacy, such as technological literacy, computer literacy, and information literacy. These new concepts extended the notion of literacy to include information communication technology (ICT) skills needed to function effectively in a society controlled by technology (Buckingham, 2006). These new notions of literacy were generally praised for their emphasis on the important relationship between technology, information, and literacy as well as the need for practical skills and application of knowledge. However, they were also criticized for being too functional and too focused on vocational and technological skills. Some other theorists, such as the New London Group (1996), emphasized sociocultural and sensory competencies that one needs to develop in addition to technology literacy and information literacy for successful meaning-making and sharing of knowledge about the world. Mills (2016) observes that this line of research has contributed to multiple notions of literacy, including the following:

- Critical literacy (competence in how language and issues of social inequality, power, and human agency are related).

- Socio-spatial literacy (competence in how literacy practices are socially produced across different geographical regions).

- Socio-material literacy (competence in issues of how literacy practices interact with material artifacts in teaching and learning contexts).

- Multimodal literacy (competence in the use of different semiotic modes for meaning-making).

In language education, this notion of literacies was made prominent by the work of the New London Group (1996). They reintroduced the theory of multimodality into language education with emphasis on the interconnection among representation, meaning-making, and communication as distinct but interrelated processes that depend on the combination of different semiotic modes (Kress, 2010, Kress & Van Leeuwen, 2001). They also developed a pedagogy of "multiliteracies" (see Shakina Rajendram's discussion on this in Chap. 5 of this volume).

Advances in digital technology and the blurring of the lines between life online and life offline, especially from 2009–2019, have led to a growing interest in digital literacy. The notion of digital literacy has gained worldwide importance as evident in various initiatives around the world. For example, the Global Digital Literacy Council project aims to develop global digital literacy standards based on input from subject matter experts worldwide (gdlcouncil.org, 2019). Initiatives also include policies and projects by governments in Africa, Asia, Australia, Europe, and the United States that aim to integrate digital literacy into national education curricula.

Today, digital technologies greatly influence how English language learners encounter and interact with the target language in and outside the classroom (Godwin-Jones, 2015). More than ever, language teachers are expected to acquire digital literacy so that they can help students develop digital literacy skills necessary to negotiate multiple discourses, as they use information and multimedia technologies to comprehend and produce multimodal texts in different cultural and linguistic contexts (Hafner et al., 2015). In what follows, I explore the conceptual and theoretical understandings of digital literacy and examine their implications for teaching English as an additional language.

Concepts and Theoretical Considerations

The notion of digital literacy was introduced into academic discourse by research that focuses specifically on how the internet and different forms of digital technology are shaping human communication and literacy practices. The concept was made popular by Paul Gilster's (1997) seminal work, *Digital Literacy*. Even though this work is criticized for its lack of clarity on the definition of digital literacy, it provided one of the earliest frameworks for understanding literacy as it specifically relates to digital technologies. One of the many definitions of digital literacy that Gilster provides is "the ability to understand and use information in multiple formats from a wide variety of sources when it is presented via computers" (p. 6). From this conceptualization, digital literacy is seen as comprising four competencies: the ability to search the internet, evaluate information, assemble knowledge, and navigate hypertext. Gilster considers technology skills and information mastering important; however, he identifies the main goal of digital literacy as "mastering ideas" but not just technology skills or "keystrokes" (Gilster, 1997, p. 15).

As a concept, digital literacy has been continuously evolving. The question of what constitutes digital literacy continues to be one of debate, as seen in the plethora of conceptualizations in the existing literature with different emphasis on skills and/or performances that one needs to master to be considered digitally literate

(Son, Park, & Park, 2017). Works that have looked at digital literacy from skills perspectives have identified the need to develop the following skills:

- *Photo-visual*: Comprehending graphic information
- *Reproduction*: Creating new and meaningful texts from existing ones
- *Branching*: Constructing knowledge using hypertexts, links, and other non-linear navigation
- *Informational*: Evaluating the validity and credibility of information
- *Socio-emotional*: Understanding and successfully applying the "rules" of cyberspace communication

(Martin, 2005).

Other theorists have identified different dimensions of digital literacy, including:

- *Operational*: Ability to use technology
- *Semiotic*: Comprehending and using language associated with the new multimedia
- *Cultural*: Integrating into the intellectual environment of the information society
- *Civic*: Ability to understand the rights and responsibilities in relation to new technological context

(Tornero, 2004).

When viewed from the perspectives of skills and dimensions, digital literacy comprises technology literacy, information literacy, and sociocultural literacy. This chapter adopts Martin's (2005) definition of digital literacy as:

> the awareness, attitude and ability to appropriately use digital tools and facilities to identify, access, manage, integrate, evaluate, analyze, and synthesize digital resources, construct new knowledge, create media expressions, and communicate with others, in context of specific life situations, in order to enable constructive social action; and to reflect on this process.
>
> (p. 135)

In second language education, the conceptualization of digital literacy is influenced by two main theoretical perspectives: the functional/skills approach and sociocultural approach (Reinhardt & Thorne, 2011). The functional/skills approach mainly sees digital literacy as using digital tools to access and use information to develop text-based literacy skills of reading, writing, listening, and speaking. Emphasis is placed on developing skills and competence in using technology and information, such as searching and using internet sources effectively. However, such skills and competencies are mostly considered "add-ons" to the language course. Teachers who adopt a functional/skills approach to developing digital literacy in ESL/EFL classrooms tend to see digital technologies as "tools" for completing formal classroom language learning tasks (Tour, 2015). They belong to a group that see literacy practices in informal language learning settings, such as online gaming and social networking sites, as "irrelevant or even as a waste of time" (Godwin-Jones, 2015, p. 9). With this approach, not much attention is paid to how digital media influences and shapes learners' sociocultural interaction beyond the classroom (Guikema & Williams, 2014). This lack of attention to sociocultural aspects of digital literacy is what is said to "confine digital literacy to a form of instrumental or functional literacy" (Buckingham, 2006, p. 267).

The sociocultural approach to digital literacy in language education is based on the view of language and language learning as a social event and cultural practice mediated and shaped by human action (Gee, 2000, Lantolf & Pavlenko, 1995). The sociocultural view of digital literacy "complexifies and contests the notion of literacy as primarily a brain-local skill involving an individual engaged in deciphering and producing graphically rendered language" (Thorne, 2013, p. 193). This means that literacy involves more than just the individual developing knowledge about language. It also involves understanding social and cultural factors that affect how language might be used to get things done successfully in different contexts in society. Proponents of this approach to digital literacy, therefore, argue that "language teaching must foster literacy, not only in terms of basic reading and writing skills but also in terms of a broader discourse competence" (Kern, 2000, p. 2). Thus, the integration of digital literacy in ESL/EFL classrooms should go beyond developing technological and informational skills and should focus on helping students gain a deeper awareness of how to use these skills in broader cultural contexts (Buckingham, 2006) and become creative and responsible citizens.

Further, from the sociocultural perspective, digital literacy is seen as involving more than just a single notion of literacy and is referred to, in plural, as "digital literacies" (Nascimento & Knobel, 2017). While digital literacy is conceptualized as part of new literacies needed for the 21st century, it is also seen as distinct from other forms of new literacies because of its unique emphasis on literacy practices in a digital environment. Conceptualizing digital literacy in its plural form (digital literacies) is usually meant to emphasize its nature as an integration of different literacies, including technology literacy (e.g., ability to use digital technology), information literacy (the ability to recognize a need for information, search, evaluate, organize, and use information from the internet and other electronic sources effectively and responsibly), and new media literacy (ability to navigate the complexities involved in issues of representation, authorship, the role of audience, and the critical use of language in digital media). It also includes sociocultural literacy (ability to identify and use social and cultural norms and rules considered appropriate in online environments) to ensure effective participation, collaboration, networking, creativity, shared expertise, as well as the creation and distribution of multimodal contents (Buckingham, 2006; Godwin-Jones, 2015; Hafner et al., 2015; Lankshear & Knobel, 2011; Tour, 2015). Some scholars have questioned the notion of "literacies" and called attention to problems that arise when literacy is pluralized. However, current scholars of second language education generally agree that there is a "blurring of boundaries among literacies" (Godwin-Jones, 2015). No single notion of literacy captures the skills, competencies, and processes that enable one to use digital technology safely, search and evaluate information on the internet, use various semiotic modes to create digital content, collaborate, and communicate with others responsibly and effectively. There is a general agreement among scholars that digital literacy is composed of an integration of different types of literacies (Nascimento & Knobel, 2017).

A distinct focus within the sociocultural approach is the critical perspective. It holds that language learning and literacy practices should focus on lived experiences of students, especially "the things in their lives that are problematic, which they might be able to change and improve through the tool of literacy or an additional language" (Crookes, 2012, p. 2). Further, the critical view posits that the digital technologies we use are not neutral but are value-laden tools that carry inherent philosophies and biases that shape the way we see, understand, and live in the world. As Jones and Hafner (2012) point out, the use of digital technologies involves the establishment of relationships and development of multiple identities through interaction with others. In second language education, people who hold the critical perspective argue that digital literacy should be taught as an aid to social equality. They call attention to issues, such as the digital divide, the colonization of the online space by the most powerful, cyber-bullying, and social isolations (Mills, 2016). They also draw attention to the relationship between language and power and the need to equip learners with critical language skills that empower them to question whose interest a particular type of communication might be serving (Machin & Mayr, 2012). Equipping learners to judge the authenticity and credibility of internet sources requires helping them to identify the "intended consumers, and assumptions about gender, age, social class, ethnicity, belief systems, and silences" (Mills & Levido, 2011, p. 84) as well as the ideological goals that a particular text might be serving.

Another theoretical perspective used to facilitate the development of digital literacy in second language education is multimodality, which refers to the "use of several semiotic modes in the design of a semiotic product or event" (Kress & Van Leeuwen, 2001, p. 20). It builds on the idea of semiotics and critical pedagogy and calls for integration of semiotic modes, such as written, visual (still and moving images), gestures, and sound in meaning-making. Multimodal composing may be in the form of digital (e.g., CDs, computers, or the internet) or print-based texts. Proponents of multimodal composing as a means of developing digital literacy in second language education argue that learners should be helped to understand the *affordance* of digital tools (how digital technologies are designed and what they allow users to do). In digital compositions, each mode in a multimodal ensemble has a distinct affordance that relates to sociocultural norms of interaction (Royce, 2007; Selwyn & Facer, 2007). In a world where almost all screen-based texts are multimodal in nature, it is "impossible to make sense of texts, even of their linguistic parts alone, without having a clear idea of what these other features might be contributing to the meaning of a text" (Kress, 2000, p. 337). Also, students need to understand *intersemiotic complementarity* (how different modes work together in an orchestration of meaning in a multimodal text) as well as their role as *designers* who integrate different modes of representation used in the production of multimodal texts (Kern, 2000).

All the theoretical perspectives discussed earlier, the functional/skills, sociocultural, critical, and multimodal perspectives, emphasize the need to expose language learners to digital literacy in a way that will prepare them to succeed in various aspects of their lives in today's digital world. This has important implications for how we teach digital literacy in second language education.

IMPLICATIONS FOR ENGLISH LANGUAGE EDUCATION

A number of studies have explored various ways of teaching digital literacy in English as a second language (ESL) and English as foreign language (EFL) contexts, including the development of digital literacy among children and adults ESL learners, marginalized school communities around the world, and ESL/ EFL college classrooms (Buckingham, 2006; Cairo, 2014; Son et al., 2017; Yeh, 2018). Because the digital environment allows the integration of several semiotic modes, most of these studies have adopted computer-based multimodal composing activities as a means of teaching digital literacy. Findings from these and other studies have shed useful light on steps that need to be taken for a successful development of digital literacy in language education.

Embracing a Broader Meaning of Literacy

Exciting research shows that teachers have used different tasks, including digital storytelling, creation of online posters, personal websites, and online portfolios to integrate digital literacy into language education. However, most activities aimed at developing digital literacy still focus mainly on written communication, such as wiki and blog posts and forum discussions (Godwin-Jones, 2015). Also, most of these activities have focused on the use of digital tools in formal language classrooms. There are only a few instances where digital multimodal composing goes beyond activities in the classroom to include informal language learning that occurs in digital environments, such as Facevolume, Flickr, and Instagram outside class assignments and projects (Hafner et al., 2015). Even though teachers are exploring digital technologies in their classroom, "language teaching with digital technologies has not been transformed and many teachers have been reluctant to acknowledge [an] extended understanding of literacy" (Tour, 2015, p. 124). They see print-based literacies and forms of assessment as superior to other forms of literacy. Successful integration of digital literacy into English language teaching requires a pedagogical shift, which admittedly is difficult to make but one that the realities of our times demand of us. English language teachers need to transcend the traditional notion of literacy and embrace literacy in a broader sense. It is important that, as language teachers, we teach our students not only the ability to speak, listen, read, and write, but also broader literacy skills, such as critical consumption and production of information, collaboration, creativity, problem solving, innovation, and digital safety. Students need all these skills to construct and decode meaning successfully as they communicate in digital environments.

Developing a Multimodal Syllabus

In addition, digital literacy cannot be taught as an "add-on" or Appendix A to a syllabus based on traditional notion of literacy. Successful teaching of digital literacy requires a multimodal syllabus. Some basic features of a multimodal syllabus include presenting language teaching and learning as both cognitive and social activity (the purpose of language learning as communication) and seeing the language learner as a social agent and a designer. A multimodal syllabus also provides specific objectives for the integration of multiple modes, such as written, oral, and visual. Assignments and in-class activities go beyond reading and writing print-based texts and require students to produce digital multimodal texts. Assessment focuses on the affordance of each mode as well as the integration (intersemiotic complementarity) of the modes. Developing a multimodal syllabus calls for student-centered approaches, such as problem-based learning and project-based learning that help extend learning beyond the classroom. Further, such projects are planned in a way that empowers students to reflect on biases inherent in different texts and use language as a means of understanding and promoting social justice.

Helping Students Develop Technology and Information Literacy

Even though digital literacy involves more than just the ability to use digital tools, helping students develop technology skills is crucial for successful development of digital literacy in English language education. While today's students might be digital natives and be able to navigate social networking and online communities easily, they need help and guidance to handle the complexities involved in reading and composing digital multimodal texts. It is important to scaffold technology use for students while making room for creativity and being opened to different ways students choose to use the tools.

In addition, successful teaching of digital literacy in English language education requires a new understanding of what it means to search, evaluate, and use sources effectively. It calls for moving away from practices that "appear to presume that objective truth will eventually be achieved through a process of diligent evaluation and comparison of sources" (Buckingham, 2006, p. 267). Since no text is ideology-free, our approach to digital literacy should be helping students understand that every text has some biases, that no text is of "higher quality" than another (Fabos, 2004, p. 95) but as Buckingham rightly points out, that every text "can be adapted for different social purposes" (p. 267). Helping students make critical use of sources in the language classroom therefore calls for helping them identify the intention, purpose, and biases of the author as well as their own biases that influence the way they read and produce different texts. This calls for creativity on the part of language teachers as they guide students to do critical reflection. Factors such as different age and proficiency levels of learners should be taken into consideration. For example, at the college level, it is also important that in addition to teaching students about plagiarism, we also teach them how translation tools can facilitate or hinder language acquisition (see Godwin-Jones's [2015] detailed discussion on this).

Models for Integrating Digital Literacy Into English Language Education

English language teachers around the world have explored different models in helping students develop digital literacy. One common model used by language teachers in the United States is the model POST (Jenkins, 2015). The model involves four main components of a lesson that focuses on integrating digital literacy in English language teaching: People (considering students' needs and ability), objectives (identifying the kind of digital literacy skills that students will develop in a lesson), strategy (choosing specific activities/tasks that will help students use a digital technology), and technology (selecting technologies that students will use in the real world). In Australia, Mills and Levido (2011) used the iPed model to integrate English language teaching and digital literacy. The model emphasizes four dimensions needed for a successful integration of digital literacy: Linking (helping students connect text production to self, culture, and the world), challenge (getting learners to understand that texts and textual practices are ideological and social), co-create (using technology more critically and effectively), and share (using texts as a means of communicating with local and global audience). In addition, Kurek and Hauck (2014) propose the Multiliteracies Training model, which involves three steps: Informed reception of multimodal input, thoughtful participation in opinion-generating acts, and creative contribution. Jones and Hafner also propose a Discourse model, which involves five dimensions: meaning, doing, relating, thinking, and being (for more on this, see Jones & Hafner, 2012). These and other models provide a useful guide on how teachers can integrate digital literacy into their English language curriculum.

FUTURE DIRECTIONS

Teacher Training

To support all of the previously-mentioned pedagogical changes that need to occur for successful development of digital literacy in English language education, some steps need to be taken. One important step is to train teachers on how to integrate digital literacy into their instruction. Scholarship on digital literacy in English language education suggests that ESL and EFL teachers are not prepared to integrate digital literacies into instruction and that a "comprehensive treatment of digital literacies may be lacking in foreign language methods materials" (Guikema & Menke, 2014, p. 280). Research also shows that within university courses that seek to help preservice teachers to develop digital literacy, most teachers are more open to print-based digital media and resist "out-of-school digital literacies" (Nascimento & Knobel, 2017). It is, therefore, important that teachers are trained to understand, use, and appreciate the affordances of digital tools because "teachers' digital mindsets and assumptions about different affordances of digital media can facilitate or hinder the incorporation of new literacies in the language classroom" (Tour, 2015, p. 136). Some policy makers, curriculum writers, and other stakeholders around the world (e.g., Australia, Canada, South Africa, United Kingdom, and United States) have began to pay attention to the need for digital literacy training for preservice teacher education programs. However, more attention needs to be paid to teacher education in digital literacy, because as Nascimento and Knobel rightly observe, "[T]here is no use in equipping schools with digital technologies and services without taking digital literacies into preservice teacher education as part of the overall curriculum and preparation experience" (p. 85). One successful way of helping English language teachers to integrate digital literacy into language teaching is training them to develop TPACK (Technology, Pedagogy, and Content Knowledge) competence. For more suggestions on strategies for training English language teachers to integrate digital literacy, see Pilgrim and Martinez (2015), Tai (2015), and Tour (2015).

Revising Current Assessment Practices

In addition, for the development of digital literacy to be more than a decorative Appendix A in English language education, assessment practices need to move beyond the current predominant focus on print-based literacy. The exclusive focus on print-based literacy assessment practices in many institutions and national standardized testing militates against the development of digital literacy. In some ESL and EFL contexts where teachers are assessed and promoted based on how their students perform on standardized exams, teachers find it extremely difficult to embrace multimodal composing in the classroom (Jiang, 2017). For example, many large-scale English language tests generally do not measure students' ability to self-monitor comprehension in online reading, collaborate in online writing, produce digital media, or critically evaluate media (Mills, 2008). While some school "authorities have begun to include multimodal and digital text production in standardized English assessments, this is currently the exception rather than the rule" (Mills, 2016, Kindle, loc. 601). It is not surprising that most teachers tend to see multimodal composing activities geared toward the development of digital literacy as a waste of time or deviation from their main job. Revising assessment practices in second language education to measure other literacies besides the traditional literacy will highlight the importance of digital literacy for students and provide a way of assessing how learners are developing other aspects of digital literacy. It will also give English teachers and school authorities confidence to include projects and activities that facilitate the development of digital literacy in the language curriculum.

In conclusion, this chapter has explored some common concepts and theoretical foundations of digital literacy and some steps that need to be taken to empower language teachers as they help language learners develop digital literacy. Given the reality of today's digital culture, helping students develop digital literacy in the language classroom is no longer optional. Not doing so is to do great disservice to our students. Teaching digital literacy should go beyond developing technological and informational skills and should help students develop a deeper awareness of the broader cultural uses of the internet. Paying more attention to how we prepare teachers to teach digital literacy, moving beyond the current predominant focus on print-based literacy practices in language assessment, and addressing other sociocultural factors that impede the development of digital literacy in the language classroom will help us empower students to develop technology, information, and other sociocultural competencies and skills they need to function effectively as critical, creative, and responsible citizens and designers of the world they dream about.

Discussion Questions

1. What is the role of language in helping students develop digital literacy?
2. What curriculum changes do you have to make in order to enhance the development of digital literacy in your classroom?
3. What are some challenges in teaching digital literacy in the language classroom? What practical steps would you propose as a way of overcoming the challenges?
4. How might ESL/EFL teachers successfully design lessons that critically empower students to engage issues of social justice as they learn English as an additional language?
5. What are your personal beliefs about using critical and multimodal pedagogies in teaching English as an additional language?

Resources for Further Exploration

1. Bow Valley College (2019). *The ESL Literacy Network*. Retrieved from https://globalaccess. bowvalleycollege.ca/networks/esl-literacy-network.
   This site provides useful resources for developing digital literacy, tools for classroom instruction and program development, as well as empirical research and stories from ESL teachers around the world.
2. Dzekoe, R. (2017). Computer-based multimodal composing activities, self-revision, and L2 acquisition through writing. *Language Learning & Technology*, 21(2), 73–95. Retrieved from http://llt.msu.edu/issues/june2017/dzekoe.
   This article provides an example of how language teachers can use computer-based multimodal composing activities to help students develop digital literacy.
3. European Center for Modern Languages of the Council of Europe (2019). *Digital literacy for the teaching and learning of languages*. Retrieved from www.ecml.at/ECML-Programme/ Programme2016-2019/Digitalliteracy/tabid/1797/language/en-GB/Default.aspx.
   This site provides training modules, webinars, workshops, and other resources on digital literacy, language teaching, and learning English and French.
4. Ortieb, E., Cheek-Jr, E., & Semingson, P. (2018). (Eds). *Best practices in teaching digital literacies. Literacy research, practice and evaluation*. Vol. 9. Bingley, UK: Emerald Publishing Limited.
   This book provides useful and current examples of best practices of teaching digital literacy in the language classroom.

REFERENCES

Arnheim, R. (1969). *Visual thinking*. Berkeley, CA: University of California Press.

Buckingham, D. (2006). Defining digital literacy: What do young people need to know about digital media? *Nordic Journal of Digital Literacy*, 4(1). Retrieved from www.idunn.no/dk/2006/04/defining_digital_literacy_-_what_ do_young_people_need_to_know_about_digital

Cairo, J. (2014). *Teaching adolescents how to evaluate the quality of online information: Edutopia*. Retrieved from www.edutopia.org/ blog/evaluating-quality-of-online-info-julie-coiro

Crookes, G. (2012). Critical pedagogy in language teaching. In L. Ortega (Ed.), *The encyclopedia of applied linguistics*. Oxford: Wiley/Blackwell.

Debes, J. (1969). The loom of visual literacy: An overview. *Audiovisual Instruction*, 14(8), 25–27.

Fabos, B. (2004). *Wrong turn on information superhighway: Education and the commercialization of the Internet.* New York, NY: Teachers College Press.

Gee, J. (2000). The new literacy studies form "socially situated" to the work of the social. In D. Barton, M. Hamilton, & R. Ivanic (Eds.), *Situated literacies: Reading and writing in context* (pp. 180–196). London, UK: Routledge.

Gilster, P. (1997). *Digital literacy.* New York, NY: Wiley.

Godwin-Jones, R. (2015). Contributing, creating, curating: Digital literacies for language learners. *Language Learning & Technology*, 19(3), 8–20. Retrieved from http://llt.msu.edu/issues/october2015/emerging.pdf

Guikema, J. P., & Menke, M. (2014). Preparing future foreign language teachers: The role of digital literacies. In J. Guikema & L. William (Eds.), *Digital literacies in foreign and second language education* (pp. 265–285). CALICO Monograph Series, 12. CALICO: Texas University.

Guikema, J., & Williams, L. (2014). Digital literacies from multiple perspectives. In J. Guikema & L. Williams (Eds.), *Digital literacies in foreign and second language education* (pp. 201–226). San Marcos, TX: CALICO.

Hafner, C. A., Chik, A., & Jones, R. H. (2015). Digital literacies and language learning. *Language Learning & Technology*, 19(3), 1–7. Retrieved from http://llt.msu.edu/issues/october2015/commentary.pdf

Jenkins, R. (2015). *Integrating digital literacy into English language instruction: Companion learning resource.* Washington, DC: U.S. Department of Education, Office of Career, Technical, and Adult Education.

Jiang, L. J. (2017). The affordances of digital multimodal composing for EFL learning. *ELT Journal*, 71(4), 413–422.

Jones, R. H., & Hafner, C. A. (2012). *Understanding digital literacies: A practical introduction.* London, UK: Routledge.

Kern, R. (2000). *Literacy and language teaching.* Oxford, UK: Oxford University Press.

Kress, G. (2000). Multimodality: Challenges to thinking about language. *TESOL Quarterly*, 34, 337–340.

Kress, G. (2010). *Multimodality: A social semiotic approach to contemporary communication.* New York, NY: Routledge.

Kress, G., & van Leeuwen, T. (2001). *Multimodal discourse: The modes and media of contemporary of contemporary communication.* London, UK: Edward Arnold.

Kurek, M., & Hauck, M. (2014). Closing the digital divide: A framework for multiliteracy training. In J. Guikema & L. Williams (Eds.), *Digital literacies in foreign and second language education* (pp. 119–140). San Marcos, TX: CALICO.

Lankshear, C., & Knobel, M. (2011). *New literacies: Everyday practices and classroom learning* (3rd ed.). New York, NY: Open University Press.

Lantolf, J., & Pavlenko, A. (1995). Sociocultural theory and second language acquisition. *Annual Review of Applied Linguistics*, 15, 108–124.

Machin, D., & Mayr, A. (2012). *How to do critical discourse analysis: A multimodal introduction.* London, UK: Sage.

Martin, A. (2005). DigEuLit: A European framework for digital literacy: A progress report. *Journal of eLiteracy*, 2, 130–136.

Mills, K. A. (2008). Will large-scale assessments raise literacy standards in Australian schools? *Australian Journal of Language and Literacy*, 31(3), 211–255.

Mills, K. A. (2016). *Literacy theories for the digital age: Social, critical, multimodal, spatial, socio-material & sensory lenses.* Bristol, UK: Multilingual Matters.

Mills, K. A., & Levido, A. (2011). Iped: Pedagogy for digital text production. *The Reading Teacher*, 65(1), 80–91.

Nascimento, A. K., & Knobel, M. (2017). What's to be learned? A review of sociocultural digital literacies research within pre-service teacher education. *Nordic Journal of Digital Literacy*, 12(3), 67–88.

New London Group. (1996). A pedagogy of multiliteracies: Designing social futures. *Harvard Educational Review*, 66, 60–93.

Pilgrim, J., & Martinez, E. (2015). Web literacy and technology integration: Moving beyond TPACK with student-centered instruction. *Journal of Literacy and Technology*, 16(2), 121–153.

Reinhardt, J., & Thorne, S. (2011). Beyond comparisons: Frameworks for developing digital L2 literacies. In N. Arnold & L. Ducate (Eds.), *Present and future promises of CALL: From theory and research to new directions in language teaching* (pp. 257–280). San Marcos, TX: CALICO.

Royce, T. D. (2007). Intersemiotic complementarity: A framework for multimodal discourse analysis. In T. D. Royce & W. L. Bowcher (Eds.), *New directions in the analysis of multimodal discourse* (pp. 63–110). London, UK: Lawrence Erlbaum.

Selwyn, N., & Facer, K. (2007). *Beyond the digital divide: Rethinking digital inclusion for the 21st century.* Retrieved from www.immagic.com/eLibrary/ARCHIVES/GENERAL/FUTRLBUK/F070530B.pdf

Son, J., Park, S., & Park, M. (2017). Digital literacy of language learners in two different contexts. *The JALT CALL Journal*, 13(2), 77–96.

Tai, S.-J. D. (2015). From TPACK-in-action workshops to classrooms: CALL competency developed and integrated. *Language Learning & Technology*, 19(1), 139–164. Retrieved from http://llt.msu.edu/issues/february2015/tai.pdf

Thorne, S. L. (2013). Digital literacies. In. M. R. Howkins (Ed.), *Framing languages and literacies: Socially situated views and perspectives* (pp. 192–218). New York, NY: Routledge.

Tornero, J. (2004). *Promoting digital literacy: Final report: Understanding digital literacy*. Retrieved from http://ec.europa.eu/education/archive/elearning/doc/studies/dig_lit_en.pdf

Tour, E. (2015). Digital mindsets: Teachers' technology use in personal life and teaching. *Language Learning & Technology*, 19(3), 124–139. Retrieved from http://llt.msu.edu/issues/october2015/tour.pdf

Yeh, H. (2018). Exploring the perceived benefits of the process of multimodal video making in developing multiliteracies. *Language Learning & Technology*, 22(2), 28–37.

Affordances of Mobile Devices in Teaching English as a Foreign Language in Brazilian Public Schools

Cristiane R. Vicentini, Inês Cortes da Silva, and Luciana C. de Oliveira

Information and Communication Technology (ICT) provides opportunities to enhance pedagogical practices and the overall learning experience (Kenning, 2007), and the ubiquitous nature of mobile technologies affords multimodal collaboration in both online and offline settings. In this case study, smartphones had different roles. For the instructor, they were used to plan, share, and obtain feedback. For English language learners (ELLs), the roles of smartphones included research, language practice, and giving feedback. This chapter discusses how these devices contributed to increasing student awareness of the various uses of mobile applications in developing their English language skills.

THE SETTING

This case study describes a ninth-grade classroom – equivalent to the last grade in middle school in the Brazilian educational system – in Sergipe, Brazil's smallest state, located in the Northeast region of the country. It focuses on a series of ninth-grade English as a Foreign Language (EFL) lessons at Northeast State School (NSS, pseudonym). NSS is a 65-year-old educational institution located in the city of Sunrise (Sunrise, pseudonym) and most students (57%) live in small towns near the school. Sunrise, with a population of 19,365, bases its economy on agriculture and trade. Moreover, a large number of Sunrise inhabitants have chosen this institution for their education due to its great historic value and prestige.

When the case study took place, NSS had 606 students enrolled in morning, afternoon, and evening classes. Morning classes run from 7:30 a.m. to 11:45 a.m., afternoon classes run from 1:00 p.m. to 5:15 p.m., and evening classes run from 7:00 p.m. to 10:30 p.m. Even though EFL is taught in the Brazilian public school system from the sixth grade, ninth-graders do not have the same level of proficiency in reading and writing. Furthermore, the public school system in Brazil does not allocate enough resources to a great majority of schools. As a consequence, these schools do not have access to the latest technology, and many campuses struggle with even the most basic infrastructure needs. Efforts to overcome these challenges have taken place in the last 12 years, with the development of initiatives such as PROUCA (Programa um computador por aluno), a computer per student initiative based on the *One Laptop per Child* model, and Tablet Educacional (Educational Tablet), a now-defunct program implemented by the Brazilian National Ministry of Education to distribute tablets to both teachers and students in the Brazilian public school system. These programs aimed to increase access to Information and Communication Technologies (ICT) in an attempt to fill the digital gap. Unfortunately, not all schools have received the equipment, especially ones not located in big cities.

The lessons discussed in this case study took place in the school library, which has four round tables – a more favorable setting to foster interaction and collaboration than the traditional classroom rows. They were taught by Mrs. Inês Cortes da Silva in May of 2018, one month before the beginning of the FIFA Soccer World Cup. The World Cup, which is held every four years, is embedded in Brazilian culture, captivating people of all ages. During the 2018 World Cup, Brazil seemed to be one of the favorites to win the championship, which brought excitement to the learners at every mention of this competition – many of Mrs. da Silva's students are soccer fans and look up to soccer players as their heroes. With this in mind, and taking into consideration that the topic of countries and nationalities was already part of the instructional content in the syllabus, Mrs. da Silva decided to make the connection between this content and the World Cup, a current event at that time.

DESCRIPTION OF ENGLISH LANGUAGE LEARNERS

The English language learners (ELLs) in this case study were in the last grade of middle school in the Brazilian public education system, and all of them spoke Brazilian Portuguese as their native language. In this class, there were 28 students (11 girls and 17 boys) ranging in age from 13 to 17. A small number of ELLs lived close to school (14%), while the majority of ELLs (86%) lived in nearby small towns and relied exclusively on public school transportation to attend classes. In this group, the level of academic proficiency varied due to disparate socioeconomic status among the learners, some of whom heavily depended on government-subsidized free school lunches as their main food intake. On the other hand, since English has a ubiquitous presence in Brazilians' everyday life (gaming, music, the internet, among others), ELLs had a higher interest in engaging in activities using the language. Yet in order to be able to make connections between the English language present in these learners' lives and the content learned in school, instructional support was needed. In this sense, mobile technology can present itself as a helpful tool in the classroom.

As of 2014, smartphones have become the main tool for internet access in Brazil due to governmental support for the development of communication technology, which enables most families to own mobile devices. This particular group of ninth graders was chosen because the majority of the learners owned smartphones and often brought them to school.

PEDAGOGICAL APPLICATION AND INNOVATION

In a world permeated with digital gadgets, smartphones are more common than ever before, and their use as instructional tools for different subjects has become particularly innovative and valuable in Brazilian teaching contexts. In fact, there have been significant advances in incorporating mobile learning into English language teaching practices, both in high- and low-technology environments (Hockly & Dudeney, 2018; Pegrum, 2014). Mobile apps offer opportunities to explore vocabulary and language features as well as practice the skills of listening, reading, speaking, and writing. Mobile technology also brings affordances such as authentic interaction between the device and the learners as well as among their peers. Likewise, smartphones enable building multimodal content which can include images, text, audio, and video. Research has shown that working with multimodal content and mobile technology can increase students' motivation to engage with material and take ownership of their learning, empowering them and improving their language skills (Olesova & de Oliveira, 2016; Pellerin, 2018).

The use of technology in instruction allows students to take an active role in learning while performing a variety of tasks. Learners can also engage in collaborative meaning-making processes and easily share their finalized projects with others (Gilmetdinova, de Oliveira, & Olesova, 2018; Vicentini & de Oliveira, 2018). Additionally, using digital technologies in the classroom offers learners opportunities to explore multimodal means of communication and collaboration, which support knowledge making (Cope & Kalantzis, 2015), develop learner autonomy (Pegrum, 2014), and prepare them for "a world in which messages are increasingly available through multimodal means" (Toohey et al., 2015).

Mrs. da Silva's choice to use smartphones in her classes was made to incorporate devices which students frequently bring to class. With this in mind, and due to increased interest in using mobile technology by

ELLs, the focus of this case study was finding out how the use of mobile apps could support vocabulary development, as well as speaking and writing practice, during the creation of learners' final projects. The lesson objectives included exploring digital technologies for pedagogical purposes, developing students' independence, and using the English language in a context of immediate interest to ELLs.

For her lessons, Mrs. da Silva linked a discussion of the instructional content of "Countries and Nationalities," present on the syllabus, to the FIFA World Cup, a championship cherished by a great majority of Brazilians. As the World Cup includes teams from different countries around the world, the connection between the topic and this major event was easily established. Moreover, Mrs. da Silva used the technology available to students – their mobile phones – to allow her ELLs to explore digital technologies in the process of their learning. There were several mobile apps utilized during the lessons. During the first two classes, the teacher utilized *Portuguese Dictionary*, a bilingual app used as a reference for key vocabulary. The choice for this particular app included (1) the ability to access the word bank without the need for an internet connection, (2) the availability of sample sentences utilizing the selected words, and (3) the integration of audio pronunciation for each word and sentence (see Figure 8.1.1).

Throughout the lessons, ELLs used the app to look up the names of 11 different nationalities. Learners also used the dictionary app as scaffolding for vocabulary development by looking up the Portuguese translation of the countries described in a vocabulary practice worksheet. Accessing the Portuguese version of these lexical items enabled ELLs to expand their linguistic repertoire without devaluing their own identities, which contributed to a fuller meaning-making experience. Moreover, as learners engaged with the mobile application, they also had

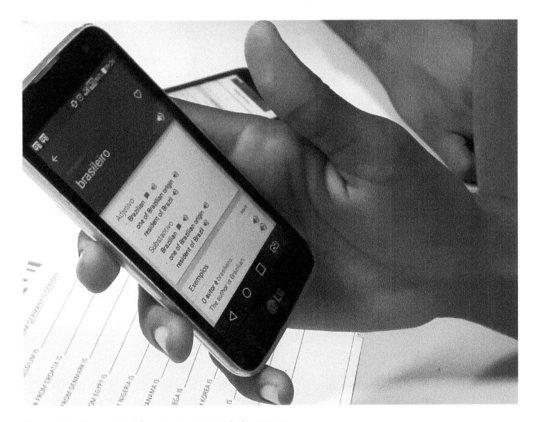

Figure 8.1.1 Screenshot from Portuguese Dictionary app.

Source: Photo by Inês Cortes da Silva (2018)

the chance to listen to the words both in isolation and in context (i.e., example sentences) by clicking on the "sound" icon (see Figure 8.1.2). Mrs. da Silva encouraged all students to practice pronouncing the new vocabulary as they looked up each word.

After these activities, learners had the opportunity to collaborate in the creation of digital posters describing their choice of one of the players who competed during the World Cup. First, ELLs used their smartphones to access a PDF created by Mrs. da Silva displaying photos and biographical information of eight soccer players taking part in the FIFA World Cup games, each of whom represented a different country (i.e., Argentina, Belgium, Brazil, Colombia, France, Germany, and Portugal).

Although most students were familiar with the players due to their constant presence in mass media, more information was needed to complete their tasks, and since access to the internet was not available in the school at the time the lesson was taught, the informational PDF served as the starting point for the activity. The PDF file, written in English and created with the JPG to PDF Converter mobile application, was shared with students in order to enable them to find data related to their favorite player (see Figure 8.1.3).

For students to access the file, Mrs. da Silva utilized Share It, a mobile application that distributes data via Bluetooth wireless connection using a smartphone. Once familiarized with the content of the PDF, learners were tasked with writing about one of the players, and ELLs made their selections individually. However, in the process of creating their digital posters describing the chosen player, learners were encouraged to collaborate with their classmates, exchanging ideas on language structure and vocabulary choice.

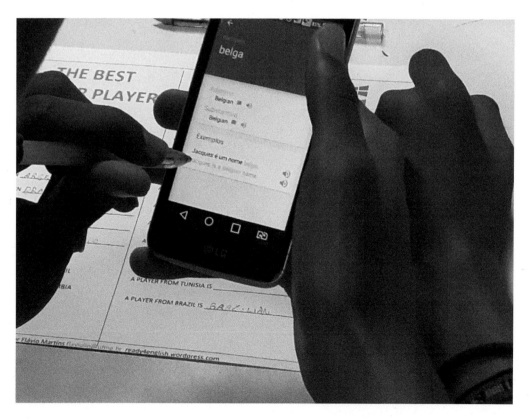

Figure 8.1.2 Using the mobile app for vocabulary and pronunciation development

Source: Photo by Inês Cortes da Silva (2018)

Figure 8.1.3 PDF handout

Source: Handout by Flávio Martins

To complete this assignment, students had the option to use two mobile apps familiar to most Brazilian students who own a smartphone: Instagram and WhatsApp. These two applications have features which can be used as text editing tools for the creation and sharing of photos and/or videos containing doodles, captions, stickers, and/or emoji. Stories, a feature of Instagram, and Status, a feature of WhatsApp, were chosen, since both can be used without an internet connection (see Figure 8.1.4).

For the remainder of the class, ELLs seemed very engaged and motivated to complete their task and share their posters with their peers. The language used in the posters contained biographical information (name, age, nationality, etc.) in the third person to describe each soccer player, which provided additional practice for this kind of descriptive writing.

By incorporating the three mobile applications to instruction, Mrs. da Silva utilized technology already owned by students (Hockly, 2014) to create opportunities for learners to interact with the apps and collaborate with their classmates. The three applications also afforded students' development of vocabulary while at the same time building up their listening, speaking, reading, and writing skills. Instagram and WhatsApp allowed students to practice writing, and the dictionary app provided students with the opportunity to practice listening, speaking, and reading. Moreover, as they looked up the soccer players' nationalities, ELLs also noticed the recurrent use of the suffix "-ese," which is very similar in Portuguese (i.e.,"ês").

At the end of the activities, ELLs were encouraged to write about their experience, take screenshots of their comments, and share them with Mrs. da Silva. For their comments, they utilized the text editing features of Instagram and WhatsApp, eventually sharing them through Share it. Learners' feedback on the use of smartphones revealed that many students had been unaware of the affordances of smartphones for educational purposes. That is, before they utilized their mobile phones as tools for language learning, these ELLs associated their smartphones with leisure activities – not with educational ones. This idea could be a reflection of cell phones being viewed as a distraction in the classroom and not welcomed in most school settings. Consequently, it can be difficult for learners to realize that a simple dictionary app can contain a great deal of information which can be used as a source for structural and lexical development without even the need for a Wi-Fi connection.

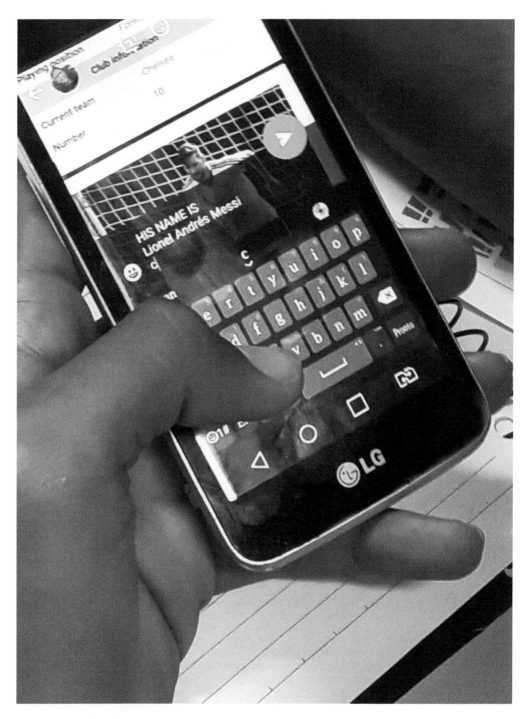

Figure 8.1.4 Creating a digital poster

Source: Photo by Inês Cortes da Silva (2018)

As a result of this experience, students commented that they could see themselves using the mobile applications utilized during the lesson more often, as a means to complete other assignments and to further develop their English language skills. Because these mobile apps can be utilized anytime, anywhere, without the need for constant teacher scaffolding, students have more autonomy in their language learning process. When asked to provide feedback on their experience, students wrote comments in Portuguese – their native language – which reflected how they benefited from the lessons. As stated by Samuel (pseudonym), "I thought last class was interesting because I learned many things and made many mistakes, but I was able to correct them." Likewise, Paulo (pseudonym) also enjoyed the activity, saying that "it is a different and great way to learn while having fun at the same time. I hope I can continue using this method for my studies!!"

The feedback on the lessons also included comments on the practicality of using devices that students already own. As Alicia and Shirley (pseudonyms) explain, they "found the class interesting, cool, easy and practical, just like smartphones make communication easier nowadays." Furthermore, Beatrice's (pseudonym) feedback revealed how she enjoyed the interaction afforded by the use of mobile technology, as demonstrated in the following quote:

> I liked the class; there are parts which are easy and some are harder, but it is definitely so much more fun to do this kind of activity because we get a better understanding of things and class gets much more interactive.

CONCLUSION

As demonstrated in this case study, the incorporation of mobile technology for educational purposes can bring higher engagement and motivation to students. Even though some might believe that teaching with technology is not attainable in low-resource contexts (see Hockly, 2014; Yang & Egbert, 2004), our case study illustrates how teachers and students in such contexts can still benefit from technology such as smartphones and mobile applications that do not require the internet to access and create content. While developing their digital posters, Mrs. da Silva's students interacted with their peers by asking and answering questions posed by their classmates and continuously referred to the mobile apps as means to learn and practice their language skills. As a consequence, the incorporation of technology in the instructional setting sparked ELLs' enthusiasm for taking ownership of their learning and further developing their English. The topic chosen by Mrs. da Silva reflected her students' interests, and the technology-based lesson activities received positive feedback from the learners. In this class, the students also developed increased awareness of the presence of English in various aspects of their everyday lives (e.g., songs, brand names, advertisements, word borrowings) and enjoyed the flexibility to use mobile applications outside of traditional classroom settings. This newfound interest and increased awareness of English language ubiquity in students' surroundings fostered their autonomy, strengthened their motivation to utilize the language, and improved their skills throughout the learning process.

REFERENCES

Cope, B., & Kalantzis, M. (2015). The things you do to know: An introduction to the pedagogy of multiliteracies. In B. Cope & M. Kalantzis (Eds.), *A pedagogy of multiliteracies* (pp. 1–36). London, UK: Palgrave Macmillan.

Gilmetdinova, A., de Oliveira, L. C., & Olesova, L. (2018). Three perspectives on TESOL courses told via a learning management system. In G. Kessler (Ed.), *TESOL voices: Online and hybrid classroom education* (pp. 15–21). Alexandria, VA: TESOL Press.

Hockly, N. (2014). Digital technologies in low-resource ELT contexts. *ELT Journal, 68*(1), 79–84.

Hockly, N., & Dudeney, G. (2018). Current and future digital trends in ELT. *RELC Journal, 49*(2), 164–178.

Kenning, M. (2007). *ICT and language learning.* New York, NY: Palgrave Macmillan.

Olesova, L., & de Oliveira, L. C. (2016). Teaching technology to ELLs. In N. Li (Ed.), *Teaching ELLs across content areas: Issues and strategies* (pp. 157–185). Charlotte, NC: Information Age Publishing.

Pegrum, M. (2014). *Mobile learning: Languages, literacies and cultures.* London, UK: Palgrave Macmillan.

Pellerin, M. (2018). iPad and iPod in the language classrooms: New learning environments and learning experiences. In B. Zou & M. Thomas (Eds.), *Handbook of research on integrating technology into contemporary language learning and teaching* (pp. 286–306). Hershey, PA: IGI Global.

Toohey, K., Dagenais, D., Fodor, A., Hof, L., Nuñez, O., Singh, A., & Schulze, L. (2015). "That sounds so cooool": Entanglements of children, digital tools, and literacy practices. *TESOL Quarterly, 49*(3), 461–485.

Vicentini, C., & de Oliveira, L. C. (2018). Using technology tools in writing instruction. *NYS TESOL Journal, 5*(2), 44–51.

Yang, Y., & Egbert, J. (2004). Mediating the digital divide in CALL classrooms: Promoting effective language tasks in limited technology contexts. *ReCALL Journal, 16*(2), 280–291.

A Lesson in Hedging With Online Corpus Data in an Academic Research and Writing Course in the U.S.

Erik Voss

The demands of an academic writing course in the United States have changed throughout the years for international students. In addition to learning about research methodology, collecting data, and writing academic reports in English, students are required to work with digital texts using word processing software and a growing number of online resources. Both the ability to compose in a digital environment and navigate online resources can be taught to foster students' digital literacy skills. This case study presents an example of an assignment to teach students how to use an online corpus of academic English to learn about hedging in the methodology section of research papers.

THE SETTING

International graduate students who are admitted to English-medium educational institutions often face many cultural, social, emotional, and linguistic challenges in their new setting. Students must be prepared to successfully communicate orally with new students, instructors, and advisors. Although students may be successful in communication outside of the classroom, academic language used specifically in academic courses (e.g., in course textbooks, research articles, and written course assignments) can be challenging.

This case study describes a lesson in a *Research and Writing* course in an English language pathway program at an English-medium university in the United States. The *Research and Writing* course was designed to introduce students to the research methods and fundamentals of writing a graduate-level course paper to prepare them for graduate school. Students are asked to conduct a literature review, annotate a reference list, design a survey instrument for data collection, and complete a research paper with APA format for the final project in the course.

The primary purpose of *Research and Writing* is to assist students with understanding the linguistic complexity of academic texts from various genres and disciplines. In addition to lessons covering the organization of a research paper, attention-raising exercises help students notice the vocabulary and grammatical patterns inherent in specific texts, as well as their functions. This case study will describe the process of helping students in this course develop hedging skills in their academic writing.

DESCRIPTION OF ENGLISH LANGUAGE LEARNERS

The *Research and Writing* course consisted of 12 students between the ages of 22 and 25. There was an even distribution of male and female students. This particular course was a group of Chinese-speaking learners of English who had completed their undergraduate degrees at universities in China in a variety of majors.

Students were preparing for graduate study in different disciplines, such as Leadership, Project Management, Digital Media, or Analytics, offered by the College of Professional Studies.

In general, students arrive with a wide range of background knowledge and language proficiency and enroll in the pathway program for either one or two semesters. Because this is a pathway program aiming to prepare students for graduate study, the standardized English language score requirement is a 61 TOEFL score for a one-semester program or a 72 TOEFL score for a two-semester program. Matriculation into their destination graduate program depends on students completing the program with an adequate GPA and the TOEFL score required by their target program. Although the maximum enrollment for the course is 18, the class size is usually 12–15 students. The course meets six hours a week for 14 weeks in the Fall and Spring semesters, and an intensive seven-week version of the course is offered in the first half of the summer semester.

PEDAGOGICAL APPLICATION AND INNOVATION

Written language in an academic research report differs in complexity from other genres of writing. One key aspect that students have difficulty with is the ability to hedge rather than state a proposition directly (Wishnoff, 2000). Hedging uses lexical or syntactic features to modify or mitigate a proposition (Hinkel, 2005). Therefore, I have included lessons on hedging in my course to help students learn the appropriate use of hedging in research writing. Specifically, this lesson focuses on the use of modal auxiliary verbs, "may," "might," and "could."

This pedagogical application demonstrates the use of corpora to investigate the use of the modal auxiliary "might" in methods sections of research reports. Traditional approaches to teaching hedging with modal auxiliaries take a comparative approach such as Swales and Feak (2012) task comparing sentences with different verbs to determine the meaning and strength of the claim in each sentence. For example, the sentence with a single verb "influences" in the present tense will have a different meaning than the sentence with the modal verb "might." Additional variations of the sentence can be developed for comparison using verbs "can," "could," and "may" (p. 159).

- "Word-of-mouth advertising *influences* a consumer's incentive to purchase a product" (italics added)
- "Word-of-mouth advertising *might influence* a consumer's incentive to purchase a product" (italics added)

Students can discuss the meaning of the sentences with other students and the instructor as well as the degree to which each statement commits to a claim. While this activity is good for awareness raising, students can also benefit from observing use of modals in authentic academic texts.

Digital Literacy

The hedging lesson builds on an awareness of modal use of hedging through a data-driven learning (DDL) approach to language learning (Boulton, 2012). This approach encourages students to explore a collection of authentic texts in a self-selected discipline. Students can search for vocabulary or grammar in a specific genre to observe how the language is used in their discipline and apply their new knowledge to their own writing.

This lesson using corpora for language learning is aligned with the functional/skills approach to digital literacy that views literacy as the ability to use digital tools "to access and use information to develop text-based literacy skills of reading, writing, listening, and speaking" (Dzekoe, 2020, Ch. 8 in this volume). In this case, there are multiple digital tools, the first of which is the word processor that the student is using. This tool could be a Microsoft Word document or an online document such as in Google Docs. While students may have experience with this document, they may not be familiar with features such as automated numbering to create a formal outline and hanging indentation to format the reference section, which are foundational formatting tools for research writing following APA formatting guidelines. The second digital tool is a collection of texts called a corpus that is accessed online through a website interface. A corpus of authentic texts that is used to look for language use is called a reference corpus. Students are expected to be able to use both the filter and search features in order to identify texts that contain linguistic features they wish to explore. Learning to use this digital tool requires guidance by an instructor. Therefore, the students must have the knowledge to use multiple tools to explore the texts and apply the information to their own writing in the digital environment.

Corpus Exploration

The reference corpus for this lesson is the Michigan Corpus of Upper-Level Student Papers (MICUSP), which was developed at Michigan University's English Language Institute to collect examples of proficient student writing (Römer & Wulff, 2010). MICUSP consists of approximately 2.6 million words in 829 different types of papers from 16 different disciplines within four subject divisions (Humanities and Arts, Social Sciences, Biological and Health Sciences, and Physical Sciences). A filter menu allows a student to narrow searches by discipline (e.g., English, Economics, Linguistics), writer level (e.g., 1st year graduate, 2nd year graduate), and writer characteristics (e.g., native-English speaker or non-native English speaker). Searches can also specify type of text such as proposal, or research paper, and textual features to select such as an abstract, literature review, or methods section, for example. Using the online MICUSP interface, students are asked to filter for representative papers in their discipline and search for the use of the modal auxiliary "might." The results display sections of texts where the word "might" occurs in authentic language samples as shown in Figures 8.2.1 and 8.2.2.

Students are then asked to copy and paste the occurrences into a word processing document for examination. Next, students create a list of sentences or phrases with the target word called concordance lines. If there are not enough examples in a student's discipline, it is also helpful to look for examples across other disciplines. For example, a student could explore methods sections in research reports in Linguistics and produce concordance lines like these examples with "might" highlighted.

> I (with assistance) brainstormed sentences or phrases that one <u>might</u> use when he or she wanted to fix a speech mistake

> Our first reaction <u>might</u> be to question the somewhat arbitrary relationship we came up with earlier,

> This <u>might</u> also help explain why this lengthening occurs only for the initial stops

> This paper is an attempt to find the weakness in this experiment so that future experiments <u>might</u> be carried out with better success.

> This <u>might</u> have something to do with their being prevocalic, or it <u>might</u> be that the lenis/fortis distinction is more relevant here than phonation.

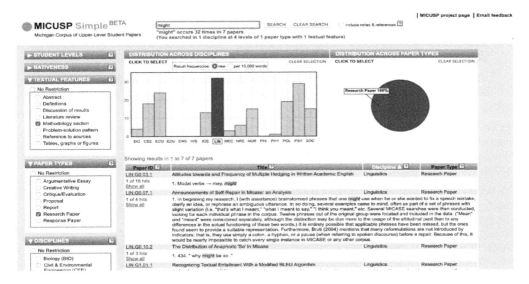

Figure 8.2.1 Screenshot of Michigan Corpus of Upper-Level Student Papers (MICUSP) Simple showing results for the word "might" in student research papers in Linguistics

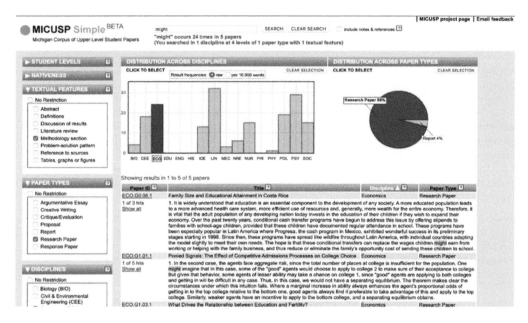

Figure 8.2.2 Screenshot of Michigan Corpus of Upper-Level Student Papers (MICUSP) Simple showing results for the word "might" in student research papers in Economics

For comparison, a student could explore methods sections in research reports in Economics and produce concordance lines like the following sentences and phrases with "might" highlighted.

> The hope is that these conditional transfers can replace the wages children <u>might</u> earn from working or helping with the family business,

> the <u>wan-xi-shao</u> policy dating from 1970 <u>might</u> actually cause the relationship itself as well as its evolution over cohorts.

> Therefore, the policy <u>might</u> be the intermediary part joining female education and fertility together and drive the relationship between them.

> Asymmetric stock price response <u>might</u> be attributed to a few factors such as earnings management and/or voluntary disclosure occurred before earnings announcement.

> a fairly straightforward way of approximating what a respondent's well-articulated beliefs <u>might</u> look like if they were forced to develop them in a rigorous way

The next step is to analyze the sentences or phrases for a relationship between structure and meaning. Structural analysis should identify phrases that are representative of the discipline-specific language. For example, Table 8.2.1 shows phrases that students find in the Linguistics and Economics texts. These examples include structural phrases and example verbs that students can learn to apply in their own writing.

The student then explores the words in the phrases in the examples. In a comparison of sentences or phrases from the two disciplines, students should clearly see that Linguistic scholars use more pronouns in subject position in hedged statements. Students are encouraged to go beyond the concordance lines to identify what the reference is for each pronoun. A takeaway from these examples is to state a claim in one sentence and explain its implications using hedging language (i.e., might) in a second sentence. Examination of the Economics examples uncovers more complex sentences and more examples of hedging in the same statement as the claim.

Table 8.2.1 Example phrases that include "might" from Linguistics and Economics texts

Linguistics	Economics
Phrases that one might use	Children might earn
Our first reaction might be to question	Policy might be the intermediary part
This might also help explain	Stock price response might be attributed to something
This might have something to do with	{a way of explaining} What a respondent's well-articulated beliefs might look like
It might be that	

Source: Erik Voss

As a final exploratory exercise, I ask students to rewrite some of the sentences and phrases without using "might" and notice how the claim changes without the modal auxiliary. These types of explorations using authentic language in academic texts usually helps students notice hedging language so they can express themselves appropriately in their own discipline-specific writing.

CONCLUSION

This case study has demonstrated the use of an online academic corpus with discipline-specific texts as a pedagogical tool to help graduate students in a *Research and Writing* course improve their ability to hedge in academic research papers. The availability of online corpora has provided both students and instructors with immediate access to authentic language that can be used as a model of language use. A growing number of corpora are now available online, making it easier for students to search for specific words and phrases in authentic language. Education and training are needed to learn how to use the rich language data available on the websites. Instructors should guide students in the selection and use of appropriate corpora for their specific context.

REFERENCES

Boulton, A. (2012). What data for data-driven learning? *EuroCALL Review*, 20(1), 23–27.

Dzekoe, R. (2021). English language education and digital literacy in the 21st century. In P. Vinogradova & J. K. Shin (Eds.), *Contemporary foundations for teaching English as an additional language: Pedagogical approaches and classroom applications* (pp.). New York, NY: Routledge.

Hinkel, E. (2005). Hedging, inflating, and persuading. *Applied Language Learning*, 15(1–2), 29–53.

Michigan Corpus of Upper-Level Student Papers (MICUSP). Retrieved from http://micusp.elicorpora.info

Römer, U., & Wulff, S. (2010). Applying corpus methods to writing research: Explorations of MICUSP. *Journal of Writing Research*, 2(2), 99–127.

Swales, J. M., & Feak, C. B. (2012). *Academic writing or graduate students: Essential tasks and skills*. Ann Arbor, MI: University of Michigan Press.

Wishnoff, J. R. (2000). Hedging your bets: L2 learners' acquisition of pragmatic devices in academic writing and computed-mediated discourse. *Second Language Studies*, 19(1), 119–148.

CASE STUDY 8.3

The Effect of Mobile Learning on Learner Autonomy in the United Arab Emirates

Hussam Alzieni

Mobile technologies and mobile learning (mLearning) offer appealing opportunities to language learners to access multiple sources of information anytime and anywhere. Recently, there has been an increasing interest in incorporating mLearning into the learning-teaching process to enhance students' academic success in different educational contexts (Al Zieni, 2019; Gitsaki & Robby, 2014). According to Ting (2015), teachers can expect that "by relating the school learning to students' digital literacy, the way of students' autonomously acquiring their digital literacy outside school may help them develop autonomy in school learning" (p. 25). This case study is an example of incorporating digital literacy in English language education in which mLearning was used as the medium of instruction. All the materials used by the teacher and students were digital, and the students used iPads as the principal tool to develop their English language skills. Students' engagement in level 3 Foundations Program at Dubai Men's College (DMC) of the Higher Colleges of Technology (HCT) was examined to explore the effects of mLearning on their academic autonomy and to promote their overall independence. The students developed their autonomy to exercise their digital literacy to resolve the difficulties they faced while using their educational apps, during Web exploration, and collecting data for their academic work.

THE SETTING

In April 2012, the decision makers in the United Arab Emirates (the UAE) decided to use mLearning as a significant model of instruction in the Foundations Programs of three Federal institutions: Higher Colleges of Technology (HCT), Zayed University (ZU), and the UAE University (UAEU) for the academic year starting in September 2012. This decision was made in order to advance active learning methods that would provide the students with the skills and experiences needed in a flexible work environment to achieve individualized and collaborative student learning and introduce the project-based and task-based instruction (Kamali, 2012). This case study took place in the Foundations Program at Dubai Men's College (DMC) of HCT. The Foundations Program has four levels, and it accepts the students at CEFR A1, A1+, A2, A2+, B1, and B1+ levels of proficiency.

The Program aims to prepare students for undergraduate university life academically and professionally. Improving English language skills is the primary concern, and students at the end of the program must pass a global band 5.0 of the IELTS exam in order to join their bachelor programs. Before the implementation of mLearning and transition to the use of mobile devices in the program, teachers used a blended teaching relying on a combination of printed and online materials. In this transition, a general Common European Framework (CEFR) based curriculum of digital resources was used, and students were provided with digital coursebooks (New Headway, Intermediate) and were asked to download some essential mobile apps to their devices. The apps were Keynote, iMovie, Pages, iAnnotate, DropBox, Creative Book Builder (CBB), iFiles, iBooks, and BlackBoard Mobile Learn (BBL).

The infrastructure, including high-speed Wi-Fi and high-tech smart boards, supported the teaching and learning process. Moreover, there were well-trained IT teams, and continuous mLearning professional development programs were designed to enhance the teachers' abilities to integrate mLearning in their instruction.

DESCRIPTION OF ENGLISH LANGUAGE LEARNERS

Young Emirati high school graduates between the ages of 17 and 19 who do not meet the minimum English language entry requirements of 5.0 on the IELTS have to complete a year-long Foundations Program before matriculating into their career programs of choice or bachelor programs at the DMC. This program is designed specifically for the UAE students whose native language is Arabic. They come mainly from public schools in the UAE, where Arabic is the language of instruction. However, some students might come from private schools with English as the language of Instruction.

Some of these students need additional support in their development of autonomous learning skills, as their prior schooling settings did not focus on this type of learning, and many had not had a chance to be active participants in their classroom learning until they began college (see Hatherley-Greene, 2014). Thus, mLearning was incorporated into the curriculum to facilitate the development of student autonomy while also integrating the development of digital literacy skills in English language classes.

PEDAGOGICAL APPLICATION AND INNOVATION

MLearning is defined as "the exploitation of ubiquitous handheld technologies, together with wireless and mobile phone networks, to facilitate, support, enhance, and extend the reach of teaching and learning" (Pegrum, 2014, p. 15). In this context, it refers to the ability to obtain or provide educational content on personal pocket devices such as tablets or smartphones inside and outside the classroom. Educational content refers to digital learning assets, which include any form of material or media made available on a personal device like video sharing, fan fiction, image sharing, and online gaming. The students at the DMC can use this content anywhere, anytime, and at their own pace.

All students at the Foundations programs were provided with iPads. A digital English language coursebook was downloaded to these devices together with such apps as Adobe Reader, Blackboard, Creative Book Builder (CBB), DropBox, iBooks, iMovie, Keynote, Nearpod, and Pages. The rationale behind choosing these apps was that they offered different functions for students to use inside and outside the classroom. For example:

- Blackboard was used for sharing course content and assessments.
- DropBox was used for filing, sharing, and getting access to any digital devices.
- iMovie, Keynote, and Nearpod were used for presentation and production of students' projects.
- Adobe Reader and Pages were used for creating documents annotations.
- CBB and iBooks were used for creating, publishing, and storing eBooks.

These mobile apps support different aspects of digital literacy development. Data literacy and information provided by BBL App, for example, push digital literacy forward and positively impact the development of autonomous learning. The apps provide an excellent opportunity for communication and collaboration among learners, thus offering the students tools for digital content creation and development of problem-solving strategies. Digital literacy, mLearning, and learner autonomy develop as a complex of strategies facilitated by various assignments and technology tools used in this class. The following examples discuss how learner autonomy and digital literacy skills can be developed together and impact each other as students engage in inquiry-based projects, emotional intelligence activities, and metacognitive tasks.

Inquiry-Based Projects Using WebQuests

According to Gibson (2010), digital literacy includes developing the skills of information location and application as well as understanding of how to use available evidence to assist in problem solving and decision making about essential questions and issues that have no clear answers. Two web-based examples of instructional strategies – WebQuests and Web Inquiry Projects – are suggested as ways to develop these and other necessary 21st-century learning skills. Inquiry-based projects using WebQuests allowed incorporation of mLearning to enhance learner autonomy in the language classroom. The projects were developed using the Inquiry-Based Learning approach and designed to create space for the learners to construct and build knowledge through personal or societal experience (see Reynolds, 2016). Engaging with WebQuests, learners read, analyzed, and synthesized information found online to complete a language learning activity. Learners cooperated and worked in groups to achieve a particular task, and each member of a group was given a "role." Every WebQuest had introduction, task, process, evaluation, and conclusion components and aimed to promote critical thinking at the levels of analysis, synthesis, and evaluation. Each student had a particular task to complete (e.g., looking up information on the topic of the WebQuest, synthesizing information, and presenting information identified and integrated by other group members) that culminated in the online collaboration of all group members. One of the WebQuests that the students worked on was "Managing Expenses WebQuest" (http://zunal.com/webquest.php? w=306445).

For example, the teacher asked the students to read the introduction to the WebQuest:

> After you graduate, there are responsibilities you will have to take on to support yourself (and your family). In this WebQuest, you will be researching how to manage your money and building your budget for after graduation.

Then, the students read the required task.

Work on a team of four people:

1. Go to Mehnaty on HCT portal and choose a job to apply for.

2. Post your CV online.

3. Watch the YouTube video www.youtube.com/watch?v=-TmxTVPuDCk.

4. Use a Budget tool like "Expenses App" to make your budget based on the salary offered.

5. Make a list of all your expenses. Include all possible costs, even entertainment, insurance, etc. Make your list using Pages.

6. Make your budget and fill in the budget sheet.

7. Evaluate the work of others. Use the peer review form.

In the end, the students were asked to look at their work and evaluate themselves using the rubric provided. Figure 8.3.1 shows the rubric of this WebQuest.

The digital literacy approach of using mLearning incorporated with inquiry-based projects helped the students develop their learner autonomy, critical-thinking skills, collaboration, and problem-solving skills. Healey (2014) points out that someone qualifies as an autonomous learner when they independently choose aims and purposes and set goals; select materials, methods, and tasks; exercise choice and purpose in organizing and carrying out the selected tasks; and choose criteria for evaluation. Working with WebQuests, the students used digital tools to develop the skills of information location and application which is one aspect of digital literacy. According to Gibson (2010), these skills include the ability to find, evaluate, synthesize, and use the information to answer questions and make informed decisions.

Emotional Intelligence (EI) Development Activities

Another example of promoting learner autonomy in English language instruction was incorporating elements of digital literacy development using emotional intelligence development activities. Emotional intelligence is defined as "an assortment of mental abilities and skills that can help you to successfully manage both yourself

#	1	2	3	4	Score
Found a job and figured the monthly gross income.	Found a job.	Found a job and estimated how much per hour or salary.	Found a job and figured weekly gross income.	Found a job and figured out the gross monthly income.	0
Figured your net monthly income by deducting other expenses.	Filled in gross monthly income figure.	Filled in gross monthly income figure and calculated some expenses.	Filled in gross monthly income figure and calculated reasonable expenses	Filled in gross monthly income figure and calculated reasonable expenses. Take gross income and subtract expenses to get net income amount.	0
List expenses and calculate total expenses for the month.	List random expenses.	List major expenses house payment/rent, car, and food.	List all expenses but does not calculate total expenses.	List all expenses and calculate total expenses for the month.	0
Presentation	Acceptable	Attractive	V. Good	Excellent showing team work/ Appropriate Language	0
		Final Score			0/16

Figure 8.3.1 The rubric for the Managing Expenses WebQuest

Source: Hussam Alzieni. http://zunal.com/evaluation.php?w=306445

and the demands of work with others" (Walton, 2012, p. 4). Goleman (1995) points out that emotional intelligence has four areas: self-awareness, self-management, social awareness, and relationship management. Buvoltz, Powell, Solan, and Longbotham (2008) studied the relationship between emotional intelligence and learner autonomy. They observed that impulse control, hope, optimism, self-confidence, adaptability, achievement drive, communication, conflict management, and collaboration competencies associated with EI had potential to impact development of learner autonomy.

In our case, there were English language tasks designed to enhance language and emotional intelligence skills. In the task shown in Figure 8.3.2, for example, the aim was to develop the students' self-awareness, self-management, social awareness, and social management skills. They first responded to a brainstorming question about the tourist attractions in the UAE as an example of raising social consciousness. Then they watched a video about the Sheikh Zayed Mosque to further tap into the four areas of emotional intelligence as described by Goleman (1995). The video has the potential to inspire the viewers by the fantastic structure of the mosque and to trigger the memories of the founder of the UAE. Thus, watching it could help learners reflect on their emotions toward the scene. Besides, it could prepare learners to understand and manage their emotions as well as convey their message of welcome to the foreigners visiting the place. In the cases where the students' communities used to have limited exposure to the world around them, these videos could help the students understand people from other cultures and develop ways to deal with this new exposure. Finally, the students responded to four questions that prompted them to think more deeply and reflect on their emotions, thus developing further their emotional intelligence. In summary, promoting digital literacy skills which are

Emotional Intelligence Development Activity

Brainstorming:

1. Name some tourist attractions in the UAE (Social Awareness)

   a. _____

   b. _____

   c. _____

   d. _____

   e. _____

2. Watch the following video about Sheikh Zayed Mosque and then respond to the questions follow:

   https://www.youtube.com/watch?v=MzZ5OvzA_mQ

(Self-awareness, Self-management, Social awareness, & Social management)

   a. What do you feel after watching this video? (Self Awareness-emotion literacy)

   _____

   b. Watch the video again and tell about your emotions this time. (Self management-metacognition)

   _____

   c. What is the importance of Sheikh Zayed Mosque to the people of the UAE and to the people of the world? (social Awareness)

   _____

   d. What are other projects do you suggest that could help the UAE community and the world community? (Social management)

   _____

Figure 8.3.2 An Emotional Intelligence Task

Source: Hussam Alzieni

in positive correlation with the autonomy of these students helped in solving problems related to their interests, hobbies, and most importantly, managing their relations with people from different cultures.

Metacognitive Tasks

To stimulate the development of learner autonomy, we also incorporated elements of digital literacy in metacognitive tasks. Metacognitive skills mean thinking about thinking and knowing what you know and what you do not know (Flavell, 1979). Dixon (2011) maintains that autonomy requires metacognition realized in conscious awareness of the learning process. He states that the autonomous person can step back from what they are doing and reflect upon it to make decisions about what they need to do and experience next.

For the metacognitive task, the students completed a weekly reflection (done at the end of each week) using the Independent Learning Reflection worksheet (see Al Zieni, 2019 for details). In this task, the students were prompted to think about their learning experience, express their learning preferences, consider what went well and what did not in their learning, and identify possibilities for improvement. This reflection contributed to the development of students' learning autonomy, as it elicited critical thinking and problem-solving skills. Developing strategies for self-reflection, the students could gain a better understanding of their emotions, strengths, weaknesses, and driving factors. Thus, by developing a better understanding of the aspects of the self, they further developed adaptability to changing and new situations.

CONCLUSION

Emotional intelligence activities, metacognitive tasks, and inquiry-based projects used in this class incorporated mLearning tools and facilitated development of digital literacy and learner autonomy. In these activities, digital literacy development enhanced autonomous learning, as the students had freedom of self-expression and could focus on the development of independent learning strategies and skills. Through various mobile applications and by using iPads and smartphones, the students engaged in interactive and collaborative activities that provided them with opportunities to learn about their classmates, develop learning strategies, and obtain self-directed learning experiences. The impact of mobile devices on the development of learner autonomy was noticeable. Their use aided in simulating learning and English language use in a real-world context, which in turn motivated the students to use English to complete the assignments and thus achieve the level of English language proficiency required in their further academic studies.

REFERENCES

Al Zieni, H. (2019). The effect of mobile learning on learner autonomy: A suggested measurement tool to assess the development of learner autonomy. *The Journal of Asia TEFL, 16*(3), 1020–1031.

Buvoltz, K. A., Powell, F. J., Solan, A. M., & Longbotham, G. J. (2008). Exploring emotional intelligence, learner autonomy, and retention in an accelerated undergraduate degree completion program. *New Horizons in Adult Education and Human Resource Development, 22*(3–4), 26–43. doi:10.1002/nha3.10315

Dixon, D. (2011). *Measuring language learner autonomy in tertiary-level learners of English* (Doctoral dissertation). Retrieved June, 2015, from http://go.warwick.ac.uk/wrap/58287

Flavell, J. H. (1979). Metacognition and cognitive monitoring: A new area of cognitive-developmental inquiry. *American Psychologist, 34*(10), 906–911. doi:10.1037/0003-066X.34.10.906

Gibson, S. E. (2010). Developing digital literacy skills with WebQuests and web inquiry projects. In A. Tatnal (Ed.), *Web technologies: Concepts, methodologies, tools, and applications* (pp. 1554–1569). IGI Global.

Gitsaki, C., & Robby, M. A. (2014). Post-secondary students using the iPad to learn English: An impact study. *Journal of Mobile and Blended Learning, 6*(4), 1–15.

Goleman, D. (1995). *Emotional intelligence: Why it can matter more than IQ*. New York, NY: Bantam Dell Publishing Group.

Hatherley-Greene, P. J. (2014). The cultural border-crossing index: Implications for higher education teachers in the UAE. *Learning and Teaching in Higher Education: Gulf Perspectives, 11*(2), 1–21.

Healey, M. (2014, October). *Developing independent & autonomous learning*. Retrieved from www.mickhealey.co.uk/

Kamali, D. T. (2012). *Al Rawi*. Higher Colleges of Technology. Retrieved from www.hct.ac.ae/content/uploads/alrawi_sep12.pdf

Pegrum, M. (2014). *Mobile learning: Languages, literacies, and cultures*. Hampshire, UK: Palgrave Macmillan.

Reynolds, R. (2016). Defining, designing for, and measuring "social constructivist digital literacy" development in learners: A proposed framework. *Educational Technology Research and Development, 64*(4), 735–762. doi:10.1007/s11423-015-9423-4

Ting, Y. (2015). Tapping into students' digital literacy and designing negotiated learning to promote learner autonomy. *The Internet and Higher Education, 26*, 25–32. doi:10.1016/j.iheduc.2015.04.004

Walton, D. (2012). *Emotional intelligence: A practical guide*. London, UK: Icon Books Ltd.

UNIT 9
Advocacy and TESOL

CHAPTER 9

Advocacy for Student and Teacher Empowerment

Heather A. Linville

An important part of any educational environment, advocacy is especially critical in English language teaching (ELT). Teacher advocates, or change agents (Adoniou, 2017), worldwide recognize the need to improve educational access and outcomes for their students as well as professional conditions for themselves. However, advocacy is also context-dependent, where the need for advocacy varies in each environment, along with the potential advocacy actions one is able to undertake in the local environment. In this chapter, I present types of advocacy actions and the skills needed to advocate, broadly distinguishing between advocacy in English as a second language (ESL) contexts, where English is a national or widely spoken language, and English as a foreign language (EFL) contexts, where English is not spoken, for the most part, beyond the classroom. At present, the majority of research on advocacy by English language teachers comes from ESL teaching contexts. Therefore, this chapter itself is a call for advocacy to widen the circle of knowledge about advocacy in all ELT contexts.

FRAMING THE ISSUE

Advocacy is defined most often as speaking up against injustice and for those who may not have a voice (Athanases & de Oliveira, 2007). Advocates first notice a situation or issue and then take action to try to remedy it. When English teaching professionals advocate, they act as an ally and are empowered to make positive changes, big and small, for English learners (ELs) and themselves. However, identifying and classifying ELT advocacy has not been an easy task. Some researchers have differentiated between within-the-classroom and beyond-the-classroom advocacy (Dubetz & de Jong, 2011), recognizing that teachers have multiple sites in which advocacy is needed and may occur. Others have explained advocacy as transformative or non-transformative, a distinction which focuses on the final intended or achieved outcome of the action and whether it has challenged ("transformed") harmful or inequitable practices (Athanases & de Oliveira, 2007; Haneda & Alexander, 2015).

We know that ESL teachers advocate for their students, including refugees and immigrants, who are often marginalized and may experience prejudice or discrimination in schools and communities because of their linguistic or ethnic differences (Hawkins & Norton, 2009). They also advocate to reduce the achievement gap between EL and non-EL students, which often exists in these contexts. ESL teachers of adults also advocate for the greater availability of English language programs (Sheppard, 2019). ESL teachers advocate for themselves as professionals, for greater recognition of their expertise and to combat professional marginalization (Harper & de Jong, 2009) or to improve working conditions, for example, through more permanent positions (Sun, 2010).

Similarly, EFL teachers advocate for their students who may be marginalized for different reasons, such as socioeconomic class (Mambu, 2012; Vinogradova & Linville, 2020). EFL teachers also advocate for themselves as professionals, especially speaking up against the marginalization of non-native English-speaking teachers (NNEST; Llurda, 2015) or to improve their working conditions, such as advocating for reduced class sizes (Vinogradova & Linville, 2020). They also advocate for more acceptance of cultural and linguistic diversity, including recognizing and strengthening mother tongue usage, multilingualism and greater linguistic rights, and for language teaching methods that may be less common or accepted in their teaching contexts or which counter the dominant expectations of the field (Canagarajah, 2008; Llurda, 2015). As can be seen, advocacy happens in numerous ways in the variety of ELT contexts.

Advocacy also occurs for a variety of reasons. In EFL contexts, feeling the responsibility to work in the best interests of students can be a motivator for teacher advocacy. EFL teachers may also feel caught between the realities of their teaching context, with limited funding, training, or support for teachers, and changing language policies which see English as a main tool for global access and success (Hoang & Truong, 2017). In such cases, teacher agency, the ability to make choices and act according to individual priorities, may allow EFL teachers to advocate by taking a "purposeful course of actions . . . chosen due to what he[/she] believes to be best for his[/her] students" (Hoang & Truong, 2017, p. 189). This focus on students' needs and providing them the best possible education is also present in ESL teachers' advocacy.

Within the United States, many ESL teachers report advocating because they feel responsible and care for their students, because they feel a need to protect or defend ELs, and/or because they believe in equality for their students and have a social justice stance in this work (Athanases & de Oliveira, 2007; Dubetz & de Jong, 2011; Staehr Fenner, 2014; Suárez & Domínguez, 2015). ESL teachers in the U.S. are also expected to advocate as part of their professional duties in states that follow the TESOL Pre-K-12 Teacher Preparation Program Standards (TESOL, 2019). Advocacy is strongly linked to ESL teachers' professional identity in Standard 5 as follows:

> Candidates demonstrate professionalism and leadership by collaborating with other educators, knowing policies and legislation and the rights of ELLs, advocating for ELLs and their families, engaging in self-assessment and reflection, pursuing continuous professional development, and honing their teaching practice through supervised teaching.
>
> (TESOL, 2019, p. 11)

Advocacy additionally appears in Standard 3 (Planning and Implementing Instruction), as collaboration and communication with other colleagues in order to support ELs' learning, and in Standard 4 (Assessment), in which teacher candidates are expected to advocate for equitable assessment for ELs.

A few scholars are critical of the growing expectation for teachers to be advocates. Morgan (2016), for one, sees the "domestication of dissent" as a way to superficially support advocacy actions but not truly push for the social or professional changes that would improve the sociopolitical status of ELs nor address pressing professional issues, such as ESL teachers being overqualified and underemployed. Kubanyiova and Crookes (2016), in the same vein, recognize this changing role for language teachers but express concern that teachers may now be seen as the solution for what are truly structural problems.

Keeping in mind this critical perspective, this chapter offers guidance on some advocacy actions English language teachers may engage in, suggestions on how to develop the skills needed to advocate most effectively, and an advocacy stance that is designed to empower all teachers to become, or continue to be, advocates in their teaching contexts.

CONCEPTS AND THEORETICAL CONSIDERATIONS

Through advocacy, English language teachers can work to improve the lives of their students and themselves as professionals, all over the world. While more research is needed to classify types of advocacy actions, one useful distinction may be between "instructional" and "political" advocacy (Linville, 2016, in press).

Instructional advocacy involves actions in teachers' own classrooms or schools. For example, when co-teaching in U.S. contexts, ESL teachers often go into other classrooms where they can advocate to support and empower ELs. In this work, the main focus is on supporting and improving the educational access and outcomes of the ELs they teach (Linville, 2016, in press). Some instructional advocacy actions include encouraging ELs to maintain their home languages and cultures to increase home-school connections and students' self-esteem; going "above and beyond" in classrooms to help ELs succeed academically, such as tutoring outside of normal class times; and empowering ELs to speak up for themselves, for example, asking for resources and modifications as needed (Athanases & de Oliveira, 2007; Linville, 2019; Staehr Fenner, 2014).

Instructional advocacy in EFL contexts may involve choosing materials or methods which go against the prescribed or traditionally expected curriculum in order to best meet the needs of students (Canagarajah, 2008; Hoang & Truong, 2017). For example, a teacher in Indonesia introduces critical pedagogy to his students and teaches "English for advocacy purposes" (Mambu, 2012) in order to harness the power of this international language to fight oppression and marginalization in their local communities and society. This teacher uses the topic of the English language itself to engage students as critical thinkers and self-advocates.

Political advocacy, on the other hand, involves challenging inequitable school or district policies, and often goes beyond teachers' school environments, to the local, state, or national community as well (Linville, 2016, in press). When engaged in political advocacy, or *activism* (Linville, 2016), teachers focus on changing policies for the benefit of all ELs, not just those in their immediate educational environment, and/or responding to policies which negatively impact themselves as ESL/EFL teachers in order to improve conditions for all. Occurring in ESL and EFL environments, examples of political advocacy include advocating for NNEST professional respect and recognition (Llurda, 2015); for teachers' better working conditions and pay, as well as more stable employment (Sun, 2010); and fighting against professional marginalization in all forms (Harper & de Jong, 2009). In EFL contexts, English language teachers may find themselves facing changing standards and expectations as more nations place greater emphasis on English language learning. Teachers' voices are often not sought in educational policy changes (Adoniou, 2017), meaning that this process can disempower and *deprofessionalize* EFL teachers as they face job uncertainty or a lack of clear guidance and support to meet the new policies (Hoang & Truong, 2017). ESL teachers may advocate politically by speaking up for ELs at school board meetings or other community meetings (Hesson & Toncelli, 2019) and writing to local and national leaders in support of linguistic and cultural diversity (Athanases & de Oliveira, 2007; Linville, 2019). In ESL contexts, this type of advocacy also includes empowering and working with EL families; for example, informing ELs and their families of their rights and of the resources available to them and coordinating with community agencies to ensure EL families receive those services (see the link for ¡Colorín Colorado! in the Resources section for more information on working with EL families).

Whether engaging in instructional or political advocacy, it is possible, and perhaps even likely, to feel an element of personal or professional risk. Athanases and de Oliveira (2007) eloquently describe teachers'

> dance between courage, strength of conviction, and persistence . . . , and realistic assessment of challenge and risk inherent in *speaking for* students in public arenas of school and *speaking up and against* practices and policies failing students in need.
>
> (p. 132, italics in original)

Perhaps because political advocacy feels more challenging and riskier, ESL teachers in the United States are less likely to report doing this type of advocacy (Linville, 2016, in press). TESOL professional organizations are also involved in advocacy, such as English Australia, and focus their work at least in part on political advocacy, no doubt recognizing its great importance in making lasting, positive changes for ELs, ELT professionals, and the profession as a whole. For example, in recent years the U.S.-based TESOL International Association has issued position statements which advocate against the discrimination of NNEST and in favor of full-time positions for adult ESL educators. This organization also sponsors the annual TESOL Advocacy and Policy Summit, an event where participants learn about relevant federal education policies and lobby their representatives directly in their offices on Capitol Hill in Washington, DC. Local associations can also be encouraged to support and promote advocacy actions if they are not doing so already. These associations can additionally help by building advocacy networks across communities and countries. In these ways, local, national, and international organizations also engage in and support teachers' political advocacy.

Perhaps due to the risk involved, all types of advocacy in English language teaching have a strong focus on empowerment. Empowered English language teachers are able to empower their students as well. Administrators and educational leaders also have a role to play in this work as they are part of the supportive teaching context which empowers and supports ESL and EFL teachers in their advocacy.

When working with ELs in classrooms, teachers aim to empower their students as multilingual individuals who know their rights and who can develop the ability and confidence to speak up. Staehr Fenner (2014) suggests using scaffolded advocacy, similar to how teachers scaffold instruction, to support ELs and their families until they are able to advocate for themselves. In political advocacy, empowerment, or a sense of agency, allows teachers to have the strength and confidence to speak up to political leaders to change policies for ELs and to better ESL/EFL teachers' living and working conditions. Teachers who feel a greater sense of responsibility, who have more confidence as advocates, and who feel they have greater support for advocacy in their teaching context, are more likely to engage in advocacy (Linville, in press). Teachers must draw upon the leadership skills they already possess but may be unaware of (Staehr Fenner & Breiseth, 2017) and recognize their own professional knowledge and expertise (Harper & de Jong, 2009). In the next section, I offer some strategies to help all English language teaching professionals develop advocacy skills and thus feel empowered.

IMPLICATIONS FOR ENGLISH LANGUAGE EDUCATION

How to Advocate

English language professionals must ask for, and in some cases demand, what they and their students deserve, yet teachers may not know how to carry out this work. I offer a framework for advocacy (Linville, 2019) which begins with noticing a problem and ends with deciding what action to take, keeping in mind the advocacy focus (ELs, EL families, teachers, and the profession) and those with whom advocacy takes place (co-advocates and stakeholders at local and national levels). The first step is for ELs and English teaching professionals to be alert, noticing situations in which inequity, inequality, or injustice are present. After noticing comes acting as skillful advocates.

Schools and classrooms are social spaces, and the ability to collaborate provides the foundation for all instructional advocacy. Establishing strong collegial relationships starts at the beginning of the school year and includes getting to know colleagues in the school, identifying co-advocates, and drawing upon professional knowledge and expertise to discuss EL rights and best practices. Many ESL teachers liken their work to that of diplomats, as they typically have to work with everyone in the school and maintain collegial relationships throughout their teaching context (Linville, 2019). Examples of such collaboration include helping non-ESL teachers modify or scaffold their lessons for ELs, speaking up in teacher and administrative meetings when negative comments about linguistic or cultural diversity are heard, or speaking on behalf of ELs in instructional meetings, such as when a student is being considered for special education services (Athanases & de Oliveira, 2007; Linville, 2019; Suárez & Domínguez, 2015). In EFL settings, teachers need to understand and work within the local hierarchy, where collaboration with an older, more experienced colleague can help newer teachers advocate even where they lack a voice (Vinogradova & Linville, 2020). Developing and maintaining positive relationships with others, and the ability to work in collaboration, are key. Some suggestions to best carry out this foundational work for advocacy include approaching colleagues at times that are convenient to them (for example, not when they are busy right before a class), having a positive and open attitude, and conveying respect for others as colleagues and experienced professionals (Linville, 2019; Staehr Fenner, 2014).

Interpersonal communication skills are also key in this work and will depend upon the cultural and pragmatic expectations of the teaching context. General advice is to approach others with empathy and understanding, using inclusive language, such as "we" and "our" rather than exclusive language, such as "I" and "my." It is also important to work strategically within the hierarchy in the teaching context (for example, knowing if teachers can talk directly to the school counselor about supporting an EL, or if they need to speak to the principal first). Just like in the work of the most successful diplomats, advocacy work is best achieved by being aware of not only what to say but also how to best say it, listening as much as talking, compromising when needed, and staying focused on the final goal, be it better access to education and improved educational outcomes for ELs or improved professional conditions for ESL/EFL teachers (Linville, 2019).

For political advocacy, I refer to the U.S.-based National Education Association's (NEA, 2015) five-step approach:

1. Identifying the root cause of the issue.

2. Engaging allies.

3. Understanding the relevant policies and laws.

4. Educating others and organizing.

5. Identifying what you can do at various levels.

In the first step, knowing the underlying cause of an issue helps tailor advocacy actions more strategically. For example, when faced with negative comments about linguistic diversity from a colleague, it is important to know if the opinion is unique to one teacher or if it is a negative viewpoint throughout the school, coming down from the school head. Learning more about the reasons behind the issue, identifying stakeholders and anyone else impacted by or who impacts the situation, and determining their perspectives on the issue help English language professionals begin to build a coalition of support that contributes to the understanding of all sides of the issue. Knowing that some stakeholders will agree and some will disagree on the issue, the NEA (2015) offers this advice:

> To be effective, you must foster relationships with others, be willing to listen to opposing viewpoints, and use conflict as an impetus for change. There will be a wide variety of perspectives for any issue, and it's important not to dismiss those who do not share your beliefs. Despite differing opinions, the advocacy process has the potential to be a consciousness-raising experience for all participants.
>
> (p. 12)

As with instructional advocacy, it is important to focus on relationship building, as we never know who our strongest allies and co-advocates may be.

The next step is to better understand the policies or laws relevant to the issue. For example, in Canada, where the Ministry of Education of each province sets the policy for English language instruction, Ontario's 2007 Policy on English language learners outlines the policies for reception and orientation, initial assessment and placement, programming, and graduation requirements for ELs (see www.edu.gov.on.ca/eng/document/esleldprograms/). No matter the teaching context, knowing what the laws or policies say relevant to the issue puts English language teachers in a better position to advocate for change. With that knowledge in hand, advocates can focus on educating others about the issue, expanding the network beyond the original stakeholders approached, and taking advantage of any meeting or gathering to raise the issue.

Empowerment in advocacy comes from knowledge; identifying the sphere of influence (Staehr Fenner, 2014), and knowing what change is possible in each teaching context at a particular moment in time. The skills needed for political advocacy, to some extent, are the same as for instructional advocacy: diplomacy skills, identifying co-advocates, and keeping the final goal in mind. Other skills needed for this type of advocacy work are building knowledge about legal rights and political processes, recognizing and engaging stakeholders, and prioritizing advocacy actions which are possible (Athanases & de Oliveira, 2007; Staehr Fenner, 2014). While political advocacy can seem more daunting, it is within English language professionals' reach with increased knowledge and skills, and in collaboration with others.

Learning How to Advocate

Everyone involved in English language teaching needs to be prepared to advocate. Advocacy might be a natural role for some, but practicing the skills helps everyone – teachers, administrators, and even affiliate leaders – become stronger advocates and feel better prepared to take on that role. TESOL teacher education programs should highlight the professional responsibility to advocate (potentially through the TESOL Standards [2019]) and teach the skills of instructional and political advocacy. Here are three ways teachers can continue developing these skills.

Teachers can use a typical language learning activity, role-playing, to develop advocacy skills (Whiting, 2019). In such a role play, teachers can imagine they are talking to a colleague who has expressed negative views about ELs, English language teachers, or linguistic diversity. They can first think about what they would say, writing down the response as a plan to articulate their ideas clearly. Because this type of advocacy usually takes place face-to-face, they can then practice saying the response to a friend or colleague, or even video-record themselves, a fairly easy-to-manage task with the embedded camera on many smartphones.

Friends or colleagues can provide feedback, or teachers can self-evaluate, reflecting on what they say and how they say it, checking in particular for the tone and approach most appropriate in the local cultural context. By practicing and reflecting this way, teachers will be better prepared for advocacy whenever such situations arise.

Teachers can also lay the foundation for advocacy by seeking out relationships with everyone in their school, university, or language center. Teachers can look for commonalities and start conversations in the hallway, in the cafeteria, or before and after teacher meetings. While these relationships may not originally be about advocacy, they can plant the seeds that will grow and serve teachers as advocates for years.

Finally, ESL/EFL teachers can make the habit of staying current not only on ELT methods and SLA theories but also on changes to educational laws and policies that may impact ELs and English language teachers locally, nationally, and even internationally. Local English teacher organizations may help with this somewhat daunting task. For example, the TESOL International Association does a good job of sending weekly emails keeping its members informed, and local affiliates often have monthly newsletters. This knowledge is essential for advocacy.

FUTURE DIRECTIONS

This chapter has laid out a framework and ideas about advocacy in English language teaching. Knowledge of the importance of advocacy in English language teaching and how to go about advocating is growing each year. However, much of the knowledge comes from research conducted in ESL teaching contexts. Knowing how context makes a difference in advocacy, more EFL-centered advocacy research is needed. Here I highlight three additional areas which I believe will continue to fuel professional conversations about advocacy in the near future.

We increasingly understand teaching to be political work and that we must prepare our students, and view ourselves, as critical consumers and thinkers (Canagarajah, 2008). Like Mambu (2012), Hawkins and Norton (2009) also see this link between critical pedagogy and advocacy, pointing out, "critical pedagogy is directly concerned with social action and educational change. . . . [C]ritical pedagogy seeks to empower people to challenge oppressive conditions in their lives" (p. 32). Advocacy is questioning and problematizing the status quo, working to change what is unjust. In a global society, unfortunately, instances of oppressive conditions and of inequity and injustice abound. ELT professionals must be empowered, and must empower their students, family members, and community members as agents of change to combat such situations.

However, many questions about empowerment and agency related to advocacy remain. More research is needed to understand the barriers to advocacy in various settings and what impacts ESL/EFL teachers' ability and willingness to advocate. When faced with a situation of injustice, how do English language teachers decide to advocate or not? How empowered do they feel in this work? What is their motivation to advocate? Having teachers talk about and reflect upon these questions can help ELT professionals understand more about teacher advocacy and better prepare themselves for this role. In addition, ELT professionals need to continually keep in mind the critical perspective on teacher advocacy and its role in addressing structural inequality. Teachers should not be seen as the only group that needs to advocate for change. More opportunities need to be offered to preservice and in-service teachers to help increase the understanding of advocacy and the skills needed to advocate in various teaching contexts. Through such support and practice, all ESL and EFL teachers recognize and claim their expertise (Harper & de Jong, 2009) and empower their students as well.

Finally, a goal of advocacy in ELT should be to encourage and seek out multilingualism and multiculturalism. A shift is occurring toward viewing all ELs as emergent bilinguals and as creative users of language rather than focusing on linguistic skills they might not yet have (García & Kleifgen, 2010). ESL/EFL teachers are experts in this language teaching and learning process as well as intercultural connections. In this era of standards and standardization, multilingualism needs to be viewed as a resource rather than a problem, and a vital element of being global citizens. Supporting and advocating for students must include supporting and advocating for linguistic and cultural diversity as well. Through advocacy, English language teachers can work to improve the lives of their students and themselves as professionals, all over the world.

Discussion Questions

1. What are the reasons that you have (or will) engage in advocacy? Explore the ways that your motivation for advocacy may relate to an awareness of social justice.
2. Reflect on the type of advocacy you have most frequently engaged in, instructional or political, and why that is the case. Imagine two or three situations in which you would feel empowered to engage in another type of advocacy.
3. Relationship building is mentioned as one of the top advocacy skills. What strengths do you already have with this skill? In what areas would you like to grow?
4. In what ways do instructional and political advocacy overlap? Provide a situation or two in which these two types of advocacy would be needed.
5. Can you imagine a time in the future in which advocacy in English language teaching will not be necessary? What would it take for that to be the case?

Resources for Further Exploration

1. Advocacy for ELLs: Event Archive & Resources. (n.d.). Retrieved from www.colorincolorado. org/advocacy-ells-recommended-resources
   The website ¡Colorín Colorado! offers a plethora of written and audiovisual information for those working with ELs in ESL settings. Their page focused on advocacy (see link) is particularly helpful. Be sure to scroll down to see all the wonderful resources available!
2. Africa TESOL (n.d.). Retrieved from www.africatesol.org/.
   TESOL affiliates are a great resource on the issues relevant for each local region and to work with as you begin your local advocacy work. A newer affiliate, Africa TESOL (see link) focuses on collaboration in the region and raising the profile of African teachers of English.
3. TESOL Advocacy Action Center: Advocacy Resources (n.d.). Retrieved from www.tesol.org/ advance-the-field/advocacy-resources.
   The TESOL International Association has the goal of increasing respect for teachers, students, and the profession as a whole. The webpage (see link) includes information about the TESOL Advocacy and Policy Summit, resources on immigration and refugee concerns, and TESOL position statements on a variety of issues, among other resources.
4. Linville, H., & Whiting, J. (2019). *Advocacy in English language teaching and learning*. New York, NY: Routledge.
   Covering theories of advocacy, constraints, and challenges, and a range of hands-on perspectives in varying teaching contexts, this text offers a deeper understanding of what advocacy is and can be, and gives teachers the tools to advocate for students, families, communities, and the profession.
5. Advocacy (n.d.). Retrieved from www.englishaustralia.com.au/advocacy/advocacy.
   Another English language teaching association, English Australia's advocacy webpage (see link), provides a wonderful blueprint on how similar associations can approach advocacy through submissions (or position statements), disseminating information on and working to change relevant policies, and a media strategy.

REFERENCES

Adoniou, M. (2017). *Professionalism and the profession as change agent*. Paper presented at the Summit on the Future of the TESOL Profession, Athens, Greece. Retrieved from www.tesol.org/docs/default-source/advocacy/misty-adoniou. pdf?sfvrsn=0

Athanases, S. Z., & de Oliveira, L. C. (2007). Conviction, confrontation, and risk in new teachers' advocating for equity. *Teaching Education*, 18(2), 123–136. http://doi.org/10.1080/10476210701325150

Canagarajah, S. (2008). The politics of English language teaching. In S. May & N. H. Hornberger (Eds.), *Encyclopedia of language and education, 2nd Edition, Volume 1: Language policies and political issues in education* (pp. 213–227). Berlin, Germany: Springer.

Dubetz, N. E., & de Jong, E. J. (2011). Teacher advocacy in bilingual programs. *Bilingual Research Journal: The Journal of the National Association for Bilingual Education*, 34(3), 248–262. http://doi.org/10.1080/15235882.2011.623603

García, O., & Kleifgen, J. A. (2010). *Educating emergent bilinguals: Policies, programs, and practices for English language learners*. New York, NY: Teachers College Press.

Haneda, M., & Alexander, M. (2015). ESL teacher advocacy beyond the classroom. *Teaching and Teacher Education*, 49, 149–158. https://doi.org/10.1016/j.tate.2015.03.009

Harper, C., & de Jong, E. (2009). English language teacher expertise: The elephant in the room. *Language and Education*, 23, 137–151. https://doi.org/10.1080/09500780802152788

Hawkins, M. R., & Norton, B. (2009). Critical language teacher education. In A. Burns & J. C. Richards (Eds.), *Cambridge guide to second language teacher education* (pp. 30–39). Cambridge, UK: Cambridge University Press. https://doi.org/10.1111/j.1540-4781.2011.01212_2.x

Hesson, S., & Toncelli, R. (2019). Making the path by walking together: A collaborative approach to advocacy. In H. Linville & J. Whiting (Eds.), *Advocacy in English language teaching and learning* (pp. 147–157). New York, NY: Routledge.

Hoang, H., & Truong, L. B. (2017). Teacher agency and autonomy in rural Vietnam. In P. C. L. Ng & E. F. Boucher-Yip (Eds.), *Teacher agency and policy response in English language teaching* (pp. 188–201). New York, NY: Routledge.

Kubanyiova, M., & Crookes, G. (2016). Re-envisioning the roles, tasks, and contributions of language teachers in the multilingual era of language education research and practice. *Modern Language Journal*, 100(S1), 117–132.

Linville, H. A. (2016). ESOL teachers as advocates: An important role? *TESOL Journal*, 7(1), 98–130. https://doi.org/10.1002/tesj.193

Linville, H. A. (2019). Advocacy skills for teachers: "A real careful little dance". In H. Linville & J. Whiting (Eds.), *Advocacy in English language teaching and learning* (pp. 3–17). New York, NY: Routledge.

Linville, H. A. (in press). A closer look at ESOL teacher advocacy: What we do and why. *TESOL Journal*.

Llurda, E. (2015). Non-native teachers and advocacy. In M. Bigelow & J. Ennser-Kananen (Eds.), *The Routledge handbook of educational linguistics* (pp. 105–116). New York, NY: Routledge.

Mambu, J. E. (2012). English for advocacy purposes: Critical pedagogy's contribution to Indonesia. In K. Sung & R. Pederson (Eds.), *Critical ELT practices in Asia* (pp. 111–136). Rotterdam, The Netherlands: Sense Publishers.

Morgan, B. (2016). Language teacher identity and the domestication of dissent: An exploratory account. *TESOL Quarterly*, 50(3), 708–734.

National Education Association (NEA). (2015). *All in!: How educators can advocate for English language learners*. Washington, DC: The National Education Association. Retrieved from www.colorincolorado.org/sites/default/files/ELL_AdvocacyGuide2015.pdf

Sheppard, R. (2019). Action required: The adult educator as advocate. In H. Linville & J. Whiting (Eds.), *Advocacy in English language teaching and learning* (pp. 121–132). New York, NY: Routledge.

Staehr Fenner, D. (2014). *Advocating for English learners: A guide for educators*. Thousand Oaks, CA: Corwin.

Staehr Fenner, D., & Breiseth, L. (2017). *You are already a leader: Identifying your leadership skills on behalf of ELLs*. Retrieved from www.colorincolorado.org/article/you-are-already-leader-identifying-your-leadership-skills-behalf-ells

Suárez, M., & Domínguez, M. (2015, October 5). Carrying that weight: ESL teacher negotiations toward advocacy and equity. *Radical Pedagogy*, 12(2), 3. Education Research Complete, Web.

Sun, Y. (2010). Standards, equity, and advocacy: Employment conditions of ESOL teachers in adult basic education and literacy systems. *TESOL Journal*, 1(1), 142–158. http://doi.org/10.5054/tj.2010.215135

TESOL International Association (TESOL). (2019). *Standards for initial TESOL Pre-K-12 teacher preparation programs*. Alexandria, VA: Author.

Vinogradova, P., & Linville, H. (2020). *Diverse voices of advocacy*. Podcast in preparation.

Whiting, J. (2019). Beyond the philosophy statement: Bringing advocacy center stage in TESOL teacher education. In H. Linville & J. Whiting (Eds.), *Advocacy in English language teaching and learning* (pp. 31–43). New York, NY: Routledge.

Educators Influencing Policy

The Language Opportunity Coalition and the Seal of Biliteracy in the U.S.

Rachel Thorson Hernández and Nicholas Close Subtirelu

The Seal of Biliteracy is as an initiative to incentivize and credentialize bi-/multilingualism in United States K-12 education. While it has been widely celebrated as a positive development in U.S. educational language policy, concerns have been raised about whether the program effectively recognizes the bilingualism of English language learners (see Subtirelu, Borowczyk, Thorson Hernández, & Venezia, 2019). In this case study, we discuss the advocacy work of the Language Opportunity Coalition (LOC), a group that has advocated on behalf of English language learners to affect the policies that established the Seal of Biliteracy in their state. The LOC is a coalition of Massachusetts teachers, parents, and students who have come together to advocate for equal educational opportunities for learners and speakers of all languages.

THE SETTING

Massachusetts, a small state in the northeastern part of the United States, has had a contentious history with bilingual education over the last few decades. In 2002, the state legislature passed a ballot measure known as the "Question 2 Initiative" that essentially outlawed bilingual education in Massachusetts public schools. Advocates for the ballot measure argued that English-only education, officially called Sheltered English Immersion (SEI), would right the wrongs of Massachusetts's previous policy of bilingual transnational education, which they described as a "failure" that prevented immigrant children from being able to "fully participate in the American Dream of economic and social advancement" (Massachusetts Secretary of the Commonwealth, 2002). Massachusetts's ban on bilingual education remained in effect until the watershed passing of the LOOK Act (a nickname for the official "Act relative to language opportunity for our kids") in 2017, when school districts in Massachusetts were awarded the right to offer research-based learning programs for English language learners (ELLs), and the state was charged with the establishment of the Massachusetts Seal of Biliteracy.

The Massachusetts Seal of Biliteracy

The Seal of Biliteracy is an initiative to incentivize and credentialize bi-/multilingualism in United States K-12 education. As of 2019, Massachusetts is one of 36 states that, along with the District of Columbia, have approved a statewide Seal of Biliteracy since the program was first adopted in California in 2011. In order to establish statewide guidelines for implementing the Seal, Massachusetts educators, along with parents and students, formed the Language Opportunity Coalition (LOC), which coordinated the 2014–2018 Massachusetts Seal of Biliteracy Pilot Program. Since 2015, an increasing number of school districts have participated in the program, with hundreds of students receiving the Seal upon graduating from high school since the pilot began.

Eligibility for the Seal is based on a student being able to demonstrate proficiency in English and another language. Students demonstrate English proficiency by attaining a score of 260 on Massachusetts's state standardized test – the Massachusetts Comprehensive Assessment System. Proficiency in another language may be demonstrated by attaining an Intermediate High score on the American Council on the Teaching of Foreign Languages (ACTFL) standardized test or by submitting a portfolio if no ACTFL test for the language in question exists.

At the same time that LOC oversaw the Massachusetts pilot of the Seal, it advocated for the passage of the previously mentioned LOOK Act. Among other important goals related to language opportunities for Massachusetts K-12 students, the LOOK Act sought to establish a state Seal of Biliteracy to encourage schools to establish language programs that would promote bilingualism and the efforts of students to learn or maintain foreign, heritage, or native languages other than English. In November 2017, the LOOK Act passed the Massachusetts House and Senate and was subsequently signed into law, thus establishing the Massachusetts Seal of Biliteracy. However, the version of the bill passed raised serious concerns about equitable access among the educators who make up LOC, which almost immediately began advocating for changes to the bill. The issues involved in Massachusetts's implementation of the Seal echo those documented in other states. In general, while many educators are optimistic about the Seal, it remains to be seen whether or not the initiative serves the interests of *all* students, especially in light of research questioning whether the Seal effectively recognizes the bilingualism of English language learners. For example, in their critical policy analysis of documents promoting and implementing the Seal in different states, Subtirelu et al. (2019) found that the purpose of the Seal has overall been aimed at promoting foreign or world language education, that the policy requirements for demonstrating biliteracy advantage native English-speaking students studying a foreign or world language, and that schools with high percentages of students of color and/or from low-income families are less likely to participate in the program.

DESCRIPTION OF ENGLISH LANGUAGE LEARNERS

Seventeen years after the passing of its ban on bilingual education and two years after the end to this ban, Massachusetts's population of ELLs continues to grow. The number of ELL students in the state has doubled to over 90,294 since 2000 (Language Opportunity Coalition, 2017), and ELLs make up around 10% of the total student population. The English-only policy put in place by the 2002 mandate did not prove to be the panacea its advocates believed it would be. Today, ELLs in Massachusetts fall behind their native-English-speaking peers in terms of high school graduation, college attendance, and standardized test results. Additionally, the four-year dropout rate for ELLs in 2017 exceeded 15%, which is three times the state average (Massachusetts Department of Elementary and Secondary Education, 2017). Unfortunately, as many teachers, administrators, and current and former ELLs can attest, Massachusetts is not an anomaly when it comes to both historic lack of equitable treatment of and performance gaps between ELLs and their native-English-speaking peers. Although it is unclear how the Seal of Biliteracy will ultimately benefit Massachusetts's ELLs, the state's recognition of the other languages these students speak is a promising shift in the discourse. Essentially, the LOOK Act establishing the Seal marks a change from a state policy announcing to ELLs that their languages aren't welcome in school to one saying that those same languages will help them achieve an award recognizing their multilingualism.

LANGUAGE POLICY APPROPRIATION AND INNOVATION

It's no surprise that teachers of ELLs, whose numbers also continue to grow, often feel powerless when it comes to (re)negotiating policies that, at best, fail to fully support their students' learning and life goals and, at worst, only support those students who tick the boxes of whiteness, wealth, and (English) monolingualism (Delavan, Valdez, & Freire, 2016). How, then, can these teachers advocate for equitable learning opportunities for the ELLs they teach? LOC's advocacy efforts on behalf of Massachusetts's ELLs are a compelling example of how teachers can resist one-size-fits-all approaches to policy decision making and become active participants in the debate on education. Key points for teachers wondering how to undertake a similar process of becoming policy-actors are discussed and center around two main ideas: shared decision-making and shared resources (Ellison, Anderson, Aronson, & Clausen, 2018, p. 161).

Shared Decision Making

Teachers are, arguably, the individuals within the educational hierarchy best able to inform society of the daily realities of K-12 education and therefore should be part of the policy-making process affecting their classrooms. Teachers are also extremely busy, and their jobs don't always make it easy for them to be involved in policy decisions, both due to lack of time and other resources and the question of how their political activity may affect them professionally. Having acknowledged these constraints, we believe it is in the best interest of state and district boards of education, schools, teachers, parents, and students that educational decisions be shared and co-created and that teachers be encouraged to participate in policy discussions and decisions. With this in mind, LOC has modeled the concept of shared decision-making via public discourse in a number of ways. For example, they have published calls for action and step-by-step guidelines to encourage teachers as well as the general public to communicate their support for legislation such as the LOOK Act. These calls for action, which have included testifying before the Massachusetts Joint Committee on Education, attending and speaking at Board of Education meetings, and contacting local and state legislators, are accompanied by guidelines, fact sheets, infographics, and summaries of current policies published by LOC. One such set of guidelines (see Figure 9.1.1) offers advice for teachers on how to communicate with legislators in an open hearing on a policy affecting ELLs in the state. The call for action and guidelines shown here encourage and model shared decision-making while also serving as an inspirational example for empowering teachers who wish to make their views on the educational policies that affect them known to the legislators who ultimately draft and vote on these policies.

Specifically, the guidelines shown in Figure 9.1.2 validate and elevate teachers' experiences and knowledge, stating, "You have so much to offer policy conversations without having to be a data or policy expert." The post and guidelines also give step-by-step suggestions for how to draft testimony to be given in front of the Joint Committee, encourage teachers to ask friends and colleagues to also give testimony, and invite teachers to contact LOC to let them know if they will testify.

The post and guidelines are just one example of the many ways LOC has embraced the idea of shared decision-making. Among other things, LOC has used social media to make public their concerns with the Seal of Biliteracy, rally support for their proposed plan to advocate for legislation to address these concerns, and keep their members and supporters apprised of and involved in their efforts to enact policy change. As such, LOC is a good model for how social networking can be used by educator-advocates who want to push for policy change. Finally, LOC's use of social media to publish their attempts, setbacks, and successes in advocating for policy changes that improve equitable educational access for ELLs also makes these public and transparent, thus giving equal access to their mission for language-learning equality.

Shared Resources

In advocating for changes to policies like the LOOK Act that shape how Massachusetts's ELLs are taught and the access they have to educational opportunities, LOC has done a great job of sharing their resources, especially those concerning the knowledge they have gained through their collective expertise as teachers, coordinators of the Seal of Biliteracy Pilot Project, and policy-actors. For example, they have published fact sheets in multiple languages that can be presented to parents, educators, and members of the Board of Education/MA Legislature. For example, here are useful resources:

- in English: https://languageopportunity.files.wordpress.com/2018/05/english-look-act-fact-sheet-for-parents.pdf)

- in Spanish: https://languageopportunity.files.wordpress.com/2018/05/spanish-look-act-fact-sheet-for-parents-dese.pdf

- in Portuguese: https://languageopportunity.files.wordpress.com/2018/05/portuguese-look-act-fact-sheet-for-parents-dese-5-2018.pdf

They have also drafted a Toolkit for implementing and starting the Seal of Biliteracy (see https://languageopportunity.org/seal-of-biliteracy2) and for contacting lawmakers to advocate for changes to current educational policy in the state (see Language Opportunity Coalition, 2018).

Language Opportunity

Massachusetts Language Opportunity Coalition

Hearing of the Joint Committee on Education

☐ May 5, 2015　☐ MATSOL　☐ Coalition News
(https://languageopportunity.files.wordpress.com/2015/05/alert.jpg)Support
the LOOK Bill and the Seal of Biliteracy Bill

Hearing of the Joint Committee on Education
Tuesday, May 12, 2015 at 10 a.m.
Massachusetts State House, Room 2A

- See our Legislation (https://languageopportunity.org/legislative/) page for
  information about the bills.
- Let us know via the Contact Us (https://languageopportunity.org/contact-us/) page if you plan to
  testify.
- Instructions on how to take action – testify and contact your legislators: English
  (https://languageopportunity.files.wordpress.com/2015/05/hearing-of-the-joint-committee-on-
  education-instructions.docx) / Spanish
  (https://languageopportunity.files.wordpress.com/2015/05/communicacic3b3n-con-familias-
  comitc3a9-de-educacic3b3n.docx)

Blog at WordPress.com. (https://wordpress.com/?ref=footer_blog)

Figure 9.1.1 LOC blog post on testifying on behalf of the LOOK Act

Source: Language Opportunity Coalition

Hearing of the Joint Committee on Education for the LOOK Bill and the Seal of Biliteracy Bill

ATTEND THE HEARING at the Massachusetts State House Room A2 on Tuesday, May 12, 2015, at 10:00 am and support our ELLs! **GIVE TESTIMONY** on why you support a change in the English Language Learner system. Contact the Language Opportunity Coalition if you plan to attend or testify.

GUIDANCE FOR TESTIMONIALS
Testimonials that tell a story about individuals are very powerful. Focus on what you know and care about. Think about what you know and have experienced and present your concerns and ideas for better solutions. You have so much to offer policy conversations without having to be a data or policy expert. Plan to speak for no more than 3 minutes.

SUBMIT WRITTEN TESTIMONY
You can submit written testimony to the Chairs of the committee and cc: your State Senator and State Representative. Here is the list of names for the Joint Education Committee Chairs and members. You could also send the testimony to Language Opportunity Coalition and we will make sure it is handed in on Tuesday.

GUIDANCE FOR WRITTEN TESTIMONIES

- Limit the text to 1.5 pages
- Include your name, address, where you work or study, what you do for work,
- State "I am a member of The Language Opportunity Coalition" or list your organization,
- State "I am in favor of the bills H422/S336 (Seal of Biliteracy) and H498/S262 (Look Bill) and this is why.
- Pick one action point listed in the <u>LOOK Bill Fact Sheet</u> and speak to that.
- State "I recommend that bills H422/S336 (Seal of Biliteracy) and H498/S262 (Look Bill) should be passed.

CALL LEGISLATORS
Call the Chairs of the Joint Committee on Education and your State Senator and State Representative to **urge them to attend the hearing** and support the bills. To find your state Rep or Senator, go to www.wheredoivote.ma.

SPREAD THE WORD to colleagues and friends!

Figure 9.1.2 LOC's guidelines for testifying before the Joint Committee

Source: Language Opportunity Coalition

It is important for teachers engaging in policy work to share their successes, failures, suggestions, and questions with other teachers so that (1) the views of teachers with different local experiences (i.e., public vs. private and urban vs. rural schools, districts with many ELLs vs. those with few, etc.) are represented, and (2) teachers can build off the experiences of others. Since teachers are always pressed for time, sharing resources and knowledge gained through experience is a great way for teachers to be able to make efficient use of these important resources. Blogs, shared drives such as Box, Google Drive, and Dropbox, email groups like Google Groups, and instant messaging systems like Slack are just a few examples of web- and cloud-based platforms that teachers can use to share resources. LOC's blog post (see Figure 9.1.3) exemplifies resource sharing. The post invites teachers to view a webinar outlining recent changes to the LOOK Act and offers clear, step-by-step guidelines on how to publicly comment on the regulations on the Massachusetts Department of Education's website.

By sharing their resources online, LOC is able to reach and involve more teachers in the policy process, thus accomplishing both the goal of sharing resources and sharing decision-making.

Suggestions for Teachers Wishing to Engage With Policy

Based on LOC's advocacy efforts, we developed suggestions for teachers to support efforts in shaping policy decisions affecting them. These suggestions are mostly applicable to teachers working in the United States K-12 context. Knowing that political activism can be harshly punished in many places in the world, we

4/3/2020 Webinar: How to provide input on proposed LOOK Act regulations | Language Opportunity

Language Opportunity

Massachusetts Language Opportunity Coalition

Webinar: How to provide input on proposed LOOK Act regulations

□ April 25, 2018May 3, 2018 □ MATSOL □ Coalition News

The public comment period is open on the proposed regulations for the LOOK Act. The proposed changes include the proposal requirement for establishing an alternative EL program, EL Parent Advisory Councils, criteria for the Seal of Biliteracy, draft requirements for the Bilingual Education Endorsement, and SEI Endorsement for Vocational Technical teachers and changes to voc-tech licensure requirements. It is important that educators of English learners provide input. This webinar will give an overview of the new regulations and provide instructions on how to comment.

Presented by the Language Opportunity Coalition and MTA

WEBINAR
LOOK Act Regulations – Public Comment 101: How to provide input on proposed regulations
Thursday, May 3, 2018 at 4:00 PM

View/print the the webinar slides (pdf) (https://languageopportunity.files.wordpress.com/2018/05/matsol-mta_public_comment_look_act_webinar.pdf)

Brought to you by GoToWebinar®
Webinars Made Easy®

Blog at WordPress.com. (https://wordpress.com/?ref=footer_blog)

https://languageopportunity.org/2018/04/25/webinar-how-to-provide-input-on-proposed-look-act-regulations/ 1/1

Figure 9.1.3 Blogpost announcement of a LOC webinar

Source: Language Opportunity Coalition (2015)

understand that these suggestions might not be applicable and implementable outside of the United States. At the same time, we hope they can be useful and provide ideas in developing advocacy action plans.

- Keep people informed – Fact sheets, guidelines, Twitter/Facebook/blog posts, infographics, and webinars are just a few ways teachers can inform and involve their colleagues and the public in their initiative.

- Invite input – Tell fellow teachers that you value their opinions and invite them to work with you to advocate for policy change.

- Validate other teachers' experiences – Let your colleagues know they have the right to participate in policy decisions; they are knowledgeable experts on their students and schools and have invaluable locally situated insights that legislators need to hear.

- Share resources – Publish shareable fact sheets, suggested guidelines for things like giving testimony and contacting lawmakers, drafts of proposed legislation and letters to legislators, and anything else you think can be of use to teachers; share your successes and failures and ask other teachers if they would be willing to do the same.

- Educate yourself and your colleagues on ELLs' linguistic repertoires; for example, the myth of semilingualism – The state of being neither proficient in an L1 nor in an L2 is one that many teachers perpetuate (Kangas, 2017).

- Do the work to involve ELLs' parents in the school. See the chapter by Carruba-Rogel in Bucholtz, Casillas, and Lee (2018) for details.

- Create opportunities for ELLs to use their home language(s) in ways that are institutionally valued; e.g., a school organization that recognizes multilingual students' translation and interpretation skills and intercultural knowledge by providing student-led language brokering services for non-English-speaking parents (see the chapter by Lopez in Bucholtz et al., 2018).

CONCLUSION

Because program decisions for K-12 world language education in the United States are almost always made at the state level, there is great potential for advocates within individual states to shape the policies that establish the implementation of policies like the Seal of Biliteracy, which currently differs greatly from state to state in terms of language requirements. Though this inconsistency implies its own set of challenges, it opens up spaces for advocates to locally enact change. LOC's advocacy on behalf of English language learners in Massachusetts is a compelling example of how educators can use spaces such as social media platforms to involve fellow teachers and the community at large in sharing resources and decision-making thereby expanding the number of voices involved in shaping educational language policy.

REFERENCES

Bucholtz, M., Casillas, D., & Lee, J. (2018). *Feeling it: Language, race, and affect in Latinx youth learning.* New York, NY: Routledge.

Ellison, S., Anderson, A. B., Aronson, B., & Clausen, C. (2018). From objects to subjects: Repositioning teachers as policy actors doing policy work. *Teaching and Teacher Education, 74,* 157–169.

Kangas, S. (2017). "That's where the rubber meets the road": The intersection of special education and bilingual education. *Teachers College Record, 119*(7), 1–36.

Language Opportunity Coalition. (2015, May 2). *Hearing of the Joint Committee on Education for the LOOK bill and the seal of biliteracy bill* [web log comment]. Retrieved from https://languageopportunity.org/2015/05/05/hearing-of-the-joint-committee-on-education/

Language Opportunity Coalition. (2017). *English learner education bills.* Retrieved from https://languageopportunity.files.wordpress.com/2015/01/look_bill_fact_sheet_may2017.pdf

Language Opportunity Coalition. (2018, April 28). *Webinar: How to provide input on proposed LOOK act regulations* [web log comment]. Retrieved from https://languageopportunity.org/2018/04/25/webinar-how-to-provide-input-on-proposed-look-act-regulations/

Massachusetts Department of Elementary and Secondary Education. (2017). *2016–2017 student dropout rate report.* Retrieved from http://profiles.doe.mass.edu/dropout/default.aspx

Massachusetts Secretary of the Commonwealth. (2002). *Full text of 2002 ballot questions.* Retrieved from www.sec.state.ma.us/ele/ele02/elebq02/bq02full.htm#q2anc

Subtirelu, N., Borowczyk, M., Thorson Hernández, R., & Venezia, F. (2019). Recognizing whose bilingualism?: A critical policy analysis of the seal of biliteracy. *The Modern Language Journal, 103*, 371–390.

Caring as a Form of Advocacy for Literacy-Emergent Newcomers With Special Education Needs

The Community-Building Pedagogical Approach in the U.S.

Luis Javier Pentón Herrera

This case study provides an example of teacher advocacy in the form of designing and incorporating a targeted intervention using the community-building pedagogical approach to help English learners (ELs) succeed in our learning environment. This case study is also an example of student advocacy, as it shows how ELs become active participants in the classroom, and their actions of supporting each other become the foundation of a respectful and inclusive learning environment.

THE SETTING

Clover High School (pseudonym) is a public secondary school located in an economically booming suburban area in a northeastern state of the United States of America. Clover High is considered a medium-size school serving approximately 2,100 students and employing more than 130 teachers. The school is racially and culturally diverse, as students' families come from many parts of the world, primarily Africa, Central America, and the Caribbean English-speaking islands. Over 15 languages are spoken as a first language by students and staff at this school.

The setting where this case study primarily takes place is in the only English for Speakers of Other Languages (ESOL) newcomer classroom. The other three ESOL classes in the school teach more advanced English levels: beginners, intermediate, and advanced. This classroom is located on the first floor of the high school's main building. The classroom is set up as a Socratic-style learning environment where all the chairs are placed in a U-shape and a big blackboard covers one of the four walls. The other three walls of the classroom are decorated with students' art projects, family pictures, and flags from their native countries.

DESCRIPTION OF ENGLISH LANGUAGE LEARNERS

This case study primarily focuses on two of the most vulnerable ELs in our classroom, Elizabeth and Oscar (pseudonyms). Elizabeth is a 17-year-old newcomer from Honduras. She arrived at school last year toward the end of the 2017–2018 school year. When she arrived, she was visibly scared and would cry when teachers talked to her in English or during period changes because the number of students walking in the hallways frightened her. For Elizabeth, formal schooling was a new experience. She lived in a rural area of Honduras and was never afforded the opportunity to attend school. According to her mother, because Elizabeth has developmental delays – cognitive, speech, and language skills, as well as fine and gross motor skills – and is hard of hearing, schools in Honduras were not able to accommodate her needs. As a result, Elizabeth did not learn to read or write and speaks Spanish, her native language, with difficulty.

Oscar is a 16-year-old newcomer from El Salvador. He arrived at school in the beginning of the 2018–2019 academic year. Oscar has acute developmental delays – cognitive, speech and language skills, social and emotional skills, and fine and gross motor skills. According to his mother, he went to school up to second grade in El Salvador; however, Oscar cannot read or write. Oscar's fingers are often curled, making it difficult for him to practice writing. In addition, Oscar has bursts of energy that prompt him to stand up, walk around the class, and sing, yell, or talk uncontrollably. At the time of this case study, neither Elizabeth nor Oscar had been offered special education services at the school.

PEDAGOGICAL APPLICATION AND INNOVATION

When Elizabeth arrived to our school during the 2017–2018 academic year with visible developmental delays, I asked our special education team to evaluate her to see if she would qualify to receive special education services. However, because she was an EL, special educators insisted that she just needed to learn English. The same situation took place with Oscar when I requested for him to be evaluated for special education services. Elizabeth and Oscar's under-identification as special education students is, sadly, not uncommon among ELs. As Zacarian (2011) notes, the fear some schools have of wrongfully referring ELs to special education evaluations (overrepresentation) has resulted in stalling the process "for such a long period of time that when the referral and identification process finally occur, it is too late to provide the types of interventions that would have helped the student the most effectively, if at all" (p. 131).

For this reason, after learning that my students were not going to receive appropriate support in a timely manner, I decided to engage in research that could further expand my knowledge to incorporate meaningful learning routines to help them. Also, my vision was to improve my approach to teaching so I could advocate for them inside our classroom and help them make meaningful social connections while building resilience. As a result, I developed the community-building pedagogical approach – a practice I found to be impactful. I observed this approach to help Elizabeth and Oscar feel more comfortable inside our classroom and gradually learn to cope with and navigate the daily routines and social interactions with their classmates.

The Community-Building Pedagogical Approach

The community-building pedagogical approach is a daily practice that has shaped my pedagogy as an ESOL educator. It focuses on creating a communal living environment within the classroom where students actively engage in activities that resemble the Japanese educational concept known as "group living" (Le Tendre, 1999). For group living to be effective, teachers are expected to take a social role in the lives of students; that is, role modeling and active participation in students' activities during and after school is necessary. Thus, teachers become trusted moral authorities who promote collective participation and compassionate social interactions within the learning environment.

The three main components of the community-building pedagogical approach are: (1) leadership, (2) sense of community, and (3) egalitarian participation. In our classroom, leadership is understood as students' ability to successfully complete individual tasks and responsibilities, be accountable for one another, and come to a consensus on how to complete class activities and projects. Sense of community is defined as having a voice and engaging in routines that promote group responsibility, reflection, and social and emotional bonds. Further, egalitarian participation is viewed as a communal process where equity and mental, psychological, and physical well-being for everyone is of utmost importance.

Incorporating thoughtful and caring routines that promote these three components are essential for this form of advocacy. The examples reflect how the components of leadership, sense of community, and egalitarian participation work in our classroom.

Leadership: Engaging in Peer Monitoring

Peer monitoring occurs when individuals notice and respond to their peers' behavior, performance (Loughry & Tosi, 2008), and feelings. In our classroom, peer monitoring takes the form of classroom routines where students encourage each other to perform well, help one another, and deter inappropriate behavior with the vision of maintaining a learning environment of mutual support as they learn English and navigate through the experience of being a newcomer. Peer monitoring gives students the opportunity to demonstrate their leadership skills as individuals and members of a group. In the beginning of the school year, discussing this topic in detail in English with my students was not possible because they were all newcomers with emergent English skills. As such, I would incorporate group and pair activities and explain to each group in their first language (in this case, Spanish, as all students were Spanish speakers at the time) what collaborative learning was and how they could learn and support one another. After a couple of months, students felt comfortable with collaborative learning and had the opportunity to interact with all of their classmates. It was only then that we started to devote time to classroom activities that slowly introduced the concept of peer monitoring.

The first activity we included to introduce peer monitoring focused on using correct forms of the present progressive (verb to be + ing). I incorporated a whole-class speaking activity where each student had to take out a sentence strip from a bag while covering their eyes. Then they had to read and act the sentence to the class. An example was "John is singing in class." Then I would ask students, "Is that ok (with my thumb up) or not (with my thumb down)?" and usually students would reply with "no" or "no good" and I would take that opportunity to show how it could be corrected: "John, please don't sing in class," and then I would ask the rest of the class to repeat after me. After a month and a half of incorporating similar activities, we talked about desired and undesired behaviors in our learning environment and, after writing acceptable behaviors down on a big poster, we all agreed to follow these behaviors by going through all of them individually and asking students to give a "thumbs up" for yes or "thumbs down" for no. In the beginning, creating a culture of peer monitoring was a challenge because students were not familiar with the concept. Nonetheless, incorporating daily activities that immersed the entire class in real-life moral situations where they could correct or praise one another proved important and helpful.

When we were first learning about collaborative work and peer monitoring, I began to pair Elizabet and Oscar with other classmates and asked those students to teach Elizabeth and Oscar how to write their names, the alphabet, and colors in English and Spanish. I explicitly showed the students how to teach Elizabeth and Oscar to accomplish small tasks one at a time. For example, Oscar needed to learn how to correctly hold a pencil before he could learn how to write. The method for involving Elizabeth and Oscar was to first show them how things were done (I or their classmates would demonstrate), then ask Elizabeth and Oscar to repeat what we were doing. Importantly, when asking Elizabeth and Oscar to repeat our actions, we would provide support as needed. For example, sometimes I would hold Oscar's hand while he traced the letters with the goal that he would develop muscle memory. After that, we would ask Elizabeth and Oscar if they could do it by themselves. Elizabeth was a fast learner and was usually able to work independently after repeating the process a couple of times. However, Oscar needed additional peer support learning to trace numbers and letters. At the time of this case study, Elizabeth was able to write by herself the alphabet with minimal support from classmates and could correctly identify the colors in English and Spanish. Oscar, on the other hand, still needed support from his classmates to trace his full name and numbers.

For Elizabeth and Oscar, peer monitoring improved their school experience and they continued to work collaboratively with their classmates. Elizabeth found her voice in our classroom community and started to often correct students who deviated from behaviors she found unacceptable. For example, when a boy pulled a girl's hair, she shouted "¡no eso!" (don't [do] that!) in front of the class. I believe that Elizabeth was comfortable to express her voice in our classroom because she knew all of her classmates and because she felt safe. Although some teachers might find Elizabeth's behavior disruptive, I see her confidence to speak up as a positive outcome of her experience in our classroom. It indicates that she felt part of our learning community and, in this sense of belonging, she found resilience to share her voice and provide feedback to her classmates.

Sense of Community: Infusing Components of Restorative Practices

The infusion of restorative practices in our weekly routines has proven healing and unifying. Restorative practices, sometimes addressed as restorative discipline, is defined as a "philosophy or framework that can guide [educators and advocates] as we design programs and make decisions within our particular settings"

(Amstutz & Mullet, 2015, p. 4). Because restorative practices is a flexible framework, we used it to learn English while building a sense of community. Once a week we came together in a circle to talk about different topics of particular interest to my students. These topics ranged from school fighting to personal life experiences. In our circles, we incorporated English to reinforce language learning and stay faithful to the guidelines previously accepted by a consensus.

When I first introduced the practice of restorative circles into our learning environment, I explained to my students the concept in Spanish to ensure full understanding. At the same time, I brought with me a list of guidelines that we needed to understand and went around the class asking students to verbally agree to them saying "I accept" or "I don't accept." I explained that the purpose was for us to use Spanish as needed but the ultimate goal was to use as much English as possible. We had a metal cookie tin full of different topics chosen by students. They were free to add a piece of paper with a topic anytime they wanted and could just walk up to the tin and throw in a piece of paper. When we came together in a circle, I would open the cookie tin and randomly grab a piece of paper with a topic and devote our circle to that topic alone. To keep English inside our circle, I would bring a few props such as sentence starters (i.e., I feel, I like, etc.) and cards that paired different adjectives with visuals (i.e., the word *sad* with a sad face). In addition, on the easel pad, I would write questions in English and Spanish to ask my students in the circle.

Recently, Oscar experienced a breakthrough in one of our circles. Before we circled up that day, Oscar and his classmates were working on colors using English and Spanish, and Oscar was coloring the flags of the United States and El Salvador. Because he tended to forget names and things, I checked on his progress and reminded him that he was coloring the flags of El Salvador and the United States. After the coloring activity, we circled up and conducted our circle as usual. However, during the check-out activity (last activity in the circle), I asked students to say the name of a color that reflected how they felt after the circle, to which Oscar shouted ";blue, *como la bandera de El Salvador!*" (blue, like the flag of El Salvador!). This was the first time in class that Oscar ever said a color in English and it was the first time he ever made a connection between a color and an object. This was a huge accomplishment! Everyone at the circle applauded Oscar and were laughing with him. This type of meaningful interaction among students shows that, in the circle, we are all one big community. Oscar was very proud of that event and repeated several times what he had accomplished in the circle. It was a great day for him.

Egalitarian Participation: Encourage Group Living and Commitments to One Another

Egalitarian participation is a daily routine in our classroom where we practice resolution of conflict by discussion and empathy for one another, a commitment to the group, and willingness to make individual accomplishments a group success (Le Tendre, 1999). Accomplishing egalitarian participation has not been an easy feat, in part because it is a new concept for many of the learners. Conflict does arise in our classroom among students, but it is rarely addressed in front of the class. Instead, I diffuse conflict by asking the students involved to step outside the classroom and discuss the situation with me. My guide for resolving conflicts is to always emphasize that we want to ensure our classroom remains an environment where we all feel safe and have the opportunity to learn without feeling worried about anything else. This message of peace and inclusion resonates with my students because many of them have experienced hardship in their lives and want to leave those experiences behind and focus on learning English to become successful in the United States.

In our classroom, no one is left behind. Students are trusted with a wide range of choices and autonomy. For this reason, we incorporate activities that focus on building group identity and empathy toward one another. At the same time, these activities also focus on developing an understanding that obstacles can be overcome when working together. In one of our restorative circles, one of the students made a comment about social media and it quickly became a topic of interest. Students asked if we could learn the meaning of some words, memes, hashtags, and phrases used in social media and text messages. We agreed that we could devote a class to those topics and the students were tasked with bringing the information they wanted to learn in class. Some students brought acronyms used in text messages (i.e., lol, ttyl), others brought hashtags (i.e., #influencer, #blacklivesmatter), and a few brought memes. As a class, we went through the list and talked about them, including those containing obscene language because I wanted my students to learn, in a judgment-free space, the content they are exposed to on social media.

CONCLUSION

In the English language teaching world, advocacy can take many forms and can include community outreach and services (Pentón Herrera, 2019), school and/or county reforms (Staehr Fenner, 2014), and political engagement (Pentón Herrera & Obregón, 2018), to name a few. I believe that classroom advocacy should remain a primary concern for ESOL educators. Specifically, when advocating for the incorporation of classroom practices that support vulnerable ELs like Elizabeth and Oscar. It is my hope that this case study sheds light on the importance of caring as an essential form of advocacy for newcomers with no prior formal education, literacy-emergent academic skills, and cognitive and physical special needs. Furthermore, this case study highlights the impact of community-building routines inside learning environments for special education newcomers as they build resilience, find a voice, and safely learn literacy and English at their own pace.

REFERENCES

Amstutz, L. S., & Mullet, J. H. (2015). *The little book of restorative discipline for schools: Teaching responsibility: Creating caring climates.* New York, NY: Good Books.

Le Tendre, G. K. (1999). Community-building activities in Japanese schools: Alternative paradigms of the democratic school. *Comparative Education Review,* 43(3), 283–310.

Loughry, M. L., & Tosi, H. L. (2008). Performance implications of peer monitoring. *Organization Science,* 19(6), 876–890.

Pentón Herrera, L. J. (2019). Advocating for Indigenous hispanic EL students: Promoting the Indigenismo within. In H. A. Linville & J. Whiting (Eds.), *Advocacy in English language teaching and learning* (pp. 161–174). New York, NY: Routledge.

Pentón Herrera, L. J., & Obregón, N. (2018). Challenges facing Latinx ESOL students in the Trump era: Stories told through testimonios. *Journal of Latinos and Education.* doi:10.1080/15348431.2018.1523793

Staehr Fenner, D. (2014). *Advocating for English learners: A guide for educators.* Thousand Oaks, CA: Corwin & TESOL International Association.

Zacarian, D. (2011). *Transforming schools for English learners: A comprehensive framework for school leaders.* Thousand Oaks, CA: Corwin.

Building Communities of Practice

Advocacy for English Teachers in Rwanda

Richard Niyibigira and Jean Claude Kwitonda

This case study describes the process of building communities of practice (CoPs) in Rwanda through an initiative that started after a major change in language policy. Aiming to create a trilingual society, the government decided that English had become the language of instruction in 2009 "with immediate effect" (Kagwesage, 2013, p. 2). Before 2009, French was the main language of instruction at high school and higher education levels, while Kinyarwanda (the native language of Rwanda) was the predominant language of instruction at the elementary school level. This major policy change required teachers to adjust to the demands of learning and teaching in English. Due to the socioeconomic realities of Rwanda, teachers felt challenged to navigate logistical and psychological demands associated with learning a new language and related teaching strategies. To meet the demands of the new government language policy, teachers became inspired by peer-led advocacy through school-based (professional) learning communities and were empowered to improve English as the language of instruction in Rwandan schools.

THE SETTING

Having been colonized by Belgium, a French-speaking nation, French has been the official language and the medium of instruction alongside Kinyarwanda, the native language of Rwanda. English was not included in Rwanda's educational system until 1995, when Rwanda introduced it as its third official language (Kagwesage, 2013). Following the 1994 repatriation of many Rwandese refugees who had been living in neighboring French-speaking countries (e.g., Burundi and the Democratic Republic of Congo) and English-speaking countries (e.g., Uganda and Tanzania), there was a need to "capture the plurality of discourses, [and] languages" (Warner & Dupuy, 2018, p. 119) of students who were now matriculating into different primary, secondary, and college levels in Rwanda. One way to do it was through the languages of instruction. The inclusion of English also found expression in the geopolitical landscapes of globalizing forces, as English is seen as a language affording its speakers economic, political, and/or cultural capital in the global labor market (Dewey, 2007). Thus, starting in 2008, the government of Rwanda undertook initiatives to train teachers to boost their English language proficiency levels and knowledge of teaching methodology. This training initiative necessitated a systemic transformation to cater to all primary and secondary teachers whose second language after Kinyarwanda was French. The transition from teaching in French to teaching in English was not easy, particularly among teachers who had been teaching in French. The transition entailed that French-speaking teachers had to teach in English while learning it at the same time.

The Association of Teachers of English in Rwanda

To support the transition to English language teaching, a group of eight English teachers got together in 2008 to establish a peer-led professional development initiative and chose the Association of Teachers of English in Rwanda (ATER) as its official designation. Today, the association has grown to 60 active members supporting more than 300 primary and secondary schoolteachers from seven districts in Rwanda, organized in ATER's Communities of Practice (CoP).

Currently there are seven CoPs countrywide that initially started with limited financial means and based operations in Kigali, where most of the members worked and lived at that time. Apart from the $15 annual membership fee, ATER did not have any other source of income that could facilitate activities outside of Kigali. However, following the 2015 conference which included teachers from rural areas, ATER received a lot of requests to establish CoPs in different regions in Rwanda. Additionally, ATER received both technical and financial support from different government partners, including the U.S. Department of State's Regional English Language Office (RELO) located in the U.S. Embassy in Kigali, The British Council, and the A.S. Hornby Educational Trust through the International Association of Teachers of English as a Foreign Language (IATEFL). All these partnerships were built as a result of different advocacy activities that ATER carried out from its early days. We approached both the U.S. Embassy and the British Council for support as the two international bodies have extensive experience in English language teacher development in Rwanda. In addition, we approached the two most established teacher associations in English language teaching, TESOL International Association and IATEFL, and applied for affiliation, which brings many networking and learning opportunities for members. From there, networking with other teacher associations around the world gave ATER a chance to learn about more partnerships and funding opportunities from inside and outside the ATER partners.

PEDAGOGICAL APPLICATION AND INNOVATION

Advocacy and Teacher Empowerment

The attention that ATER received by the end of 2015, particularly for the amount of support the association was offering to teachers in rural areas, was not only a sign of success but also an indication of a greater need for advocacy through teacher empowerment. At the time of writing this case study, ATER and its partners had focused on two vital advocacy processes, namely, empowerment through modification of the environment and nurturing self-efficacy (Johnson & Hackman, 2018) among CoP members.

Providing Financial and Logistical Support

Professional development programming in Rwanda requires more than intrinsic motivation to learn on the part of teachers to be successful, because of both logistical and financial challenges. For example, in Rwandan rural areas, neighboring schools may be a two-to-three-hour walk one way. Most teachers and students in Rwanda walk to school, as the cost of private and public transportation is prohibitive. As a result, it was hard to convince teachers to walk that long distance for a training at a local school and expect them to function optimally without any form of support. To support teachers in their professional development, several local and international organizations provided meals, which indicated to the teachers the meaning and value placed on professional development in the CoPs. Although this type of support was necessary in the economic context of Rwanda, it was not enough to foster and sustain intrinsic motivation among CoPs. In fact, ATER needed to redefine its ways of seeing the CoPs and how they worked by providing a model where CoP members could run their own activities without direct involvement of ATER. We see this type of approach to ATER and CoP governance as nurturing self-efficacy and peer-led advocacy and discuss it in the following section.

Nurturing Self-Efficacy and Peer-Led Advocacy

As a crucial component of advocacy and empowerment, self-efficacy impacts sustainability precisely because empowered people develop a greater sense of self-efficacy and are more likely to set and reach higher goals and less likely to give up when they encounter impediments (Bandura, 1977; Bandura & Wood, 1989). To foster self-efficacy, ATER started training CoP leaders using the Professional Learning Communities (PLCs) model (Dufour, 2004) and protocols adapted from McDonald's and Allen's (n.d.) tuning protocol. According to McDonald and Allen (n.d.), the tuning protocol involves educators in sharing and reflecting on pedagogical challenges with fellow colleagues. As reflective collaboration, the tuning protocol aims to refine teaching approaches and improve pedagogical outcomes. In particular, the PLC model fits the case of CoPs in Rwanda because it encourages English teachers to confront challenges that necessitate a stronger support system in order to navigate psychological and pedagogical processes of transitioning from one linguistic culture to another. The adaptation of tuning protocols helped us structure the teachers' conversations as deliberate peer reflections about students' learning and about challenges and potential solutions in their work. To ensure the CoPs' continuity without direct involvement of ATER, we adapted the tuning protocol by training CoP leaders on the PLC meeting protocols and tasking them with reporting on a monthly basis about their progress. In addition, ATER's professional development coordinator was available to answer questions regarding implementation of the protocols.

PLCs in Practice

The idea of using PLCs was inspired by a presentation made at the 2015 ATER conference by a group of university instructors in Rwanda. Their presentation showcased how PLCs worked in their school. The ATER leadership team approached the school for a partnership on bringing the PLC concept to the CoPs. Following McDonald and Allen's (n.d.) tuning protocol, a PLC workshop took place in Kicuriro, Kigali, on May 14, 2018. The workshop used an adaptation of this tuning protocol (see Appendix A for the Sample Tuning Protocol) to familiarize the participants with the protocol process. First, a presenting teacher described a pedagogical challenge or dilemma to participating PLC members, outlining the issue and what had been done to resolve it. Second, PLC members asked probing questions, reflectively exploring and offering possible scenarios that could clarify the pedagogical challenge. Third, individual PLC members shared with each other what they would like to offer as feedback in order to address the pedagogical issue. Fourth, participating PLC members reflected and agreed on final takeaways based on the individual view of how they could handle that pedagogical challenge. At the end of the collective reflection, the presenting teacher took time to reflect on what they had learnt from the process and how that would affect their teaching. For example, in a follow-up on the impact of the tuning protocol workshop, one teacher explained that they had changed the way they used to approach teaching letter writing by focusing on the content of each paragraph separately and by using peer reviews in the process of writing. These changes were informed by tips and ideas discussed during the workshop, and these new ideas helped the teacher implement strategies they had not used before. As a result, the teacher was able to run more successful letter-writing sessions with the students.

Conclusion

The case of the CoPs of English teachers in Rwanda highlights the process of advocating and empowering English language teachers through CoPs. In particular, the case illustrates the social-economic context of teaching English in a pluralistic and changing society with limited resources. In this regard, advocacy was instrumental in mobilizing initial financial resources to help teachers access the information and pedagogical resources they needed to promptly adjust to meet the new professional demands. Moreover, advocacy sought to increase teachers' intrinsic motivation through peer-led activities, which we hope, buttressed long-term continuity of the CoPs.

REFERENCES

Bandura, A. (1977). Self-efficacy: Toward a unifying theory of behavioral change. *Psychological Review*, 84, 191–215. http://doi.org/10.1037/0033-295X.84.2.191

Bandura, A., & Wood, R. (1989). Effects of perceived controllability and performance standards on self-regulation of complex decision making. *Journal of Personality and Social Psychology*, 84, 805–814. http://doi.org/10.1037/0022-3514.56.5.805

Dewey, M. (2007). English as a lingua franca and globalization: An interconnected perspective. *International Journal of Applied Linguistics*, 17(3), 332–354. http://doi/abs/10.1111/j.1473-4192.2007.00177.x

DuFour, R. (2004). What is a "professional learning community"? *Educational Leadership*, 61(8), 6–11.

Johnson, C. E., & Hackman, M. Z. (2018). *Leadership: A communication perspective.* Long Grove, IL: Waveland Press.

Kagwesage, A. M. (2013). Coping with English as language of instruction in higher education in Rwanda. *International Journal of Higher Education,* 2(2), 1–12. doi:10.5430/ijhe.v2n2p1

McDonald, J., & Allen, D. (n.d.). *Tuning protocol.* Retrieved from www.nsrfharmony.org/wp-content/uploads/2017/10/tuning_0.pdf

Warner, C., & Dupuy, B. (2018). Moving toward multiliteracies in foreign language teaching: Past and present perspectives . . . and beyond. *Foreign Language Annals,* 51, 116–128. http://doi.org/10.1111/flan.12316

Appendix A

Sample Tuning Protocol – Kicukiro CoP Meeting: PLC Model

Kicukiro CoP meeting

DATE: 14/5/2018
MEMBERS:

1. DILEMMA: Tuning protocol

I have been teaching cover letter for the last two weeks. Students are not writing their cover and complaint letters using the format provided despite the fact that these have been scaffolded, they have hard copy samples and soft copy samples of these letters. They are also able to outline the requirements for body paragraphs but they don't write their letters using the format.

2. FOCUS QUESTION/S:

Clarifying and probing questions

- Did they do a diagnostic for these letters? This might mean that they are still writing as they used to before they learnt?

- Have they watched a video with an outline for these letters?

- Have they done editing for content for their peers?

- Do they have sample outlines and complete letters?

- Is it possible that they have memorized the content for each paragraph but do not know how to write each complete paragraph? Is it possible that they have not internalized the information?

- Is it possible that the complaint letter has been borrowed from an evening student? Because I have read and graded that letter last trimester?

3. DISCUSSION AND/RESOLUTION:

- It might help to go to class with a flip chart which has the requirements for each paragraph and have ss look at it as they write

- It might help to have more peer editing practice from students. Guide ss on the content areas to edit

- It might also be useful to have a mixed letter and have ss arrange the sentences in order

- Organize your lessons focus on paragraph by paragraph practice.

- Help the ss to understand the function of each part of the letter

4. MEMBERS' REFLECTION AND "TAKEAWAYS":

- Provide students with step by step practice of the letters

- Have a flip chart or write on the board the outline of information needed for body paragraphs

- Encourage students to use papers sometimes to hand in work.

- Give room for peer review and guide learners while they are editing

- Help students to practice writing proper topic sentences

UNIT 10
TESOL Teacher Education

CHAPTER 10

Preparing English Language Teachers for Participatory Teaching

Polina Vinogradova

FRAMING THE ISSUE

The topic of English language (EL) teacher education and professional development is vast and complex. The TESOL profession is global. EL education is globalized and localized. Global and local dynamics and realities of life together with questions of EL variation and change impact decisions of teaching methods, teaching and learning standards, and approaches to learning assessment. When conceptualizing this volume and selecting topics for it, we wanted to highlight how global and complex our teaching profession is. With this perspective, we can see the complexities and demands of English language teacher education, which is tasked with preparing compassionate, knowledgeable, creative, and flexible language educators.

Prior chapters in this volume provide excellent discussions and definitions of terms crucial for contemporary EL teacher education. All of them highlight various domains and aspects of participatory EL teaching in the postmethod era. As such they set a charge for teacher educators to prepare EL teachers who understand and recognize (1) the global scale and local dynamics in our profession, (2) the fallacy of viewing a native English speaker as the model for English language learning, (3) the need for culturally responsive pedagogy to become an essential component of EL teaching, (4) translanguaging as a source of productive practice in EL teaching, (5) the need for multiliteracies development and for incorporation of projects that develop digital literacy skills, (6) the use of technology for interactive and collaborative language learning, and (7) ways to advocate and support EL learners, their families, colleagues, and the profession. Preparing such teachers is certainly a huge undertaking that requires the understanding of practicalities, particularities, and possibilities (Kumaravadivelu, 2003; Murray, 2009) of each teacher's community, environment, and setting. The great complexities that the seven aspects represent deserve a separate book for EL teacher educators, and it is impossible to imagine one chapter in a volume that can address all nuances and implications for EL teacher education. Thus, in this chapter, I focus on concepts and theoretical considerations that are essential to contemporary EL teacher education – EL teacher expertise, identity, and empowerment within the context of critical participatory pedagogy. These concepts are crucial and relevant in any teacher development setting and are paramount aspects that make affordances for initial and continuous EL teacher development. These are the concepts that enable teacher agency and the ability to understand their teaching environments and support their students and colleagues.

The teaching profession is a lifelong learning experience; thus, teacher education and development goes beyond undergraduate or graduate programs in TESOL or language education. It includes continuous and regular professional development of in-service teachers in the form of professional discussion groups, professional associations, and professional development workshops and programs. For the purpose of this chapter, I focus specifically on academic preparation of TESOL candidates and discuss concepts and practical implications with this teacher population in mind. At the same time, these concepts and considerations are applicable and important in professional development of in-service English language educators as well.

CONCEPTS AND THEORETICAL CONSIDERATIONS

If we think about TESOL programs, we often envision a great diversity of students and environments. In some programs, students come from various places around the world, planning and getting ready to go and teach around the world; many are going to places which might not be where they came from or socioculturally familiar to them. In others, still quite diverse, there are students sharing a common local knowledge, having a common cultural framework, and expecting to teach students in settings rather familiar to them. What are the principles and knowledge that TESOL candidates need to be exposed to and explore in order to be teaching professionals who are able to research, explore, and understand the nuances of their teaching settings?

In this chapter, I focus on aspects that define contemporary teacher education and that can enable teacher candidates and practicing teachers to implement critical, culturally responsive pedagogy that creates space for translingual multimodal practices, views literacy as multilingual and multimodal, and recognizes advocacy as an essential component of teaching and professional development.

EL Teacher Expertise

A substantial part of teacher preparation and professional development undoubtedly focuses on the development of teacher expertise. But what does this expertise mean in the postmethod era when we need to prepare TESOL candidates to implement critical participatory pedagogy? Following Farrell (2013) and Johnson (2006), we can suggest that EL teacher expertise has historically included learning about the subject of teaching, in our case English; learning about teaching methods or, in postmethod terms, professional theories; observing and practicing professional theories through microteaching and practicum activities; and developing pedagogical expertise during the first years of teaching. Thus, from being a novice teacher, we observe a gradual movement toward developing expertise that Farrell (2013) views as both a state and a process. Expertise as a state refers to teacher's knowledge after years of teaching, while expertise as a process describes teacher's development over time. Johnson (2006) further expands on the development aspect of teacher expertise and describes teacher learning as

> lifelong, as emerging out of and through experiences in social contexts: as learners in classrooms and schools, as participants in professional teacher education programs, and later as teachers in the settings where they work. . . . L2 teacher learning [is] socially negotiated and contingent on knowledge of self, students, subject matter, curricular, and setting. . . . L2 teachers [are] users and creators of legitimate forms of knowledge who make decisions of how best to teach their L2 students within complex socially, culturally, and historically situated contexts.
>
> (p. 239)

Studying EL teachers' perceptions of teacher expertise, Farrell (2013) identified five main expertise characteristics. They include (1) knowledge of learners, learning, and teaching, (2) engagement in critical reflection, (3) accessing prior experiences, (4) informed lesson planning, and (5) facilitating active student involvement. Farrell notes that these characteristics don't exist separately from each other but rather form a complex body of teachers' praxis that allows for a more holistic and fluid understanding of EL teacher expertise.

These five characteristics of EL teacher expertise are significantly informed by teachers' self-perceptions, their view of their roles in language development of their students, and the role of English in their local settings and globally. This includes perceptions of what makes a legitimate EL speaker and what makes a legitimate EL educator. Thus, development of EL teacher expertise includes constant teacher identity negotiation and renegotiation.

EL Teacher Identity

EL teacher identity has been an area of extensive analysis and investigation in recent years (see Charles, 2019; Fan & de Jong, 2019; Peercy, Sharkey, Baecher, Motha, & Varghese, 2019; Pennington, 2015; Yazan,

2018). Overall, language teacher identity is viewed as dynamic, multilayered, transformative, and constantly negotiated through personal and professional interactions, sociocultural contexts, existing ideologies, and power dynamics (Fan & de Jong, 2019; Vinogradova & Ross, 2019; Yazan, 2018). As Fan and de Jong (2019) put it, "[I]dentities are not context free, but are enacted, constructed, negotiated, and projected with others within local and global contexts" (p. 2).

Scholars explore teacher identity in connection to practice and individual experiences; language, context, and discourse; and raciolinguistic ideologies (Charles, 2019; Fan & de Jong, 2019). Pennington (2015) offers a *frames perspective* for understanding of a TESOL teacher identity that seems particularly relevant when exploring identity factors that are at play for TESOL candidates. It can guide EL teacher educators in creating opportunities for explicit discussions of and reflections on identities in academic TESOL settings and in professional development programs for practicing and experienced EL teachers.

In the frames perspective, Pennington (2015) recognizes EL teacher identity aspects informed by various dimensions of teaching and learning practice (practice-oriented frames) and identity aspects informed by a variety of settings and contexts (contextual frames). Practice-oriented frames include: (1) instructional identity that "defines classroom persona" (Pennington, 2015, p. 20) and is informed by the teaching content and methods, (2) disciplinary identity informed by teachers' academic preparation, qualifications, and their teaching setting, (3) professional identity informed by "individual interpretation of disciplinary knowledge, standards, and practices acquired through education and experience in work contexts" (Pennington, 2015, p. 22), (4) vocational identity informed by "teacher's dedication to the students and to the teaching job" (Pennington, 2015, p. 23), and (5) economic identity informed by the TESOL marketplace and reward and satisfaction associated with it.

While practice-oriented identity frames focus on various professional and personal acts that encompass teaching, contextual frames focus on how the teaching setting is positioned locally and globally. This local and global positioning of EL teacher identity is informed by sociocultural and raciolinguistic ideologies that play a significant role in perceptions of EL teacher legitimacy and professional expertise (Charles, 2019; Fan & de Jong, 2019). Thus, they have significant implications for all identity aspects in practice-oriented frames.

The frames approach to understanding EL teacher identity is particularly useful for EL teacher education and professional development. Identity frames can serve as a guide for teacher educators when developing activities that recognize the central role of EL teacher identity and create space for its negotiation. This will also help in recognizing emotions that accompany teaching and teacher development (Fan & de Jong, 2019; Yazan & Peercy, 2016). Thus, the frames perspective reminds teacher educators that we need to cultivate identity negotiation in order for TESOL candidates to develop their teacher expertise.

EL Teacher as a Transformative Intellectual

In the context of participatory pedagogy and sociocultural approach in second language teacher education, we see a call for language teachers to become *transformative intellectuals* (see Johnson, 2006; Kumaravadivelu, 2003; Murray, 2009). Kumaravadivelu (2003) describes three concepts of a language teacher – passive technician, reflective practitioner, and transformative intellectual – that are important for TESOL candidates to understand in order to develop their own transformative teaching practices.

To this day, many of our TESOL candidates are well familiar with a passive technician approach in which a teacher places particular value on professional theories and prescriptive grammar and views themselves as an objective vehicle for information delivery and assessment of learner knowledge. For some TESOL candidates, this approach might be a part of their *apprenticeship of observation*, defined by Lortie (1975) and Johnson (1999) as teachers' memories of their own learning experiences and of their teachers. Further, not all TESOL candidates have apprenticeship of observation of a learner of an additional language. Some are monolingual English speakers with no or limited experiences of learning an additional language. Thus, they can struggle to relate to their students' learning experiences and rely on learning memories outside of language education.

Teacher reflection becomes an important activity for TESOL candidates that allows them to explore teaching practices more attuned to EL learners' needs, motivation, environment (including sociocultural context), and other variables that define and influence their language learning. Seeing an EL teacher as a reflective practitioner (Kumaravadivelu, 2003; Wright, 2010) and developing strategies and habits of regular reflection is one of the goals in contemporary TESOL education. An EL teacher as a reflective practitioner understands the importance of reflection, regularly engages in reflection *in* action and reflection *on* action, and uses reflection to adjust and redefine their teaching practices and approaches with the goal of developing their personal theories of teaching (Farrell, 2016; Kumaravadivelu, 2003). In Kumaravadivelu's words, reflective teaching is "a holistic approach that emphasizes creativity, artistry, and context sensitivity" (p. 10). Thus, as Kumaravadivelu points out, a reflective practitioner is an educator who recognizes their perceptions and the influences of their apprenticeship of observation; is involved in curriculum development and change in their teaching setting; works on improving classroom practice; and engages in continuous professional development.

Reflective practice that challenges teachers' own assumptions and perceptions of teaching and language learning is an important part of being a transformative intellectual. Here, this regular reflection is done not only to improve teaching practices, but to achieve personal ideological transformation. A transformative intellectual is someone who understands that teaching is never neutral, it is a political act that should create possibilities for growth and advancement for all participants in the learning process; should account for particularities of the teaching setting, the learners in this particular setting, and the teachers; and has conditions for the teacher to create their own theory of practice informed by continuous teacher reflection. This allows for the integration of the principles of possibility, particularity, and practicality that are central to participatory teaching and the postmethod condition (Kumaravadivelu, 2003; Murray, 2009). (For a detailed discussion of postmethod pedagogy and its principles of particularity, practicality, and possibility, see Chap. 3 of this volume.) Thus, social transformation through learning, and not just learning to acquire new knowledge and develop language skills to complete particular tasks, becomes the goal of the learning process. This goal also includes transformation of the teacher as well as of the learners that further creates possibilities of the transformation of life outside of the classroom.

This potential for transformation and connection to the community, including families and communities of learners, requires inquiry-oriented socially contextualized activities that include creativity, experimentation, and development of a critical lens on the role of language, its function, and its variation in a larger society. It requires from EL educators careful and meticulous preparation which provides learners with options and robust engagement with language and its context. This is the connection to the teacher-centered classroom in Auerbach's (2000) view of participatory pedagogy. It takes a transformative intellectual to enact and engage their learners with the participatory approach. As Johnson (2006) powerfully puts it, "L2 teacher education is to sustain a teaching force of transformative intellectuals who can navigate their professional worlds in ways that enable them to create educationally sound, contextually appropriate, and socially equitable learning opportunities for the students they teach" (p. 235).

IMPLICATIONS FOR ENGLISH LANGUAGE TEACHER EDUCATION

From the discussion earlier as well as from previous chapters and case studies in this volume, we see that EL teacher education is tasked with developing flexible and reflective teachers who:

- recognize that their expertise goes well beyond the knowledge of the structure and function of English
- understand the principles and theories of language acquisition
- have the knowledge of historically developed language teaching methods
- are able to develop clear learning objectives, detailed lesson plans, and assessments.

Further, EL teacher education includes the understanding of the transformational power and potential of EL teachers' roles not just in the classroom but in the learners' lives and in the lives of their communities. It includes the ability and knowledge to recognize that the process of teaching is the process of constant learning that challenges us to develop and further redefine our personal theories. To prepare EL educators who can grow as transformative intellectuals, we need to create experiences of participatory learning for TESOL candidates.

Participatory Pedagogy

In Chap. 2 of this volume, Chang and Salas offer an in-depth discussion of critical pedagogy and its crucial role in EL education. Participatory pedagogy is a form of critical pedagogy (see Auerbach, 2000; Kumaravadivelu, 2006), and in Chap. 4 of this volume, Thomas and Carvajal-Regidor discuss its role in culturally relevant teaching (CRT). With the focus on the impact of participatory pedagogy for English learners, and following Auerbach (2000), Lee (2014), and Kesler (2011), Thomas and Carvajal-Regidor emphasize that participatory pedagogy revolves around the knowledge of language learners' lives and experiences and prepares the learners to challenge social inequalities. Thus, participatory pedagogy contextualizes language learning and connects it with the learners' immediate and broader sociocultural community.

Participatory pedagogy also acknowledges the central role of the language teacher, thus making it significant to teacher development and teacher empowerment. What makes participatory pedagogy so important for EL teacher education, specifically in Auerbach's (2000) understanding of it, is acknowledgement of expertise of a teacher that leads to teacher empowerment. Auerbach problematizes the notion of a learner-centered classroom that equates learner-centered with participatory. In various TESOL literature, we see the term "learner-centered" and hear our TESOL candidates use it regularly. While acknowledging the need to put language learners at the center of the pedagogical process, Auerbach (2000) problematizes the concept of a learner-centered classroom, finding it to be misleading and identifying it as a "false construct" (p. 145). She also finds the concept of learner-centered as potentially culturally problematic. For example, it can be viewed as individualistic since it focuses on individual needs of the students and assumes that the students know what their needs are.

Participatory pedagogy, informed by Paolo Freire's view that "both the content and process of education can either reinforce or challenge the powerlessness of marginalized people" (Auerbach, 2000, p. 145), aims to empower teachers as well as learners. This is why participatory pedagogy is so important for EL teacher education and development. In a sense, it acknowledges that a language classroom is teacher-centered because it is the teacher who knows how to incorporate the learners' knowledge and experiences into the language learning process. It is the teacher who has the knowledge of professional TESOL and language acquisition theories and over the years will be and has been developing their personal theories, as defined by Kumaravadivelu (2003). It is the teacher who has the knowledge of approaches, activities, and techniques and who carefully incorporates them in lessons, materials, and curriculum in order to create a participatory classroom for English learners based on the principles of participatory practice described by Auerbach (2000). These principles are:

- The needs and concerns of the participants in the language learning process are central to curriculum content.

- All are equal participants in the learning process – "everybody teaches, everybody learns."

- In the learning process, collective knowledge gets developed through dialogue and collaboration – "classroom processes are dialogical and collaborative."

- Learning is linked to individual experiences that also get positioned in a larger sociocultural context.

- Language skills are taught in context and are "appropriated as new knowledge to be used in service of action for change."

- The content of learning is connected to the social context – "language learning is not the end in itself, but rather a means for participants to share their reality."

(p. 148)

For a language teacher to incorporate these principles and enact participatory pedagogy requires careful preparation, planning, and flexibility. It also requires teacher expertise that includes knowledge of approaches, tools, and techniques that can be used to incorporate ELs' interests and lives and create possibilities for language and social growth. Thus, TESOL candidates need to recognize the expertise they already have and develop new knowledge, skills, and practices to enact participatory pedagogy.

In other words, TESOL candidates themselves need to be viewed not from a deficit perspective by teacher educators, colleagues, and supervisors, but from a perspective that sees their multilingualism, prior learning and teaching experiences, and overall socializations as strengths and assets crucial to their development as EL educators. Thus, viewing TESOL teacher education from a participatory perspective and using a participatory approach in teacher education creates space for EL teacher identities to develop and flourish. This results in TESOL candidates' empowerment that leads to ability and eagerness to be transformative intellectuals and participatory educators.

In order to empower EL learners and create educational spaces that embrace critical participatory pedagogy, implement CRT, create translingual space, and foster development of digital literacies, TESOL candidates need to experience this type of learning themselves. We as teacher educators, need to remember that our TESOL candidates come to our programs with prior socializations as language learners, students, and teachers; that they rely on their apprenticeships of observation; and that many have substantial and well-developed views as to what language teaching entails and how language learning should be structured. Many TESOL candidates have ideas of what types of knowledge and skills they need to develop in order to go and teach, thus coming with expectations of what they want to leave with and be able to do after graduating from their teacher education program. As a result, as Wright (2010) points out, as teacher educators, we are presented with the challenge of moving from a "transmission model" (p. 275) of teacher education to a model where we create space for TESOL candidates to move from experiencing various pedagogical approaches (such as those discussed in this volume) under the overall umbrella of participatory teaching and learning to adopting it in their own teaching. Thus, modeling of participatory teaching and the critical reflective practices that it entails becomes essential in TESOL teacher education. This modeling creates an environment that fosters "cognitive apprenticeship" (Wright, 2010, p. 275) for TESOL candidates that entails engagement with contemporary and diverse TESOL/Applied Linguistics research; various field experiences; engagement in action research; and continuous critical reflection that provides space for identity negotiation and recognizes the role of emotions, worries, and doubts of TESOL candidates.

Postmethod in EL Teacher Education

The postmethod approach in EL education is a form of participatory pedagogy that demands the need for continuous and regular reexamination and redevelopment of classroom practices. In Chap. 3 of this volume, Rashed discusses postmethod in detail, with a focus on a contemporary EL learner. But what are its implications for EL teacher education that needs to create conditions for TESOL candidates to work toward becoming transformative intellectuals who understand the particularities, practicalities, and possibilities of their work?

The postmethod condition calls on EL teacher educators to guide TESOL candidates in their development of "flexibility, adaptability, and contextual awareness" (Murray, 2009, p. 17) and to see teaching as culturally relevant, caring, nurturing, and supportive (see Chap. 4 of this volume for a detailed discussion of CRT). This creates the potential for TESOL candidates to develop knowledge and sensitivity in order to adjust their instruction and assessment approaches to their future teaching environments, including environments that they cannot predict and anticipate during their studies.

Following Kumaravadivelu (2003, 2006) and Murray (2009), we should model postmethod teaching through macrostrategies – maximizing learning opportunities, facilitating negotiated interaction, minimizing perceptual mismatches, activating intuitive heuristics, fostering language awareness, contextualizing linguistic input, integrating language skills, promoting learner autonomy, raising cultural consciousness, and insuring social relevance. (For a detailed discussion of postmethod and macrostrategies, see Chap. 3 of this volume.) This prompts the incorporation of activities of inquiry, collaboration, and exploration, thus creating space for TESOL candidates to develop their own personal theories, further leading to the development of teacher autonomy that requires competence, confidence, and flexibility (Murray, 2009). Competence, confidence, and flexibility are in turn necessary parameters for the enactment of participatory pedagogy – a pedagogy that creates space for both EL learner and teacher empowerment.

The macrostrategy of maximizing learning opportunities becomes essential. It helps teacher educators develop robust instructional experiences for teacher candidates, decolonize and diversify materials and readings, offer various formats for group work, and find alternative and multimodal formats for class projects. Thus, teacher educators constantly model diverse and engaging classroom practices that TESOL candidates can adopt in their own teaching. This requires integration of various materials (readings, videos, podcasts, new media) and activities of various formats – creating space to collaborate in small and large groups, work individually, write, reflect, video record their own teaching, develop lesson plans, and constantly explore their visions of themselves as language educators.

For example, incorporating elements of a flipped classroom can create space and offer time to engage TESOL candidates in substantive and robust activities during class time. These can be peer-reviews and analysis of teaching philosophies and lesson plans, discussions of classroom observations and tutoring sessions, and brainstorming and planning of participatory activities and assessments, to name a few. Further, in these various individual and group activities, continuous and regular reflection becomes one of the central practices that maximizes learning opportunities of TESOL candidates (see Baecher, McCormack, & Kung, 2014; Coffey, 2014; Farrell, 2016; Lazaraton & Ishihara, 2005). As Farrell (2013) points out, "teaching expertise does not automatically translate into teacher expertise unless teachers consciously and actively reflect on these experiences" (p. 1080).

As mentioned earlier, TESOL candidates might have preconceived notions of what language teaching entails and how it should be done. These views can be informed by their apprenticeship of observation; their personal experiences, including prior teaching; and their views on the role and function of education overall. Here, the macrostrategy of bridging perceptual mismatches can help teacher educators acknowledge the candidates' prior knowledge and socializations while providing explicit contextualization and reasoning for their new teacher development experiences and new approaches to EL teaching. For example, narrative inquiry, which "seeks to understand, determine, and examine ways in which historical periods, locations, and contexts shape individual experiences" (Charles, 2019, p. 7) can support TESOL candidates in their understanding of who they are as language teachers. Further, narrative inquiry provides a platform for the voices and experiences of historically marginalized TESOL candidates to be heard – Black, Latinx, NNEST EL educators as well as the ones who identify as LGBTQ+ (Caldas, 2019; Charles, 2019; Fan & de Jong, 2019; Paiz, 2015).

One of the preconceived notions that I have seen TESOL candidates express and sometimes defend is the need to teach "standard" English and create an English-only setting in class and sometimes in the whole school or program. In exposing TESOL candidates to critical language awareness, translingual practices, dismantling the myth of "standard English," and challenging monolingual ideology, macrostrategies of fostering language awareness, raising cultural consciousness, and ensuring social relevance become central guiding principles. With these macrostrategies, TESOL candidates can be introduced to CRT and translanguaging that EL learners engage in outside of formal learning environments. For example, TESOL candidates can explore community language practices and ideologies as they engage in ethnographic projects and case studies. They can conduct interviews with and observations of multilingual learners. They can also study language ideologies in various EL programs and explore what informs these ideologies. Here, TESOL candidates can get acquainted with advocacy work, learn advocacy tools and resources, and design advocacy action plans for their own current and future work.

While we want TESOL candidates to reflect on their prior socializations as students, language learners, and language teachers, we want them to know that their experiences are valuable and valued. Again, as we want to approach EL teaching from an asset and not a deficit perspective, we want to model this approach in EL teacher education. Here, the macrostrategy of activating intuitive heuristics and promoting learner autonomy come into play. Asking TESOL candidates to write their learning and teaching autobiographies, interview experienced language educators, and develop their own teaching philosophies are activities that promote reflection and explicit understanding of what informs TESOL candidates' teaching values and beliefs.

Becoming transformative intellectuals who practice participatory pedagogy and advocate for their learners and communities requires substantial agency on the part of a language teacher. This agency develops with experience, through critical reflection, and comes from the knowledge of the professional theories that result in the development of personal theories of practice (Kumaravadivelu, 2003). A part of this practice is developing a teacher's personal stance in the profession, which requires extensive identity work. Thus, EL teacher education and teacher educators are tasked with designing and offering TESOL candidates substantial participatory experiences that recognize "complexities of who teachers are, what they know and believe, how they learn to teach, and how they carry out their work in diverse contexts throughout their careers" (Johnson, 2006, p. 236).

FUTURE DIRECTIONS

In this chapter, I built on discussions offered by the authors in this volume who illustrate the need to see EL education from a critical participatory lens. This volume argues for a substantial ideological reform in EL language education and TESOL – a reform that views EL education as teaching and learning English as an *additional* language, thus acknowledging and emphasizing that our language learners are multilingual and learn English in culturally and linguistically diverse settings with various goals and motivations. This reform needs to explicitly recognize that English does not belong to a particular group of people in a particular geographical area, thus dismissing an idealized native English speaker as the model for all English language learners. This reform will recognize a great diversity of people who grow up speaking English, thus acknowledging English linguistic diversity. This reform will argue for "situation-specific" (Murray, 2009, p. 18) EL education that accounts for the English learners' local realities and demands. It also needs to decolonize learning materials and activities and bring in voices and representation of racially, social, and culturally diverse communities as well as people with disabilities. Further, this reform will need to change hetero-normative discourses and representations and create LGBTQ+ inclusive environments.

This reform has already started, as we see from the case studies in this volume where EL teachers from all over the world implement critical participatory pedagogies embracing a pedagogy of caring that builds on multilingualism, multiliteracies, and community engagement and emphasizes creativity, collaboration, and empowerment. In order to continue and carry through this reform, teacher educators are tasked with reimagining and redesigning our own roles and ideological stances in EL teacher education. How do we transform our own curricula and teaching, our own views of what makes a "good" EL educator and a "good" EL education program? How do we rely on a pedagogy of caring and compassion with our TESOL candidates to in turn enable them to carry out this type of pedagogy in their own teaching? As Peercy et al. (2019) put it, "[T]eacher educators have to be able to consciously, intentionally examine how they bring their identities to bear, in order to engage in more dynamic, responsive, meaningful teacher education" (p. 2). This requires our own continuous reflection and learning, our own recognition of privilege and limitations of our own experiences, and our own conscious and systematic transformation through action, advocacy, and research.

Discussion Questions

1. Who are you as an EL educator? How do you see your role in the classroom? How do you think your students and colleagues see you? How would you describe your instructional, disciplinary, professional, vocational, and economic identities? How does your teacher identity inform your teaching acts and personal theories?

2. How do you define EL teacher expertise? What expertise informs your teaching and how? What professional development would you like to receive in order to enhance your teacher expertise? What would you like to add to your existing expertise?

3. If you are a current TESOL candidate or EL educator, what are some of the concepts and themes in this book that are particularly relevant to you? How are you implementing them in your work right now? What are some of the new ways that you would like to explore to introduce these concepts to your teaching?

   If you are an EL teacher educator, what are some of the concepts and themes in this book that are particularly relevant to you as an EL teacher educator? How are you implementing them in your work right now? What are some of the new ways that you would like to explore to introduce these concepts to your work with TESOL candidates and/or EL teachers?

4. If you are a teacher educator, think about a TESOL class that you are currently teaching or a professional development program or course you are currently running. What macrostrategies are currently present in your teaching? How do you introduce them into your students' work?

   If you are a current TESOL candidate or a teacher completing/recently completed professional development, what are some macrostrategies that you have observed your teacher educators use? With what activities and projects are these macrostrategies incorporated?

5. When developing this volume, we wanted to provide opportunities to our readers to engage in teacher reflection while reading chapters and case studies. What are some of the chapters and case studies that triggered this reflection for you? Why do you think they triggered this reflection? How can you translate this reflection into your teaching and work with EL learners and TESOL candidates?

Resources for Further Exploration

1. de Oliveira, L. C. (Ed.). (2013). *Teacher education for social justice: Perspectives and lessons learned*. Charlotte, NC: Information Age Publishing.
   In this edited volume, teacher educators of diverse ethnic, cultural, and linguistic backgrounds explore concepts of social justice and how they are relevant and can be incorporated in teacher education. While the chapters are mostly focused on social justice and teacher education to support culturally and linguistically diverse students in the United States, they are informative and relevant to a broader global readership of EL educators and TESOL candidates.
2. Farrell, T. S. C. (2018). *Reflective language teaching: Practical applications for TESOL teachers* (2nd ed.). New York, NY: Bloomsbury Academic.
   This book is an excellent resource for EL teacher educators and preservice and in-service teachers of English as an additional language. It explores various aspects of EL teacher reflection and includes such themes as self-reflection, action research, teaching journals, teacher development groups, and collegial friendships. This book offers case studies, sample questions for reflection, and practical suggestions to TESOL candidates, experienced EL educators, and teacher educators that are applicable in various teaching and professional development settings around the world.
3. IATEFL TDSIG (n.d.). *DEVELOPOD – The IATEFL TDSIG Podcast*. https://player.fm/series/developod-the-iatefl-tdsig-podcast
   A website by the Teacher Development Special Interest Group (TDSIG) of the International Association of Teachers of English as a Foreign Language (IATEFL) offers a collection of podcasts devoted to various topics of TESOL teacher education and development. These podcasts can be used in various professional development activities to facilitate analysis, reflection, and discussion.
4. Nero, S., & Ahmad, D. (2014). *Vernaculars in the classroom: Paradoxes, pedagogy, possibilities*. New York, NY: Routledge.
   As the authors of this book state, "[A] critical examination of the ways in which language (both oral and written) operates in the classroom can yield great insight into teaching and learning" (p. 3). This book is a great resource for TESOL candidates to develop understanding of vernacular Englishes – "the varieties of English spoken as a mother tongue or a second language in the U.S. and around the world" (p. 4) that are usually not included in EL curricula. This can help TESOL candidates to develop appreciation of the richness of the English language, further problematizing and questioning the concepts of the "standard English" and idealized "native English speaker."

5. We Teach Languages (n.d.). *We Teach Languages Podcast*. https://weteachlang.com/
This website offers a series of podcasts that present diverse voices and perspectives of language teachers. While the podcast does not focus specifically on teaching English as an additional language and features teachers of various languages, it presents a number of relevant topics useful for discussion and reflection for TESOL candidates.

REFERENCES

Auerbach, E. R. (2000). Creating participatory learning communities: Paradoxes and possibilities. In J. K. Hall & W. Eggington (Eds.), *The sociopolitics of English language teaching* (pp. 143–163). Clevedon, England: Multilingual Matters.

Baecher, L., McCormack, B., & Kung, S. (2014). Supervisor use of video as a tool in teacher reflection. *TESL-EJ*, 18(3), 1–16.

Caldas, B. (2019). To switch or not to switch: Bilingual preservice teachers and translanguaging in teaching and learning. *TESOL Journal*, 10, e485. https://doi.org/10.1002/tesj.485

Charles, Q. D. (2019). Black teachers of English in South Korea: Constructing identities as a native English speaker and English language teaching professional. *TESOL Journal*, 10, e478. https://doi.org/10.1002/tesj.478

Coffey, A. (2014). Using video to develop skills in reflection in teacher education students. *Australian Journal of Teacher Education*, 39(9), 86–97. http://dx.doi.org/10.14221/ajte.2014v39n9.7

Fan, F., & de Jong, E. J. (2019). Exploring professional identities of nonnative-English-speaking teachers in the United States: A narrative case study. *TESOL Journal*, 10, e495. https://doi.org/10.1002/tesj.495

Farrell, T. S. C. (2013). Reflecting on ESL teacher expertise: A case study. *System*, 41, 1070–1082.

Farrell, T. S. C. (2016). The practices of encouraging TESOL teachers to engage in reflective practice: An appraisal of recent research contributions. *Language Teaching Research*, 20(2), 223–247. https://doi.org/10.1177/1362168815617335

Johnson, K. E. (1999). *Understanding language teaching: Reasoning in action*. Boston, MA: Heinle Cengage Learning.

Johnson, K. E. (2006). The sociocultural turn and its challenges for second language teacher education. *TESOL Quarterly*, 40(1), 235–257.

Kesler, T. (2011). Teachers' texts in culturally responsive teaching. *Language Arts*, 88(6), 419–428.

Kumaravadivelu, B. (2003). *Beyond methods: Macrostrategies for language teaching*. New Haven, CT: Yale University Press.

Kumaravadivelu, B. (2006). TESOL methods: Changing tracks, challenging trends. *TESOL Quarterly*, 40, 59–81.

Lazaraton, A., & Ishihara, N. (2005). Understanding second language teacher practice using macroanalysis and self-reflection: A collaborative case study. *The Modern Language Journal*, 89(4), 529–542.

Lee, M. W. (2014). A participatory EFL curriculum for the marginalized: The case of North Korean refugee students in South Korea. *System*, 44, 1–11.

Lortie, D. (1975). I think it's this. In D. C. Lortie (Ed.), *Schoolteacher: A sociological study*. Chicago, IL: University of Chicago Press.

Murray, J. (2009). Teacher competencies in the post-method landscape: The limits of competency-based training in TESOL teacher education. *Prospect: An Australian Journal of TESOL*, 24(1), 17–29.

Paiz, J. M. (2015). Over the monochrome rainbow: Heteronormativity in ESL reading texts and textbooks. *Journal of Language and Sexuality*, 4(1), 77–101.

Peercy, M. M., Sharkey, J., Baecher, L., Motha, S., & Varghese, M. (2019). Exploring TESOL teacher educators as learners and reflective scholars: A shared narrative inquiry. *TESOL Journal*, 10, e482. https://doi.org/10.1002/tesj.482

Pennington, M. C. (2015). Teacher identity in TESOL: A framework perspective. In Y. L. Cheung, S. B. Said, & K. Park (Eds.), *Advances and current trends in language teacher identity research* (pp. 16–30). New York, NY: Routledge.

Vinogradova, P., & Ross, E. H. (2019). Fostering volunteer ESL teacher identity through reflection on apprenticeship of observation. *TESOL Journal*, 10, e480. https://doi.org/10.1002/tesj.480

Wright, T. (2010). Second language teacher education: Review of recent research on practice. *Language Teaching*, 43(3), 259–296.

Yazan, B. (2018). Toward identity-oriented teacher education: Critical autoethnographic narrative. *TESOL Journal*, 10(1), e388. https://doi.org/10.1002/tesj.388

Yazan, B., & Peercy, M. M. (2016). ESOL teacher candidates' emotions and identity development. In J. Crandall & M. Christison (Eds.), *Teacher education and professional development in TESOL: Global perspectives* (pp. 53–67). New York, NY: Routledge and the International Research Foundation for English Language Education (TIRF).

CASE STUDY 10.1

Reflective Teaching and Critical Language Pedagogy in a Thai EFL Context

María Díez-Ortega and Hayley Cannizzo

This case study illustrates how an international teaching practicum supported and gave graduate student-teachers the tools needed to develop and engage with critical reflective practices in their language classrooms. It further examines how, through these practices, one student-teacher developed, implemented, and refined a critical and culturally responsive pedagogy in her Thai EFL classroom.

THE SETTING

Eight graduate students in an Applied Linguistics program from a U.S. university spent the summer in the North-Eastern Isaan region of Thailand, completing an international teaching practicum. The student-teachers taught their own English classes at North-Eastern University (NEU, pseudonym). The university is located on the edge of a metropolitan region bordering on agricultural areas, far from major tourist destinations. As such, students have little contact with English outside of the university. Additionally, English classes at NEU tend to be extremely large in size (80–200 students). Consequently, teachers tend to adopt a lecture-style classroom, primarily focused on grammar, with little opportunity to practice speaking. This results in students who, while having studied English for a number of years, remain low-proficiency learners. While students were able to write short sentences, they lacked fundamental listening and speaking skills and knew only basic vocabulary and grammar.

In order to improve their English, students at NEU take voluntary English courses every other summer taught by a group of graduate student-teachers. These student-teachers are enrolled in a practicum course at their home university and come to Thailand to teach at NEU for five to six weeks.

The overall purpose of the practicum is to help these student-teachers deepen their pedagogical knowledge and teaching practice in second language teaching while developing a reflective pedagogy. A reflective pedagogy, or reflective teaching, is a cyclical process in which teachers examine and evaluate the "what," the "how," and especially the "why" of their practice, attitudes, and beliefs (Bailey, 2012; Richards & Lockhart, 1994). Reflective teaching is meant to provide teachers with the opportunity to "question, articulate, and reflect on their own teaching and learning philosophies" (Gebhard, 2009, p. 251). Since reflective teaching was an essential component of this practicum, student-teachers were required to complete several assignments throughout the practicum that revolved around this practice.

The student-teachers met once a week for a three-hour seminar to discuss relevant articles, share issues from the classrooms, and try out new activities. The practicum assignments included peer-observations, weekly group reflections, a reflection journal, a philosophy of teaching statement, and observations of student-teachers by their practicum professor and teaching assistants (TAs). In addition, student-teachers were encouraged to conduct action research in their classes. This case study further examines how one student-teacher's engagement with reflective practices allowed her to create and revise a critical participatory approach in her classroom.

Description of Student-Teacher Population and English Language Learners

Eight graduate student-teachers enrolled in an Applied Linguistics Master's Program at a U.S. university participated in the teaching practicum. The student-teachers' ages ranged from early twenties to late thirties, and their nationalities (Japanese, Chinese, Korean, Filipino, and U.S.) and levels of teaching experience were diverse. For the majority, the practicum was their first experience with their own classroom. While many planned to continue on in a teaching career after their master's, some hoped to pursue a PhD and focus on research.

Hayley, the student-teacher in this case-study and one of the chapter authors, was a second-year master's student. At the start of the practicum, she had three years of EFL teaching experience in Europe. Her class at NEU consisted of 17 second- and third-year university students majoring in Chemistry. The class met Monday through Thursday for five weeks during the months of June and July, for two-hour sessions. Most of her learners had studied English for an average of 14 years and could express themselves in short, written sentences and basic vocabulary. However, they lacked oral communication skills, struggling to produce simple sentences when asked questions such as "What's your name?" or "How are you today?". While Hayley was expecting low-proficiency learners, she was surprised by her students' almost "complete beginner" level and soon realized her students did not possess the linguistic knowledge needed to engage with her original teaching plan.

Pedagogical Application and Innovation

The pedagogical innovations and applications of this case study are the product of Hayley's learning to use and engage with reflective pedagogy during the practicum. This case study demonstrates how by engaging in systematic, reflective practices, such as journaling, observations, and action research, Hayley better understood her students' needs. As a result, she was able to employ a culturally responsive pedagogy in which she developed materials and activities to help scaffold her Thai English language learners into engaging with Critical Language Pedagogy (CLP).

Hayley entered the practicum knowing that she wanted to attempt to use CLP in her classroom. Critical pedagogy is defined by Crookes (2013) as "teaching for social justice, in ways that support the development of active, engaged citizens" (p. 8). CLP thus, is the interaction between the theory and practice of critical pedagogy with that of language learning and teaching (Crookes, 2013). However, once Hayley met with her students, she realized her materials were too advanced and that students lacked the basic communication skills needed to engage in her CLP lessons. Through the reflective assignments required by the practicum, Hayley engaged in critical reflective teaching that allowed her to rethink, adapt, and successfully implement CLP with her low-proficiency learners. To demonstrate how Hayley's reflective practices allowed her to identify students' needs and implement change, we have included both classroom techniques and reflections from her teaching journal.

The first classroom technique Hayley used was implementing the Freirean and CLP concept of classroom negotiation. This may involve negotiating a syllabus, classroom rules, or even grades with students. However, through reflective practices, Hayley realized her students were not proficient enough to hold a discussion-based negotiation. Thus, she developed step-by-step worksheets that made negotiation an attainable and realistic task for her students (see Figure 10.1.1).

In her journal, we observe this reflective process:

> I spent a lot of the day trying to figure out how to scaffold my students while negotiating classroom rules and a language policy. I came up with a heavily scaffolded worksheet to try and help them. For example, I ask: "Should food be allowed in the classroom?" and then they circle "yes", "no" or "I don't know/ I prefer not to say". I want my students to engage in CLP but I definitely think it is important to get them used to the idea of having more choice and voice in the classroom first.

Another technique Hayley used was the teaching of critical vocabulary. Through reflection, Hayley realized early on that her students would be unable to participate in any kind of critical dialogue without vocabulary that expresses critical concepts. Thus, Hayley introduced a few critical words along with more "conventional" second language vocabulary.

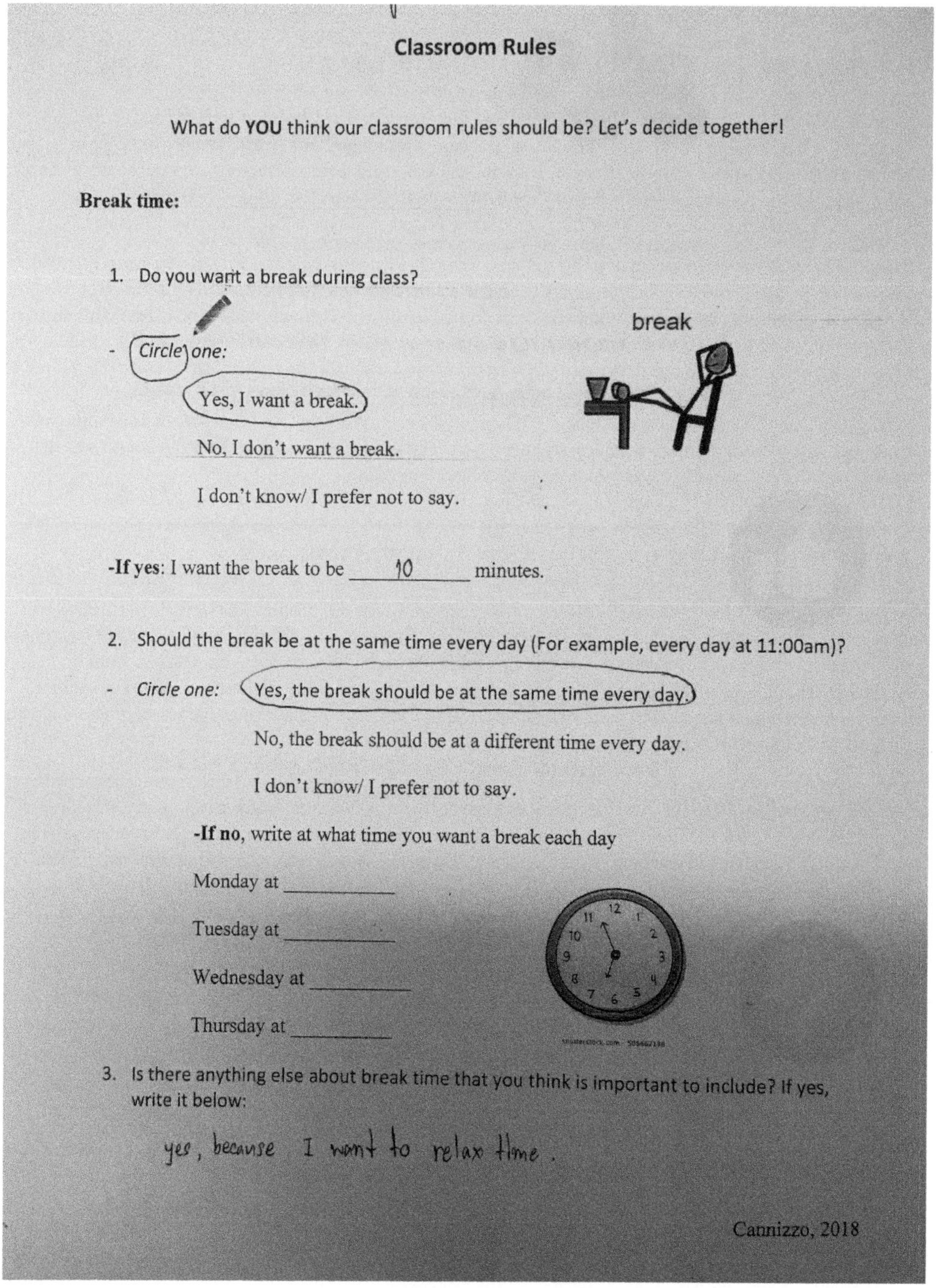

Classroom Rules

What do **YOU** think our classroom rules should be? Let's decide together!

Break time:

1. Do you want a break during class?

 - *Circle one:*

 Yes, I want a break.

 No, I don't want a break.

 I don't know/ I prefer not to say.

 break

 -**If yes**: I want the break to be _____10_____ minutes.

2. Should the break be at the same time every day (For example, every day at 11:00am)?

 - *Circle one:* Yes, the break should be at the same time every day.

 No, the break should be at a different time every day.

 I don't know/ I prefer not to say.

 -**If no**, write at what time you want a break each day

 Monday at _____

 Tuesday at _____

 Wednesday at _____

 Thursday at _____

3. Is there anything else about break time that you think is important to include? If yes, write it below:

 yes, because I want to relax time.

 Cannizzo, 2018

Figure 10.1.1 Scaffolded worksheet for classroom rules negotiation

Source: Student of Hayley Cannizzo

I taught them verbs such as read, write, walk but also vote, protest, fight and help. I think it is important to start building students' critical vocabulary from the start. This way, once they are able to form more complex structures, they will already have some of the vocabulary needed to be critical.

Since learners already had many of the concepts (e.g., vote) available in their L1s, Hayley realized that her students only needed to be taught the word in English in order for them to use it (Parba, 2018). Along with a critical vocabulary, Hayley also worked to build students' "critical expressions" such as agreeing, disagreeing, and stating opinions so that, early on, students had a voice and the linguistic tools needed to use that voice in the classroom.

The nature of the practicum provided Hayley with the opportunity to implement and revise her teaching plan. Through the supportive network cultivated by the practicum, along with feedback from observations and daily reflections, Hayley was eventually able to adopt and adapt a critical participatory approach. As a final project, Hayley asked her students to pick a problem in Thailand that they thought was important. The students then had the task of creating a critical poster project based on their chosen topic (see Figure 10.1.2). Some examples of problems students picked were waste separation, driving against the flow of traffic, and the overuse of plastic bags.

Once students had chosen their problem, Hayley scaffolded learners toward creating their projects and toward deciding what should be included on their posters. In the brainstorming worksheet for the critical poster project (see Figure 10.1.3), the intentional use of Thai allowed students to express their ideas first in their L1, before using these same ideas in English for their posters. While Hayley was aware of the importance of translanguaging in the classroom, the practicum gave her the flexibility to create a space in which students' L1 was validated and encouraged. This opportunity may not have been available in a more conventional, often constrained, teaching environment.

Even though Hayley was, overall, successful in scaffolding her students into CLP, she experienced a series of failures and triumphs along the way. These failures forced her to reflect critically on her teaching practices and beliefs as well as on how she could then meet her students' needs. Hayley explains this further in her journal:

> I think I have experienced some victories, as well as failures, in my teaching. Especially with CLP. The first time I tried to do something with CLP it completely failed. My students didn't understand anything. My second attempt was a bit better but still not anything near a success. However, I see these failures as also being a success. By failing at what I tried to do, I learned a lot and now have a much better understanding of how to use CLP with beginners.

By engaging in a reflective pedagogy and the open supportive nature of the practicum, Hayley was able to identify what was not working in her classroom and adjust accordingly. In doing so, she successfully adapted a critical participatory approach best suited to her beginner learners' needs. This included building students' critical vocabularies and expressions, giving them a voice in the class, allowing them intentionally to utilize their L1, scaffolding them using step-by-step worksheets, and introducing CLP in small, digestible amounts.

CONCLUSION

This case study illustrates how implementing reflective pedagogies in teacher education can help teachers develop more culturally responsive pedagogies suited to their students' needs. During an international teaching practicum, the student-teacher in this study engaged in a reflective pedagogy that helped her better assess her own understanding of her students, their needs, and her own beliefs. In doing so, she identified problems in her classroom and took action to implement change that eventually led to successfully scaffolding her learners into CLP. Through learning about and engaging with reflective practices such as journaling, observations, group reflections, action research and seminar meetings, student-teachers such as Hayley were given the opportunity to grow as language teachers in ways that may not have otherwise been possible in a more conventional context.

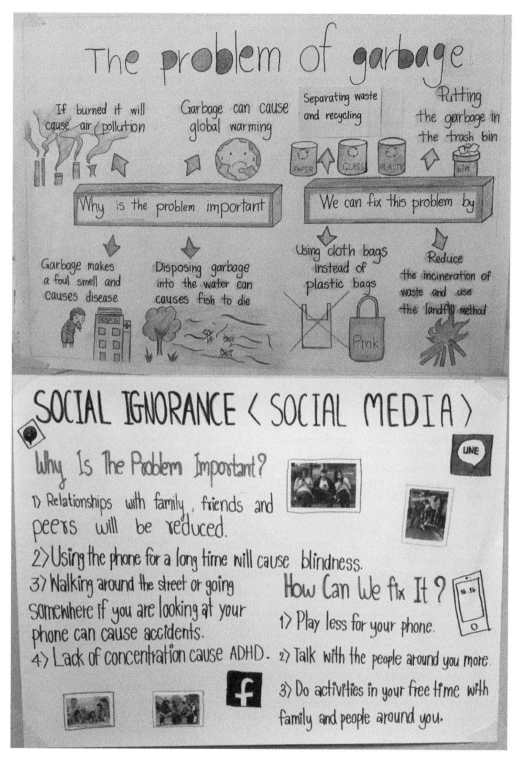

Figure 10.1.2 Examples of students' final Critical Poster Project

Source: Student of Hayley Cannizzo

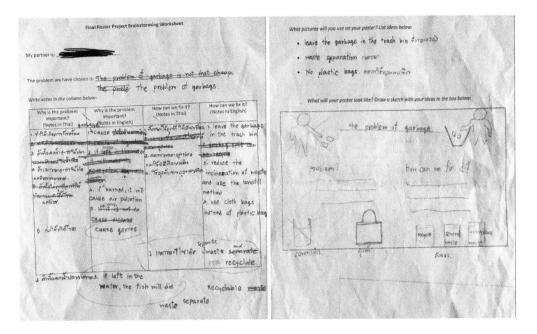

Figure 10.1.3 Scaffolded brainstorming worksheet for final poster project

Source: Student of Hayley Cannizzo

REFERENCES

Bailey, K. M. (2012). Reflective pedagogy. In A. Burns & J. C. Richards (Eds.), *The Cambridge guide to pedagogy and practice in second language teaching* (pp. 23–29). New York, NY: Cambridge University Press.

Crookes, G. (2013). *Critical ELT in action: Foundations, promises, praxis.* New York, NY: Routledge.

Gebhard, J. G. (2009). The practicum. In A. Burns & J. C. Richards (Eds.), *The Cambridge guide to second language teacher education* (pp. 250–258). New York, NY: Cambridge University Press.

Parba, J. (2018). *Empowering the Filipino language classroom: Towards critical pedagogy and curriculum* (Unpublished doctoral dissertation). University of Hawai'i at Manoa, Honolulu, HI.

Richards, J. C., & Lockhart, C. (1994). *Reflective teaching in second language classrooms.* Cambridge: Cambridge University Press.

From Teachers to Young Learners

Integrating Personal Development Instruction into Foreign Language Teaching in Serbia

Danijela Prošić-Santovac

This case study illustrates the education of 21st century English language teachers by presenting a segment of their preparation for higher-quality teaching. It enriches the common syllabuses of methodology courses by shifting focus from language skills and a relative disregard of content importance to a constructive use of content for both language and personality development. In this process, the teachers' 21st century skills were enhanced, especially in the domain of personal and social responsibility, with a focus on developing the "ability to communicate constructively in different social situations (tolerating the views and behavior of others; awareness of individual and collective responsibility)" (Binkley et al., 2012, p. 58).

THE SETTING

The case study was set in the context of a master's level course, *Teaching English at Preschool and Early School Age*, taught at a Department of English Studies, within a university in south-eastern Europe. The course aimed to provide opportunities for students to learn about different theories and approaches in teaching English to young learners as a foreign language and to enable them to function competently and thoughtfully as a basis for further development and improvement in the course of their own professional practice. The syllabus covers topics such as characteristics of young and very young learners, as well as those of effective teachers, and the role of their presentation skills and nonverbal communication in teaching young learners. In addition, alternative methods of evaluating the acquired knowledge are addressed within the course, as well as creating and maintaining a positive learning environment. The latter topic is developed through understanding causes of disruptive behavior and using emotional intelligence and positive communication in classroom management. For this purpose, the use of social stories, rhymes, fairy tales, and other forms of children's literature is elaborated on, with an emphasis put on defining criteria for selection of works to be used in language teaching. Also, discussions center around developing adequate activities around the works of children's literature in the context of theme-based instruction, and their use as a basis for creating a final exam play, either a puppet show, shadow play, or a play with masked actors. All this is done with the aim of stimulating teachers to integrate language teaching and students' personal development in their future practice.

DESCRIPTION OF ENGLISH LANGUAGE TEACHER CANDIDATES

The learners in this case study were both English language learners themselves in the course of their professional development, albeit at the C2 level of *Common European Framework of Reference for Languages*, and English language teachers to young learners in their professional life. They were attending their master's level studies after completing four years of undergraduate studies in order to gain the title of English language and literature teachers. Therefore, for the sample in question, the course presented both pre- and in-service training. At the time of their course attendance, 71.1% of teachers were employed, while the rest had not had any previous teaching experience apart from a brief teaching practicum in primary schools provided by the faculty during their undergraduate studies. In all, during the period between the years 2015 and 2018, there were 90 students attending this course, with the number for each academic year ranging from 15 to 25. Their mean age was 24.6, and their gender was distributed in accordance with the general tendency in the country for language teachers to be mostly female (85.6% female and 14.4% male). As the status of the course within the master's program was elective, only the students interested in the subject chose to attend it, and were, therefore, active participants in the planned activities and discussions.

Pedagogical Application and Innovation

An examination of practice in methodological training of preservice foreign language teachers, both locally and internationally (e.g. Wilbur, 2007), led to the discovery that university teacher education courses most frequently include instructions on teaching grammar, vocabulary, and language skills. However, they much more rarely emphasize the importance of some other "life" skills, preparing preservice teachers to focus only on language teaching and disregarding the opportunities that the inevitable use of content for context provision offers. Taking into account the statement that "language is always about something, so it might as well be about something of consequence" (van Lier, 2004, p. 82), the challenge was to create a course syllabus that would not treat pedagogy and methodology separately from the content and that would include both self-development and value education in the instruction (Tal & Yinon, 2009).

Thus, the focus of the *Teaching English to Young Learners* (TEYL) course in question shifted from the common content of methodology courses to one in which, through theme-based language instruction, both the ways of developing the teacher trainees' and their future pupils' emotional intelligence received due prominence. This was done, among other things, by using children's literature with the aim of unraveling the underlying subtexts and ideology permeating the texts and by discovering ways of using them to enhance classroom relationships among the children themselves and between teachers and pupils. For example, in the practical activity to be showcased, well-known fairy tales were used to develop thematic units around the theme of bullying by finding ways to connect and develop language skills and the knowledge related to other subjects in the curriculum. Shin and Crandall's (2014, p. 74) thematic unit web served as the template, with teams of teachers working on the main theme from the point of view of art, music, science, social studies, math, and physical education (see Figure 10.2.1).

Simultaneously, they were required to design and integrate into the web the activities that would aim at developing young learners' reading, writing, listening, and speaking skills when applied in the classroom. They also had to distribute these activities across four lessons dedicated to the theme. The stories used in this activity were tales whose plot contained abuse of the main characters in one form or another. These stories were used as a starting point for conversations about bullying (Table 10.2.1).

By designing their own thematic units to be delivered to young learners, the teachers could move away from an approach to foreign language teaching based on a passive reliance on textbook materials and toward a more independent approach to curriculum design. This way, they were able to contribute to their learners' personal development and enhance their learners' emotional intelligence. Simultaneously, this approach raised the teachers' awareness of the importance of working on their own attitudes and "attend[ing] to their own 'inner' work" (Whitmore, 2009, p. v), both personally and professionally. This is important, as the teachers themselves were a product of traditional approaches to language teaching and learning and have gone through traditional ELT methodology courses, which, as mentioned at the beginning, usually focus on teaching language skills only. In addition, the preservice teachers had a mostly nostalgic attitude toward traditional fairy tales and did not view them as a potential source of examples of problematic relationships. In the course of their study, the preservice teachers gradually traveled the road from reluctance to acceptance of literature as a medium for learning, moving away from viewing it only as a source of vocabulary and grammar examples for practice or reading comprehension exercises. They developed an understanding of its potential as authentic material for use in ELT classrooms which can contribute to their own students' personal development and enhance their emotional intelligence.

1. Sample Materials

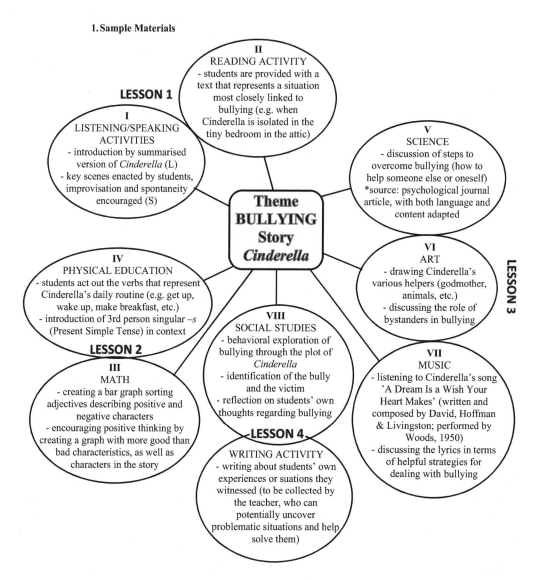

Figure 10.2.1 An example of a thematic unit web created by the teachers

CONCLUSION

This case study focuses on the 21st-century English language teacher training context, interwoven with teacher activism and care for students' well-being, in addition to their general language education. In modern educational systems, "as teachers are feeling more and more pressure to prepare their students for testing, there is less and less time to help [them] to learn what it means to be a wise, caring and courageous person of character" (Pearmain, 2006, p. 1). However, English language teachers can and should be much more than a vehicle of transmitting linguistic knowledge. Due to the nature of ELT classes, they have a great opportunity to influence children's personal development in ways that most other subject teachers cannot. The language taught and used in an ELT classroom can be meaningful, if teachers choose to exercise agency (Prošić-Santovac & Radović, 2018) and include topics highly relevant to their students' lives.

Table 10.2.1 Stories used in the activity

Story title	Forms of abuse of the main character	Topics for class discussions related to bullying
The Ugly Duckling	Continually rejected by peers due to different appearance in youth	Bullying because of difference (of any kind); exclusion of one individual from group
Cinderella	Used for providing menial service; experienced psychological abuse and deprivation of social life	Psychological bullying; exclusion of one individual from group, but using their resources for group gain and interest
Rumpelstiltskin	(Girl) used by a socially dominant individual (king) to provide riches in order to become his wife, or be killed in case of failure	Repeatedly using someone in order to allow them into a certain social circle, by creating an illusion that it is the only option for the person
The Three Little Pigs	Hunted by a stronger individual (wolf); repeated destruction of personal property (houses)	Taking away or destroying the bullied individuals' property by the stronger ones
The Little Red Riding Hood	Followed and attacked by a stronger individual (wolf) while on the road alone; saved by another strong individual (hunter)	Being stalked or intercepted by stronger peers on the way to school; encouraging asking for adult help, organizing in groups to prevent bullying opportunities
Beauty and the Beast	Isolated by a stronger individual and treated in a psychologically cruel way (depending on the version of the story)	Bullying in a personal relationship (of any kind); isolating an individual from their social circle
Rapunzel	Isolated by a stronger individual and prevented from contact with the outside world	Bullying by adults; isolation; preventing others from socializing with excluded person

REFERENCES

Binkley, M., Erstad, O., Herman, J., Raizen, S., Ripley, M., Miller-Ricci, M., & Rumble, M. (2012). Defining twenty-first century skills. In P. Griffin, B. McGaw, & E. Care (Eds.), *Assessment and teaching of 21st century skills* (pp. 17–66). Dordrecht, Germany: Springer.

Pearmain, E. D. (2006). *Once upon a time: Storytelling to teach character and prevent bullying.* Boone, NC: Character Development Group, Inc.

Prošić-Santovac, D., & Radović, D. (2018). Children's vs. teachers' and parents' agency: A case of a Serbian-English bilingual preschool model. *Language, Culture and Curriculum, 31*(3), 289–302.

Shin, J. K., & Crandall, J. A. (2014). *Teaching young learners English: From theory to practice.* Boston, MA: National Geographic Learning.

Tal, C., & Yinon, Y. (2009). Teachers' values in the classroom. In L. J. Saha & A. G. Dworkin (Eds.), *International handbook of research on teachers and teaching* (pp. 259–276). New York, NY: Springer.

van Lier, L. (2004). The semiotics and ecology of language learning: Perception, voice, identity and democracy. *Utbildning & Demokrati, 13*(3), 79–103.

Whitmore, J. (2009). Foreword. In S. Neale, L. Spencer-Arnell, & L. Wilson (Eds.), *Emotional intelligence coaching: Improving performance for leaders, coaches, and the individual* (pp. v–vi). Philadelphia, PA: Kogan Page.

Wilbur, M. L. (2007). How foreign language teachers get taught: Methods of teaching the methods course. *Foreign Language Annals, 40*(1), 79–101.

Preparing Teachers to Create LGBTQ+ Inclusive Classrooms in the U.S.

Joshua M. Paiz

> Educators have a social responsibility to promote human dignity and to further social justice for [LGBTQ+ students].
>
> (Nelson, 2006, p. 19)

This case study outlines an activity to help prepare ESL practitioners to build more LGBTQ+ inclusive pedagogies (see Nelson, 2006; Paiz, 2018). LGBTQ+ here stands for the lesbian, gay, bisexual, transgender, queer, question, same-sex-loving, twin-spirited, intersexed, and ally community. In recent years, LGBTQ+ issues have received increasing attention in TESOL, but the matter remains largely ignored in teacher education (Merse, 2015; Paiz, 2019). This case study seeks to equip teacher educators with a useful starting point for their critical practice.

THE SETTING

I have used the activity described here in two different ESL educator professional development settings – as a pedagogy presentation at a meeting of a regional TESOL affiliate and as a professional development workshop delivered at a community college in western Maryland in the United States. In both instances, the activity was carried out in a classroom-style space with fixed tables and chairs, expansive whiteboard space, and a digital projector. Here, I will focus my description largely on the workshop as it was delivered to ESL instructors in the two-year community college setting, although there are implications for teacher education at all levels.

In the summer of 2018, I was invited to give a two-hour professional development workshop at a community college in western Maryland that enrolls over 6,000 students. In the summer of 2018, I was contacted by their director of diversity, equity, and inclusion about my potential interest in visiting their campus to deliver a professional development workshop to their ESL educators. These educators came from a variety of professional backgrounds, having worked previously in testing and assessment, language tutoring, and literacy education in both educational and private sectors. Many of the faculty members who attended the workshop were part-time, adjunct faculty members who also worked at other institutions in the area. At this institution, their primary focus was on teaching academic literacy development and acculturation courses to students who were new to the area and to U.S. higher education. Their driving motivation was that their school enrolled a large number of immigrant and migrant English language learners. Moreover, the school had a large and active LGBTQ+ student group, reflecting the strong sexual diversity of the college campus. Both the directors of Diversity, Equity, and Inclusion and of the ESL program commented on the strong LGBTQ+ student organization, which regularly held well-attended events on campus. And, when I arrived for the workshop, flyers for two different events – a beginning of the year meet-and-greet and HIV/STI awareness and testing were present throughout the student union building. Both speak to the relatively high visibility of LGBTQ+ concerns on this campus. The director of the ESL program felt that additional teacher education opportunities would help the ESL faculty members to address this very visible sexual diversity in their classes with English language learners, with the goal of facilitating understanding, respectful engagement, and greater acculturation to the local campus.

DESCRIPTION OF WORKSHOP PARTICIPANTS

The workshop participants were ESL educators focusing on the two-year college setting. While the majority were native English-speaking teachers (NESTs), a small subset was non-native English-speaking teachers (NNESTs) predominantly coming from South America, the Middle East, and Eastern Europe. Their time in the field ranged from three to fifteen years of ELT experience in primary, secondary, and tertiary educational settings around the globe.

At the community college professional development workshop, approximately 12 educators participated in the professional development workshop, which was offered as an optional event but for which the participants received professional development credit as part of their ongoing renewal and promotion schemes. The majority of participants were mid-career professionals with at least a master's degree in TESOL or a related discipline. Of the participants, the majority identified as cisgender women or men. Cisgender status refers to individuals whose biological sex assigned at birth match their gender identity, while transgender refers to individuals whose biological sex assigned at birth and gender identity are misaligned (see Aultman, 2014; NCTE, 2016). In their current positions, they work in English for Academic Purposes (EAP) and literacy acquisition classes at the two-year college level.

PEDAGOGICAL APPLICATION AND INNOVATION

To prepare the participants for the workshop activities, I began with a series of attitudinal and reflective questions through a quick survey, which included prompts focused on teacher awareness of LGBTQ+ lives in their classroom, their feelings about LGBTQ+ representation in ELT materials, and their comfort with incorporating LGBTQ+-aware pedagogies into their practice. (See Appendix A for the Opening Attitudes Survey.). These questions prompted educators to reflect on their thoughts about LGBTQ+ issues, their relationship to English language teaching (ELT), and the need for students – straight- or LGBTQ+-identified – to engage with LGBTQ+ content and conversations in the classroom. During this step, I used live, anonymous polling software (e.g., Poll Everywhere, DirectPoll.) and presented the responses to questions to the group on the screen at the front of the class, pausing briefly to discuss the trends that we were seeing in the response patterns. The goal in this step was to help create an open environment and to highlight the different points of entry we all had regarding this topic. Throughout this stage, I reminded the educators that this was a judgment-free space and that our goal was to critically reflect on our teaching practices and how they may reify heteronormative practices. *Heteronormative practices* are those linguistic, education, and ideological acts that present reproductive, monogamous heterosexuality as the only culturally valued and acceptable way of life (see Nelson, 2006). I also started with this activity to help ease participants into the workshop and lower affective barriers to participation. I find one effective approach to help ensure this goal is always met is to include an option for participants not to respond to individual survey items, a fact that I make clear from the beginning of the workshop. I do, however, remind them that their responses will help the group to work together to address concerns unique to their context.

Once this "pulse-taking" was completed, I moved on to introducing basic ideas about queering the classroom, tying them to large goals of critical pedagogy such as engaging with issues of power, privilege, and marginalization in the classroom. I began by introducing educators to what was at stake when we ignore LGBTQ+ issues in our language classrooms. Specifically, that this erasure – even through some might just see it as non-engagement – serves as a tacit endorsement of heteronormative discourses and linguistic practices that can, at best, demotivate language learners or, at worst, cast LGBTQ+ individuals as deficient language learners. Ignoring issues of sexual diversity can only serve to reinforce other discourses of deficiency that they may encounter in society or the institution by being English language learners. I then set the stage for our conversation on approaches to queering the ESL classroom. *Queering*, here, refers to how to make our classroom spaces that both acknowledge and critically engage with how language and culture create options for selfhood as understood through the lens of sexuality. It should be noted, however, that the focus of the queered classroom space is by no means limited to issues of sexual identity. A queer approach can also be used to challenge the status quo of other identities, such as professional identity. It is well documented that each discipline uses language and disciplinary culture to outline a set of identity options that are more valued and valid than others, and a queer approach to professional education can help to make these options more salient to professionalizing students while also equipping them with tools to critique and resist these normative views of professional selfhood (see Deters, 2011).

I centered our workshop conversations around the idea of queer inquiry (see Nelson, 2006), which is the notion that all identities are mediated through language and maintained by social discourses. Only by understanding how language and discourse work together to make certain identities more valid and valuable than others can we come to understand our place in the world better and to advocate for those who find themselves in marginalized positions. To arrive at this understanding often requires us to engage with how dominant social discourses prime us to see the world in a certain way. Two examples make this point rather salient. First, consider how we think of romance in a predominantly heteronormative society. From a young age we are primed to consider people in love as referring to a monogamous heterosexual male/female coupling. This means when we hear someone talking about being in love, we almost immediately assume that they mean an opposite sex partner, unless we are close friends and have been told otherwise. While this may be changing in some contexts, another example shows how society positions certain lives and bodies as having more valid access to certain identities. Take the professional identity of ESL teacher. In many contexts, a native-speaker bias means that this identity position is often immediately ascribed to white, monolingual, so-called native speakers, and that non-white, non-monolingual, so-called non-native speakers are given marginalized access to this identity position and often cast as less-than their native speaker peers by broader society (TEFL Equity Advocates, 2018).

After reviewing the concepts and terminology within the idea of queering, I had ESL teachers engage in a short narrative illustration activity to help underscore the ways that dominant discourse colors our knowledge about the world for the educators. This also became a modeling activity for the teachers, an activity that they could use with their learners. In this activity, I had the teachers read a short story (see Appendix 10.3.B) that deals with a queer theme but that treats that queerness as unmarked in much the same way that heterosexuality is treated in daily life. That is, the story focuses on queer issues or characters, but does not have the characters engaging or overtly mentioning their sexual identity. Before reading, I gave the participants instructions that they in turn could give to their students. They had about twenty minutes to read the story, underlining new words and words that seemed to mean something different in this story. Once they were done with the reading, they were to choose one scene from the short story to draw. Here, I stressed that simple stick figures were fine, as I could do no better than that myself. Once the reading and drawing were done, I asked the participants to share their illustrations with a peer and explain their choices. I then asked a few of them to share their drawings with the whole group and to explain their artistic decisions.

Almost without fail, their drawings began to reflect a heteronormative worldview as the participants drew a cisgendered, heterosexual nuclear family or a little boy trying to go into the girls bathroom, as opposed to a transgender boy attempting to use the boys bathroom (see Figures 10.3.1a and 10.3.1b for sample drawings).

When this kind of picture was shared, I asked the teachers to show where in the text they had seen this identity and what language in the text could back up their decision. These kinds of questions open the door to discussions about gender-neutral relationship markers and hypocorisms (nicknames). They also open the door to critical discussions about how language and our presuppositions color how we see a text. At no point did I say that their interpretation was wrong. Rather, I modeled the kind of critical questioning we want our students to start doing when it comes to encountering possibilities for selfhood.

Once a few of the teachers had shared their drawings and we had discussed the text and the new or novel-use words in it, I wrapped up the activity by asking the workshop participants to reflect on how they might

(a)   (b)

Figure 10.3.1 Recreations of participant drawings from narrative illustration activity

Source: Joshua M. Paiz

integrate this style of activity and a queer perspective into their teaching. Here, I did not ask them to share. Rather, I asked them to take that reflection with them and to revisit it in a week or so, after they have had time for additional thought and possibly experimentation on the topic.

CONCLUSION

The example shows one possibility for equipping 21st-century TESOL/ELT practitioners with knowledge and tools that can enable them to create more inclusive classrooms. I would point out that the approach used, informed as it has been by Nelson's (2006) queer inquiry approach, has the added benefit of modeling critical thinking and analysis skills that are highly valued in U.S. higher education, where I currently teach. As such, it can serve the purpose of further acculturating students to U.S. academic norms. In other settings, queer inquiry can be used to advance a critical pedagogical agenda that is centered on broader social justice considerations. Specifically, it can help to raise students' awareness of how sexuality is represented and policed by dominant social discourses in their local contexts. This can be made even more salient for students by incorporating local queer voices into the curriculum whenever possible either through guest speakers or stories/narratives created by local authors. Most importantly, however, is that it prepares students and teachers to engage with sexual literacy in a way that better prepares them to participate in conversations about sexuality and selfhood that have been identified as a central social discourse in the West.

Moreover, regardless of context, queering ELT allows us to create classroom spaces where all students are represented, even if only symbolically through our practice and teaching materials. By creating space in our teaching for marginalized voices and identities, we can equip our students with the linguistic tools needed to be advocates for themselves and others by modelling advocacy in our pedagogical approach. Finally, as Ó'Móchaim (2006) showed in his discussion of deploying queer pedagogy at a Japanese women's college, this approach can also be empowering to students to both challenge normative discourses and also to come to a better understanding of their own sexual identity.

REFERENCES

Aultman, B. (2014). Cisgender. *TSQ: Transgender Studies Quarterly*, 1(1–2), 61–62. https://doi. org/10.1215/23289252-2399614

Deters, P. (2011). *Identity, agency, and the acquisition of professional language and culture*. London, UK: Continuum.

Merse, T. (2015). Queer-informed approaches and sexual literacy in ELT: Theoretical foundations and teaching principles. *Language Issues*, 26(1), 13–20.

NCTE. (2016). Understanding Transgender people: The basics [white paper]. *National Council for Transgender Equality*. Washington, DC. Retrieved from https://transequality.org/sites/default/files/docs/resources/Understanding-Trans-Short-July-2016_0.pdf

Nelson, C. (2006). *Sexual identities in English language education: Classroom conversations*. New York, NY: Routledge.

Ó'Móchaim, R. (2006). Discussing gender and sexuality in a context-appropriate way: Queer narratives in an EFL college classroom in Japan. *Journal of Language, Identity, and Education*, 5(1), 51–66. doi:10.1207/s15327701jlie0501_4

Paiz, J. M. (2018). Queering ESL teaching: Pedagogical and materials creation issues. *TESOL Journal*, 9(2), 348–367. https://doi.org/10.1002/tesj.329

Paiz, J. M. (2019). Queering practice: LGBTQ+ diversity and inclusion in English language teaching [The forum]. *Journal of Language, Identity, and Education*, 18(4), 266–275. https://doi.org/10.1080/15348458.20191629933

TEFL Equity Advocates. (2018, April 13). Students prefer "native speakers". *TEFL Equity Advocates and Academy*. Retrieved from http://teflequityadvocates.com/2018/04/13/students-prefer-native-speakers/

APPENDIX A
Opening Attitudes Survey

1. I have students who are members of or have a connection to (e.g., a family member or close friend), the LGBTQ+ community.

    a. Yes

    b. No

    c. Don't know

    d. Prefer not to answer

2. LGBTQ+ issues do not receive adequate representation in English-language classroom materials and activities.

    a. Agree

    b. Disagree

    c. Unsure

    d. Prefer not to answer

3. LGBTQ+ issues impact straight-identified students as well as LGBTQ+-identified ones.

    a. Agree

    b. Disagree

    c. Unsure

    d. Prefer not to answer

4. I would like to include LGBTQ+ content but feel under-prepared to facilitate such discussions for English-language students.

    a. Agree

    b. Disagree

    c. Unsure

    d. Prefer not to answer

5. I am nervous about incorporating LGBTQ+ content and themes into my English-language classroom because of potentially negative student responses.

    a. Agree

    b. Disagree

    c. Unsure

    d. Prefer not to answer

Appendix B
Instructions for Narrative Illustration Activity

In this activity, you will do three things. First, you will read the story carefully to understand what it is about. Second, you will underline any new words or word uses that you see in the text (we will discuss them later). Finally, you will pick a scene from the story to illustrate. It does not have to look pretty. Personally, mine will be rather ambiguous stick figures.

Text for Narrative Illustration Activity

Steel gray clouds hung low in the sky, and the rain was coming down in sheets, cascading over the cars that were idling at the intersection. Madison tapped her fingers impatiently on the steering wheel while glaring up at the stop light, willing it to change. This was a traditionally long light, she knew, having waited at it countless times over the years on her way to the Columbia County School campus. That knowledge, however, did nothing to make her less edgy. She exhaled sharply, glaring at the pickup in front of her. Her eye was drawn to the bumper stickers on the window and tailgate – decals for the local baseball team, a sticker for a local conservative politician, and – there it was – the Stars & Bars, a flag that's come to represent oppression, hatred, and backward thinking.

On a typical day, Madison would have been able to blow off the backward thinking affront presented by the car in front of her. But, today was far from typical. She had been just getting out of a meeting with her team of lab assistants when she'd received a message from her son's school. There was a flash of irritation as she considered the likely mindless reason for the call. Knowing Tommy, it was likely that he'd forgotten his lunch again or some homework assignment for one of his more martinet-minded teachers. *Why can't Al just take care of this?* She huffed as she walked back to her office to return the school's call. After returning the school's call, she realized that this would not be a simple issue to fix, nor was it one that her spouse could handle on their own. So, grabbing her messenger bag, car keys, and phone, she dashed off to her car to make for the school. Thanks to her impeccable luck and the weather's brilliant sense of timing, it left her stuck here at this godforsaken light in the driving rain staring at this racist, spiteful truck in front of her. She just rolled her eyes. Now wasn't the time to vent her frustration; she'd need every ounce of rage in her to deal with Tommy's drama at school.

After pulling into the school parking lot, she rushed to the principal's office. As she rounded the corner, she saw Tommy sitting on a low bench outside of the office – his face buried into a handkerchief and his shoulders bouncing up and down, obviously sobbing. Next to him sat Alex, gently rubbing his back. Madison's and Alex's eyes met, a glance filled with recognition and frustration. A heavy sigh escaped Madison as she ducked into the receptionist's office to sign in.

"Madison Gonzales to see Principal Strickland." she barked at the young-looking, unfamiliar receptionist, "I'm Tommy Moore's mother."

There was a moment of hesitation before the receptionist responded. Madison found herself mentally taking bets on just what asinine and vaguely bigoted thing would come out of his mouth. Perhaps the mismatched skin tone between mother and son would elicit comment.

"Oh. Ms. Gonzales, I thought Tommy's mom had already arrived." The receptionist looked genuinely befuddled.

"Yes, one of them has, and now the other is here as well." She replied with fire in her words, "And, it's *Doctor Gonzales* if you don't mind very much. Principal Strickland. Now."

Just as she was getting ready to unleash an even angry tirade on the increasingly confused receptionist. Principal Strickland walked into the room. "Now, Dr. Gonzales, I'm sorry to bother you, but Tommy was reported for using the wrong restroom again. As you well know, when the Public Bathroom Privacy and Security Act passed a few days ago, Tommy was told that she —"

Madison clenched her fist so tightly she could feel the nails bite into the skin on the palm of her hand, "I'm sorry, but I believe that you mean he. And, I'm going to stop you right there. This seems to be a conversation where I'd like my lawyer to sit in as well." She held up a finger in the principal's face while she fished her phone out of her suitcoat pocket. It could never be anything simple, could it? Another school, another administration that would be more at home in the "simpler times" of 1950's America – a time when men were men, women were women, and everyone else could just shut up about it. As she waited for the call to connect, her thoughts turned to her son sobbing in the hallway, the poor kid.

Index

Note: Page numbers in *italics* indicate figures and page numbers in **bold** indicate tables.

academic autonomy 51
Academic Expertise Framework 153
accessibility 195–196
accidental plagiarism 132–133
action research 17; *see also* participatory action research (PAR)
active citizenship 23–24, 27
activism 251
additive bilingualism 123
adjacency pair 95
Adobe Reader 241
adult ESL literacy class case study: metalinguistic conversations about language in 136–138; translanguaging vs. traditional approach **137**; translingualism in 135–138
adult learners 95
advocacy: beyond-the-classroom 249; critical pedagogies and 254; defining 249; educational policy and 257–258, 261, 263; EFL and 249–252, 254; empowerment and 251–254; English language teaching (ELT) and 249–254; ESL and 249–252, 254; ESOL students and 269; framework for 252–253; instructional 250–251, 253; interpersonal communication skills and 252; multiculturalism and 254; multilingualism and 254; peer-led 271; personal risk and 251; political 250–251, 253; scaffolded 252; social justice and 250; teacher agency and 250, 254; teacher education and 253–254; teacher empowerment and 271–272; teachers and 249–251; within-the-classroom 249
African American students 91
agency 155–156, 176, 250, 254
agroecotechnology students 204–205
Akbari, R. 30
Allen, D. 271–272
Allwright, R. L. 50
alternative journalism 23
Altherr Flores, J. A. 95
American Council on the Teaching of Foreign Languages (ACTFL) 258
Anderson, M. 68, 191, 194

Aneja, G. 127
Ant and the Grasshopper, The: activity based on 81, 83; illustrations for 84, 85, 86, 87, 88; sample worksheet for 88
Ares, N. 38
Argentina 66–68
Arnheim, R. 217
Arsic, N. 83
arts-based discussion case study: art used in 170; critical reflections and 166–167, 173; English language learners and 160; multiliteracies pedagogy and 160–167, 169; overt instruction in 164–166, 171; pyramid of inquiry and 161–164, 168, 171–174; self-advocacy and 167–169; transformed practice and 167–168
Asher, J. 48
A.S. Hornby Educational Trust 271
assessment: authentic EAL 95; distributive assessment models 156; educational technology and 196–197; holistic 156–157; multiliteracies pedagogy and 156–157; peer-to-peer 156, 202; translingualism and 128
assets pedagogy 94
Association of Teachers of English in Rwanda (ATER) 270–272
Astor Educators Initiative 160–161, 169
Athanases, S. Z. 251
Audiolingual Method 48
Auerbach, E. R. 280–281
Autonomous University of Entre Ríos, Argentina 66
autonomy: academic 51; digital literacy and 241, 243–244; emotional intelligence (EI) and 243; metacognitive tasks and 244–245; mobile learning and 240, 242–245
available technology 196

Basque Autonomous Community 95
Battelle for Kids 4
Benemérita Universidad Autónoma de Puebla (BUAP) 38
Bergmann, J. 196
bilingual education 257
bilingualism 123, 257–258

"Bilingual Speech Contest" 145–146
bi/multilingual text activity 145
Biography-Driven Instruction (BDI) 94–95
BlackBoard Mobile Learn (BBL) 240–241
blended learning 197, 205
Blommaert, J. 121
Bloom's Taxonomy 15, 213
borderless learning 204
Brazil 227–229
British Council 3, 10, 271
Brooke Astor Fund 160
Brown, A. F. 100
Bucholtz, M. 93, 263
Buckingham, D. 222
Buvoltz, K. A. 243

Canada 95, 253
Canagarajah, A. S. 123, 124, 125, 127
Canale, M. 49
Cannizzo, H. 289, 291
Carnegie Mellon University 193
Carvajal-Regidor, M. 281
Casillas, D. I. 93, 263
Chang, B. 281
Chapelle, C. A. 196
Cherry, C. 165–166
Chicago 102
China 107–108
Chinese 121, 201
Chun, D. 194, 197
Cisneros, S. 100
civic engagement 161
classroom negotiation 289, 290
CLT see Communicative Language Teaching (CLT)
code-switching 123
Cole, D. R. 153
collaborative learning: collaborative writing and 192;
    defining 193; digital technology and 191, 193;
    digital tools for 193; peer monitoring and 267;
    second language learning and 192; TESOL and 18
collaborative technologies: blended learning and 197;
    ESL teaching and 191, 197; flipped classrooms and
    191, 196; individualized second language learning
    and 191; learners and xiii; selected tools for 193;
    writing and 194
collaborative writing 192, 194
Collins, T. 177
Common European Framework of Reference for
    Languages (CEFR) 24, 39, 57, 107, 210, 240, 294
communication: as 21st century skill 79; call-response
    95; digital technology and 151, 218; interpersonal
    252; multilingual 122, 124–126; multimodal 3,
    122–123, 126; styles of 93; translingualism in 123
communication skills course (ENG 311) case study:
    critical pedagogy in 29; email writing task in 32,

36–37; English language learners in 29; meeting
    tasks in 31–32, 35; presentation tasks in 30–31, 31;
    reflective dialogue and 29–33; student-generated
    rating scale in 30, 34; syllabus design 28–30
communicative competence 49
Communicative Language Teaching (CLT) 49, 59
communities of practice (CoPs) 270–272
community-building pedagogical approach 266–268
community-building pedagogy case study: egalitarian
    participation and 268; ESOL students and 265;
    leadership and 267; peer monitoring and 267;
    restorative practices and 267–268; sense of
    community and 267–268; special education students
    and 266; student advocacy and 265, 269; teacher
    advocacy and 265–266, 269
community-informed discourse 93
Community Language Learning 48
competence: communicative 49; cross-cultural 200–
    201; cultural 91; discourse 49; grammatical 49;
    language proficiency and 124; linguistic 66, 95, 183;
    multimodal 126; performative 124, 126;
    sociolinguistic 49; strategic 49; symbolic 183
Computer-Assisted Language Learning (CALL) 192,
    194–195
co-narration 93
Content and Language Integrated Learning (CLIL) 95
Content-Based Language Teaching 49
context-sensitive pedagogy 66–71
continuous professional development (CPD) 38
Cope, B. 153, 175
corpus/corpora 235–237, 238, 239
course planning 56–60
Crandall, J. A. 295
Creative Book Builder (CBB) 240–241
critical consciousness: active citizenship and 24, 27;
    arts-based discussions and 166–167; English
    proficiency and 24; social justice themes and 109; in
    student journalism 23–27
critical discourse analysis (CDA) 17
critical framing: activity for 173; arts-based discussion
    and 166; multiliteracies pedagogy and 152–153,
    161, 164, 169, 175
critical language pedagogy (CLP) 289
critical language pedagogy (CLP) case study: classroom
    negotiation and 289, 290; critical participatory
    approach and 291; critical poster project 291, 292,
    293; critical vocabulary and 289, 291; reflective
    teaching and 288–289, 291; translanguaging and
    291
critical literacy: authentic resources and 157; defining
    218; digital podcast projects and 155; multiliteracies
    pedagogy and 154–155; multimodal activities and
    155; TESOL and 17
critical pedagogies: action research and 17–18;
    advocacy and 254; collaboration and 18;

context-specific enactments of 19; disruption and 19; English language education (ELE) and 281; feminist scholarship and 16; participatory pedagogy and 281–282, 284; pedagogy of caring and 284; postmethod pedagogies and 47–48; recognition and 18; reflective dialogue and 29–33; social justice and 16–19, 39; solidarity and 18–19; students as resources in 30; TESOL and 15–20, 47, 53
Crookes, G. 250, 289
cross-cultural competence 200–201
CRP see Culturally-Responsive Pedagogy (CRP)
Crystal, D. 3
cultural competence 91
cultural differences 113–114, 125, 200
cultural diversity 155, 204, 251–252, 254
culturally relevant pedagogy 91, 97, 100, 107
culturally relevant teaching (CRT) 281
Culturally-Responsive Pedagogy (CRP): academic achievement and 91; distance learning and 97; English as a Foreign Language (EFL) and 96; English as an additional language (EAL) and 94–95; English as a second language (ESL) and 101, 103, 107, 113–116; English language education (ELE) and 92, 94, 97; English language teaching (ELT) and 9; English medium instructional sites (EMIs) and 95–96; language-in-education policies and 97; local ways of knowing and 93; marginalized students and 91–92, 96; multicultural education and 91; pedagogy as caring 93–94; pedagogy as participatory 93; pedagogy as sociocultural phenomenon in 92; pedagogy as supportive of students' linguistic rights 93; pedagogy as sustaining and revitalizing 92–93; principles for 100; problem-posing pedagogy 101, 103; social construction theory and 115; student cultural knowledge and 113; teachers as change agents for 97; TESOL and 91–92
culturally responsive teaching 108, 113
Culturally Responsive Teaching (Gay) 91
culturally sustaining pedagogies 9, 91–92, 94–95
Cummins, J. 153
Curiel, L. C. 155
curriculum: critical pedagogies and 18; culturally-responsive pedagogy and 91–93; LGBTQ+ inclusive pedagogy and 301; multiliteracies pedagogy and 156; P21 framework for 5; participatory pedagogy and 281; postmethod pedagogies and 56, 66, 71; SDGs and 5; translingualism and 125, 127

Danzak, R. L. 154, 155
Darabi, R. 51
da Silva, I. C. 228–231, 233
data driven learning (DDL) 236
Davidoff, K. 132
Debes, J. 217
deep thinking 29

de Haan, J. 7
de Jong, E. J. 279
de los Ríos, C. V. 125
democratic participation 200
democratic teaching 93
de Oliveira, L. C. 251
de Pareja, J. 167
Design concept 152
Dewey, J. 23
digital literacy: concept of 218; critical reflections and 222; defining 218–219; development of technology skills and 222; dimensions of 219; first language (L1) literacy and 151; functional/skills approach to 219, 236; initiatives for 218; learner autonomy and 241, 243–244; metacognitive tasks and 244; mobile apps and 241; models for 222; multimodality and 220–221, 223; multimodal syllabus and 221–222; second language education and 219–223; skills for 219; sociocultural approach to 219–220; teacher training and 222–223; 21st century skills and 7
Digital Literacy (Gilster) 218
digital natives 191
digital podcast projects 155
digital technology: accessibility and 195–196; active learning and 228; as add-on 151, 219; collaborative learning and xiii, 191, 193, 193, 228; communication and 151, 218; digital natives and 191; English language learners and 192, 218; knowledge-sharing through 183; learner training and 195; multiliteracies and xiii; multimodal communication and xiii, 151; social equality and 220; standards for 195; teachers and 192; see also collaborative technologies; educational technology
Direct method 48
discourse competence 49
Discourse model 222
distance learning 97
distributive assessment models 156
diversity: cultural 155, 204, 251–252, 254; language 122; linguistic 250, 253–254, 284; sexual 298–299; student 41, 100; in teaching and learning 19
Dixon, D. 244
Domnauer, T. 177
Dreamkeepers, The (Ladson-Billings) 91
Dressing for the Carnival (Homer) 162, 162
DropBox 240–241, 261
Dubai Men's College (DMC) 240–241

Earl, R. 163
Eberly Center for Teaching Excellence and Educational Innovation (Carnegie Mellon University) 193
educational policy: advocacy work in 257–258, 261, 263; LOC and 259, 260, 261, 261, 262; shared decision-making and 258–259, 260, 261; shared

resources and 258–259, 261, 262; teacher activism and 262–263; teachers and 258–259

educational technology: accessibility and 195–196; assessment and 196–197; backup plans and 196; collaborative learning and **193**; defining 192; different learning styles and 196; feedback and 196–197; flipped classrooms and 191, 196; language teaching and 192, 194–195; standards for 195; student learning goals and 195; student learning outcomes and 194; student training and 195; teacher training and 195; *see also* collaborative technologies; digital technology

Education for Sustainable Development (UNESCO) 9

egalitarian participation 268

Egbert, J. 194, 196

ELE *see* English language education (ELE)

Electronic Journal for English as a Second Language, The (TESL-EJ) 195

Elijah Boardman (Earl) 162, 163

ELLs *see* English language learners (ELLs)

EL teacher education: advocacy skills development in 253–254; apprenticeship of observation and 279; cognitive apprenticeships and 282; critical pedagogies and 38; digital literacy and 223; expertise and 278, 282–284; frames perspective for identity 279; global/local dynamics and 277; historically marginalized candidates and 283; identity and 278–279, 282, 284; LGBTQ+ inclusive pedagogy and 298–299; life skills in 295; multilingualism and 126–127; multiliteracies pedagogy and 156; narrative inquiry and 283; participatory pedagogy and 277–284; personal development instruction in 294–296; postmethod approach in 282–284; professional development and 277; reflective teaching and 279–280; teachers as transformative intellectuals 279–280, 283–284; TESOL programs and 277–278; translanguaging-focused 127; *see also* Professional Development Portfolio course case study; student-teachers; *Teaching English to Young Learners* (TEYL) case study

emergent bilingual xiii, 126, 254

emotional intelligence (EI) 242–243, 244, 245

empowerment *see* student empowerment; teacher empowerment

engagement *see* student engagement

English as a Foreign Language (EFL): advocacy and 249–252, 254; collaborative technologies and 191, 197; culturally-responsive pedagogy and 96; digital literacy and 219–221, 223; educational technology and 192; linguistic imperialism and 96; mobile technologies and 227

English as an additional language (EAL): adult EALs and 95; authentic assessments in 95; bi/multilingual learners and 3, 9; Biography-Driven Instruction (BDI) and 94–95; culturally-responsive pedagogy and 94–95; English as a Foreign Language (EFL) and 96; English medium instructional sites (EMIs) and 95–96; Koryoin children and 139–140; multiliteracies pedagogy and 156; multimodal communication and 3; teacher education and 284

English as an International Language (EIL) 96

English as a Second Language (ESL): advocacy and 249–252, 254; collaborative technologies and 191, 197; content-based instruction 175–176; critical literacy and 155; culturally-responsive pedagogy and 101, 103, 107, 113–116; digital literacy and 219–221, 223; educational technology and 192; international students and 113–114; LGBTQ+ individuals and 298–301; pedagogical recommendations for 116; presentation skills and 108, 111; presentation task grading rubric **112**; problem-posing pedagogy 100–103; queering the classroom 299–300; social justice themes in 107–111, 117

English Effect, The (British Council) 10

English for Academic Purposes (EAP) 30

English for General Academic Purposes (EGAP) 181

English for Speakers of Other Languages (ESOL): classroom advocacy and 269; community-building pedagogy and 265–266; multimodal graphic stories and 155; special education students and 266

English language: as global lingua franca 3, 8–10; international development and 10; myth of Standard English and 122; in Rwanda 270

English language (EL) teacher education *see* EL teacher education

English language education (ELE): culturally-responsive pedagogy and 92, 94, 97; identity-erasing texts and 92; imposed knowledge and 92; multiliteracies pedagogy and 154; translingualism in 124; unequal access and privilege in 92; *see also* English as an additional language (EAL); English language teaching (ELT)

English language learners (ELLs): academic autonomy and 51; arts-based discussions and 160; campus tour movie project 103, 105, 106; communication skills course and 29; digital technology and 192, 218; discourse competence and 49; eclectic approach and 49; ESL programs and 100–103; filmmaking and 101–103; grammatical competence and 49; leadership skills and 267; liberatory autonomy and 51; literacy and 217–218; method and 48–49; mobile technologies and 227–229; multimodality and 218; peer monitoring and 267; political socialization and 161; positionalities and 101; postmethod pedagogies and 49–51; problem-posing pedagogy and 101–103; research-based learning programs for 257–258; sociolinguistic competence and 49; strategic competence and 49

English language teachers: advocacy and 249–253; as change agents 97, 249; concepts of 279; continuous professional development (CPD) and 38; culturally-responsive pedagogy and 97; digital literacy training and 222–223; educational policy and 258–259, 261, 262, 263; identity and 278–279, 300; inquiry-oriented activities 280; monolingual ideology and 126–127, 147; native English-speaking (NESTs) 299–300; non-native English-speaking (NNESTs) 299–300; professional development (PD) and 77–78, 299; professional identity and 250; reflection and 279–280; Serbian 77–78; shared decision-making and 258–259, 260; shared resources and 258–259, 261, 262; TPACK competence 223; as transformative intellectuals 279–280, 283–284; translingualism and 127, 140, 142; translingual strategies instruction and 143

English language teaching (ELT): accidental plagiarism and 132–133; advocacy and 249–254; "banking method" of 24; collaborative 193; collaborative technologies and **193**, 197; collaborative writing and 192, 194; content-based instruction 77; culturally-responsive pedagogy and 9; digital literacy and 218; digital technology and 151, 193–195; eclectic approach to 49; goals and assumptions about 57; inclusive pedagogy and 41; learning outcomes and 194; LGBTQ+ inclusive pedagogy and 298–301; MA program in 38–43; method and 47–49; Mexican programs in 38; mobile technologies and 228; monolingual ideology and 122, 127–128; multiliteracies pedagogy and 10, 151; multimodal literacy and 151, 156; multimodal resources for 157; as political act xii, 20; postmethod pedagogies and 50–52; self-reflexivity in 128; skills in 193–194; social justice and 38, 43; student diversity and 41; student funds of knowledge and xii, xiii, 176; technology standards for 195; training for xiv; translingualism in 122, 124–127; 21st century skills and 8; *see also* English language education (ELE); second language (L2) teachers

English medium instructional sites (EMIs): culturally-responsive pedagogy and 95–96; deficit ideologies and 95–96; postsecondary institutions and 95; project-based course development in 56; remedial English classes and 95; translanguaging pedagogy and 128

English proficiency exam (EPE) 28

English Program for International Communication (EPIC) 23–24

ESL *see* English as a Second Language (ESL)

ESL composition course case study: culturally-responsive pedagogy and 114–116; international students and 113–116; reading materials for 114

ESOL *see* English for Speakers of Other Languages (ESOL)

"Everyday Literacy Project" 144, 145, 146

Exploratory Practice framework 50

Facebook 197, 221

Facultad de Humanidades, Artes y Ciencias Sociales (FHAyCS) 66–67

Fadel, C. 5, 7–8

Fan, F. 279

Farrell, T. S. C. 278, 283

Feak, C. B. 236

feminist scholarship 16

first language (L1) literacy 135–136, 151

First Nations people 93

Flickr 221

flipped classroom case study: Bloom's Taxonomy and 213; English language learners and 209–211, 213; internet reliability and 210; teacher workload and 213; use of Google Classroom 209–210, 211, 213; use of Telegram 209, 211, 212, 213

flipped classrooms (FC): active learning in 210; available technology and 196; collaborative technologies and 191, 196; defining 209; participatory pedagogies and 283; TESOL and 197

Flores, N. 127

Forde, T. B. 100

Foreign Language Didactics 1 (FLD1): collaborative reflection and 69; communicative language teaching reflection 76; context-sensitive pedagogy and 68–71; English language learners and 67; English teaching contexts and 69, 74; implementation of CLT 70; language teaching method reflection 75; language teaching methods and 69, 75; local teaching context and 69, 73; postmethod pedagogies and 67, 69–71; syllabus innovation and 67–71; *see also* Initial English Language Teacher Education (IELTE) case study

foreign language instruction 192

frames perspective 279

Fredricks, L. 96

Freire, P. 16, 23, 24, 29, 32, 70, 281

French language 270

García, O. 123–124, 126

Gay, G. 91, 93

Gee, J. P. 39

Generation Z 191

Gheitanchian, M. 53

Gilster, P. 218

Giroux, H. A. 70, 71

Global Digital Literacy Council 218

Goleman, D. 243

Google Classroom 192, 209–210, 211, 213

Google Docs 200–202, 236

Google Drive 261

Google Earth 177–178, 178, 179, 203

Google Groups 261

Google Sites 177

Google Translate 142–143

Gouin, F. 48

Graddol, D. 8
Graduate Record Examinations (GRE) 201
Grammar-Translation Method 48
grammatical competence 49
Green, B. 151
group living 266, 268

Haffner, A. 136
Hafner, C. A. 220, 222
Harcup, T. 23
Harvest, The 102
Hauck, M. 222
Hawai'i: academic writing and 200; campus tour movie
    project 103, 105, 106; English language learners in
    100–103, 200; immigrants in 101–103; *see also*
    Intermediate Academic Writing 3 (IAW3) case study;
    problem-posing pedagogy case study
Hawai'i Plantation Village 101, 102
Hawkins, M. R. 254
Hazratzad, A. 53
Healey, D. 196
Healey, M. 242
hedging 236, 238–239, 239; *see also Research and Writing*
    course case study
Heller, M. 122
Herrera, S. G. 94
heteronormative practices 299–300
Higher Colleges of Technology (HCT) 240
Holmes, M. A. 94
Homer, W. 162, 162
Hopper, E. 164, 164, 165–166
Horner. B. 125
House on Mango Street, The (Cisneros) 100
How I Learned Geography (Shulevitz) 176
Hubbard, P. 195
Huda, M. E. 52
hybridity 152

iAnnotate 240
iBooks 240–241
identity: communication styles and 93; cultural 114–
    115; culturally-responsive pedagogy and 96–97; EL
    teachers and 278–279; frames perspective for 279;
    linguistic 91; multimodal 155; practice-oriented
    279; professional 250, 279, 300; sexual 300;
    translingualism and 123, 125–127
IELTE *see* Initial English Language Teacher Education
    (IELTE) case study
iFiles 240
If Your Name Was Changed at Ellis Island (Levine) 176
immigrants 249
immigration 101–103; *see also* migration and
    immigration project case study
iMovie 240–241
inclusive classrooms 298–300

inclusive pedagogy 41
individualized learning 191
Indonesia 204–207
information and communication technology (ICT) 217,
    227
information literacy 218–220
Initial English Language Teacher Education (IELTE) case
    study: context-sensitive pedagogy and 70;
    development of content knowledge in 66–67;
    pedagogical content knowledge and 66–67;
    pedagogical knowledge and 66–67; postmethod
    pedagogies and 71; power relationships and 70;
    program content and 66–67; social issues and 70;
    syllabus design and 66–70; *see also Foreign Language
    Didactics 1* (FLD1)
Inquiry-Based Learning 242
Instagram 221, 231
instructional advocacy 250–251, 253
intensive English course: international students and
    131–132; role-play projects and 132–134; student-
    centered 132; student dialogue and 132–133;
    translanguaging and 132–134
Intensive English Programs (IEPs) 95
interdisciplinary learning 5, 18, 155–156
Intermediate Academic Writing 3 (IAW3) case study:
    critical thinking in 203; EAL learners and 200–201;
    peer assessment and 202; process-oriented approach
    to 200; self-editing and 202–203; student-created
    rubric in 201–202; 21st century skills and 203; use
    of Google Docs 201–203; writing skills and 200–202
International Association of Teachers of English as a
    Foreign Language (IATEFL) 271
International General Certificate of Secondary Education
    (IGCSE) 107
Internationals Network for Public Schools 160
International Society for Technology in Education
    (ISTE) 6–7, 195
international students: academic writing and 235–236;
    cultural identity and 114–115; ESL teaching and
    113–116, 131–132; social needs and 114
interpersonal communication skills 252
intersemiotic complementarity 221
intertextuality 152
Into the West (Collins) 177
iPads 100–101, 103, 240–241
iPed model 222
Isemonger, I. 25
ISTE *see* International Society for Technology in
    Education (ISTE)

Jacobs, G. M. 193
Japan: "banking method" of language learning in 24;
    English language teaching (ELT) in 181–184; online
    collaborative writing and 204–207;
    videoconferencing and 207

Japanese 201
Johnson, K. E. 278–280
Johnson, S. I. 124
Jones, R. H. 220, 222
Juan de Pareja (Velázquez) 166, 166, 167

Kachru, B. B. 3
KAHOOT! 196–197
Kajee, L. 156
Kalantzis, M. 153, 175
Karakalpakstan 209–210
Kavimandan, S. K. 94
Kesler, T. 93, 281
Kessler, G. 194
Keynote 240–241
Keynote textbook series (National Geographic Learning) 157
Khany, R. 51
Kinyarwanda language 270
Kirkwood, C. 39
Kirkwood, G. 39
Kiss, T. 154
Kochi National University (Japan) 23–24
Korean 121, 201
Koryoin children 139–140, 142–144
Koryoin children case study: English language learning and 139–140; image searches and 143, 144; translingual activities 144–145, 145, 146, 146; translingual practices and 139–140, 141, 142–143, 143, 144, 146
Kostka, I. 195, 196
Kubanyiova, M. 250
Kumaravadivelu, B. 47–51, 56, 68–69, 279–280, 281, 282
Kurek, M. 222
KWL charts 78
Kyoto University (KU) 181–184

L1 *see* first language (L1) literacy
L2 learners *see* second language (L2) learners
Ladson-Billings, G. 91
language: holistic perspective on 124; identity and 47, 51, 101, 300; as ideology 51, 54; learner understanding and 38; linguistic rights and 93; linguistics and 48–49; meaning-making and 121, 123–124; monolingualism and 122; policy and 52, 92, 97, 258–259, 270; power relationships and 220; social discourse and 300; sociocultural practices of 217–221; sociopolitics of 48; structuralism and 123; *see also* English language; English language teaching (ELT); multilingualism; translanguaging/translingualism
Language Education Center (University of Miyazaki, Japan) 205
language-in-education policies 97

Language Opportunity Coalition (LOC) 257–259, 260, 261, 261, 262
language play 183
language practice: classroom 125; critique and 127; multilingualism and 123–126; translingualism and 122, 126–127; use of smartphones 227
Language Teaching and Technology 196
Lankshear, C. 151
Larsen-Freeman, D. 68, 191, 194
learner autonomy: digital technology and 228; EL teacher education and 282–283; emotional intelligence (EI) and 242–243; macrostrategies for 50; metacognitive tasks and 244; mobile technologies and 241–243, 245; postmethod pedagogies and 52–53, 282; theme-based instruction and 81
learner-centered classrooms 281
Learning by Design 181, 184
learning outcomes 194
learning styles 53, 58, 79, 94, 154, 196
Lee, E. 127
Lee, J. S. 93, 263
Lee, M. W. 96, 281
Lee, T. S. 93
Lesbian Gay Bisexual Transgender Queer Intersex (LGBTQI) communities *see* LGBTQ+ individuals
Levido, A. 222
Levine, E. 176
LGBTQ+ inclusive pedagogy case study: dominant discourse and 300–301; ESL teachers and 298–300; gender-neutral relationship markers and 300; narrative illustration activity 300, 301, 304–305; opening attitudes survey 303; professional development (PD) and 299–300; queer inquiry and 300
LGBTQ+ individuals 16, 298–300
Li, J. 197
Li, M. 197
Li, W. 123–124
liberatory autonomy 51
"Life in Kochi Project" 23–26, 26, 27
Lin, A. 125, 128
Lingley, D. 24–25
linguistic diversity 10, 155, 250, 253, 284
linguistic rights 92–94, 97, 250
literacy: defining 217; information 218; language learning and 217; multimodal 218; print-based 221, 223; socio-material 218; socio-spatial 218; technological 217–218; traditional approaches to 152, 221; visual 217; *see also* critical literacy; digital literacy
literacy-emergent newcomers 265, 269
LOC *see* Language Opportunity Coalition (LOC)
Lomicka, L. 191, 192
Longbotham, G. J. 243
LOOK Act 257–259, 261
"Loom of Visual Literacy, The" (Debes) 217
Lord, G. 191, 192

Lortie, D. 279
Lozanov, G. 15

Mackey, M. 156
macrostrategies 50, 282–283
Malang, Indonesia 204
Malderez, A. 68–69
Mambu, J. E. 254
Mandarin Chinese 107–108
Mardani, M. 52
Marshall, S. 95
Martin, A. 219
Martinez, E. 223
Massachusetts: educational policy and 258–259, 260, 261, 261; ELLs in 258; English-only policy in 257–258; LOOK Act and 257–259, 261; Seal of Biliteracy and 257–259
Massachusetts Comprehensive Assessment System 258
May, S. 123
McCarty, T. L. 93
McClay, J. K. 156
McDonald, J. 271–272
McGill, D. 25
meaning making: collaborative 160–161, 228; digital technology and 193, 229; hybridity and 152; language and 121, 123–124; methodology and 17; multilingual 160–161; multimodal 126, 152, 183, 218, 220; practice of 123–124; pyramid of inquiry and 162; semiotic resources for 139
metacognitive tasks 244
method 48–49; see also postmethod pedagogies
methodology 48
Metropolitan Museum of Art 160–161, 168–169
Mexico 38
Michigan Corpus of Upper-Level Student Papers (MICUSP) 237, 237, 238, 238
Microsoft Word 236
migration and immigration project case study: analyzing and 177, 179; application of knowledge and 178–179; books and websites for 180; conceptualizing and 177; content-based ESL instruction 175–176; creation of wikis and 177; experiencing and 177, 179; Google Earth and 177–178, 178, 179; multiliteracies pedagogy and 176–177, 179; student personal journeys and 176–177
Mills, K. A. 218, 222
Mizusawa, K. 154
mobile devices: as instructional tools 228; internet access and 228; mobile apps and 228–233; mobile learning and 240; multimodal collaboration and 227–228; online collaborative writing and 206; see also mobile technologies case study; smartphones
mobile learning (mLearning) 240–241
mobile learning (mLearning) case study: digital literacy and 241–244; ELLs and 241; emotional intelligence

(EI) development activities 242–243, 244, 245; inquiry-based projects and 242, 245; learner autonomy and 240, 242–245; metacognitive tasks and 244–245; mobile apps and 240–241; Web Inquiry Projects 242; WebQuest rubric 243; WebQuests and 242
mobile resources 121
mobile technologies case study: EFL instruction and 227–231, 233; mobile apps and 228–229, 229, 230, 230, 231, 231, 232, 233; multimodal collaboration and 227–228, 230, 233; student engagement and 228, 231, 233; text editing and 231; vocabulary development and 229–231, 233
Moll, L. xii
monoglossic ideology 128
monolingualism 122–123, 127–128, 147
Moodle 205, 208
Moradian, E. 52
Morgan, B. 250
multicultural education 91, 94–95, 113, 115
multiculturalism 18, 154, 254
multilingualism: advocacy and 254; as an asset 127; code-switching and 123; performative competence and 124; Seal of Biliteracy and 257; student empowerment and 123; student practices and 124, 126; translingualism and 125; transnational movement and 122; value of xiii; Word Walls and 140, 142
Multilingualism Programme (MP) 95
multiliteracies pedagogy: Academic Expertise Framework and 153; analyzing and 179; application of knowledge and 179; arts-based discussions and 160–167, 169; assessment and 156–157; background of 152; benefits of 156; challenges of 156–157; conceptualizing and 177; critical literacy and 154–155; cultural diversity and 155; Design concept in 152; digital technology and xiii; dimensions of 175; English language education (ELE) and 154, 218; English language teaching (ELT) and 10, 151–152; experiencing and 177, 179; hybridity in 152; inclusiveness and 154; interdisciplinary learning and 155; intertextuality in 152; key components of 152–153; linguistic diversity and 155; New Literacy Studies (NLS) and 153; second language acquisition and 154; situated practice and 153, 161; student engagement/agency and 155–156, 176; translanguaging approach and 155
Multiliteracies Training model 222
multimodal communication: digital technology and xiii, 151; English learners and 3; everyday literacy and 126; meaning-making and 126, 152, 218, 220; translingualism and 122–123, 125
multimodal composing 220–221, 223
multimodal literacy: academic rap video as 183; defining 218; digital technology and 220–221, 223;

English language teaching (ELT) in 156–157; first language (L1) literacy and 151; intersemiotic complementarity and 221; mobile technologies and 227–228, 230, 233; multiliteracies and 152; students as designers in 221
multimodal syllabus 221–222
Murray, J. 282

NACTIC model 39–41, 43
narrative inquiry 283
National Education Association (NEA) 252–253
National Geographic Learning 157
Native Americans 93, 108
native English-speaking teachers (NESTs) 299–300
Natural Approach 48
Nearpod 241
Necesidades de alumnos en su Contexto por medio de TIC see NACTIC model
Nelson, C. 301
"New Freedom" (Cherry) 165–166
New Literacy Studies (NLS) 17, 153
New London Group (NLG) 152, 154, 156, 218
new media literacy 220
NLS *see* New Literacy Studies (NLS)
non-native English-speaking teachers (NNESTs) 299–300
North Korean refugee students 96
Norton, B. 38, 254
Notional-Functional Syllabuses (NFS) 49
Nukus State Pedagogical Institute (NSPI) 209–210
Nurture or Nature 181, 186–187

Ó'Móchaim, R. 301
online corpus data 235–237
Online Culture Exchange Program (OCEP) 205–206, 206
online learning 97
online writing case study: blended learning and 205; classroom preparation for 207; collaborative technologies and 204, 206–207; collaborative writing and 204–207; English language learners and 204–205; preparation for 206; study buddy system and 206; topic discussions 206; use of smartphones 206; videoconferencing and 204–208, 208; writing exchange structure 205
OpenCourseWare channel (Kyoto University) 181–182
Ortega, L. 123
overt instruction 164–166, 171

P21 *see* Partnership for 21st-Century Learning (P21)
Pages 240–241
PAR *see* participatory action research (PAR)
participatory action research (PAR) 17–18, 53
participatory pedagogy: critical 278, 282, 284; EL teacher education and 277–284; empowerment and

281–282; English language learners and 281–282; English language teachers and 281–282; flipped classrooms and 283; pedagogy of caring and 284; postmethod approach in 282; principles of 281; teacher-centered classroom and 280; teacher expertise and 278, 282–283; teachers as transformative intellectuals 279–280
participatory teaching 277
particularity 50, 52–54, 69
Partnership for 21st-Century Learning (P21) 4, 4, 5–8
pedagogy: adjacency pair and 95; assets 94; as caring 93–94, 284; community-building approach 266–268; critical language (CLP) 289; culturally sustaining 9, 91–92, 94–95; as participatory 93; problem-posing 100–103; responsive 94; as sociocultural phenomenon 92; as supportive of students' linguistic rights 93; as sustaining and revitalizing 92–93; translanguaging and 95, 122, 125–126, 128; translingual 125; *see also* critical pedagogies; Culturally-Responsive Pedagogy (CRP); multiliteracies pedagogy; participatory pedagogy; postmethod pedagogies
pedagogy of multiliteracies *see* multiliteracies pedagogy
peer monitoring 267
peer-to-peer assessments 156
Pennington, M. C. 279
Pennycook, A. 39
performative competence 124, 126
personal development instruction 294–296
Pilgrim, J. 223
political advocacy 250–251, 253
political socialization 161
Poll Everywhere 108
Portuguese Dictionary 229, 229
possibility 50–54, 70
postmethod era xii, 9–10, 56, 277–278
postmethod pedagogies: constraints on teachers 52–54; context-sensitive 67–69; critical pedagogy and 47–48; effectiveness of 53; EL teacher education and 282–284; frameworks for 50, 56, 59; learner autonomy and 51–52; macrostrategies for 282–283; model for course design 59; multilingualism and xiii; particularity and 50, 52–54, 69; possibility and 50–54, 70; practicality and 50, 52–54, 70; project-based course and 56–60; Rashed, D. xiii; resistance to 52; second language (L2) teachers and 50; sense of plausibility and 50–51, 67; support for in-service teachers 52–53; teacher autonomy and 51–52; teacher empowerment and 48–53; textbooks and 51–52, 54; types of xii
POST model 222
postsecondary institutions 95
Powell, F. J. 243
Prabhu, N. S. 50
practicality 50, 52–54, 70

practice-oriented identity 279

practicums 56–59, 288–289

presentation skills 108, 111, **112**

presentation tasks 30–31, 31, **112**

preservice teachers 223; *see also* EL teacher education

problem-posing pedagogy case study: culturally-responsive pedagogy and 103; ESL and 100–103; immigration and 101–103

Probyn, M. 125

professional development (PD): digital technology developments and 195; EL teacher identity and 279; global/local dynamics and 277; LGBTQ+ inclusive pedagogy and 299–301; primary teachers and 77–79, 81–82; Rwandan teachers and 271

Professional Development Portfolio course case study: course organization **40**; critical pedagogy and 38–39; digital autobiography and 41, 41; digital technology and 41; final project in 42–43; inclusive pedagogy and 41; NACTIC model and 39–41, 43; teaching time line in 42

Professional Learning Communities (PLCs) 271–272, 274

project-based course development case study: action research and 58; authenticity in 58; culturally-responsive pedagogy and 101; descriptive writing in 58, 64; final course and project schedule **63**; guest teacher interviews 58–59, 65; language teaching goals and assumptions 57; model for postmethod approach 59; postmethod planning and 56–60; student language needs and 57–58; student survey 62; teaching philosophy graphic organizer 61

PROUCA (Programa um computador por aluno) 227

Pullen, D. L. 153

Pyramid of Inquiry 161–164, 168, 171–174

queer inquiry 300

Rajendram, S. 156

rap video project case study: authentic learning environment and 184; description of 182; knowledge-sharing through technology 183; language play in 183; learning by design and 181, 184; multiliteracies pedagogy and 181, 183; multimodal literacy and 183; song lyrics 186–187; team learning and 181, 183

Rashed, D. 282

recognition 18

reflective dialogue 29–33

reflective teaching: critical 289; participatory pedagogy and 279–280; student-teachers and 288–289, 291

Regional English Language Office (RELO) 271

Reinhardt, J. 194, 197

Research and Writing course case study: academic writing and 235–238; corpus exploration 237, 237, 238, 238; hedging in 236, 238, 239

responsive pedagogy 94

restorative practices 267–268

revitalizing 91–95, 97

Richards, H. V. 100

Richards, J. C. 48

Riley, R. 4

Rodgers, T. 48

role-play project case study: cultural identity and 132; improvisations in 134; minimizing of accidental plagiarism and 133; translanguaging and 131–134

Rosa, J. 127

Russian-Korean children *see* Koryoin children case study

Rwanda: communities of practice (CoPs) in 270–272; language policy in 270; professional development in 271–272

Salas, S. 15, 281

Sams, A. 196

scaffolded advocacy 252

SDGs *see* United Nations Sustainable Development Goals (SDGs)

Seal of Biliteracy 257–259

Seal of Biliteracy Pilot Program 257, 259

second language (L2) learners: collaborative learning and 191; digital literacy and 151; digital technology and 191; educational technology and 192; funds of knowledge and 155; multimodal literacy and 151; writing and 200; *see also* English language learners (ELLs)

second language (L2) teachers 50; *see also* English language teaching (ELT)

second language acquisition 122–124

second language education: critical perspective and 220; data driven learning (DDL) in 236; digital literacy and 219–223; functional/skills approach to technology in 219, 236; intersemiotic complementarity and 221; literacy and 217; multimodality and 220–221; sociocultural approach to technology in 219–220; *see also* English as a Foreign Language (EFL); English as an additional language (EAL); English as a Second Language (ESL)

self-efficacy 271

self-reflexivity 128

Seltzer, K. 124, 125

Serbia: EL teacher education in 294–295; English language teaching (ELT) in 77–79, 81–82; professional development (PD) in 77–79, 81–82

Series method 48

sexual diversity 298–299

sexual identity 300

Share It app 230–231

Sheltered English Immersion (SEI) 257

Sheltered Instruction Observation Protocol (SIOP) 15

Shih, R. 197

Shin, J. K. 295

Shulevitz, U. 176
Silent Way 48
Situated Practice 153, 161
Skype 207–208
Slack 261
smartphones: as instructional tools 228; internet access and 228; mobile apps and 228–229, 229, 230, 231, 231, 232, 233; multimodal collaboration and 227–228; online collaborative writing and 206; see also mobile technologies case study
Smith, F. 24
Snyder, I. 151
social construction theory 115
social justice: advocacy and 250; critical pedagogies and 16–17, 19, 39, 289; digital technology and 220; English language teaching (ELT) and 38; LGBTQ+ individuals and 16, 298, 301; TESOL and 16–19
social justice themes case study: critical consciousness and 109; ESL teaching and 107–111; vocabulary for 110; writing prompts 117
sociocultural frameworks: critical perspective and 220; digital literacy and 219–220; TESOL and 17–18
sociocultural literacy 219–220
sociolinguistic competence 49
socio-material literacy 218
socio-spatial literacy 218
Solan, A. M. 243
solidarity 18–19
South Korea 96, 139–140, 142–144
Spain 95
Spanish language 39, 67, 93, 95, 121, 266–268
special education 81, 252, 266, 269
Staehr Fenner, D. 252
Standard English 122, 126–127, 283
standards: accessibility and 196; English language education (ELE) and 194–195, 251, 254, 277; global digital literacy and 218; ISTE framework for 6; prescriptive 154; state and local 91; teacher identity and 279; TESOL teacher preparation 250, 253; TOEFL exam and 131
Stankovic, D. 83
Stern, H. H. 50
Stockwell, G. 195
Storch, N. 191, 192, 194
strategic competence 49
student empowerment 251–253, 281–282
student engagement: advocacy and 254; mobile technologies and 228, 231, 233; multiliteracies pedagogy and 155–156, 176
student journalism case study: active citizenship and 23–24, 27; awakening critical consciousness in 23–27; local news and 24–25
student-teachers: collaborative reflection and 69, 74; communicative language teaching reflection 76; context-sensitive pedagogy and 66, 68; language

teaching method reflection 75; local teaching context and 69, 73; pedagogical content knowledge and 67; pedagogical knowledge and 67; postmethod pedagogies and 70–72; reflective teaching and 288–289, 291; see also EL teacher education
student voice 6, 30
study buddy system 206
Subtirelu, N. 258
Suggestopedia 15, 48
Süleiman the Magnificent 168
sustaining pedagogy 92, 97; see also culturally sustaining pedagogies
Suzhou, China 107–109
Swain, M. 49
Swales, J. M. 236
symbolic competence 183

Tables for Ladies (Hopper) 164, 164, 165–166
Tablet Educacional (Educational Tablet) 227
Tajikistan 96
talk-story 93
Task-Based Language Teaching 49, 59
teacher advocacy case study: communities of practice (CoPs) and 270–272; international support for 271; peer-led advocacy and 271; Professional Learning Communities (PLCs) and 271–272; self-efficacy and 271; teacher empowerment and 271–272; tuning protocol and 271–272, 274
teacher-centered classroom 280
teacher development see professional development (PD)
teacher education see EL teacher education
teacher empowerment: advocacy and 271–272; participatory pedagogy and 281–282; postmethod pedagogies and 48–53; sense of plausibility and 50–51
teachers: activism and 251; advocacy and 249–253; agency and 250, 254; collaborative technologies and 196; digital technology and 192, 195; expertise and 278; Google Classroom and 192; identity and 278–279; see also EL teacher education; English language teachers; professional development (PD); second language (L2) teachers
teaching: academic achievement paradigms and 15; "banking method" of 23–24; contemporary approaches to 7–8, 8; democratic 93; as political act 20; traditional approaches to 7, 8; see also English language teaching (ELT)
Teaching English to Young Learners (TEYL) case study: children's literature in 295, 297; personal development instruction in 294–296; thematic units and 295, 296
Teaching of English to Speakers of Other Languages (TESOL) see TESOL
Team Learning 181, 183
technological literacy 217–220; see also digital literacy

TED Talks 157
Telegram 209, 211, 212, 213
Ten Macrostrategies framework 50
TESOL: academic achievement paradigms and 15; action research and 17–18; advocacy and 251; collaboration and 18; critical discourse analysis (CDA) and 17; critical literacy and 17; critical pedagogies and 15–20, 47, 53; culturally-responsive pedagogy and 91–92; EL teacher education and 277–278; LGBTQ+ communities and 16; methodology and 15; NLS and 17; postmethod era in xii; recognition and 18; social justice and 16–19; sociocultural frameworks and 17–18; solidarity and 18–19; teacher education and 278–279; teacher identity and 279
TESOL Advocacy and Policy Summit 251
TESOL candidates see EL teacher education
TESOL International Association 9, 15, 195, 254
TESOL Pre-K-12 Teacher Preparation Program Standards 250
TESOL Technology Standards (Healey) 196
Test of English as a Foreign Language (TOEFL) 192, 201
Text-Based Language Teaching 49
Thailand 56–59, 288–289
Thai language 201, 291
Theme-Based Instruction (TBI) 49, 77–78
Theme-Based Instruction in Teaching English to Young Learners (TBI in TEYL) case study: contextual factors in 79, 81; pedagogical innovation and 81–82; professional development (PD) and 77–79, 81; sample materials and activities 79–81, 83, 84, 85, 86, 87, 88; stages of 78–79
theory of practice 49–50, 52, 77, 280
Thomas, M. 281
Three-Dimensional framework 50
Ting, Y. 240
Tomlinson, B. 197
Toohey, K. 38
Total Physical Response (TPR) 48
TPACK competence 223
Transformed Practice: multiliteracies pedagogy and 152–153, 161, 164, 167–169, 175; self-advocacy and 167–168
translanguaging corriente 125
translanguaging/translingualism: adult ESL and 135–138; assessment and 128; bilingualism and 123; "Bilingual Speech Contest" 145–146; bi/multilingual text activity 145; classroom language practices and 125; defining 123; in English teaching 121–122, 124–127; "Everyday Literacy Project" activity 144, 145, 146; individual practices and 123–124; Koryoin children and 139–140, 142–146; language competence and 124; multiliteracies pedagogy and 155; multimodal communication and 123, 125–126; pedagogical 95,

122, 125–126, 128; pedagogy for 125, 127; practices for 140, 142–143; principle of 122; research on 127–128; role-play projects and 131–134; strategies for 140, 142–143; student empowerment and 123; trans-semiotic system and 123; use of Google Translate and 142–143
translingual approach 122
translingual practice 122
Trilling, B. 5, 7–8
Tughra (Insignia) 168, 168
tuning protocol 271–272, 274
Turkey 28–33
Turnitin 197
21st century skills: collaborative rubric and 203; communication and 9–10; contemporary teaching approaches and 7–8, 8; contextual skills and 7; core skills and 7; digital skills and 7; English language and 9–10; frameworks for 4–7; ISTE framework for 6–7; P21 framework for 4, 5–6, 8; peer assessment and 203

UAE University (UAEU) 240
UNESCO 9
United Arab Emirates 240
United Nations Sustainable Development Goals (SDGs) 5, 5
United States: academic writing courses and 235–236; adult ESL and 135–138; bi/multilingualism in 257; content-based ESL instruction 175–176; culturally-responsive pedagogy and 91–92, 94, 107; educational policy and 263; ESL teacher advocacy in 250; immigration to 101–103; international students and 113–114, 131–132, 235–236; racial constructs in 167; see also Massachusetts
University of Miyazaki, Japan 205
U.S. Department of State 271
Uzbekistan 140, 209–210, 213
Uzbekistan State World Languages University (UzSWLU) 209–210

van Deursen, A. J. A. M. 7
Van Dijk, J. A. G. M. 7
Vandrick, S. 101
van Laar, E. 7
Velázquez, D. 166, 166
videoconferencing: assessment of speaking and 208; cultural exchange and 207, 208; online collaborative writing and 204–207; use of Skype 207–208
visual literacy 217
Visual Thinking (Arnheim) 217
Vocación de San Mateo, La (de Pareja) 167
Voss, E. 195–196, 196

Web 2.0 technologies 192
Web 3.0 technologies 197
Web Inquiry Projects 242

WebQuests 242, 243
Wedell, M. 68–69
Westward Expansion (Domnauer) 177
WhatsApp 231
WIDA K-12 Can Do Descriptors 15
Williams, C. 122
Wilson, A. A. 155
Word Walls 140, 142
world Englishes 18
Wright, T. 282
writing skills: collaborative 192, 194; descriptive
    writing 58, 64; EAL learners and 200–202; email

writing task 32, 36–37; online collaborative
204–207; peer assessment and 202; second
language (L2) learners and 200; self-editing and
202–203; standardized testing and 201; writing
prompts 117

Yi, Y. 156
youth PAR (YPAR) 18
YouTube 181–182

Zacarian, D. 266
Zayed University (ZU) 240